THE
EARLY POETIC
MANUSCRIPTS
AND NOTE-BOOKS

OF

Gerard Manley Hopkins

PLATE 1.

PORTRAIT OF GERARD MANLEY HOPKINS
by Rita MacKenzie, PSC.

This pastel portrait represents Hopkins at about the time he wrote the last poems in this volume.
Rita MacKenzie studied all the surviving paintings and photographs of Hopkins before she composed it
and, from them and his writings, interpreted his personality— high intelligence, a strong determination
with a touch of the stubborn, a somewhat withdrawn inner self capable of hurting others if attacked,
and great sensitivity tinged with sadness.

JUL 2008
Received
Ohio Dominican

THE
EARLY POETIC
MANUSCRIPTS
AND NOTE-BOOKS

OF

Gerard Manley Hopkins

IN FACSIMILE

Edited with Annotations

Transcriptions of Unpublished Passages

and an Explanatory Introduction

BY

NORMAN H. MacKENZIE

Norman H MacKenzie

Garland Publishing, Inc.

NEW YORK & LONDON   1989

F 821.8 H794cpm 1989
Hopkins, Gerard Manley
| The early poetic manuscripts
and note-books of Gerard...

For Father Leonard Cochran, OP,

with pleasant recollections of our meetings in

Philadelphia and Providence and admiration

of your own Hopkins research

Norman MacKenzie

All previously unpublished variants of Hopkins' works, and Note-books C.i and C.ii,
copyright © 1989 Trustees for Roman Catholic Purposes Registered,
114 Mount Street, London, WIY 6 AH

Introduction and textual commentary copyright © 1989 Norman H. MacKenzie.
Portrait of Hopkins © Rita MacKenzie
All rights reserved.

LIBRARY OF CONGRESS CATALOGING-IN-PUBLICATION DATA

Hopkins, Gerard Manley. 1844-1889
The early poetic manuscripts and note-books of Gerard Manley
Hopkins in facsimile / edited with annotations, transcriptions of
unpublished passages, and an explanatory introduction by
Norman H. MacKenzie.
p. cm.
Includes index.
ISBN 0-8240-3898-3
1. Hopkins, Gerard Manley, 1844-1889—Notebooks, sketchbooks,
etc.—Facsimiles.   2. Hopkins, Gerard Manley, 1844-1889—
Manuscripts—Facsimiles.   3. Manuscripts, English—Facsimiles.
I. MacKenzie, Norman H.   II. Title.
PR4803.H44A6   1989
821'.8—dc20   89-32239

The volumes in this series are printed on acid-free,
250-year-life paper.

PRINTED IN THE UNITED STATES OF AMERICA

Contents

ABBREVIATIONS AND SIGNS

Signs Used by Hopkins

∪ of   (sometimes these signs are confused with
∩ and   each other by the poet)

ϑ Θ   the, or th/Th (Greek theta; l.c. and u.c.
        are at times indistinguishable)

——   a dash (for "ditto"), the same length as
      a word to be repeated, drawn in the line
      below it. [See e.g. C.i.108, Plate 53, bot.
      left, where all are used.] GMH also writes
      cd., shd., wd., fr. for could, should, would,
      and from.

Abbreviations for MSS

A   An album of Hopkins's poems kept by Robert
     Bridges to preserve his autographs or
     transcripts. It is paginated, with odd numbers
     on the left in reversal of the convention.
     (Bridges Loan Collection, Bodleian Lib.,
     Oxford.)

B   An album of transcriptions of Hopkins's poems
     made by Bridges, and corrected by the poet
     himself in 1884. Hopkins later pasted in
     or inscribed poems in autograph. (Bodleian
     MS. Eng. Poet. d.149)

C.i.   Early Note-book (miscalled "Diary") kept
        at Oxford Sept. 24 1863 to Sept. 9 1864.
        Reproduced on Plates 29-77. (Campion Hall,
        Oxford.)

C.ii.   Continuation to Lent, 1866 (i.e., Feb. 14
         to Easter-eve, Mar. 30). Reproduced on Plates
         82-151. (Campion Hall, Oxford.)

D   MSS sent to Canon R.W. Dixon.

H.i.   A modern album into which the Bodleian guarded
        all the loose Hopkins MSS. bought from the
        Hopkins family in 1953—along with MSS. B
        and H.ii. (Bodleian Lib., MS. Eng. Poet.
        c.48)

H.ii.   An album created by Bridges in 1889 from
         poetic MSS. found after Hopkins's death.
         (Bodleian Lib., MS. Eng. Poet. d.150)

Initials of Hopkins Editors

RB   Robert Bridges (1844-1930)
RWD   Richard Watson Dixon (1833-1900)
WHG   William H. Gardner (1902-69)

GMH   Gerard Manley Hopkins (1844-89)
HH   Humphry House (1908-55)
NHM   Norman H. MacKenzie (1915-)
CLP   Catherine L. Phillips

Abbreviations for Published Hopkins Volumes
(all published by Oxford University Press)

P.   Poems. 1st edn. ed. RB,London: 1918
              2nd edn. ed. Charles Williams,
                  Lon.: 1930
              3rd edn. ed. WHG, London: 1948
              4th edn. ed. WHG and NHM,
                  London: 1967
              OET (Oxford English Texts), ed.
              NHM
              Oxford Authors (Poetry and Prose),
                  ed.CLP, London: 1986

N.   Note-books and Papers, ed. HH, Lon.: 1937

J.   Journals and Papers, ed. HH, completed
      by Graham Storey, Lon.: 1959

S.   Sermons and Devotional Writings, ed.
      Christopher Devlin, SJ, Lon.: 1959

L.i.   Letters to Robert Bridges, ed. C.C. Abbott,
        Lon.: [1935] rev. 1955

L.ii.   Correspondence of GMH and R.W. Dixon,
         ed. C.C. Abbott, Lon.: [1935] rev. 1955

L.iii.   Further Letters, ed. C.C. Abbott, [1938].
          All refs. are to rev. and enlarged 2nd
          ed., Lon.: 1956

Scale

⊢——————————⊣ 50 mm of the original MS.;omitted
from most pages of C.i. and C.ii., as these all
measure c. 7 cm. wide x 12 cm.

Acknowledgements

For long-sustained encouragement, as well as generous permission to reproduce the Hopkins material in this, the first of two volumes of facsimiles (much of it previously unpublished), I express my gratitude to the British Province of the Society of Jesus. This warm co-operation was extended to me first by Fr. Ronald Moffat and the permission was confirmed by Fr. Edward Ennis as Secretary of Trustees for Roman Catholic Purposes Registered (in whom the Hopkins copyright is now vested). The two early Note-books, C. i and C. ii, part of the rich collection of Hopkins manuscripts in Campion Hall, Oxford, have never before been published in full. They appear here complete at the request of the British Province and by their kind leave, thus making accessible to careful scholars new material the value of which is outlined in Part II of the Introduction. That part has been composed with the professional advice of Felix Letemendia, M.D. (Madrid), F. R. C. Psych. (London), who for many years, as a psychiatrist attached to an Oxford college, was closely associated with undergraduates. To his deep interest and insights I am much indebted.

The owners of the Hopkins manuscripts have offered me every assistance as well as their blessing on this edition. I am specially indebted to the late Edward, first Lord Bridges, and to his son Thomas, the present baron, both of whom among many kindnesses made special arrangements so that I could over prolonged periods compare the manuscripts they owned with other versions in Oxford. The staff of the Bodleian Library have treated me with great courtesy over the years: their Hopkins treasures include MSS.B, H.i and H.ii, besides collections of letters from and about the poet. I have been much indebted to the late Robert Shackleton, former Librarian, to Douglas Vaisey the present Librarian, David Rogers who gave me special assistance on many occasions, and Colin Harris. Edward Hall, Director of the Oxford University Research Laboratory for Archaeology and the History of Art has provided expert help in differentiating Hopkins's inks from those used by Robert Bridges.

Other owners who have provided me with photographs are the late Christabel, Lady Pooley, a direct descendant of Grace Hopkins, who sent me copies of sonnets the poet transcribed for his sister; the rector of Stonyhurst College; the President and Librarian of Holy Cross College, Worcester, Massachusetts, and of the College of Notre Dame of Maryland; the Harry Ransom Humanities Research Center, University of Texas at Austin; the Archivist of the Irish Province in Dublin; Fr. Francis Edwards, SJ, Archivist of the British Province, Mount Street, London; the Very Rev. C.J.Q. Whitaker, The Oratory, Birmingham; the Archivist of the Northamptonshire and Huntingdonshire Archives in

Delapre Abbey; and the Department of Manuscripts of the British Library.

For assistance in checking doubtful readings in the classical poems I thank Colin Hardie, late of Magdalen College, Oxford, and Ross Kilpatrick of Queen's University, Ontario; and for help with the poems in Welsh, Marie Surridge, also of Queen's.

My many return visits to Oxford to study the manuscripts have been generously financed by the Canada Council and its successor, the Social Sciences and Humanities Research Council; or, during 1979–1981, the Killam Trust. The Dean of Graduate Studies and the Dean of Arts and Science at Queen's have also provided support. Among colleagues who have lent me practical encouragement I must name John Stedmond and the late George Whalley. Lesley Higgins drew my attention to the rare pamphlet reproduced in Plates 152 to 154 and has assisted me in other ways. Early transcriptions of the manuscripts were prepared by Bronwyn Wallace, now a rising Canadian poet.

Successive Masters of Campion Hall, Oxford, offered me hospitality while I was examining the poems; for this kindness I have been indebted to Jesuit Fathers Deryck Hanshell, E.J. Yarnold, the late Benjamin Winterborn, Paul Edwards, and Peter Hackett. Among helpful librarians and archivists I particularly remember Philip Endean, SJ, and the late Basil Fitzgibbon, SJ. I thank Penelope Bulloch of Balliol College and Christine Butler of Corpus Christi College, Oxford, for permission to use manuscripts in their care.

To Fr. Anthony Bischoff, SJ, I owe a particular debt. In the 1940s, before the two notebooks C. i and C. ii had suffered further impairment through heavy use, he arranged for them to be carefully microfilmed, and even persuaded a metropolitan police department to take photographs of the most difficult pages through special filters. Although he is still opposed in principle to the publication of Hopkins's Anglican notes of spiritual self-examination (an attitude which I long shared with him), he has at the request of the Provincial of the British Province of the Society of Jesus supplied me with his microfilms and the transcriptions he made when the manuscripts were somewhat more legible. His continued friendship and co-operation have been vital for this volume.

Fuller acknowledgements will be found in my Oxford English Texts edition of *The Poetical Works of Gerard Manley Hopkins*. The origin of these Facsimiles in that edition and their eventual separation from it are outlined in Appendix A below. To my Oxford editors I should add Thomas Collins, now Vice-President of the University of Western Ontario, who persuaded me to produce the Hopkins volumes. Ralph Carlson, former Vice-President of Garland Publishing, showed exemplary patience over delays caused by an eye condition which eventually required surgery.

I owe more than can easily be put into words to my family for their unfailing support during the Hopkins editing that has preoccupied me for so many years. My wife Rita helped me in the initial stages as far as her own professional pursuits in music and art permitted. Her pastel portrait of Hopkins is reproduced as Plate 1. Our daughter Catherine was of considerable help in the early stages of the *OET*, and I have also benefited from her careful study of the texts.

NORMAN H. MACKENZIE
Queen's University at Kingston, Ontario
M A R C H 1988

Introduction

This is the first of two volumes of Hopkins's *Poetic Facsimiles*, which have been planned to include every known autograph of his verse, along with any transcriptions which have some authority. Very few of them have been previously reproduced in facsimile, and some of the early drafts have been hitherto known only in brief extracts.

PART I
ARRANGEMENT OF PLATES

My main purpose in editing Hopkins's manuscripts has been to encourage a closer study of his poetic development—both during his successive phases and, on a smaller scale, in his reshaping of individual pieces. With this two-fold objective, the poems are set out in more or less chronological sequence, and the various versions of a poem are placed side by side—a design which has often required many calculations before the demands of legibility could be reconciled with those of close proximity, especially in his more mature verse.

These facsimiles have gradually evolved alongside my new edition of Hopkins in the Oxford English Texts series, a work passing through the press as this volume has reached its final stages. The OET is not a Fifth edition of Oxford's *Poems of Gerard Manley Hopkins*, to replace the Fourth edition that W.H. Gardner and I first issued in 1967: like its OET predecessors for other poets, it is intended for more specialized and scholarly use. As the OET Hopkins arranges the poems in the approximate order in which they were composed, its poem and line numbers are recorded in the margins of these plates. Each of the extensive headnotes in the OET commentary (too long to be repeated in the facsimiles) describes every MS in turn and attempts to assign it a place in the sequence, either from its provenance, or its physical layout (subject to his changing preferences), or from subtle modifications in Hopkins's handwriting.

In this last respect I am deeply indebted to Dr. Catherine Phillips, herself the editor of the latest edition of Hopkins in the new Oxford Authors series. She undertook at my request the laborious investigation of the many little changes through which Hopkins's hand modified itself, letter by letter. This pioneering work proved so demanding that she was at times ready to abandon it as too complicated to provide reliable data, but in the end it proved an irreplaceable tool. Checking her conclusions with different reference material to guide me, I have in nearly every case reached the same broad dating for each

manuscript. Hopkins, on the all-too-few occasions when he dated an interim autograph, tended to assign each revision the date of his earliest draft, a rather misleading practice.

Dr. Phillip's own chronological sequence, refined independently, inevitably varies from mine in the arbitrary positions we have each chosen for longer poems, such as "A Voice from the World" or "Floris in Italy," the composition of which overlapped scores of shorter lyrics. Moreover, because of my special interest in comparing successive versions of a particular piece, I have tended to group these together under a single number: thus four handlings of the St. Dorothea legend, which in our Fourth edition were scattered from pp. 20 to 344, are here and in the OET brought together as No. 42(a), (b), (c), and (d)—a collocation I decided upon after the frustrations of trying to compare them in depth.

The Early Note-books, C.i and C.ii.

The basically chronological sequence in this volume of facsimiles is both intensified and yet interrupted by the inclusion of the two little Note-books that contain most of his early poems along with much rich material for poetry. These two Note-books, C. i and C. ii, owned by Campion Hall, Oxford, and never before published in full or reproduced in facsimile, are included here at the request of the British Province of the Society of Jesus. The reasons for the request and for my carefully considered agreement are set out in Part II of this Introduction.

These tiny unruled note-books, their pages measuring only 7.2cm. by 11.8, were designed to fit into a waistcoat pocket so as to be readily available. Hopkins used them for coming engagements, social or academic, for capturing in words or sketches the inscapes of trees or the traceries of windows. He developed poetic fluency by composing snatches of verse which often seem to be passages from some rousing lost play, but which, I am convinced, are really exercises in embodying some visual or philosophical discovery in a form easily adaptable to an as yet unwritten verse drama. There was no market for purely descriptive fragments. Of special fascination are his ingenious philological speculations, cultivated in preparation for Moderations—an ordeal which is not even mentioned in the pages following C.ii.25 when it must have confronted him.

The familiar title, "Early Diaries," is clearly a misnomer. They only occasionally record the day's events, except indirectly through the informative daily notes of self-examination. The first little book, C.i., is dated "September 24, 1863," but in the course of a year and some 200 pages it yields only just over a dozen dates, more than half of them attached to pencil sketches. With C.ii. also, after the initial date "Sept. 9. 1864" on its inside front cover, dates are equally rare till we reach C.ii.62 when the daily notes of so-called "Sins" begin, invaluable for dating the poems scattered between them. I have emphasised dates throughout by entering some of them in the outer margin.

Attention should be drawn to sections of C.i and C.ii where pages have been cut out, in most cases probably by Hopkins himself. He alludes (C.ii.88) to a rough sketch on C.ii.85–86 which he had torn out so that a more finished drawing could be made from it: only the stub remains. Many earlier drafts of poems must have been sacrificed in a similar way, such as drafts of "Floris in Italy" when it was in narrative stanzas instead of dramatic form. Hopkins inserted page numbers in C.i up to p. 198: from this point the pagination is mine (ignoring a missing leaf after C.i.202). The gaps revealed by Hopkins's own

pagination of C.i are pp. 1–12; the top halves of 13 and 14; 19, 20; 109–22; 125–32; 181–82; 185–86. The top half of C.i.191 ("Gerard Hopkins reflected in a lake") was "borrowed" by an admirer but later recovered. Hopkins's own numbering of C.ii ends with p.8. Two leaves, C.ii.29 to 32, were cut out but preserved separately. About half of C.ii was left blank—perhaps just as well since Hopkins's writing had been shrinking towards illegibility. With forty or more lines to the page, and deletion strokes wavering through letters scarcely a millimeter in height, there have been considerable editorial problems in producing a transcription. Though Hopkins entrusted poems, both drafts and faircopies, to his Note-books, he probably copied out separately any verse he wanted to show others, in the process converting his private shorthand signs and abbreviations into normal script.

It seemed vital to reproduce each of the Note-books in its entirety without interruption. The first, C. i, occupies Plates 29 to 77, beginning after the last poem he composed before entering Oxford and ending in September 1864. Then we have to retrace our steps briefly to catch up with the separate manuscripts of some poems copied into his first tiny Note-book: these engross only Plates 78 to 81. To save turning back to the C. i pages for comparison I have reproduced again the relevant entries from the Note-book. Thus with No. 17, "Barnfloor and Winepress," the version published in the *Union Review*, which varies from the first form in nearly every line, is surrounded on Plates 78 and 79 by transcripts made by Hopkins's friends from a now-missing autograph. The draft in C.i reappears (along with "New Readings") on Plate 80ᴬ, a right-hand plate. Any left-hand plate in these volumes may be brought within the same field of simultaneous view as a later right-hand plate by the simple expedient of holding up the intervening leaf or leaves at right angles. This has been taken into account in planning the layout, asserting priority at times over the marshalling in strict chronological order of the different versions of a particular poem.

The second early Note-book, C. ii, which flows straight on in time from C. i, absorbs Plates 82 to 151. Immediately after these plates I have inserted a very rare pamphlet, no copy of which I have been able to find in North American libraries, Questions for Self-Examination, discovered in Keble College, Oxford, among Dr. Liddon's papers by one of my research students, Dr. Lesley Higgins. It is probable that Hopkins was handed this or a similar guide to self-scrutiny by his confessors. After this association item we have once again to overtake a few manuscripts of poems contemporary with the second Note-book: Plates 156 to 165 accommodate them all.

PART II
NOTES ON THE DAILY EXAMINATION
OF CONSCIENCE

Through editorial work on poems that Hopkins composed at Oxford I had from the sixties onward spent a great deal of time scrutinizing the two tiny Note-books, C.i and C.ii. I made no attempt, however, to transcribe the notes of his sins or scruples which are scattered through the second half of volume two. They have been looked at by many scholars with the consent of Campion Hall. The spiritual entries cover a period of ten troubled months from March 25, 1865, during which Hopkins was trying to reach a higher plane of spiritual life, and debating within himself whether his greatest sin might not be membership of a schismatic church. They end on January 23, 1866, some two and a half years before he entered the Jesuit Novitiate (Sept. 1868).

Though there has been a general understanding that they could not be published without explicit permission, many scholars have referred to them and drawn their own conclusions, sometimes of a controversial nature. The Jesuits at Campion Hall showed no special sensitivity about these records while I was working on the manuscripts: indeed, at one stage a former Master of the Hall asked me whether I could see any objection to the two little books being deposited on loan in the Bodleian Library, since they contained the drafts of so many early poems. In advising strongly against this my prime consideration was the vulnerable state of the pencil entries, already seriously smudged even before they were loaned to Humphry House for the preparation of *The Note-books and Papers of Gerard Manley Hopkins* (1937) and the subsequent *Journals* (1959). I had over the years observed the deterioration of the Hopkins manuscripts generously loaned to the Bodleian by Lord Bridges, although they were in ink and on stouter paper. But I also argued that the notes of his sins and misgivings were essentially private documents which I would prefer to see respected.

I was certainly not alone in taking this stance: it was one which had been adopted around 1947 by W.H. Gardner, Humphry House, Anthony Bischoff, SJ, and the Very Rev. Martin D'Arcy, SJ, and later by other leading scholars such as Graham Storey. However, during the seventies a number of younger scholars pointed to the greater openness now prevailing in the availability of diaries and the study of sexual orientation. In addition to many gifted writers who, secretly or openly, responded to masculine physique more than to feminine, there were numerous Victorians, educated at school and university alike in an almost entirely male setting, who felt drawn towards both sexes, but whose friendships with women were severely limited by their environment. They seem to have remained celibate in most cases: in fact, many were Anglican High Church members with austere codes of conduct in all activities.

There have been increasingly frequent references to this aspect of Hopkins's life in the last ten years, notably by Paddy Kitchen in her *Gerard Manley Hopkins* (London: 1978), Chapter IV. After studying all the notes of his self-scrutiny and thoroughly investigating the Victorian background, Kitchen dismissed as misplaced any inference that Hopkins's reputation would be "tainted with . . . abnormality" by an

> admission and discussion of an involuntary capacity to find men attractive
> . . . Since he was to become a celibate, and since his life as an undergradu-

ate was apparently very chaste, it may fairly be claimed that his sexual orientation was never conclusively evolved. Awareness of male beauty, palpa-
bly expressed, appears in some of his later poetry, but whether it indicates
the direction in which his feelings might finally have deepened and expanded under a different life-style is not established (p. 62).

Though these deductions seem reasonable, there were protests from some Hopkins critics that the notes of conscience had been used without warrant, and the Society was asked
to protect the poet's privacy. The developments which made me change my own convictions should therefore be explained.

Disappointed that Hopkins's *Journals and Papers* had long been out of print, scholars
began to ask the Society of Jesus whether they could urge Oxford University Press to
reprint it, possibly with revisions. Before deciding whether to make a recommendation,
the Master of Campion Hall, Fr. Peter Hackett, SJ, carrying out some enquiries, mentioned the matter informally to me and invited my reactions. I repeated what I had often
said in writing about the superb levels reached by the edition: Humphry House devoted
two decades and more to meticulous research into all the circumstances surrounding
Hopkins, his family and friends during the years covered by the journals, with the aid of
his talented wife Madeline and after his death of Graham Storey. Half the volume consists
of invaluable annotations, and though there are inevitably some errors, the abundance of
detail (thought excessive by some captious reviewers when the book first appeared) has
been of increasing benefit to subsequent research. If reprinting were decided upon, I
offered to supply some corrections, along with transcriptions of a few unimportant items
such as lists of names which had probably been inadvertently omitted. The inclusion of
the notes of daily self-examination was an entirely separate matter.

Reasons for Publishing the Notes

I had already obtained permission from Trustees for Roman Catholic Purposes to reproduce all the autographs of Hopkins's poems in facsimile. These were originally intended
to form the second volume of my Oxford English Texts edition of the Poetical Works of
Hopkins, but when I reported to Oxford the interest prompted at Garland Publishing by
Dr. Thomas Collins, Oxford withdrew in Garland's favor. After the release by the Tennyson trustees of all that poet's long-restricted poetic note-books, Garland asked me to
make my Hopkins facsimiles as complete as possible. A further factor arose when it was
learned that all House's accumulated research notes for his unfinished biography of
Hopkins, along with complete (though not necessarily accurate) transcriptions of the
daily notes of sins and scruples, had passed into other hands on the death of his widow,
and (so rumor had it) were likely to be used without detailed ascription or verbatim quotation.

This possibility raised two concerns. If the entries were paraphrased in a generalized
way without acknowledgement, the balance and fairness of deductions based on them
could not be appraised by anyone without the laborious checking of the whole document. Unsympathetic comments had greeted the scholar who some years ago maintained
that Hopkins's well-known contrition over feeling tempted by a man had to be judged
within its full context: the "context" was not available to prove his argument. Moreover
the notes are in a minute script, made all the more difficult to decipher by deletion lines;
and though Hopkins made no effort to render them completely illegible by erasing them

or using looped lines, transcriptions of an obscured entry by different readers may vary dramatically.

Rather than a separate publication of the "sins," a less sensational scheme eventually commended itself and was approved: the British Province of the Society of Jesus invited me to incorporate the two tiny note-books C. i and C. ii entire in the facsimile volume that I had already almost completed. This offered the additional advantage of showing readers how casual and chaotic the jottings of poems and observations were from which House had constructed a volume to which every Hopkins scholar constantly refers. But, as I also pointed out, it complicated my task, since it would considerably delay the publication and involve a special arrangement with the publishers for the inclusion of an Introduction much longer than they normally allowed, yet necessarily not long enough to deal with all the arguments in an area where opinions have been, and probably will remain, divided. I foresaw that the publication of these private notes would seem a betrayal to many whose opinions I respected, and no commentary interpreting them could possibly satisfy everyone. People in all ages, however, have been helped in their own efforts at self-discipline by the knowledge that others whose achievements they admired faced temptations which sometimes reduced them to despair.

Those who feel that the image of Hopkins has been damaged by these revelations should consider whether the partial and more casual disclosures—bound to occur in the publicity surrounding his centenary—might not have led to serious misconceptions. Hopkins kept the note-book C.ii with him throughout his many moves in England, Wales, and Ireland. Three weeks after he began to enter the results of his daily examination of conscience, he wrote a memo, "Little bk. for sins" (Plate 105, C. ii. 65, *l* 14, April 12, 1865, four days before Easter Sunday). Yet he continued to intermingle verse with self-examinations and other notes: their juxtaposition does not seem to have worried him. The "Little book," probably bought on the advice of his confessor, seems to have been intended for summaries of shortcomings under different headings, prepared from the repetitious daily entries, for periodic confession to an Anglican priest. This we may deduce from C. ii. 68, *ll.* 10, 12, April 28 (Plate 108): "Note. [Sins *del.*] confession for Easter Communion, it is entered." This little book, recording his confessions properly so called, has not survived. He tore out of both C. i and C.ii many leaves that carried sketches or drafts of poems, whereas not a single page of his spiritual notes appears to me to be missing. The journal that follows C.ii in sequence, A.I, covering May 2 to July 24, 1866, has the top right hand corner cut away to reveal "PRIVATE J.," and inside the front cover he added below his name and the date "Please not to read." No one, however, has objected to this journal having been published in full, first by Fr. Anthony Bischoff in the Jesuit house journal *Letters and Notices* (55, no. 295, May 1947, 147–55), and subsequently by Humphry House in *Journals and Papers* (133–47). The inside cover of C.ii has no such indication of privacy: the page below his name and date remained blank for the rest of his life, twenty-three years. One of the note-books of another Balliol student, Arthur Hugh Clough, now being edited by the Master of Balliol, Anthony Kenny, has "PRIVATE" written some ten times on the cover: it also contains admissions of moral failure, though much less frankly and systematically entered. Some time before 8 May 1885, Hopkins attempted to thin out his accumulated papers, and had destroyed most of the letters received since he was a school-boy before he grew so reluctant even to re-read, let alone destroy that, fortunately for posterity, he allowed the rest of his letters and note-books to remain, "ruins and wrecks" as he diffidently called them (L. iii.255).

Dr. Felix Letemendia

I agreed to the undertaking on two conditions: that the Society of Jesus should make their sponsorship clear, and that I might have the cooperation of a medical and psychiatric expert in fields where I had no competence. I was very fortunate in enlisting Dr. Felix Letemendia, a psychiatrist with long experience of Oxford undergraduates. The analysis of the sins and scruples that follows has been extensively discussed between us and agreed upon. Dr. Letemendia has appended his own professional assessment of Hopkins's sexual orientation and problems during this period—before his conversion, Jesuit training, and emergence as a mature poet. His considered opinion, combined with my recent study of the latest medical and psychiatric investigations, has modified my own privately held views of these notes and won my full support. During a series of long discussions, we have reached the conclusions set out in the following pages. They culminate with his own professional diagnosis of the sexual aspects of the confession notes. His judgements seem to me to be in line with the most responsible analyses of sexual orientation in the recent literature of psychological medicine I have studied. I am deeply grateful to have had the collaboration of Dr. Letemendia in this delicate undertaking.

Many general readers may be somewhat impatient of the repetitious detail in these daily self-scrutinies. But the Society might have engendered suspicions if they had decided upon the printing of extracts only. Instead they agreed to a full facsimile edition along with a transcription of every word that I have been able to decipher with any assurance. Most scholarly books have portions provided for reference rather than mere perusal: here the day-by-day entries will be found to furnish new means of approaching the poems written at any particular point they cover. Even scholars were at first put off by the historical minutiae in that invaluable source-book by the late Fr. Alfred Thomas, SJ, *Hopkins the Jesuit*, (London: 1969), seriously underestimated when it first appeared. Yet it has been steadily growing in repute because it provides a solid floor of fact. Norman White, in a negative review of Thomas, expressed his own preference for "an impressionistic literary study." Fortunately he has since changed his mind; his long-awaited biography of Hopkins (he assures me) is to be accompanied by detailed references reflecting the results of his primary research, and I regret that this Introduction has been composed without the benefit of his discoveries.

Attempts To Censor the Hopkins Letters

When Professor Claude Abbott was editing the three volumes of Hopkins's correspondence, a number of people urged that certain passages should be omitted: they argued (as he later told me) that Hopkins himself, so loyal to the Church and the Society, would never have approved the publication of such remarks about the Society as "Our institute provides us means of discouragement, and on me at all events they have had all the effect that could be expected or wished and rather more" (L.i.248). Yet our insights into Hopkins have benefited immensely from Abbott's insistence upon virtually complete publication. We read such observations not only with deep empathy for the poet-priest who turned his miserable sense of isolation and failure into the superb Sonnets of Desolation, but for the Society (often short of members with particular qualifications) in its efforts to use this unique man, with his gifts and limitations, in a setting where his talents could be of best service. And Fr. Christopher Devlin, SJ, did not prune from the *Sermons and Spiritual Writings* that he collected the tormented confessions in the poet's meditation

notes in Ireland. Hopkins criticism would have remained acrimoniously controversial if censorship had been applied to these four basic volumes.

Some Biographical Gains from Publishing the Self-Examinations

The deeper understanding of the poet's life flowing from the release of these notes includes the realization of how much wider his circle of acquaintances was than the other journals disclose. They provide the means of judging who at this time were his nearest friends. Luxmoore remembered him when a Highgate School boarder being "both popular and respected" (L.iii.395), and his frequent invitations to wines, dinners, and desserts at Oxford extend this description to his residence in Balliol. Edward Bond, supposed by some to have been among the closest to him in the Oxford period, is barely mentioned. Scores of people crop up about whom the printed journals and letters are mute, inviting annotation which is really beyond the scope of the present work, but is nevertheless squeezed in here and there in compressed cross-references.

That we must not take these self-analyses at their face value appears time and again. George Saintsbury figures only once—these notes, after all, cover less than a year—and then in a hostile context: "Malicious feelings against Saintsbury at a celebration at Merton" (Plate 108, *l*.15). This reaction was probably concealed and certainly overcome, for forty years later, when Saintsbury was a distinguished Professor of English Literature in Edinburgh, he referred to "my friend of long ago, the late Father Gerard Hopkins" (*History of English Prosody*, 1906, i.382). Because it was the state church, the Church of England was interlinked with the government: the Prayer Book included a "Prayer for the High Court of Parliament." After the Prime Minister's death on October 18, 1865, Hopkins confided to his note-book "Violence abt. Lord Palmerston" (Plate 140, *l*.7). When Palmerston had been buried in Westminster Abbey with public honors and many obituary notices, Hopkins began to wonder whether his criticism of the former head of the government really was a sin: on October 29 he notes "To enquire abt. talking agst. Lord Palmerston, wh. I did today" (Plate 141, *l*.3). We do not know what advice he received. Nowhere else does Palmerston appear in his published writings, but a successor, Gladstone, comes in for some uninhibited abuse from the mature Catholic priest (July 1887) as "the Grand Old Mischief-maker loose, like the Devil, for a little while and meddling and marring all the fiercer for his hurry" (L.i.257; but see S.260).

Future research may wish to follow up such entries of considerable interest as "Conceit after hearing what Miss Tennyson said" (Plate 136, *l*.12), for which the published volumes have not prepared us; and mysterious ones: "Speaking impertinently to Liddon (about Jowett). Was it deception about my Plato paper?" (Plate 103, *l*.11, March 28–29, 1865, well before his Platonic dialogue "On the Origin of Beauty," 12 May, J.86–114); "No work done in evening through going to Addis about the Canada business" (p. 74, *l*.4).

From these notes we can generally determine within a day when Hopkins moved from Hampstead to Oxford, Manchester, or Devon and even the rough dates of his visits to relatives at Paddington or Croydon: it is often useful to know the environment in which his poems or poetic descriptions were conceived. I have interpolated notes on these, and recorded when terms ended or began. We learn a great deal about his gregariousness at this stage, his brief spells of despondency and elation, the journals he dipped into (e.g., *Athenaeum, Lancet, The Saturday Review*, not mentioned in the printed *Journals*), books he felt guilty about reading when he should have been mastering the textual emendations

proposed by this classics editor or that (the poems of Canon Dixon and Edgar Allan Poe, a Thackeray novel, a story by George Sand, etc.).

"Temptations" and "Scruples" Distinguished from "Sins"

In interpreting the "Sins" we should observe the distinction between what can fairly be called a sin and other categories: a "temptation" (which may be no sin), "temptations somewhat yielded to" (Plates 124, *ll*.7, 9, 19; 146, *l*.10; 148, *l*.9; etc.), and "scruples." A "scruple" (Hopkins was exceptionally prone to them) arises when someone is uncertain whether a particular action or thought is wrong or not. Jeremy Taylor spoke of it as a "great trouble of mind proceeding from a little motive," and Fr. F.W. Faber in his *Growth of Holiness* (1854) dismissed it as "a vain fear of sin where there is no reasonable ground for suspecting sin." Dr. Letemendia enumerates many instances scattered among Hopkins's so-called "sins."

Poems Illuminated by Notes of Self-Examination

A particular privilege conferred on critics by these notes is the opportunity of relating the poems that appear in their interstices with this intimate, though mostly negative, journal of his thought life, and the incidental revelation of how he had been spending leisure hours. The poems sometimes act as a necessary corrective to the lopsided lists of "sins." Some pieces were displaced in time: two sonnets "To Oxford" (*OET* No. 56, a and b) are dated "Low Sunday and Monday, 1865" (i.e., April 23–24) but were not entered till about June 26. From the page covering the time of composition (Plate 106) we see that he had just passed a few unhappy days at home, and that the tribute to Oxford was started on the first full day after his return (Easter term had technically begun on April 19). Another displaced reference (Plate 105, *l*.31: "In looking over the above poem an evil thought seemed to arise fr. the line before"), entered on Easter Eve, most probably alludes to the draft of "Easter Communion" (No. 53) on Plate 101: the "evil thought" could then possibly be from the prose notes above the poem on C.ii.58 *ll.* 6–8. On Good Friday he recorded "Foolish and proud thoughts abt. fasting" (Plate 105, *l.* 30)—such austerities must be hidden not only from others but from the Pharisaic mind within.

Plate 113 opens with his guilt because he had been "Idling in looking out of window in Geldart's upper room." But these value-judgements were not the product of Gerard Manley Hopkins the future internationally acclaimed poet, but of his co-tenant (as it were)—little Hopkins of Balliol, who was expected to prove himself as bright a classical scholar in Greats as he had in Mods., and who appeared so solemn in chapel and church, an "unusually exacting Anglican" (L.iii.23). That self-condemned "Idling," looking out of a high window, combined with staying up late, was presently transmuted on the same page into the haunting phrases of "The Alchemist in the City" (*OET* No. 60), gazing down from his high tower:

> My window shews the travelling clouds,
> Leaves spent, new seasons, alter'd sky,
> The making and the melting crowds:
> The whole world passes; I stand by.

Here, in fact, were some gleams of the gold which the alchemist laments as beyond his creative reach. Moreover, other admissions preceding this poetic embodiment of failure contradict the impression that he was isolated from his fellow-students. He chided himself on May 12 for "Conceited talking to Geldart (as often) about Ilbert and Art, and to Coles. Conceited things." Ilbert was a more brilliant scholar than Hopkins, a Fellow of Balliol, Librarian of the Union Society 1864–65 and its President 1865: he had befriended Hopkins shortly after his arrival (L.iii. 70–73), and seems to have complimented him on his drawing. The poem is also followed by "conceited looking forward" (Plate 114, *l.* 12). This may be sin to a saint, but every stimulating teacher encourages his students to aim high. It is commonplace for patches of despondency to be interspersed (Plate 113, *l.* 6), but less common for these too to be regarded as sinful.

The self-reproaches and the related verse can be seen as mutually corrective in the next poem also, No. 61: "Myself unholy, from myself unholy/To the sweet living of my friends I look—"; they are better than he is, though admittedly not perfect. We would expect the surrounding "Sins" to reveal "Envy of X . . . and Y." What we find is the opposite (Plates 117–18): these bristle with criticisms of M'Neill, Coles, Myers, and Gallop. The sonnet makes some amends for his censorious spirit: the spiritual notes on the other hand indicate that he was not as blind to character-defects around him as the sonnet implies.

With No. 62, "See how Spring opens with disabling cold," the admission that it gave rise to a "scruple" (a doubt whether there was something sinful about it) seems to confirm Rudy Bremer's guess that Hopkins was thinking partly about this poem when he told Urquhart (L.iii.27) that though he had nourished a "silent conviction" that he would become a Catholic for about a year before his conversion (July 1866), "when it formed itself into words" (as in this sonnet), he found himself resisting it.

That delightful lyric sung by Daphne in "Castara Victrix," "Who loves me here and has my love" (Plate 130) carries a beautiful promise of married delights in its second stanza: "And I can teach him happiness/That shall not fail in winter-time." It is significant that this song follows immediately after his spiritual note, "Temptation to adultery of the heart with Mrs. Gurney listened to" (*ll.* 8, 9). Alice Gurney was a newly married girl of twenty-one at the time (cf. L.i.l; L.iii.50; J.166, 295, 385). We may plausibly conjecture (though there are no confession notes to corroborate it) that less fleeting encounters with other young women who attracted him lie behind the more deeply felt passages in "Floris in Italy" (No. 31) and "A Voice from the World" (No. 38). These cannot have been inspired by Digby Dolben, since they were written before Dolben's brief visit to Oxford when Hopkins became so enchanted with him. Had some woman he liked become a Catholic? Some friend's conversion might account for his record on 6 September 1865, when he had stayed up late writing a subsequent portion of "Castara," that the last lines, including "Much cause to go because Castara goes" (Plate 132), produced a "wholly illogical association or alarm." His note "Putting off answering Miss Robinson" (C.ii.99, *l.* 11) probably has a much more mundane explanation.

What were the unanswered prayers that (Plates 132–33) failed to penetrate the "brazen heaven" above him (No. 67)? A hint occurs at the bottom of Plate 134: "Want of faith in God abt. temptations." We may, I think, discern through these self-examinations that his inability to cope with certain tendencies (including the "dreamy idling" we associate with the creative temperament) was one of the forces that impelled him towards the Catholic Church.

How skewed an impression the notes may convey is well illustrated from his unfinished sonnet "Shakspere" (No. 68). The question raised here seems parallel to the poet's concern in "Henry Purcell" (No. 131): how does God judge the soul of a superb artist? His admiration for Shakespeare is obvious. Yet in his "Sins" we learn only "Slight tempt. in Shakspere" (Plate 132, *ll.* 4, 5), and "Reading weakly a thing in 'Love's Labour [sic] Lost,'" which ends the notes above what must surely have been intended as a panegyric (Plate 135). It is strange that this comedy rather than a greater tragedy precipitated the tribute. These negative entries nevertheless assure us that while completing Jacobean type dramas such as "Floris in Italy" (Plate 133, etc.) he was steeping himself in Shakespeare. The inclusion of *Henry V, VI,* and *VIII* with *Richard III* in a list of works to be read (J.35) is no proof that he did read them, for the same plays recur in another list six months later (J.56, Plates 71 and 100).

Some poems completely contradict expectations based on the tone of the "Sins" preceding them. "Trees by their yield" (No. 69, Plate 137) laments his barrenness, a cry we hear among poems in his final phase in Ireland. But his notes on the previous page (Plate 136) detect "Pride and looking forward," "Conceit after hearing what Miss Tennyson said," and "Conceited forecasts." "Trees by their yield" is followed by equally unexpected entries, such as "pride and foolish self-will in thinking of preaching unaccepted Catholic truths," and "Spiritual pride." Clearly in interpreting the earlier poems, which in the Hopkins canon appear to be self-analyses, we must remember Keats's remark about the chameleon poet's ever-shifting moods. His poems written in Ireland, on the other hand, correlate closely with the sustained periods of depression shown in his confessions to Bridges and among the meditation notes published by Fr. Devlin (see my *Reader's Guide to Hopkins,* pp. 170–71). Indeed, when Hopkins was reborn as a Catholic poet in 1875 with the stranding of the "Deutschland," he seems to have resolved on a new transparency of self-revelation (L.i.47; 225, etc.).

The irritable self-dissatisfaction shown around Christmas 1865 in Plate 146 should be offset against the prayerful aspirations in "Moonless darkness stands between" (*OET* No. 73), composed on Christmas Day. His entry that night, "Idling in going to bed," is bisected by the poem that probably explains this miscalled "Sin." I like to think of that "idling" as spent at the window of his darkened room, drawing new resolution from the night sky. Nothing else he did that day has had the permanent value of this little nine-line lyric. A true poet will compose in spite of circumstances and himself.

One further reference to his poems calls for comment. On December 21, 1865 (Plate 145, *ll.* 32, 40; see also Plate 141, *l.* 9) he notes "Dangerous scrupulosity abt. finishing a stanza of *Beyond the Cloister* for Dolben," and the next day "Repeating to myself bits of" that poem when he was trying to work. Another reference to this otherwise unknown piece eleven months later (L.iii.36) enables us to identify it as probably a revision in stanzas of "A Voice from the World" (*OET* No. 38). Neither Dr. Letemendia nor I can read that poem without a conviction that some intense (even if perhaps shortlived) heterosexual experience provoked it. Sending a revised stanza of it to Dolben involved him in a conflict between prudence and impulse.

The Purification of His Ambitions

During his earlier years at Oxford Hopkins fostered multiple ambitions: to obtain a First in his classical examinations, and also to become a poet and a painter (e.g., like Dante

Gabriel Rossetti: see L.iii.214). Throughout the ten-month period covered by his notes of daily self-scrutiny we can see the last of these objectives beginning to wither, and the main thrust of his life changing to the desire for moral perfection. It might even be argued that the unruliness of his passions was the principal hidden emotional spur to this determination to devote his whole being to God, and for his choice of the Order reputed to be the most exacting, the Jesuits (cf. L.iii.226–27). Certainly his decision against the life of a painter was associated with his resolve to avoid a dangerous "strain upon the passions" (L.iii.231).

When he decided to become a Catholic, Dr. Newman urged upon him "your first duty is to make a good class" so that his friends would realize that his conversion had not deflected him from this "first duty" (L.iii.405). But readers should be reminded that these daily notes were written while Hopkins was an Anglican. It would be interesting to investigate how far their tone reflects the special attitudes of Dr. E.B. Pusey and Rev. H.P. Liddon, two Anglican High Church leaders at Oxford to whom Hopkins made his confessions at apparently infrequent intervals. His respect for these two men certainly delayed his abandonment of the English church (L.iii.94).

Hopkins was familiar with one of the most celebrated High Anglican manuals of advice for those seeking perfection, Jeremy Taylor's *The Rule and Exercises of Holy Living* (1650): the author, a Fellow of All Souls, was chaplain to Charles I before retreating to "Golden Grove" in Wales. Manley Hopkins had a copy (*Hopkins Research Bulletin*, 5, 1974, p. 37), and Gerard quoted its subheading on "The Evil Consequents [sic] of Uncleanness" in July 1864 (J.30, Plate 61). That he had studied it carefully we might surmise from a few special points of correspondence between it and his spiritual notes, along with many general parallels in matters found also in other manuals on Christian Perfection. Among "Remedies against Uncleanness" (ch.II, sect.iii) the old divine suggested not only mortifying the flesh (using if necessary "violent pain" to drive out passion—cf. "Easter Communion," *ll.* 3a, 4a, Plate 101), but "painful postures in prayer, reciting our devotions with our arms extended at full length, like Moses praying against Amalek [Exod. 17:9–13], or our blessed Saviour hanging upon . . . the cross" (cf. "Pilate," *OET* No. 10, last section). This explains Hopkins's otherwise enigmatic entry "Speaking abt. holding up my hands in prayer in Lent to Coles" (Plate 106, *ll.* 36–37). Hopkins was unsure about mortification, and noted the need to ask his mentors about it (J.59). His frequent references to "danger" may reflect Taylor's advice that the seeker after the Grace of Humility should undertake to confess to some spiritual guide "his very thoughts and fancies, every act of his, and all his intercourse [dealings, conversations] with others *in which there may be danger* [our italics]; . . . every idle thought . . . every vanity of his spirit" (ch.II, sect.iv). Another dictum that Hopkins decided was in need of clarification is also laid down in *Holy Living*: "Speak not evil of the ruler of thy people" (ch.III, sect.i), which appeared to condemn his outbursts against Lord Palmerston (Plates 140–41), but which a conscientious citizen in a modern democracy might feel part of his duty. On wandering thoughts in private and public prayers, Jeremy Taylor stressed that the important thing was the earnest desire to worship whole-heartedly, and to contend against inattention: "whatsoever wanderings after this do return irremediably, are a misery of nature and an imperfection, but no sin" (ch. IV, sect. vii). Hopkins certainly found no remedy for inattention during this spell as an Anglican: his reiterated record of his failure registers his continual desire to feel himself in the presence of God. Finally, we might note that although *Holy*

Living presents exacting "Rules for Employing our Time" (another perpetual source of guilt to Hopkins), Taylor urges that prudence and moderation be used in applying the rules (which "are not Divine commandments") according to circumstances, "not with scruple and vexation," worrying about every minute and half-hour (ch.I, sec.i). If he had been Gerard Hopkins's confessor, he would not have needed to urge on him the prayer "Give me a tender conscience" (ch. I, sect. iii), but rather, "Deliver me from vexatious scruples."

In March 1865 Hopkins makes a note to pursue "Liddon's tracts" (J.59, Plate 102). It is likely that these included *Questions for Self-Examination* (reproduced on Plates 152–154), a rare twelve-page pamphlet that one of my graduate students, Lesley Higgins, found among the Liddon Papers in Keble College during research for a Queen's Ph.D. thesis on Hopkins and Pater. She also discovered in Liddon's diary the dates on which Hopkins had confessed to him, beginning over a year earlier than these notes: 10 February and 1 March 1864; 25 March 1865 (C.ii.61, *l* 4, Plate 102 confirms this); 6 February and 17 May 1866 (after these notes end). The notes themselves mention three other occasions when he apparently intended to confess: [? 11 November 1865], 20 November and 9 December (Plates 142, ll. 23–24; 143, *l* 24; 144, *l* 37). Just before going home for the Christmas vacation he records "I confessed to Dr. Pusey Dec. 16, 1865."

One of the questions that the little pamphlet included under the Second Commandment was "Have I gone to any worship other than that of the Church of England? or in any way encouraged such schismatical worship?" This might have disinclined Hopkins from discussing with his confessors his growing misgivings about the authority of the Anglican Church, and thus deprived them of an essential insight into his divided mind. The daily reciting of the penitential psalms for a certain period was probably either prescribed as a penance or suggested as a beneficial exercise (see Plate 115, *l* 6, etc.: the "pen. ps.," as Hopkins abridges them, are in the King James or A.V., Psalms 6, 32, 38, 51, 102, 130, 143, and in the Douay, 6, 31, 37, 50, 101, 129, 142). Pusey certainly recommended that Christians should confess their sins "in sorrow, with the use of the Penitential Psalms, especially . . . the fifty-first" (see his *Sermons from Advent to Whitsuntide*, London: 1848, 148–51).

Benjamin Franklin's Autobiography

Such daily cross-examinations are quite common in the formative years of men and women who have made a mark on the world. Benjamin Franklin (1706–1790) combined in a distinguished self-made career the talents of a community-leader, philosopher, scientist, inventor, statesman, and author. Finding the Presbyterian Church in which he had been brought up little help towards the achievement of high standards of conduct, he gave up attending it: the minister concentrated on polemical matters, which promoted ill-feeling between neighbors rather than the best interests of Philadelphia. Instead Franklin at about the age of twenty-two determined to attempt to reach moral perfection through a system of nightly self-examination. From philosophers reaching back to the ancient Greeks he compiled a list of thirteen moral virtues, defining each in a short precept. What Hopkins attempted as an ascetic High Anglican bears some remarkable resemblances to Benjamin Franklin's aspirations as recorded in his famous *Autobiography*.

1 *Temperance.* Eat not to dulness; drink not to elevation.   2 *Silence.* Speak
not but what may benefit others or yourself; avoid trifling conversation.

3 *Order.* Let all things have their places; let each part of your business have its time. 4 *Resolution.* Resolve to perform what you ought; perform without fail what you resolve.   5 *Frugality.* Make no expense but to do good to others or yourself; i.e., waste nothing.   6 *Industry.* Lose no time; be always employ'd in something useful; cut off all unnecessary actions.   7 *Sincerity.* Use no harmful deceit; think innocently and justly, and, if you speak, speak accordingly.   8 *Justice.* Wrong none by doing injuries, or omitting the benefits that are your duty.   9 *Moderation.* Avoid extreams; forbear resenting injuries so much as you think they deserve.   10 *Cleanliness.* Tolerate no uncleanliness in body, cloaths, or habitation.   11 *Tranquillity.* Be not disturbed at trifles, or at accidents common or unavoidable. 12 *Chastity.* Rarely use venery but for health or offspring, never to dulness, weakness, or the injury of your own or another's peace or reputation. 13 *Humility.* Imitate Jesus and Socrates.

Beginning each day with a prayer to the divine Goodness and Wisdom he ended it with the painful filling in of a chart in which a black dot opposite any precept indicated his failure to preserve it that day. Franklin confessed to the strain of "constant vigilance . . . against the unremitting attraction of ancient habits, and the force of perpetual temptations." Hopkins confessed "Old Habits," never defined, frequently abbreviated "O.H.," which we will confront later. His stress upon "silence" in "The Habit of Perfection" (*OET* No. 77) coincides with the high priority awarded that virtue by Franklin in his efforts to "break a habit I was getting into of prattling, punning, and joking, which only made me acceptable to trifling company." And a recurrent refrain in Hopkins's self-examinations is "Waste of time," though on that imputed offence we are convinced that his verdict was very frequently thoroughly mistaken. We of course enjoy the benefit of hindsight, and the scientific study of the mind's methods of operating.

Over-scrupulosity

Hopkins's painful self-accusations make evident what has long been deduced from well-known incidents in his biography—that he was one of those over-conscientious people, with profound religious convictions, who levy unreasonable demands on themselves. Only in the desperation of his last years, perhaps on the advice of his Catholic confessor, did he resolve to extend to himself the sympathetic consideration he showed others.

> My own heart let me more have pity on; let
> Me live to my sad self hereafter kind,
> Charitable; not live this tormented mind
> With this tormented mind tormenting yet. (*OET* No. 163).

A religious called to a life of contemplation may have his apparently featureless days filled, like those of St. Alphonsus Rodriguez the door-keeper, hero of "Honour is flashed off exploit" (*OET*, No. 176), with strenuous battles to preserve his mental activities on a plane of perfect love and purity. Those whose duties are more distracting, however, requiring more extrovert attention, have to achieve a compromise. Hopkins as a Jesuit earned the reputation of not being a *practical* man because he tended to convert relatively routine tasks (such as marking matriculation papers) into exacting ordeals. When he was a Professor of Classics in Ireland, in his attempt to reach absolute fairness, though each

paper was marked out of 600, we find him on some pages of his Dublin Note-book using half-marks, worth one-twelfth of one percent. He reduced himself to nervous wreckage in the process. Much earlier, his lectures on rhetoric to Manresa Juniors in 1873–74 (J.267 ff.) were of such a penetrating exploratory nature that we are still mining their wealth with profit. That year's teaching had been given him as a rest (L.iii.122–23), yet he wore himself down with it because he prescribed too ambitious a programme for himself and his students. Characteristically, he reckoned that he had been a failure because "I taught so badly and so painfully" (L.i.30).

"Unkindness"

If we relied solely on his relentless self-scrutiny, Hopkins during the ten months from March 1865 to January 1866 might emerge as a discourteous and unpleasant companion, particularly with the Rev. Edward Urquhart. We note time and again his contrition over "laughing at Urquhart," or "Talking abt. Urquhart less kindly than I could have." Yet Urquhart constantly sought out his company, and his daughter reported that "To the very end [27 years after Hopkins's death] he spoke of the charm of Gerard Hopkins" (L.iii.438). There were certainly short spells when Hopkins could be disagreeable—e.g., at home when he was secretly wrestling with the fateful decision between the Anglican and Roman communions, and during the final crisis (L.iii, 397, not covered by spiritual notes)—but while he was a senior boy in his Highgate school, where we might expect his assertiveness to have been more pronounced since he was "cock of the walk at Elgin" (L.iii.l), the school-house in which he boarded, Charles Luxmoore, who used the phrase, described him as "both popular and respected . . . good for his size at games," "one of the very best and nicest boys in the school." Gerard's uprightness, Luxmoore affirmed, was of "far away a higher standard than that of his fellows" (L.iii.394–96). His hypersensitive ammeter as an undergraduate registered among his sins "Talking either unkindly of Fyffe or near it," or, swinging to the extreme amplitude, "Feeling contempt for Mr. Ransome's friend," when possibly no one in the group noticed anything more than a certain aloofness. Though we are seldom told what provoked such reactions, here the next sentence is "Irritation with Geldart abt. *pock-bitten*" (Plate 123, *ll.* 5, 6), which sprang from that sympathy for unfortunate victims of the dreaded small-pox shown in his later letter to his sister Kate (L. iii. 115–16).

Among those by whom Hopkins found himself, in spite of repeated contrition, most frequently irritated or amused were (like the Rev. Edward Urquhart) Anglican curates, at Hampstead, Oxford, or in country churches where he worshipped during reading vacations. He may have measured them unfairly against such veterans as Dr. Pusey. But most of these young clerics had received virtually no professional training. The Church of England seems to have assumed that the normal education of an English gentleman—twelve or more years at school and university largely devoted to mastering pagan classics—if accompanied by attendance at Anglican chapels and churches, were major contributions to the nurture of a future priest. The more earnest undergraduates paid attention to the comparatively few lectures on Biblical books or "Divinity," ignored by many able classicists (cf. J.16, 22; L.iii.77), but they were not properly instructed in how to conduct public services, nor counselled in the elements of pastoral care. After graduation most ordinands merely "got up" the Thirty-nine Articles of the Church under no formal supervision; many clergymen accepted only their broad principles, and subscription to

these was relaxed for clergy in 1865. Up to 1860 only a few small seminaries for Anglican priests had been established for the whole of England, the oldest founded within Victoria's reign. If the Rev. Gerard Herklots, curate at the Hampstead Church attended by the Hopkins family, "borrowed his sermons" (*OET* No. 32g), this was the almost inevitable outcome of his lack of theological background. It was unfortunate for him that volumes of sermons were in Manley's library. Balliol Chapel substituted a metaphysical lecture for a Sunday sermon (L.iii.71). Urquhart had taken a first in Law and History, but was not very successful as a young curate at the Oxford church of St. Philip and St. James which Hopkins normally attended (L.iii.438).

Misgivings about the Church of England

A more profound cause of the "Inattention at church," which echoes throughout the lists of "Sins," was Hopkins's undermining doubts concerning the validity of the Church of England. Hints begin to thicken in the poems from No. 62 onwards. But his notes absolutely refute the anguished accusations of his father after he had announced his reception into the Church of Rome the following year, October 1866: "Have you not dealt hardly, may I not say unfairly by us in leaving us in absolute ignorance of all till your decision was finally taken?" (L.iii.96). His father must have wishfully dismissed as mere passing fancies the many indications that Gerard had been pouring out for twelve months at least. The page of his Note-book on which he copied Newman's "Lead, kindly light!"— an appeal for divine guidance in his dilemma—records that he had on October 8, 1865, a year earlier than his father's letter, poked fun "at Mr. Ayre's sermon" delivered during a service presumably attended by the family. This may have been the one in praise of Luther (see Plate 145, l. 17) or on a parallel topic since it led Gerard to "Repeated forecasting abt. the Ch. of Rome," and at the Sunday dinner (when his father was probably present) into "Talking abt. Dr. Newman . . . in a foolish way [i.e., with admiration] likely to produce unhappiness and harm" (Plate 138, *ll.* 11, 12). This entry follows those on October 5 and 6: "Unwisely speaking long abt. leaving our Church. And on 6 some of this and more or less forecasting." Was Manley so remote from the rest of the family that he was unaware of the turbulent religious difficulties of his eldest son?

During the Michaelmas term that followed (October 8–December 18), Hopkins chided himself for "Too little reticence in talking to Challis abt. my profession," i.e., his contemplated entry into a religious order (5 November, Plate 142, *ll.* 5, 6). One of the factors holding him back from Rome was his deep admiration for Dolben, the person who combined beauty of body, mind, and spirit in the rarest perfection, but who was a member of the Anglican Order of St. Benedict (L.i.16–17). We must return to Dolben presently.

When Gerard came home to Hampstead from a stressful term (December 16, 1865) he was in an extremely unsettled frame of mind. On 20 December we read of Gerard's "Unwisely arguing and speaking in other ways abt. Catholicism to Cyril, Arthur, and Mamma." "Foolishness at Grandmamma's with talk abt. Catholicism" on 22 December is followed by further "Vehemence and unkindness in argument" with Cyril and Mamma the next day. The day after Christmas he brought his mother to tears through expressing Romish views of the "Saints etc." After the New Year on January 6, 1866, he was staying with Manley's brother, the Rev. Thomas Marsland Hopkins and his wife Kate. He noted

down "Unreticence and too much confidence to Aunt Kate abt. self" and on 8 January, "Weakness in going on talking to Aunt Fanny at night." There are, rather significantly, no allusions to private discussions of his religious dilemma with his father.

"Idling," "Lateness to Bed"

What a turmoil Gerard must have been in during that Christmas vacation. It is typical of his relentless efforts at self-discipline that he expected to be able to settle down to his classical studies immediately he reached home from Oxford: he heaps on his weary distracted brain the accusations "Indolence . . . Languor . . . Dilatoriness . . . Laziness . . . Idling and weakness over work" (Plate 145). This exhibits the Victorian work-ethic at its most unwise extreme. There are periods of readjustment during which, once practical tasks have been performed, the mind cannot concentrate upon abstractions. Hopkins was facing a major crisis that would not only make him an outsider at home, but radically endanger his status in a university whose colleges required regular attendance at Church of England services, and whose graduands were expected to subscribe to the Thirty-nine Articles of that state institution before receiving their degrees. Every circumstance of his career and his relationships with many of his friends would be fundamentally changed if he became what was contemptuously called a "pervert" to Rome.

In translating the monotonous charges of "Laziness," "Idling," "Wasting time," etc., which Hopkins enters against himself, we must bear certain facts in mind. He had obtained a First in Moderations, and in a few years was to be not only among the select company of those equally distinguished in the final examinations, but (according to Professor John Wilson, one of the examiners) "for form" he was "by far the best man in the first class" (*The Poems of Digby Mackworth Dolben*, edited with a memoir by Robert Bridges, Oxford University Press, 1911, p. xcvii). We must certainly not be fooled into thinking he spent these ten months among Oxford's lotus-eaters. So far from resting on his laurels after proving his powers with a First in Part I, November 1864, we learn from his spiritual notes, and nowhere else, that the very next term he entered (perhaps prematurely) for the most prestigious classical scholarship at Oxford, the Ireland. He may have been trying to emulate that distinguished Fellow of Balliol, Courtenay Ilbert (see Plate 113; L.iii, 70–71; J.134, 347), about to become President of the Union, who collected the Ireland the same year as a First in Mods. Though Hopkins did not win the coveted prize, he felt guilty about mentioning, in spite of a scruple, how well he had scored in it (Plate 103, *ll* 8, 9: "Repeating my [success *deleted, since he had not won the prize*] doing well in the Ireland, agst. a scruple"). Then an exhausted reaction set in and for a while he could settle to nothing, filling himself with guilt.

In many Oxford colleges at this time students were examined orally at the end of each term by a group of tutors. In Balliol the Master himself took part (along with such tutors as Benjamin Jowett or James Riddell), and the results were entered in the Master's Report Book; after Lent 1867 only those who needed to be warned were called before the tutors. Carl Schmidt has published all the entries except the earliest referring to Hopkins (in *Balliol Studies*, ed. John Prest, London: 1982, 181–82). I draw from the original manuscript remarks on other Balliol students. The texts being prepared by each student were noted, along with brief comments. These ranged, with many variations, from "Admonished for irregularity" (Algernon Swinburne, Michaelmas 1858) or "Rather idle" (Hopkins's

friend, V.S. Coles, Michaelmas 1866), through reserved judgements such as "Industrious but Eccentric" and "Satisfactory but conceited" to the heights, "Exemplary," "Highly praiseworthy," and so forth.

It is instructive to contrast Hopkins's perfectionist self-evaluations in his notes for 1865–66 with the official verdict of the Master and tutors. At the end of his first term, Easter 1863, he was ranked as "Very promising," but the following term he must have been re-adjusting to the realities of Oxford study, since he was only "very fair except in Divinity": the latter was an area often neglected by the best academics, including Ilbert.

The official comments on his three terms in the 1864 calendar year varied from "Very satisfactory," then down somewhat to "Satisfactory" and up again to the top as "Extremely satisfactory." Lent Term 1865 saw the beginning of his own self-judgements, with such regrets as "Wasting much of morning in quad," "No reading done or anything" (Plate 103), yet the official record was "very steady and creditable." For Easter and Act (or Trinity) 1865, which ran from April 19 to June 2, he accuses himself of such breaches of his ideals as "Nothing done all day but Papa's translation," or "Being late in getting to work in evening" (Plate 108); the Master's Record Book however describes him as "Very industrious but not quite regular at chapel." This was a mild reproach: his friends Addis and Paravicini, both of whom became Catholics, were often reproved for being "Very neglectful of chapel." After the summer, Michaelmas Term 1865 (October 10 to December 17) is full of Hopkins's laments over "Losing time," "Waste of time . . . in Union etc.," "Allowing Coles to talk and myself going on talking in morning," "Obstinacy abt. drawing Bramley's picture agst. warning of idleness and scruple" (Plates 140–43). The master and tutors nevertheless regarded him as "Very creditable." The spiritual notes end just after the beginning of the Lent Term of 1866 (mid-January to March 24), but the self-accusations for the first week run true to form: "Self-will in writing down (past 12) corrections in *The Nightingale* agst. warning [i.e., of conscience]," "Weak dilatoriness twice," "Wasting time in morn. over picture-hanging and in evening over that and wine in Coles' rooms so that almost nothing done all day." Yet the master and tutors reported that he was "working hard" on texts ranging from three historical books in the Old Testament, to six books of Aristotle's *Ethics*, along with four of Plato's *Republic*, and Bacon's *Novum Organum* 1–60.

Handbooks designed for intending undergraduates generally cautioned over-conscientious students about the danger of too much study. It is a relief to note that Hopkins generally conformed to the custom of spending his afternoons in non-classical pursuits, frequently taking a long walk into the surrounding countryside. This also allowed him time for writing poetry and sketching. An hour and a half or two hours in the evening was considered sufficient even in 1887 when standards had probably risen a good deal (*Oxford: Its Life and Schools*, ed. A.M.M. Stedman, London: 1887, chap.iv): "to begin reading immediately after dinner is not only useless but harmful" (p. 100). And Jowett, one of Hopkins's tutors, is said to have declared that "six hours' study a day will get the best out of a man" (*A History of Balliol College*, H.W. Carless Davis, rev. edn. Oxford: 1963, p. 217). All the vacations, however, were supposed to be devoted to academic reading; the North American custom of finding unrelated employment each summer to earn tuition fees was rarely followed; the whole financial burden not covered by scholarships fell on the "gentleman's" family.

Most educators will be disturbed by these incessant entries "Wasting time," like recur-

rent cracks of his slave-driving will. The sheer monotony of Victorian academic studies, far too often revolving around narrowly interpreted classical learning, must have made concentration hard after some ten years of the same basic diet. Hopkins would have thrived on our broader educational programmes. Especially mistaken are the entries "Wasting time in Union" (e.g., pp. 64, *l* 2; 102, *l* 13; 103, *l* 18): the Oxford Union Society possessed a fine library covering the whole gamut of subjects that were excluded from the narrow band of formal university studies, judging from its Catalogue of 1875, the closest to his own day that I have found. The Balliol College Library (as set out in its 1871 catalogue) was far narrower, and normally reserved for fellows. The great repository of the Bodleian was little used since its hours of opening conflicted with college lectures which undergraduates had to attend: Hopkins did not enrol as a reader. Perhaps his "Wasting time in morning in reading *Athenaeum* etc." (Plate 110, *ll* 24–25) was classified as a "Sin" because it intruded on an inflexible timetable, a rigidity of scheme which experienced tutors discouraged then as they do now. "Wasting time in looking at Poe's poems" (Plate 116, *l* 5) betrays too constricted an outlook: Marcus Clarke, about to emigrate to Australia, had given Hopkins Poe's poems as a parting gift. In later life Hopkins had often to admit that his acquaintance with English Literature was blushingly sketchy. In view of the support that Canon Dixon was later to provide the lonely poet, we recognise as short-sighted his verdict "Wasting time in reading Dixon" (Plate 143, *l* 30).

Another perpetual echo is "Lateness to bed"; in fact his earliest note is "Dawdling in going to bed (not very much)" (Plate 102) and one of his last entries shows him still grappling with the problem: "Resolution made to be in bed by 11 and not in bed by 12, mostly own fault" (Plate 149, *ll* 21–23). But many academics will recall from their student days how discussions became more animated and confidences more frank around midnight. "Sitting late in Geldart's room" (Plate 102) was probably occasioned by the news of how well Hopkins had done in the Ireland Scholarship examination, and we are almost relieved to see during a vacation (September 26, 1865) "Reading [*Henry*] *Esmond* on and on when I should have gone to bed" (Plate 136). On other occasions a poem commandeered his powers, postponing his retirement (e.g., Plates 132, *l* 1; 149, *ll* 24–26). Hopkins's "inattention" at chapel and family prayers was sometimes clearly due to his shortage of sleep, e.g., (Plate 109, *ll* 5ff.) "Lateness to bed, after getting up before 5 [a.m.]. Inattention at chapel. . . . [Next day] Lateness in rising, later than excused by fatigue. . . . Inattention at evensong."

"No Lessons"

In both morning and evening family prayers the Book of Common Prayer was followed, another factor contributing to the poet's frequent inattention. The "Lessons" Hopkins so often forgot were of course the scripture readings set out at the beginning of that Prayer book. Those who attempt to correlate the readings appointed for a particular day with a poem written by Hopkins during it should use a mid-Victorian edition: the passages prescribed at that time are entirely different from their current counterparts. They used to include most of the apocryphal books printed between the Old Testament and the New in the Authorized Version. He records (Plate 143, *ll* 28–29) "Evil curiosity in hearing Susannah read": "The History of Susanna" was one of the Lessons for November 22, the day of his note.

Intemperance," "Self-indulgence"

The daily notes of self-examination begin in Lent, which in 1865 extended from March 1 to Easter Eve on April 15. From the fourth century onwards this forty-day period in preparation for Good Friday and Easter was observed by certain abstinences or restraints at meals. Hopkins was quite capable of doing his physical health serious harm by imposing unwise discipline on himself; at school he had once abstained from all liquids for three weeks to prove he could match seamen's endurance when adrift in a boat (L.iii.395), a feat of will-power so liable to have ended fatally that for once we can forgive the headmaster's reactions. His mother forbad him to fast in Lent, a prohibition he told Baillie was probably sensible (L.iii.207, March 1864). After he became a Jesuit his superiors generally also realized that he should not be permitted to keep Lent strictly (L.iii.121, 138, 144); on an occasion when he did fast he admitted that he became "thinner than I ever saw myself in the face, with my cheeks like two harp-frames" (L.iii.150, April 1878: see A. Thomas, *Hopkins the Jesuit*, p. 39, n. 3 for Catholic rules of 1869 on fasts in Lent and during other days of abstinence).

These self-scrutinies of 1865 show him trying to deny himself small extras that would have pleased his palate though they were not necessary to keep him in health. He recorded as "Sins" any failure in restraint. On April 4 he was one of the guests invited to tea by the Master of Balliol, and that night he entered as a "Sin" "Eating two biscuits at the Master's" (Plate 104, *l.* 8). Undergraduates entertained each other to desserts after dinner or Hall, serving drinks and fresh or candied fruit. When Hopkins records "Intemperance at dessert at Brooke's" (Plate 105, *l.* 1) he is accusing himself of taking perhaps a second candied pear—certainly not of being intoxicated. During Holy Week he became unwell (too many austerities? *l.* 7) but refused to accept this as an excuse for not studying, and went on assailing his conscience with "No self-denial to speak of" (*ll.* 12, 13).

Even after Lent was long past we find such ascetic records as "Greediness from having had no dinner towards some dessert I saw and with my own biscuits" (Plate 115, *ll.* 7–9). At some point he resolved to make "one act of self-denial at every major meal"; on November 4 we hear that he has been letting his resolution lapse (Plate 141, *l.* 25). When he enters against himself the charge of "Self-indulgence at lunch with Macfarlane" (Plate 140, *l.* 12) this does not mean that he had over-eaten—simply that he had accepted something which he thought he ought to have refused to assert the control of spirit over body. "Intemperance" seems also to be used in a more general context of "lack of restraint"; thus "intemperance after hall [i.e., dinner] (with Emerton)" is certainly not a reference to drunkenness, but is glossed by what follows: "talking lightly about Millais etc." (Plate 108, *l.* 1). He had been expressing himself on art with too much vigour—a troublesome "sin."

"Cruelty" and "Unkindness" to Insects and People

Modern readers who have felt the influence of Eastern religious thought will have more empathy than Hopkins's fellow students would over such notes of contrition as "Killing a spider" (Plate 115, *l.* 12) or "Cruelty to a moth" (Plate 124, *l.* 6): study illuminated by an open flame would be seriously interrupted by the flutterers. We hear too of his "Killing an earwig" (Plate 130, *l.* 12), and "Cruelty to insects" (Plate 137, *l.* 10). It is this sensitivity to creatures to whom little attention was then paid that we must also remember in

interpreting his "Talking unkindly of people" (Plate 121 and numerous other places). If he lost his temper with his brother Cyril, who knows what exasperations were the cause or what good he achieved, unknown to himself, by speaking his mind? On other occasions he must himself have been in the wrong.

Summary

It would be equally foolish to pretend that Hopkins was either the only perfect or the only imperfect undergraduate in his time. Others no doubt worked harder and achieved more outward distinctions, yet will be forgotten sooner than Gerard Manley Hopkins. The comparative rarity of men with Firsts in both Mods and Greats shows that he was among the best in the period from 1863 to 1867. We have seen that "Idling" must often have been in fact preoccupation with religious difficulties or with nascent poems that insisted upon being born. His "self-indulgence" was probably much less over-eating than his failure to refuse a second spoonful or another quarter of fruit or a sugar plum. His "inattention" to the recital of routine formulae at chapel or family prayers may have sprung from lack of sleep (he was too frequently "late to bed"), or preoccupation with more fundamental problems of faith and the settling of the momentous question as to whether he should devote his whole life to priesthood in an alien Church that claimed greater authority. Clearly a large number of these "Sins" were scruples that a more experienced confessor might have brushed aside.

Sexuality

When we enter the delicate area of sexual mores we encounter in these notes a similar exaggeration of guilt. Judgements of Hopkins on this score, however, will necessarily diverge because of the widely differing blends of "prejudice," experience, and dispassionate factual knowledge that people bring to this subject. The crudest misrepresentations may still be encountered in letters to the press. Even geneticists and experts in psychological medicine cannot yet say with finality how much of the wide spectrum of sexual preferences found in any representative community is due to genetic factors in which the individual has no say, and how much to the environment, which may be very hard or impossible for people with certain inherited characteristics to overcome, if they feel compelled to attempt it because of social pressures or their own concepts of an ideal pattern.

In one of the most difficult and speculative passages of his *Spiritual Writings*, "On Personality, Grace and Free Will" (S.146ff.), Hopkins theorizes on the apparently arbitrary way in which different selves or supposits or personalities, each potentially distinct from any other, are severally "clothed in or overlaid with a nature." These natures or essences or "inscapes" are also individually varied, but the selves added to them are not selected to produce a particular blend but according to "the will of the Creator." Other men of genius or spiritual aspirations have also on occasion lamented an apparent mismatch between their spirit and their physical frame. Hopkins was self-conscious about his unusual lack of inches (not much over five feet): at Highgate this had handicapped him in sport (Luxmoore says he was "good *for his size* at games," L.iii.395, our italics), and at Balliol he could be mistaken for a schoolboy (L.iii.84). Moreover, all his life he was

subject to physical fatigue, and his last surviving meditation notes regret that God will not allow him "bodily energy and cheerful spirits" (S.262). But his sexual urges, apparently dormant until about January 1864, probably also occasioned him concern.

One minor category among his "Sins" reminds us of the prudishness with which parents from the turn of the nineteenth century onwards shielded their children from the facts of life. Bawdy jokes and whispered conversations among school boarders disseminated a tainted knowledge, but Hopkins was not one to invite such communications (cf. L.iii.394–95; 213, and n.1). At Oxford he felt guilty for having sought information in the medical journal the *Lancet* (Plate 115, *l.* 23), and often recorded "Evil thoughts in dictionary etc." (Plate 105, *l.* 12), or "Temptation to see things in newspaper yielded to" (Plate 142, *l.* 20). Paddy Kitchen (*GMH*, p. 70), though usually perceptive, seems to make insufficient allowance here for the appalling ignorance of the reproductive organs of both sexes that sprang from nineteenth century prudery and censorship. What Hopkins categorized as "Impure curiousness" stemmed from the absence of enlightened sex education.

There are many places in which Hopkins carefully differentiates between "Old habits" and "acts of uncleanness. Temptations somewhat yielded to." (e.g., Plate 124 *l.* 7). "O.H." and "impurity" (Plates 136, *l.* 14; 138, *l.* 8, etc.) probably referred to touching erogenous zones. The analysis below Plate 151 confirms that "O.H." can scarcely refer to masturbation: it seems to have been some act which, if not vigilantly suppressed, could have led to "impurity" (cf. "O.H. thrice," Plate 139, *l.* 24). Where there was emission, even between sleeping and waking, we find a far more serious note: "I fear mortal sin" (Plate 143, *l.* 19).

Hopkins makes numerous references to his encountering temptation by taking part in conversations on "the dangerous" or "forbidden" subject (e.g., Plates 139, *ll.* 9, 10; 144, *ll.* 19, 29; 145, *ll.* 6, 7). Occasionally this is associated with his rather one-sided friendship with Dolben (Plates 106, *l.* 34; 111, *ll.* 4, 5). It is probable that the reference in some, perhaps most, of the instances is to subjects that threatened his attempt to achieve perfect purity mentally and physically. His later letter to Bridges after his ordination (L.i.95, October 1879) illumines his attitude as an undergraduate also: "I think . . . no one can admire beauty of the body more than I do, and it is of course a comfort to find beauty in a friend or a friend in beauty. But this kind of beauty is dangerous." John Robinson seems to imagine that a Catholic priest in mid-Victorian times should have lived by the easy ethos that was widespread in the 1970s (an era already outmoded because of new accompanying dangers); he criticises Hopkins's poem "To what serves Mortal Beauty" for praising human beauty as surpassing any other kind only to sheer away from it as "dangerous." The poet, he says, does not follow "where the logic impels," failing to urge readers (and the priest himself) to "Love frame and face" (*In Extremity*, Cambridge University Press, 1978, p. 96). Hopkins "goes into the emptiness of 'merely meet it' and the intellectual and emotional shut-down of 'let that alone'." Yet in Victorian times any professional, whether teacher, doctor, or priest, could have endangered his own reputation and that of his institution by indulging his physical appetites with either women or men. To suggest otherwise would surely be historically naive.

Novels and memoirs dealing with Oxford in mid-Victorian times often emphasize the overwhelming predominance of males. Education in the colleges was confined to men. Worse still was the dire sparsity for girls of any equivalent of the public schools that prepared boys for admission to the universities. Though there were a few non-celibate

fellowships, dons were still liable to forfeit their fellowships if they married, and fortunate indeed was the academic who managed to find a wife whose natural aptitude for reading and study had been trained by a family governess or "indulgent" father. Students complained of the "unintelligent" chatter of the girls and wives they generally met when their tutors entertained them. Only on special occasions did Oxford take on a festive and bisexual air when sisters and parents thronged the city for Commemoration or the Summer Eights, but ordinarily it was more common to see only men walking the streets arm in arm. Heterosexual friendships were inevitably rare during men's residence in Oxford, since they met so few women, and still fewer with cultivated minds.

If friendships between men had not developed, Oxford would have become the unhealthy retreat of lonely eccentrics, ill-fitted for future social life. In fact little groups of men, especially within individual colleges, were drawn together by common enthusiasms, and established links that lasted their whole lives, scarcely weakened by their subsequent marriages and distance from each other.

That some homoerotic attraction also occurred was to be expected. In most cases this led merely to romantic exchanges (sometimes enshrined in letters or verse), rather than physical expression. The risks involved when such friendships became obsessive may be illustrated from Phyllis Grosskurth's 1964 biography of John Addington Symonds, who preceded Hopkins at Balliol (1858–62). At Harrow Symonds had been Head of the School (i.e., the top scholar), under the celebrated Dr. Charles Vaughan, a clergyman who is counted among the great headmasters of Victorian England. Between 1844 and 1859, when he suddenly resigned, Vaughan transformed Harrow from a small institution notorious for misbehavior and drunkenness into one of Britain's leading public schools. Grosskurth reveals the cause of his abrupt departure: he had allowed his attraction towards one of the senior boys, Alfred Pretor, to develop until he was unable to control his feelings. With a headlong precipitation that risked the school's newly-won reputation and terminated the educational mission to which he had dedicated all his energies, Dr. Vaughan sent Pretor passionate love-letters, which the boy showed to John Symonds.

Symonds brooded miserably over them; Vaughan attempted to fondle him also when he brought his essays to the Headmaster's study, though as a priest on Sundays he offered him the Sacraments as he knelt beside Pretor. Even after Symonds had left Harrow for Balliol the knowledge unsettled his undergraduate studies; the school of which Symonds had been proud to be Head was in danger of being torn by scandal. Only after keeping the tragic secret for a year and a half did he consult Professor John Conington during a reading party in the summer. Conington, in the interests of Harrow, urged Symonds to show his father (a medical doctor) the correspondence. Dr. Symonds, in concert with a few other worried and influential parents, quietly induced Vaughan to resign with the promise that there would be no public exposure. Dr. Vaughan's subsequent career was somewhat muted: he became vicar in a small Yorkshire market-town, but was forced to refuse the bishopric offered him after a few years. No further incidents occurred. He became Master of the Temple, and eventually Dean of Llandaff. The reputation of Harrow was saved. Gerard Hopkins seems to have picked up no scandal in Balliol about the school: we find him in July 1867 accompanying his youngest brother Lionel (then thirteen) to Harrow, where Lionel "tried for a vacancy but failed [the examination]" (J.150).

John Addington Symonds's own academic advancement also suffered from unwise friendships. He fell romantically in love with a chorister at Bristol Cathedral in his home

city, and wasted part of his first Oxford year dreaming about him. Their clandestine meetings continued for years, idealistic rather than physical. Grosskurth reports that a mutual interest in High Church ritualism brought Symonds close to Edward Urqu[h]art (the later butt of Hopkins's jokes), but that he broke the friendship when he realized that Urquhart was "becoming inordinately fond of him" (p. 45). Symonds found another Balliol man, G.H. Shorting, quite attractive physically, but his efforts to stop Shorting from ruining his own life brought savage retaliation after Symonds had won an open Fellowship at Magdalen. Under the pretext of needing Symonds to coach him in philosophy, Shorting planned to use his friend's residence in that college to facilitate his pursuit of one of the Magdalen choristers. The motive was too transparent, however, and Symonds arranged that their philosophy sessions would be held elsewhere. Shorting, infuriated by this attempt to block him from a suit which was already causing Magdalen dons some annoyance, achieved a vicious revenge by circulating among Magdalen Fellows poems and extracts of letters addressed to him by Symonds, skilfully spliced together to suggest that Symonds had encouraged his affair with the chorister. Symonds had the embarrassment of having to gather testimonials in his own defence, and of facing a full investigation of the scandal by a General Meeting of his new college. Two of his letters to Shorting that were read out were censured as in execrable taste, but he was acquitted of the charge. His probationary year as a Fellow of Magdalen, however, was so full of tension that presently in the Spring of 1863 he suffered a breakdown and left Magdalen, to spend the balance of his life as a semi-invalid (Grosskurth, 58–69). In his secret Memoirs, on which Dr. Grosskurth was able to draw for her biography, he attributed his collapse to unfulfilled passion for another chorister, Alfred Brooke.

When Hopkins entered Balliol in Symonds's final Oxford term, he must have been shocked by the rumors of such homosexual intrigues and the sudden end which they appeared to have brought to the tutorship of Symonds. Symonds had won the Newdigate with a poem on "The Escorial," the subject of Hopkins's own first extant composition. His collapse must have warned Hopkins of the danger of allowing his own response to male physique to develop beyond mere temptation. Only by contrasting the excessively conscientious behaviour of Hopkins with the stories of others who allowed their natural instincts freer expression can we see how misguided is the enthusiasm of those who wish, for whatever motive, to "recover" Hopkins as a gay poet (see, e.g., Michael Lynch on "Recovering Hopkins, Recovering Ourselves," in HQ, VI, No. 3, Fall 1979).

Hopkins's daily spiritual notes show momentary attractions to boys or fellow students, but they also demonstrate his determination to prevent their leading him into an affair. He reproaches himself (C.ii. 105, l. 46, Plate 143) for "Looking at a chorister at Magdalen." The fine music and anthems in Magdalen chapel drew members of all the other colleges, but the Magdalen dons became suspicious of any visitor who attended too frequently. This information we learn from one of Hopkins's friends, himself a young organist and choir-master, Samuel Brooke (see Plates 105, l. 1; 139, l. 14; L.iii. 76, 81, 223–24), whose diary for November and December 1862 records this vigilance. Brooke denied himself the pleasure of attending Magdalen chapel as frequently as men like George Mylne and Frederick Gurney of Balliol in all innocence did, for fear lest his interest might be misconstrued. He notes that a scholar of his own college, Corpus, had been expelled the previous February for becoming too fond of a choirboy, and he felt, since there was so much dubious interest in the boys, that the dons ought to take such further precautions

as restricting the congregation to the nave where they could hear but not see. The significant point about Hopkins's reference to the Magdalen chorister is that it was limited to looking and to one single occasion. He seems to have kept himself away from this source of "danger," since no further reference occurs.

Hopkins tried to catch at the earliest stage any natural physical impulses that might cripple his ambition to develop to their highest degree his mental and spiritual capacities. He enters against himself (C.ii. 82 *l.* 5, Plate 122) "Looking at temptations, esp. at Geldart naked." Hopkins was at the time staying with the Geldarts in Manchester, and could not suddenly leave, but any notion that he felt infatuated with Edmund Geldart is dissipated when we read the physical description he had included in his first letter home from Oxford (L.iii.70). Judging Geldart only from his appearance, he mentioned his "grey goggle eyes, scared suspicious look . . . , shuddering gait or shuffle, pinched face." In Manchester the next day he made a note to avoid as unwise "playing with Nash and the Geldarts" (bot. Plate 122).

One of his reasons for abandoning painting as a career was the "strain upon the passions" (L.iii.231)—art training involved drawing men and women in the nude. During a reading holiday at Chagford in Devon with Bond and Phillimore (who was to become a Fellow of All Souls, a Lord Justice, and President of the English Church Union, J.378), Hopkins was repeatedly ashamed of his "unkindness," "snappishness" and ill-will towards Phillimore (Plates 128, *l.* 13; 129 *ll.* 23, 27, 29; 130 *l.* 1). Yet a purely physical temptation arose one day when he set out to draw him (Plate 129, *l.* 15). Though predominantly aroused by males in this unisex community, Hopkins, mostly when away from Oxford, also recorded his attraction to beautiful Alice Gurney ("adultery of the heart" Plate 130, *l.* 9), his cousin Magdalen (three entries, Plates 146–47), a girl in a shop (140), and to others whose sex is not mentioned ("Newman's friend," a "face in the theatre," etc., Plates 113, 117).

The intensity of these temptations varied greatly. Some show minimal anxiety: "Scruples not temptation in seeing men at Worcester sports" (C.ii.105, *l.* 13, Plate 143) and "Imprudent looking at organ-boy and other boys" (C.ii.82, *ll.* 1, 2, Plate 122). Very occasionally we meet the far extreme: "Looking with terrible temptation at Maitland" (C.ii.101, *l.* 10, Plate 139). The reaction of a man who felt that such encounters were essential to his sense of well-being would have been to create opportunities to meet the attractive stranger again. This Hopkins appears to have shunned since the note does not recur—the avoidance was the easier because Maitland was not a Balliol man. At a lower level but entered some seven times come "Looking at Fyffe," or "Temptation from Fyffe and from pictures in Blake" (C.ii. 72, 75, 76, 77, 105, 111). Fyffe was a very able and influential member of his own college, who rose, like Hopkins's friend Ilbert, to become President of the Union. Before the spiritual notes begin he had invited Hopkins to join a party at breakfast (J.55, 325; see also 159 on his First in Greats). Hopkins's attitudes should be contrasted with the contrite entries, sometimes close to despair, made by an earlier Balliol man, Arthur Hugh Clough, whose notes make veiled references to a succession of "follies," "beastliness," and the ardent pursuit of "false hopes," some involving members of other colleges. Clough failed to achieve at Oxford the outstanding academic success that had been predicted from his brilliance at Rugby. His entries record human shortcomings to which Hopkins also confesses, such as vanity, oversleeping, and periodic lack of application to his studies.

The world of Hopkins's imagination to a large extent corrects the imbalance of the unisex university around him. The compositions to which he most frequently returns center upon women. There are no fewer than four versions of the delicate St. Dorothea lyric (androgynous though the graceful young saint sometimes is, like Pre-Raphaelite angels). In "Floris in Italy," spread over two note-books, Giulia, with her intense but self-sacrificing love, is no unfelt echo of Shakespeare's disguised heroines such as Viola; and even the simple ballad "The Queen's Crowning" has some emotional force. In another composition on which he lavished time, "A Voice from the World" (probably revised or extended as "Beyond the Cloister"), we meet a man's passionate heterosexual love pleading against a woman's threatened retreat into a convent. On the other hand "Richard," which presents the friendship between two men, exceedingly common in the Victorian age, holds no trace of emotional interest. It expires unmourned, to be replaced presently by "Castara," where a heroine is again the pivotal figure.

Equally significant is his preference, among contemporary poets to read and imitate, of Coventry Patmore, the poet of married love, above Walt Whitman, who might have encouraged a side of himself that he did not care to develop (L.i.154–58). His early poem "The Lover's Stars" (OET No. 13, Plates 60–61) is "a trifle in something like Coventry Patmore's style" (L.iii.213), and his journal some four months after the end of Note-book C.ii records "Walking down towards Sandford [-on-Thames] with Coventry Patmore in hand" (J.135). When he re-read *The Angel in the House* in 1883 to help the poet to revise it for a new edition, he reported: "Much of it I remember without reading (I do not say word for word) and of the rest there is little I do not at least remember to have read; though I believe I never read it but once" (L.iii.298–99). He later discussed Patmore's "The Unknown Eros" with Bridges, but his mention of that volume (not published till 1877–78) as one he had read "well before I left Oxford" is a slip due to its having been the subject of a recent letter (L.i.82, 93). He probably meant *The Angel* or its sequel, *The Victories of Love.*

One special male friendship Hopkins did attempt to form, with Digby Dolben, a young cousin of Robert Bridges, whom he met briefly when Dolben spent a few days with Bridges in Corpus during February 1865. Bridges, Coles, and Dolben had all been to Eton, where they shared a devotion to the High Church movement. Dolben himself was so strongly attracted to a monastic life that before Easter 1864 he joined the Anglican Brotherhood of St. Benedict established by Fr. Ignatius in Sussex, adopting the title "Brother Dominic of the Third Order" together with a monkish habit and crucifix (see Robert Bridges, ed., *The Poems of Digby Mackworth Dolben, with a Memoir*, London: Oxford University Press, 1911, xxxvii ff.).

Evangelicals took an unholy pleasure in reviving against High Church practices some insinuations that had been rife against Catholic monasteries at the time of the Reformation—that such institutions were hot-houses of unhealthy friendships between males. Occasional scandals gratified them, but these erupted also in public schools and in the two great universities, where the facile implication of homosexual tendencies might be tagged to any male who did not take naturally to the rough and muddy tumble of English playing fields. Hopkins's slight frame and gentle manners have led literary writers to such a positive identification, sometimes relying upon over-inclusive Freudian interpretations.

David Hilliard's article "Unenglish and Unmanly: Anglo-Catholicism and Homosexuality" (*Victorian Studies*, 25:2, Winter 1982, 181–210) provides numerous examples of this

suspicion and good bibliographies of modern investigations. The author may have been led into imperfect judgements himself simply through attempting to analyze so many different personalities, but some of the cautions he delivers (pp. 186–87) deserve particular attention: it is not possible, he concludes, "on the basis of passionate words uttered by mid-Victorians, to make a clear distinction between male affection and homosexual feeling. . . . There is the general question of whether intimate friendships between members of the same sex can legitimately be labelled homosexual when the individuals concerned may not be conscious at the time of an underlying erotic attraction."

Those who are more interested in Hopkins's sexual orientation than his evolution into poet and priest will naturally try to make as much of his friendship with Dolben as possible. Dolben in his brief visit to Oxford stayed in Bridges's college, Corpus, not Balliol, though Michael Lynch in his efforts to "recover Hopkins" indulges in such airborne fancies as that Dolben's visit had transformed Hopkins's college (of which he was in fact immensely proud from the start, L.iii.70, etc.), from "Belial" to "Bellisle" (*OET*, No. 56d, Plate 107), making it into "paradise incarnated" (*HQ*, 6:3, p. 113). There can be no doubt that Hopkins was aesthetically attracted to Dolben at all levels—physical, mental, and spiritual. But neither Hopkins nor Dolben indulged bodily desires at the expense of higher aspirations, and the evidence of Note-book C.ii, dispassionately viewed, is that Hopkins was not infatuated with him. Paddy Kitchen, after studying all the entries in his note-books, pointed out in 1978 that "if Dolben had affected his life, it was in a stimulative way, throwing him with renewed ambition and energy into a broad programme of study" (*Gerard Manley Hopkins*, p. 69). She alludes to the formidable list of "Books to be read" (C.ii.56), which I date March 1 or 2, within a week or two of their only meeting. After discussing Dolben's earlier friendship at Eton with Martin Gosselin (disguised as "Manning" in Bridges's *Poems of . . . Dolben, ed. with Memoir*, pp. xx ff; and its reprint at the beginning of *Three Friends*, Oxford University Press, 1932, pp. 19ff.), she adds "Whatever their involuntary feelings for other people, Hopkins and Dolben both soon admitted in their poetry that they would find resolution of their needs only in Christ" (p. 75).

Hopkins certainly did not allow his new enthusiasm to divert him from his preparation for Greats. As we have seen, his tutors' reports for the Lent and Easter Terms of 1865 (covering January 14 to July 8) were that he was "very steady and creditable" (Lent) and "Very industrious but not quite regular at Chapel" (Easter and Act). The services of the Church of England were becoming increasingly insipid to him, but he was inevitably hesitant about deserting the church with which his family and college existence was so intertwined. It would have been a great help to have been able to argue out the wisdom of this momentous step with Digby Dolben, and I have ventured to suggest that one of the considerations impeding such a break was that it would also breach his incipient friendship with so admirable a person.

Well before Dolben's early death (June 28, 1867) Hopkins had himself been converted (July 17, 1866, J.146) and received into the Catholic Church (October 21, L.iii.100). His own emphasis in wishing for a deeper friendship with Dolben was on the spiritual. Writing to Bridges after the news that Dolben had drowned, he began "I looked forward to meeting Dolben and *his being a Catholic* more than to anything" (L.i.16, August 30, 1867, my emphasis).

References to Dolben in Note-book C.ii. are not numerous. In February 1865, at the time of Dolben's visit, we read (p. 54) "Dolben's *carte*" (i.e., his photograph). The notes

of self-examination begin about a month later (March 25, Plate 102), but Dolben does not appear until a month later still when Hopkins records his new address, care of his private tutor in South Luffenham, Leicester—apparently after hearing from Bridges that Dolben's intended return visit to Oxford had been abandoned owing to serious eye trouble (Bridges, *Memoir*, lxviii–lxx). Simultaneously Hopkins thwarted in himself "Dangerous talking about Dolben" (C.ii.66, *ll.* 30, 34). After another two weeks we read "Desire to hear things coupled with forbidden subject, as questions about Dolben" (C.ii.71, *ll.* 4, 5, Plate 111). Then Dolben fades from the notes for five and a half months—until October 22 (Plate 140). Meanwhile physical temptations occasioned by other males and females are mentioned and dealt with. We come across "Too affect[ionate] signature to Addis. . . . Despair of God" (Plate 121), and many admissions of irritability.

The first extant letter to Bridges (August 28, 1865) was written from Torquay where Hopkins was staying with Frederick Gurney and his very attractive young wife (cf. C.ii. 92, *ll.* 8). Bridges had arranged a reunion with two of his High Church Eton friends, Coles and Dolben, but his invitation to Hopkins to join them unfortunately failed to reach Hopkins in time: he replied "nothing cd. have been so delightful as to meet you and Coles and Dolben." Sending his love to Coles and Dolben, he added "I have written letters without end to the latter without a whiff of answer" (L.i.1; cf. p. 3). Dolben was too busy cramming Greek and Euclid in the faint hope of being accepted by Balliol, and was also mulling over the establishing of an Anglican Brotherhood. He was intellectually no match for Hopkins, and was himself passing though a period of religious confusion. His tutor at Luffenham from February to July or August 1865, the Rev. Constantine Pritchard (who had himself been a Fellow of Balliol from 1842 to 1854), had courteously deployed such arguments against Roman beliefs and practices that Dolben was in a quandary, and in no state to respond to the religious dilemmas of a senior Oxford man (Bridges, *Memoir*, lxx–lxxvi). Since Hopkins's "letters without end" did not repeatedly figure in his rigorous self-scrutinies as dabbling with the forbidden subject they cannot have been romantic in tone.

Dolben resurfaces in the Note-book C.ii in October 1865, shortly after an explicit hint that Hopkins might "leave the English Church" (p. 101): "Running on in thought last night unseasonably against warning onto subject of Dolben, and today and some temptation" (October 23, Plate 140, *ll.* 1–3). On November 6 Hopkins records "Going on into a letter to Dolben at night agst. warning" (i.e., of conscience). But this is followed, clearly the next day, by an entry not deleted, which as shorn of its context has been generally misapplied: "On this day by God's grace I resolved to give up all beauty until I had His leave for it; and also Dolben's letter came for wh. Glory to God" (J.71). The last phrase must not be dismissed as equivalent to our pagan "thank heaven!" It indicates that their correspondence had been a subject of Hopkins's prayers. Critics have tended to exclaim over the spiritual refinement of a young man who was so heavenly attuned that he would not admire a violet or a landscape without Christ's permission—and his "Habit of Perfection" (January 18, 19, 1866) certainly aspires to this other-worldliness. But the reference here is surely to a more agonizing and nobler surrender—of human friendships, anticipating "To what serves Mortal Beauty?" (*OET*, No. 158). Hence too the entry that follows it: "Rebellion and spiritual pride about sacrifice," made more explicit on November 8: "Spiritual pride abt. Dolben" (Plate 142, *l.* 14). His self-sacrifice must have been costly.

The final two references to Dolben in the notes, dated December 14 and 22 (C.ii.107,

ll. 9, 10, 33, Plate 145), show a not altogether successful attempt to change the basis of their correspondence to a more artistic and intellectual level: "Waste of time in evening, conceit over letter to Dolben," and just before Christmas, "Dangerous scrupulosity abt. finishing a stanza of *Beyond the Cloister* for Dolben," when he should have been working on his classical texts. Note-book C.ii. covers only another month, and holds no further allusions to Dolben.

That Dolben's long-awaited letter to Hopkins for which he gave "Glory to God" contained poetry we must conclude from Dolben's subsequent note to Bridges, also dated November 1865: "You were very welcome to see my verses, though I certainly should not have selected them to show you. *Did Coles or Hopkins give them you, and why?*" (*Memoir*, lxxxvi). This indicates that though the poems were not of a very personal nature, they were not Dolben's best work. In the absence of Hopkins's letters to Dolben, biographers have anxiously examined his verse to detect love poems intended for him. One so identified is "Not kind! to freeze me with forecast,/Dear grace and girder of mine and me" (*OET*, No. 86, Plate 176). Attempts to give it an autobiographical interpretation ran into so many puzzles that in 1983 I concluded it must be a translation, a surmise Ross Kilpatrick of our Queen's Classics Department confirmed by identifying it as a very free translation of Horace *Odes* II. no. 17, st. 1 (see *English Languages Notes*, 23:3, March 1986, 41–42).

Another poem tantalizing to biographers has been "Where art thou friend, whom I shall never see,/Conceiving whom I must conceive amiss?" (*OET* No. 57, Plate 107). Paddy Kitchen's paraphrase (*GMH*, p. 72) is a valiant endeavour to make it fit Dolben as the least unlikely candidate: "Friend, whom I am either not going to see again, or who has gone away until some vague, future time, when I try to grasp you with my mind, I fall short of my object. . . ." It was left to Winifred Nowottny (Hopkins Society, Fourth Annual lecture, 1973, p. 16), finely elaborated by Rudy Bremer (*HQ* 7:1, Spring 1980, 9–14), to show that the sonnet was addressed individually to each of his unknown future readers. I interpret it, further, as in effect a dedication of his poetry to Christ. There is no room here to discuss other poems that have been assigned to Dolben, including the pseudo-Shakespearian sonnet trio, "The beginning of the end" (*OET* No. 59, Plates 111–12). Readers may consult my commentary in the Oxford English Texts *Poetical Works*.

After Dolben's early death, June 28, 1867, Hopkins wrote to Bridges a letter he had difficulty in drafting (L.i.16–17, August 30; cf. Plate 172). He made two very positive statements about Dolben, each followed by a major reservation beginning "At the same time." He had been looking forward, he writes, to meeting Dolben "and his being a Catholic more than to anything. At the same time from never having met him but once I find it difficult to realise his death or feel as if it were anything to me." This indicates that his surrender of all beauty to God, made in the context of Dolben (November 6, 1865, Plate 142), had been effective. He continues: "You know there can very seldom have happened the loss of so much beauty (in body and mind and life) and of the promise of still more as there has been in this case—seldom I mean, in the whole world, for the conditions would not easily come together. At the same time he had gone on in a way wh. was wholly and unhappily irrational." He agreed with Bridges that "there was a great want of strength in Dolben—more, of sense" (L.i.18). Whatever the intensity of his earlier admiration had been, it had been diluted by stories of Dolben's eccentric behavior, and the weakness of body and intellect that made him fail the matriculation exams for Oxford

entrance (L.i. 7, 15). However Dolben does appear to have been converted in mind and heart to the Catholic Church, though he was not formally received (Dom Aelred Watkin, *Dublin Rev.*, 225, no. 453, 1951, 65–70). Hopkins's last reference to him (J.236) seems to reflect an assurance of his salvation.

The self-analyses may obviously provoke controversy about Hopkins's mental and physical condition at the time they were made. Dr. F.J.J. Letemendia—M.A. (Oxon.), M.D. (Madrid), D.P.M. (Lon.), F.R.C.P.(C.), Professor of Psychiatry and Psychology, Queen's University, Ontario—is also a Fellow of the Royal College of Psychiatrists in England who practiced psychiatry in Oxford from 1960 to 1977. Together with Fr. George Croft, S.J., M.A., Ph.D. (who pursued special studies in Experimental Psychology at Oxford and in the United States), he lectured to Jesuit theology students in a course on Pastoral Theology at Heythrop College, Oxon.; it was then under Pontifical auspices before becoming part of the University of London. He has had considerable experience in the treatment of Oxford undergraduates and has done research on diagnostic aspects of sleep in psychiatry. Here he has brought his professional judgement to bear on Hopkins's reports of how he reacted to the people around him. Such subjective accounts have to be appraised in the light of the subject's views of those other behavioral patterns that can be gauged from independent sources. Dr. Letemendia therefore refers back where necessary to material presented above, while drawing upon psychological literature and his own clinical experience for an assessment of Hopkins's emotional balance and sexual orientation.

PART III
MEDICO-PSYCHOLOGICAL COMMENTARY
by Dr. Felix Letemendia

I shall begin with some comments about Hopkins's physical appearance. R. W. Dixon, looking back on the time when he taught Hopkins in Highgate school, recalled him as "a pale young boy, very light and active, with a very meditative and intellectual face" (L.ii.4). It would seem that he retained this boyish appearance into middle age for he is referred to in Katharine Tynan's *Memories* (London: 1924, p. 155) as "being small and childish-looking" in 1886. Hopkins was barely five-foot four-inches high. Photographs of him as an adult show that he was of slender body build and had a long, lean face. However, his physical attributes did not prevent him from engaging in acts of endurance and physical courage. Norman White, in an article "Hopkins the Athlete" (*HQ.* XIII, nos. 1, 2, April–July 1986, pp. 3–4) has reminded us of his delight when a boy in climbing the highest trees. When he was thirty-two he was one of the four "theologians" who completed a gruelling cross-country walk from St. Beuno's to Moel Fammau (L.iii, 137). Later still, after he had been ordained, he showed sufficient nerve to venture out onto a narrow ledge on the west façade of Stonyhurst College, three storeys above the pavement, to rescue the astronomer's pet monkey that was too frightened to return (*Hopkins Research Bulletin*, no. 4, 1973, 29).

There are several mentions of Hopkins's appearance being attractive to others, though it is not easy to separate physical attraction from that exerted by moral qualities. An account by a fellow Jesuit, Br. Henry Marchant, raises the question of effeminacy only to reject it, saying "Some would perhaps say that he appeared 'effeminate': he was *certainly not* that. He had a certain *natural* grace of carriage that was pleasing and attractive but he was quite unconscious of the fact and too manly to wish to be taken notice of, and would have hated being noticed. He had a strong manly will of his own. . . . He spoke out pretty straight what he thought; once he said to me 'I admire you and I despise you.' I quite understood why. It gave no offence" (*Note-books and Papers of GMH*, Oxford: 1937, 385).

This observation was made concerning Hopkins in his middle twenties, well past the age at which he wrote his daily self-criticisms. But the mention of effeminacy in nineteenth-century Victorian England had the implication of homosexuality, and this still applies to a large extent in our own time, in spite of the evidence provided by the careful surveys carried out by Alfred Kinsey and his fellow workers, Wardell, Pomeroy, and Clyde Martin, over a ten-year period, during which they, and a team of colleagues, compiled more than twelve thousand case histories through personally conducted interviews, an unparalleled sample that remains the only source of large-scale statistical information to date (*Sexual Behavior in the Human Male*, Philadelphia and London: 1948). Kinsey and his co-workers state that "there are a great many males who remain as masculine, and a great many females who remain as feminine, in their attitudes and their approaches in homosexual relations, as the males or females who have nothing but heterosexual relations. Inversion and homosexuality are two distinct and not always correlated types of behavior" (p. 615).

Hopkins was decidedly late in developing full sexual maturation, judging by his private note in C.i.217 (Plate 76), recorded when he was nineteen-years five-months old.

Such late development is usually associated with a lower sexual drive and activity, which continues into adult life: a typical outlet for these late-starters is that of sexual dreams, sometimes followed by emission (Kinsey, pp. 303–07). Hopkins probably noted down only those occasions that troubled his conscience (Plates 103, 143, 151).

We now know that, during sleep, cycles of rapid eye movement and dreaming occur when awakening or near awakening takes place, during which penile tumescence or erection is common, and in the young, sometimes with loss of semen. To a man like Hopkins, with such a highly developed scrupulous conscience, such an event, taking place in a state of partial consciousness, must have presented worries about his having consented to sexual pleasure. It was also a common medical view in the late nineteenth century, and even in the first quarter of the twentieth, that loss of seminal fluid diminished physical and nervous energy.

A question that arises in the mind of the reader of the Notes is that of Hopkins's sexual orientation. If a count is made of the instances of temptation or self-accusation of sins, those in which the subjects were masculine far exceed those in which they were feminine. Sexual thoughts about women, recorded in three or more instances (Mrs. Gurney, etc.) are sufficient to show that he was capable of forming a clear heterosexual intention, on one occasion explicitly stated as "adultery of the heart." The significance of this predominance of male interest, to me as a psychiatrist, is that his life had been, up to the time of the notes, one of a socially enforced male environment at boarding school and university. After graduation he lived in all-male religious communities, taught in schools confined to boys, ministered to soldiers in Cowley Barracks, and finally lectured in the Royal University of Ireland where students of Latin and Greek were almost exclusively men. Interspersed were less than three-and-a-half years of parish duties, during which his charges included women.

It is not surprising then, in terms of probability, that Hopkins's emotional affections should fall on his male friends, knowing as we do from the notes that he was easily moved by beauty of body and character (cf. L.i.16–17) and that such emotions could have sexual undertones. His scrupulous conscience recognized such experiences as serious signs of moral danger to be dispelled from the mind, and he tried to screen out discussion of Dolben as one "forbidden subject" (Plate 111, *ll.* 4, 5). His decision to abandon the possibility of a career as a painter is an indication of his awareness of the moral danger of exposure to bodily beauty (L.iii.231). He was constantly on his guard against showing too much warmth to friends (e.g., Baillie, Plate 144, *ll.* 1, 2).

Many of his fellow undergraduates had somewhat intense male friendships, such as I observed among young men at Oxford in the permissive climate of the sixties and seventies of our own century, when the opportunities for heterosexual contact were plentiful in comparison with those prevailing in Hopkins's undergraduate days. Many of these men in both eras later settled into a dominant heterosexual pattern. Hopkins, however, opted for a celibate life, and I am in broad agreement with Paddy Kitchen's conclusion that all that can be said with certainty about Hopkins's sexual orientation is its lack of maturity: it "was never conclusively evolved" (p. 62).

Because of the high degree of scrupulosity that Hopkins reveals in the Notes, it is impossible to know what significance can be attached to references to "old habits" and "temptations" or "impurities." Mention of occasion of sin while washing (e.g., C.ii.106, 108, Plates 144, 146) may in theory have referred to anything from touching the genitals,

having a penile tumescence, or even to seminal loss. He judged the last very seriously, as a unique note (Plate 143 *ll.* 19, 20) reveals: "I fear mortal sin, effluximina nulla adhibita mora"—emissions in the night which were not in any way restrained. From Plates 76 and 151, we discover that he recorded night emissions even when he was doubtful whether he had been sufficiently awake to render them sinful. The absence of any such record for his waking hours would therefore argue against their having occurred.

It is clear from his confession notes that it was the possibility of sin that was prevalent in his thoughts, but the entries register no explicit evidence of sexual acts. There are, however, entries about thoughts and about acts related to other aspects of moral behavior that provide a guide or measure by which to judge his entries on sex. "Self indulgence at my wine" he notes on one occasion (Plate 141, *l.* 5). But as our remarks above under "Intemperance" have shown, this no more indicates that he was drunk than "self-indulgence" at a tea-party, where he reproached himself for having accepted a second biscuit, reveals him a glutton. Only someone aspiring to the most strict moral perfection would consider such actions sinful. The same can be said of the other acts such as looking at a boy, a girl, a man, or touching them. Examples: "Looking at something with impure curiousness immediately after communicating" (Pl. 142, *ll.* 26–27), indicating perhaps that for such a look to have occurred after communion made the act more sinful; "Looking at Buchanan" (Pl. 143, *l.* 40); "smiling to girl" (Pl. 140, *l.* 9); "Looking at face in the theatre" (man or woman? Pl. 117, *l.* 9); "Looking at a temptation in Newman's friend" (male or female? Pl. 113, *ll.* 10, 11); "Looking at a boy at Tiverton" (Pl. 125, *l.* 6).

Some observations on scrupulosity are pertinent. It is abundantly clear in the Notes that Hopkins suffered from a scrupulous conscience (see *OED* on "Scrupulous"; "over-nice or meticulous in matters of right or wrong"). This has been remarked on by others (e.g., W.H. Gardner, Fr. A. Bischoff, SJ) and was admitted by Hopkins himself, who in the Notes refers explicitly to "scruples" in many instances. He chided himself after Christmas 1865 for his "Folly about making a scruple abt. a sugar-plum" (Plate 146, *l.* 20). Meticulousness, intense attention to detail, doubts about having done something properly, are normal mental events when the individual is concerned with grave matters, or where error can have serious consequences for others.

In the case of Hopkins his most urgent concern was the avoidance of sin and the failure to attain high spiritual goals. Scrupulosity in spiritual life is a painful, tormenting condition, well known to confessors and sometimes to experts in psychological medicine. When the ideas dominate the mind without reason, and interfere with other thoughts and activities of everyday life they are then, in the narrow technical sense, obsessional ideas. Hopkins recognizes some of his ideas about sin as scruples, so in some sense as unreasonable, but there is no evidence in the Notes that he thought that they dominated his mind to such an extent as to interfere with his life. It is of some importance to mark this technical distinction between scrupulosity and obsessional states, particularly when we consider as an example of his meticulous conscience the method he used in marking examination papers, mentioned above; such attempts to achieve absolute fairness would be considered excessive even by the most careful of examiners, but not by Hopkins himself.

It is clear from the Notes that he was often uncertain about having sinned. This is not surprising if one considers the processes involved in normal thinking in the light of modern psychology and psychopathology. Thoughts often arise in the mind as a result of

emotional or affective states, following associative processes. At some later point in time—perhaps after only a fraction of a second—the thought is reflected upon and a judgement is made about its content and meaning, and whether to pursue it or reject it. Sometimes rejection is not instantaneous and complete, as we all know when we try to forget a tune, a word, or an expression.

These processes present real difficulties to the scrupulous person. The time that elapses between the emergence of the thought or feeling and the judgement varies with the state of consciousness and alertness, as does that of the second stage between the judgement and rejection. The Notes reflect moral doubts about consent during those time periods when volition could have been exercised more swiftly and decisively; as Hopkins puts it, "Wicked thoughts have occurred and not been at once driven away. . . . Not acknowledging at once a P.O.O. [Post Office Order, i.e., money] fr. Papa" (Pl. 103, *ll.* 11–15). The second failure to do something "at once" helps us to measure the culpability of the first one.

Here are some examples from the Notes in which Hopkins recognizes the mental act as a scruple: "Drawing agst. scruple" (Pl. 145, *l.* 6); "Dallying with that temptation abt. Magdalen, wh. indeed I think was never a tempt. in itself but a scruple and a wicked careless predisposition of mind" (Pl. 146, *ll.* 25–28). [This sentence contains three aspects of interest: (a) that a "temptation" was never a temptation but a scruple; (b) that the content of the scruple was about a girl, Magdalen; and (c) that the origin of such thoughts was a predisposition of the mind, implying by this something constitutional and beyond the scope of the will.] A few other examples of his awareness of scruple out of many include "Scrupulous fear and two at least evil thoughts and one lewd curiosity" (Pl. 146, *ll.* 32–33). On the following page he twice again refers to "scruples abt. Magdalen" (*ll.* 2, 3).

Statements abound indicating moral doubts and uncertainty about whether he had really sinned (the part of the sentence that expresses doubt is italicized): "talking to Addis . . . on a dangerous subject, *pursued more than it need have been* . . ." (Pl. 104, *l.* 10); "Thought rose while I was making some poetry in fields but I was only guilty of not dismissing the subject *as far as I understand*" (Pl. 106, *ll.* 15, 21); "Got up late by il[l]ness, but *might have got up earlier*" (Pl. 108, *l.* 17); "Sin in dream *perhaps.*" (Pl. 115, *l.* 17); "Temptations *somewhat* yielded to" (Pl. 124, *l.* 7); "Giving way to *one or two* evil thoughts" (Pl. 125, *l.* 8). "Dictionary, *once I think*" (Pl. 138, *l.* 7); "*Two or three* tempts. given *some* way to" (*l.* 14); "Proud thoughts, *somewhat* yielded to" (Pl. 146, *l.* 10). This statement on pride has the same parallel form as those on sexual temptations somewhat yielded to, confirming that he was troubled by scruples about all sins: cf. "Nothing read, not very culpable *perhaps*" (Pl. 108, *l.* 22).

States of emotional disturbance are very common among undergraduates. The stresses they undergo are many. Hopkins took academic achievement very seriously. In spite of his repeated self-accusations of laziness, he distinguished himself academically. During the span of time covered by the Notes he had to find his vocation, and within it his religious faith. This entailed a major change in his life, bringing him into conflict with his family. Yet though the Notes reflect some of the difficulties he experienced, they reflect very little in the way of affective or emotional upsets. There are only a few entries in which the word "depression" is mentioned. One seems a simple reaction to a friend's comment, a passing mood, "Depression about what Addis said abt. genius" (Pl. 143, *l.*

38); the other, on the same page, the following day, "Inatt. with deep depression" (*l.* 39). For the most part this important mood is absent and so are its tell-tale physical accompaniments of loss of sleep and appetite. His complaints run in the opposite direction: he goes to bed late and has difficulty in getting up early enough to start his duties, and he often accuses himself of over-indulgence in food. There is no indication in the Notes that he suffered as an undergraduate from pathological depression. The term commonly used at the time was melancholia. Hopkins refers to it only in his poetry: "Yields to the sultry siege of melancholy" (Pl. 118, *l.* 8); and "The melancholy Daphne doats on him" (Pl. 125).

Other moods are entered in the Notes. On a number of occasions he refers to negative feelings, usually short-lived, that he calls "despondency": "Despondency and ill humour in walking to and fr. nr. Abingdon" (Pl. 104, *l.* 12). Sometimes he describes the causes of the mood: "the prospect of not being a painter" (Pl. 136, *ll.* 17, 18), or "hearing something against me" (Pl. 144, *ll.* 33–34). At others he notes the results: "Despondency leading to want of devotion at H.C." (Holy Communion, Pl. 113, *l.* 6) or "Despondency and want of control" (Pl. 143, *ll.* 3, 4). His "Languid despondency" on November 4, 1865 (Pl. 141, *l.* 22) is soon overcome by his resolution to give up all beauty not according to God's will; he then has to contend with spiritual pride (Pl. 142, *ll.* 12, 22). But in December and the Christmas vacation his dilemma over whether to become a Catholic makes him short-tempered with everyone: "despondency" recurs on December 4, 7, 18, and 20. Everything annoys him; he mentions "Being wearied about Papa's illness and Cyril's eyes." Interspersed, however, are upsurges: three allusions to "proud thoughts" and two to conceit (Plates 144–45).

From the examination of the mood states that Hopkins refers to in the Notes, no evidence of a clinically important mood disorder can be found. On the contrary, he does conform to the strong, resilient mental disposition of those who have a meticulous, scrupulous, and even obsessional tendency in youth and adult life. Those with such a disposition may show a proneness to depression in late middle and old age.

Although these medico-psychological comments are based only on the evidence contained in the Notes of self-examination for the relatively short period March 1865 to January 1866, they are of value for two main reasons: because they cover an important time in Hopkins's psychophysical development, and because the Notes were intended to be short-hand entries to serve as an *aide-mémoire* for a good confession. They differ radically from writings with an autobiographical and (as so often) a literary or self-exculpatory purpose.

Because they are remarkably explicit on sexual matters it is possible to say that his psycho-sexual development was delayed, but that there was nothing unusual in his sexual orientation. Kinsey's survey, in spite of many smaller-scale investigations in more recent years, remains the most thorough and scientifically reliable study of sexual practices and attitudes, one which is constantly quoted by specialists in the field. It reveals that it was the norm to experience both homosexual and heterosexual erotic attraction, even at a time in our century when the expected bias would have been towards under-reporting of homosexual behavior and feelings. These are still held by many members of society to be reprehensible. How far from the average, in what Kinsey calls the heterosexual-homosexual balance, Hopkins would have been placed if he had not been a celibate man, will remain the subject of speculation. In this respect, I agree with Bernard Bergonzi's conclu-

sion in his *Gerard Manley Hopkins* (New York: Macmillan, Masters of World Literature Series, 1977):

> Unlike the Victorians, we know that human sexuality is by no means stable and that the male-female division is far from absolute. Yet to assume that all close friendships between men are "really" homosexual, as is often done now, is to succumb to a very simplistic form of Freudianism. In the case of Hopkins I think a degree of open-mindedness, even agnosticism, is necessary. There is, in any event, a logical difficulty in saying what the actual sexual proclivities of a committed celibate might be (p. 149).

POSTSCRIPT
by Norman MacKenzie

Dr. Letemendia's comments are deliberately confined to Hopkins's undergraduate period and his daily examination of conscience, apart from a passing reference to the wholly male communities in which he spent all but three-and-a-half of his remaining years. I therefore add highly compressed observations on some very one-sided quotations from Hopkins's mature poetry on which deductions concerning his sexual orientation have been based.

There can be no question that throughout his life Hopkins admired men of strength and courage. But why have his numerous references to womanly grace and fortitude not been marshalled along with them? In "The Wreck of the Deutschland" (st. 16), the sailor "handy and brave," who sacrifices himself in an effort to rescue the "wild woman-kind" from the North Sea breakers, earns only four lines, whereas the five Franciscan sisters almost monopolize the remaining half of the ode. The tall nun is called a courageous "lioness," and Hopkins uses erotic imagery reminiscent of the Canticles (Song of Solomon) in describing the response of the maiden's breast to the caressing finger of her "lover" Christ (sts. 25, 31). The result of his night of glory spent with her is the conception once again of the Word and his re-birth (sts. 30, 34). This is the plainest heterosexual imagery.

To his earlier heroines, St. Dorothea and St. Thecla (*OET* Nos. 42 and 52), Hopkins adds St. Winefred (Nos. 98, 148, 153) and [St.] Margaret Clitheroe (No. 108). Margaret's fortitude under unspeakable physical pain ends a poem that earlier alludes to the beauty of body that made her admired. It would be hard to match among his paeans to male physique the enumerated evidences of feminine "gallantry and gaiety and grace" sung by St. Winefred's maidens in the "The Golden Echo" (No. 148), such as:

> Winning ways, airs innocent, maiden manners, sweet looks, loose locks,
> > long locks, lovelocks, gaygear, going gallant, girlgrace. . . .

In his play, "St. Winefred's Well," the beautiful young heroine draws responses full of lovely metaphor from her apprehensive father: "this bloom, this honeysuckle, that rides the air so rich about thee," and from her lover turned murderer, Caradoc: her head "lapped in shining hair . . . like water in waterfalls. . . ."

> Her eyes, oh and her eyes!
> In all her beauty, and sunlight | to it is a pit, den, darkness,
> Foamfalling is not fresh to it, | rainbow by it not beaming,
> In all her body, I say, | no place was like her eyes,
> No piece matched those eyes | kept most part much cast down
> But, being lifted, immortal, | of immortal brightness.

The lithe grace of boys is hedged with warnings and foreboding. The young bugler kneeling before the St. Clement's congregation for his first communion is praised for his "Breathing bloom of a chastity in mansex fine," triumphant so far in the barracks, but liable under army field conditions to be molested by "hell-rook ranks" (No. 137 *ll* 9, 16, 18). Hell also threatens not only the young man in his prime described in the middle

stanza of "Morning, Midday, and Evening Sacrifice" (No. 139), but the lyrically fresh young girl or boy—the description might fit either—with whom the poem opens. The poet prays that the owner of "The Handsome Heart" (No. 134), who might also have had a handsome face, may run all his race as nobly as he had begun it.

Admiration for the "lovely manly mould" of the drowned seaman in "The Loss of the Eurydice," quoted from a news report, is in no way reminiscent of the drowned Dolben: the emphasis is upon the disciplined skill, the product of years of service, that has been lost to the British navy—and probably to Christ (*ll.* 77–96). The Felix Randal with whom he developed a deep affinity was not the boisterous cursing blacksmith of his younger manhood but the shrunken penitent, slowly dying as he contended with "Fatal four disorders" (No. 142).

When the priest in a sermon at Bedford Leigh enumerated the physical attributes that Christ is believed to have shown while he was a man on earth (*Sermons*, 34–38), he was quoting from ancient traditions; moreover he devoted more time to Christ's mental and spiritual powers than to his appearance. His meditation note for March 8, 1884 (S. 255), on Christ's glorious transfiguration while still a man, refers to the "sight of our Lord's body as a remedy for Temptation," and the "thought of his mind and genius [as a help] against vainglory." We can also balance this vision of male perfection with his poems in praise of the Virgin Mary: "Ad Mariam" (No. 94), "Rosa Mystica" (No. 96), "The May Magnificat" (No. 126), and "The Blessed Virgin compared to the Air we Breathe" (No. 151). Andromeda is a more arresting figure in his Oxford sonnet than her rescuer Perseus (No. 138). The poem by Bridges that Hopkins most admired over the years and eventually translated into Latin was a lover's fervent worship of a woman's superb beauty (No. 166). These few examples must suffice for this Postscript.

Among many discussions of the treatment of male strength and grace in Hopkins are John Robinson, *In Extremity* (Cambridge: 1978, pp. 95–98), criticized above; the partisan paper by Michael Lynch (*HQ* VI, no. 3, Fall 1979, pp. 107–17), attacked by Donald Walhout (*HQ* VII, no. 3, Fall 1980, pp. 122–23); Wendell Stacy Johnson's "Sexuality and Inscape" (*HQ* III, no. 2, July 1976, pp. 59–65); Bernard Bergonzi, *Gerard Manley Hopkins* (London, N.Y., 1977, pp. 148–51); and David Downes, *The Great Sacrifice* (N.Y., London, 1983, p. 24ff.). Paddy Kitchen's *Gerard Manley Hopkins* (London: 1978, chap.4) shows considerable insight.

Since Hopkins realized that all passionate love, whether between the same or opposite sexes, may burgeon out of control, impoverishing the more important human gifts of intellect and spirit, his own strong-willed choice, from his Oxford days onward, was to sacrifice physical love for a life of celibacy. As a result, a century after his death in Dublin, he still lives on for us in his poetry, his journals, his letters and spiritual writings.

How to Interpret the Plates and the Notes

Even scholars familiar with Hopkins's handwriting are liable to misread him. No instant expertise can be imparted by a few pages of advice, but readers who are able to devote time to "Some Sources of Difficulty in Reading the MSS" will be able to avoid the commonest pitfalls. The legibility of the original MSS varies considerably, from stylishly written fair copies in ink to hurried pencil drafts scribbled in a miniature vest-pocket notebook and at times as hurriedly deleted. Some plates have been reproduced by the Copyflo process, because of its sensitivity to ranges of tones, while his two early Note-books have been made from glossy prints. The deleted daily notes have been prepared from plates made by a forensic document department with the use of special filters. The text might sometimes have been made plainer by employing maximum contrast, but subtle differences in the inks and in the pencil entries would have been sacrificed in the process.

Deletions. Where cancelled entries are particularly difficult to read I have tried to supply the original version, preceded by a query where uncertainty exists. Readings are given in the notes in the sequence in which they were probably developed, although Hopkins occasionally uses a caret to direct attention to a revision first.

When a word has been begun, then cancelled, I have at times tried to complete it, using square brackets. Thus in C.i.158 (Plate 60), Hopkins wrote, below a sketch of "Caen Wood," "Lord" followed by what looks like a sanserif "I," but as Lord Mansfield owned what is now called Ken Wood this is probably the beginning of an "M" (cf. C.i.160.2d). All such completions are necessarily conjectural.

Deleted words may prove to be homophones. In C.i.170 "bare" is changed to "bear" ("Barnfloor and Winepress," l.30), as "ring" and "wring" replace each other elsewhere.

Deleted words are normally indicated by "orig," (i.e., "originally"), or else enclosed in square brackets followed by "*del.*" Occasionally they are printed and then crossed through, but in the MSS themselves the cancelling stroke through words may lose hyphens and dashes: on Plate 162, e.g., (MS. H.i.23 recto, line 5a) there is a hyphen that I recovered only by means of an Infra-red Image Converter. Moreover, in type small enough to fit below the plates, horizontal lines cutting through words may, especially with names and unfinished words, confuse the distinctions between *e*, *c*, and *o*.

"Mended." This term is used when one word or phrase is changed into another merely by writing the correction more heavily on top of the original in the same space. It is sometimes hazardous to say which came first. A clear example follows on Plate 51, *l*.14, where "burs" was mended to "burns" — the note may indicate this with an arrow ("burs"→ "burns").

Scale. The MSS have been variously enlarged to take account of smaller writing or reduced so that different versions of the same poem can be juxtaposed for easier comparison. The scale line (usually at the bottom of the MS) indicates 50mm. of the original. The scale lines are omitted from the crowded pages of C.i. and C.ii. because these are all approximately 7.2 cm. wide by 11.8 cm. high.

Comparing Versions. The version on any left hand page can be readily compared with one on any later right hand page by simply holding the intervening page(s) at right angles to the other two. To facilitate this comparison the sequence of the drafts has sometimes been deliberately rearranged, or else particular plates have been reprinted on a smaller scale on the opposite side of a later opening.

The Numbering of the Lines

a) *Prose.* In the Note-books C.i. and C.ii., the lines in prose entries, even if they occur in separate paragraphs, are numbered consecutively on each page. Where no poem number precedes it, the line number will generally refer to a prose passage.

b) *Verse.* To facilitate the study of the stages through which a poem evolved, where there are drafts the line numbers are usually based on their counterparts in the final version as printed in my Oxford English Texts edition. When a draft version of a piece differs radically from its revision the *OET* may print both separately, and number them separately too (see Nos. 20, 77, and 100, e.g.). In surprisingly many cases, however, individual lines in a rough draft reappear in the polished fair copy, though they are often masterfully modified, and one line in a draft may be expanded into two later (see, e.g., Plate 97, C.ii.47, where I have numbered the early version of a line "155/6a" because it partially anticipates lines 155 and 156 on C.ii.48).

No two occurrences of a handwritten line are ever exactly the same. Every repetition or variant of a line in a series of drafts is assigned a unique code; they are lettered *a, b, c, d,* etc., in the sequence through which they *probably* evolved, though subsequent study may modify my tentative conclusions. Hopkins will often be found veering back to some discarded wording after vain efforts to improve the sense, sound, or rhythm.

Stanza 2 in my rearranged edition of the "Soliloquy of One of the Spies Left in the Wilderness" occurs in no fewer than five versions, the rhymes and arrangement of lines differing so widely that I have attached the *a, b, c,* etc., to the stanza number rather than the individual lines (see Plates 58, 60, etc.). The marginal references direct readers on to each fresh revision.

The line letters may mark the evolution only within a single draft, or attempt to track it through all the versions, depending on circumstances. With No.17, "Barnfloor and Winepress," the changes are mostly in punctuation or the application of capitals for which Hopkins himself may not have been responsible—one document is a contemporary published version (subject to editorial tinkering) and another a transcription by a friend, liable to slips. With Plates 63–64 and 78–79 therefore I have lettered the line numbers in only the first two versions. On the other hand, Hopkins's restless pursuit of a perfect translation for a hymn attributed to St. Thomas Aquinas (No. 100) can be tracked through six folio pages in which differences in pen and handwriting are sufficient to

show their probable order. The letters run on consecutively through all the drafts: some troublesome lines (e.g., *l*16) sounded the gamut from *a* to *k*, representing almost as many verbal changes, yet others only as far as *d* with minimal variation. Where a line was not begun afresh but by means of several deletions and interlineations made "substantially different" (a rather subjective criterion), I have usually given its revised form a letter of its own. Sometimes three or more versions are represented by these interlineations (see e.g. Plates 196–97, 214). I have occasionally set each of these out in full transcriptions below the MS.

Imperfections. The MSS are sometimes immensely complicated and liable to variant interpretations. I shall be grateful to receive queries or corrections in cases of doubt.

Detailed Interpretation of Plate 51 (Note-book C.i.p.100) follows on pages 42 and 43.

N.12	C.i.	100 2	Pilate
OET	100	Unchill'd I thinidle stinging	
No.10	8 b / a	~~I am not chill'd by staff~~ snow;	
(begins here)	9 a	O sun whose vast afflictive heat	
	10a	Does lay men low wiθ one blade's	
Pilate		sudden blow	
	11 a	~~before upon my brain to beat~~	
	b	Cleaves not my brain, burns not	
Lines 8-11 rev. c.i. 108 Pl.53	12 { a b / c	my feet, [albeit	
		When θ blue skies are ~~blackish~~ almost black.	
		When θ fierce — } are blue & black.	
		albeit [wiθ θeir blaze	
	13	the shearing rays contract me	
	14	Most dead - alive upon θose days.	
	15	3	
		θen I seek out θ shadow ~~stones~~	
	16	And to θose stones ~~almost~~ become akin	
	17a	My soundless moans are distant	
		in θeir tones	
	18a	As θo θey came not from wiθin	

PLATE 51

The inner column is headed by the MS. reference—here Note-book C.i, p.100. The outer column records the poem number in the Oxford English Texts edition; also whether (and where) the passage is to be found in the printed *Journals* (J.) or *Note-books and Papers* (N. page 12). Drafts scattered over many pages are linked by means of marginal cross-references.

8 a   This deleted line is legible and is therefore not transcribed in the notes to the plate. It is however quoted in the OET Commentary.

9 a   Theta stands for "the" or "th"—u.c. and l.c. are often indistinguishable (cf. "those" in 14). The apparent comma after "heat" is the apostrophe in "blade's" (10 a).

11 a   "to" is usually like "te" or (as in 12 c) "le."

11 b   "burs" → "burns" (i.e., one is altered or "mended" to the other without being rewritten). The first "not" is like "hot," the second "not" like "rot": *n* often resembles *r*.

12 a   "When the blue skies are blackish. Albeit"—"blackish" was deleted, its revision creating 12 b:

12 b   "When the blue skies are almost black. Albeit"

12 c   "When the fierce skies [dash below "skies" is ditto mark] are blue to black albeit"—the faint dot after "blue to black" in the photograph is almost invisible in the MS, so is probably not a period. Moreover the "a" in the "albeit" in 12 c is the same size as the small "a" in "rays" below it and in "are" in 17 a. The brace linking the second halves of lines 12 a, b, and c is deleted.

13   "rays"—note that *r* may resemble a *v*.

14   "Most dead"—stray dots and other marks appear on nearly every MS page, whether in pencil or ink. Did GMH really dot his *o* (thinking he had written "Mist") and what is the little "bird" above "dead"?

15   "and stones"—the cross-bar to *t* is not visible: $\cap$, the sign for "and," may here (as often elsewhere) be a slip for its reverse, $\cup$, "of."

17 a   "distant"—the *a* appears to be dotted, but this may be a stray dot since this *a* is fully formed.

Some Sources of Difficulty in Reading the Manuscripts

Hopkins's handwriting is often aesthetically pleasing, and readers can guess their way through it happily enough, yet no editor has so far succeeded in presenting a perfect transcription. Problems multiply when forty lines crowd a tiny page, with individual letters barely two millimeters high. The pencil has smudged with use—by Hopkins as well as his admirers. Letters and punctuation marks on so small a scale tend to be misshaped: *a* is often open like *u*; *e* may look like an *i*, having no loop; *t* may be uncrossed like an *l*; descenders in *f, g, j, p*, and *y* may scarcely drop below the line; capitals may be almost the same size as lower case letters. The poet sometimes misread his own writing, dotting the wrong vowels or crossing an *l* absent-mindedly. Examples of confusing words follow, greatly enlarged, for readers to examine, followed by detailed analyses and references to pages in the two Notebooks where the context often solves them. I avoided providing simple transcriptions because these short-circuit the process of observation. Misshaped letters considerably complicate the reading of names in the deleted notes of self-scrutiny. This facsimile edition is somewhat unusual in transcribing many of the less legible passages, while readers who have difficulty with others can consult the printed versions referred to in the outer margins. Notebook pages are cited for precision, followed after a period by the line number. C.i. runs from Plate 29 to 77, and C.ii. from 82 to 151.

1 stirred

2 ush

3 beast-eyed = bee.

4 receive

5 abolish'd

6 preed

7 bowls

8 laugh,

9 live a day.

10 ctr O,

11 wool.

12 Clock

13 So,

14 over

15 without

16

17 And the quantly

18 Orch

19 Vaxe

20 Blaze with him

21 { Oak lich O shelly leaves at flory deepe,
In O flesh paparee o trolling pines,
Under O cloister-light o green house trees,

22 You must ever back will your
sxie.

23 O moon as O stars.

24 { Can only be
be written

25 young

26 grateful god

27 O dented primrose, Slight-edged,

28 We meet together you & I,
Meet on one acre o one land,

29 (a) O unseen'd glass   29(c) borrowed
(b) nerve a vein.   29(d) harvest

30 To be a judge or ruler over us?

31 Weeping,—with now

32 All-heal

33 vey

34 to speak so,

35 Quadrant.

36 Square-cut stieb.

37 And would not have Oat legion o wing'l | Legion

38 forth

39 flesh.

40 skirt

41 Oox unokotd of thee

42 { knot of feathery locks
feathery knot ——

43 { contends about its
And Aosts confront

44 Sometimes Lree O summit stake
[Nos. 45 to 62 in col. c above]

45 existin

46 dex

47 tones

48 soand

49 Vance

50 bores

51 locks

52 bound

53 bound

54 { bound
slow

55 hitteh

56 list
surprise

57 gloomy

58 { O time
Told off

59 O tree

60 : Love when
Love's proper

61 creold

62 Goodnight te

REFERENCES FOR STRANGE WORDS

1   Not "strict" (four letters have deceptive shapes). Fortunately this was a rhyme word, and a revised version was transcribed by Coles—C.i.171, bot. line (Plates 64, 80ᴬ).

2   Two letters are peculiar—C.ii.5 (No. 31g, line 2). Cf. example 18.

3   "beast-eyed"? So I read it at first glance (a *u* for *a* being so frequent), then I noticed that the Greek did not match—C.i.165.2.

4   A seven-letter word with only six countable letters, the missing one being the size of a mere speck—C.i.209.5a.

5   The first letter is an open trough: cf. examples 16, 17—C.i.171.1.

6   "pieeed"? Easy once you realise that *c* is like an ordinary (not Greek) *e* —C.i.207 (No.30f, line 3).

7   The first two letters may be deceptive, though encountered in its context the word is simple enough—C.i.171.7b.

8   Two words, no comma—C.i.172 (No. 19, line 17).

9   The stroke above the *i* could be its dot (cf. example 46), but *i* is often left undotted, and the poet may have abstractedly crossed an *l* —C.i.209 (No. 32.c, line 2).

10 The first word is "mended," i.e., corrected, not by a deletion stroke and interlineation, but by the revised word being superimposed in the same space. Though the second word is written more firmly, an editor may have difficulty in deciding which is on top. In the notes the direction of change may be shown by an arrow: here "at" → "on"—C.i.206.43.

11 Letters are quite often squeezed laterally—C.i.170.33. The dot over the second *o* is simply a "stray," where the pencil touched the paper accidentally. There are some on every page.

12 The bottom lines of a tiny note-book are hard to fill accurately, especially if the book is unsupported—C.i.207, bot. (Next two examples are from the same plate.)

13 Both letters are peculiar—C.i.206.38c.

14 The first supernumerary down-stroke also occurs with some forms of *a* and *n* (see example 47)—C.i.206.34.

15 An abnormally large letter upsets this word—C.i.218 (No.31b.9).

16, 17 Thought by Alan Ward (J.523, note 44.1) to be a slip in GMH's Latin quotation, "conveniunt" for "conveniant"; but compare example 17, the word below it on the same page (C.ii.5.1 and 2), where the *a* in the unrecognisable "quantity" is more open than even the *u* before it.

18 *h* and *k* are often indistinguishable; the *i* frequently has no dot—C.i.172.16. Cf. example 34.

19 A not uncommon case of two homophones being superimposed—C.i.170.30.

20 This enlargement clarifies the revision. I misread it in 1967 as "from" revised to "for," thinking that the *f* had not been deleted.—C.i.151 (No.12, line 24).

21 Hyphens are often mere points, as in "cloister-light"; but is "shelly leaves" a hyphenation?—C.i.164.4. Cf. example 27. The little trough sign for "of" occurs twice.

22 "ever" or "even"? The first makes better sense and is the traditional reading; but I find it hard to match the last letter with an unarguable final *r*, whereas *n* often has a second limb like this one (cf. examples 23, 24, 25). Note the peculiar *x*.—C.i.221.46.

23–25 C.i.213.14; 212.12 and 13; 173.6.

26 The first *g* is not a capital, but it stands on the line instead of descending below it, and is half as large again as the next *g*.

27 If "slight-edged" was mended to "Slight-edged," was the comma before it changed to a period?—C.ii.53, prose line 1.

28 C.i.172.10 and 11. There are several cases of *e* like *i* ; one *t* is like an *l* ; and there are squeezed versions of *o* and *e*. But in the sentence these unravel themselves. The dot above "acre" has always been taken as a comma after "together," but it is so much smaller than other commas in adjacent pages that I think it is merely a stray dot.

29 Nine examples of almost interchangeable *r* and *v*. (a) C.i.151.17 was incorrectly printed from 1937 (N.23) till 1984 (Ruskin wrote of the "unveined" sky): "glare!" is on the edge of the paper; (b) C.i.103.51; (c) C.i.211 (No. 32g) (d) C.i.172.15.

30 GMH often confused his own shorthand signs for "of" (a breve) with one for "and" (a sort of circumflex). Here he caught his own slip, but in example 42 he did not—C.i.153.44.

31 C.i.206.40b. Words beginning with a Greek short *e* (ε) often appear to be u.c. when they are probably not. Cf. C.i.136.13; 137.10 and line 3 in the verse below it. There is a true u.c. *E* in "Egyptian"—137.16.

32 Here the hyphen is more like a conventional one, but the words are unusually widely separated—C.i.206.77.

33 "vey"? One of the few words which baffled Humphry and Madeline House (I solved it in 1967).—C.i.101.20. The closing parenthesis after the turn-over ["wharves)"] is a slip.

34 The *k* is like an *h*, and the comma curves the wrong way (as an apostrophe may also do)—C.i.206.37.

35 A mended name (if this is one and not an instrument) may cause serious uncertainty—C.i.172.1. Humphry House left no annotation.

36 Another hyphenation. GMH may have misread an *e* as *i* and dotted it—C.i.192.1. There are also two stray dots between "cut" and "steep" however.

37 There is often little difference between a capital *L* and its l.c. form. Here "Legion" in an early draft of "New Readings" appears to be u.c. (see its enlargement on the right)—C.i.171.14. Cf. example 60 (above "Legion" enlarged).

38 Two letters could be mistaken—C.i.169.23.

39 Another simpler example of a descender that did not descend—C.i.151.20a.

40 The *p* is like a *b*—C.i.173.8.

41 A celebrated crux, on a page crowded with some 44 lines of verse and prose. Here two words are each mended so obscurely that neither the original text nor the revision can be read with certainty. HH left a blank in J.67—C.ii.91 (No. 64c, *l* .4).

42   "knot of feathery locks" bracketed with "feathery knot *and* locks," the wrong shorthand sign being used—C.i.215.14a and b. The dash is a ditto sign: many such dittos occur on C.i.155, and are reproduced in J.

43   Confusion over capital letters: "contends" ought to have a recognisable u.c. *C* since it begins a line. The u.c. of "Hosts" is easily overlooked. Plate 166, "Nondum, " *l.*32.

44   Four words begin with *s* : note how irrational their variations in size are. The initial "S" (which must be u.c.) is twice the size of the one in "see" (l.c.) but "Summit" begins with one almost as large, yet what editor could justify u.c. for it?—C.i.101.22.

45   Note that *x* is often like a little *k.* The "tr" is merely "in": the dot (or rather dash) brushes the top of the *i*, and the final *n* recalls examples 22 to 25—C.i.213.24.

46   The dot over the *i* is again a dash. The word is not "dix" but "air" with a dash almost crossing the *r*—C.i.101.23 (very confused corrections).

47   The *n* starts with a long stroke like an *h* (cf. example 14 where an *o* begins too high)— C.i.101.17b: contr. line 17a on p. 100.

48   This example and the next show *a* and *u* exchanging shapes—C.i.101.27.

49   C.ii.5.16.

50   "pores, and"—the comma could be easily overlooked—C.i.151.20b.

51   The context shows that this is not "locks" but "looks"—C.i.172.12.

52-54   Two of these three examples are of the same word. Which is the odd man out? 52— C.i.170.29; 53—C.i.206.77; 54—C.i.211 (No. 32g).

55   The *l* seems to have been idly crossed during re-reading—C.ii.53.7.

56   "No surprise" revised to "lest surprise." GMH must surely have dotted his compressed *e* when glancing back over the line—C.i.133 (No. 11, line 3). Note that though it is universal practice to place the caret before a deletion so that the original reading may be ignored, my transcriptions follow the time sequence, quoting the original reading first, then its replacement.

57   Two unexpected shapes for *o* : the chances of misreading a name with such letters would be excellent—C.i.79.17.

58,59 In these three examples of *t, T,* how many are capitals?—C.i.214 (No. 30k), and C.i.169.23. The apparent stress in No. 59 is a comma meant for the line above.

60   GMH sometimes differentiated his *l* from *L* by rounding the down-stroke of *l* into the horizontal. The distinction can sometimes be debatable. If the second "love" has been mended to l.c., as I suspect, that would suit the theological implications, as I point out in the OET commentary—C.ii.102 (No. 71, lines 9 and 10).

61   Momentary problems arise when words are run together (complicated here by interchangeable *e* and *c*)—C.i.172 (No. 19, line 5).

62   Before dogmatising as to whether two words should be printed as separate or a compound critics might be wise to make a detailed study of GMH's pen-lifts. This splitting of a word in two before an *i* is much less common than splitting it after an *i* (which he does so as to dot it before he forgets)—C.i.206.41b.

Plates

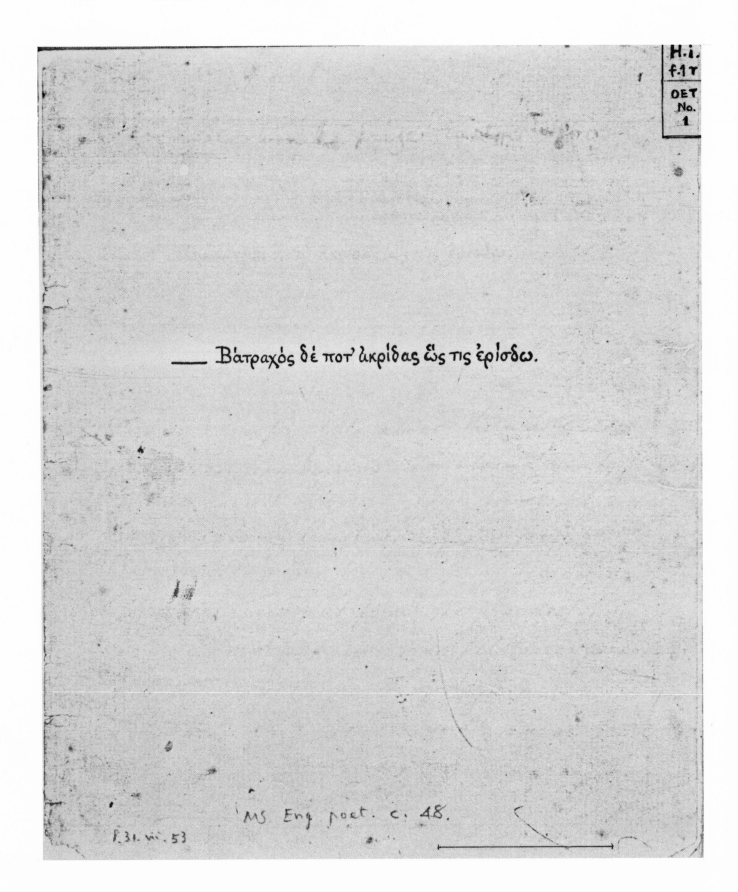

H.i.
f.1ʳ

OET
No.
1

— Βὰτραχὸς δέ ποτ' ἀκρίδας ὣς τις ἐρίσδω.

'MS. Eng. poet. c. 48.

f. 31. vii. 53

Plate 2   OET No.1: The Escorial--MS.1

H.i.f.1r. To preserve anonymity in the competition for the Highgate school poetry prize, this poem was submitted under the "pseudonym" of a Greek motto (Theocritus, <u>Idylls</u>, 7.41), and the text was copied out in ink in a formal clerical hand by GMH's father, Manley Hopkins. He used the long "s" whenever that letter was doubled (e.g., 4). The paper was folded to make a booklet of 18 folios, each 18.6 cm wide x 22.5 high. The motto occupies 1r on its own; 1v is blank (though smudged from the addition on 2r of "Won the prize. Easter - 1860."); 9v to the end were not used. The Notes were neatly printed on the versos of 2 to 8, the ink showing through on the rectos. They, and the motto, were prob. penned by GMH himself: he uses the form "Laurence" (twice transcribed as "Lawrence" in st.2), and elaborate five-pointed asterisks (contr. Manley's in st.11). An embossed rose design, not visible in photographs, adorns the top left corner of 1r and 7r.

PLATE 3. OET 1. *The Escorial* • 53

H.i.
2ʳ

The Escorial. won the prize. Easter. 1860.

— Βάτραχός δέ ποτ' ἀκρίδας ὥς τις ἐρίσδω.

1.

There is a massy-pile above the waste
Amongst Castilian barrens mountain-bound;
A sombre length of grey—; four towers placed
At corners flank the stretching-compass round,
A pious work with threefold purpose crown'd—
A cloister'd convent first, the proudest home
Of those who strove God's gospel to confound
With barren rigour and a frigid gloom—
Hard by a royal palace, and a royal tomb.

Plate 3   OET No.1: The Escorial—MS.2
    H.i.2r—transcription by Manley Hopkins (cont. on rectos of 3 to 9). In line 2 "barrens" may have puzzled
the copyist: it seems to have been added later (cf. "laver'd" in 31). Corrections were needed where "-ed" had
been written out in full (6,28,72,74, etc.).

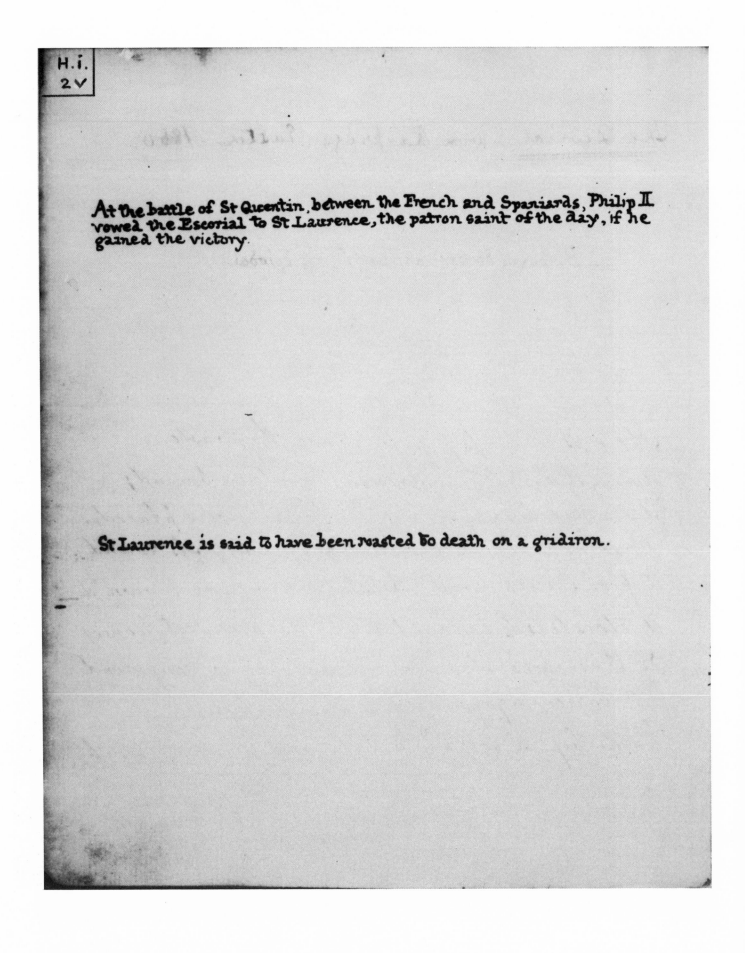

H.i.
2ᵛ

At the battle of St Quentin, between the French and Spaniards, Philip II vowed the Escorial to St Laurence, the patron saint of the day, if he gained the victory.

St Laurence is said to have been roasted to death on a gridiron.

PLATE 5. OET 1. *The Escorial* • 55

H.i.
3r

2.

3

10　They tell its story thus; amidst the heat
Of battle once upon St Lawrence' day
Philip took oath, while glory or defeat
Hung in the swaying of the fierce mélée,
"So I am victor now, I swear to pay
15　The richest gift St Lawrence ever bore,
When chiefs and monarchs came their gifts to lay
Upon his altar, and with rarest store
　×　To deck & make most lordly evermore."

───────────

3.

For that staunch saint still prais'd his master's
　　　　　　　　　　　　　　　　　　　name
20　While his crack'd flesh lay hissing on the grate;
Then fail'd the tongue; the poor collapsing frame
Hung like a wreck that flames not billows beat—
　×　So, grown fantastic in his piety,
Philip, supposing that the gift most meet　×
25　The sculptur'd image of such faith would be,
Uprais'd an emblem of that fiery constancy.

───────────

OET
No.
1

Plates 4 and 5　　　OET No.1: The Escorial--MSS.3,4.
　　Plate 4: H.i.2V--the first of the annotations, prob. printed in by GMH. He uses the spelling "Laurence".
　　In Plate 5 (f.3r) the copyist transcribed the name as "Lawrence," a spelling GMH failed to correct [printed "Laurence" in OET edn.]. At the end of 16 there is a smudge (not a comma) after "lay"; after "grate" (20) a semi-colon seems intended (contrast 113).
　　A pencil "X" beside 18 may have been added during the judging of the poem: the last line of a Spenserian st. should be an Alexandrine, not a pentameter. So too with the pencil "X" after ℓ.22, where a line rhyming with "beat" and "meet" is missing (either the composer's or the copyist's slip--unless the poems had to be no longer than 125 lines).

H. i.
3v

The Escorial was built in the form of a gridiron, — the rectangular
convent was the grate, the cloisters the bars, the towers the legs inverted, the palace the handle.
The building contained the royal Mausoleum; and a gate which
was opened only to the newborn heir apparent, and to the funeral
of a monarch.

⁂ Philip endeavoured to establish the Inquisition in the Netherlands.

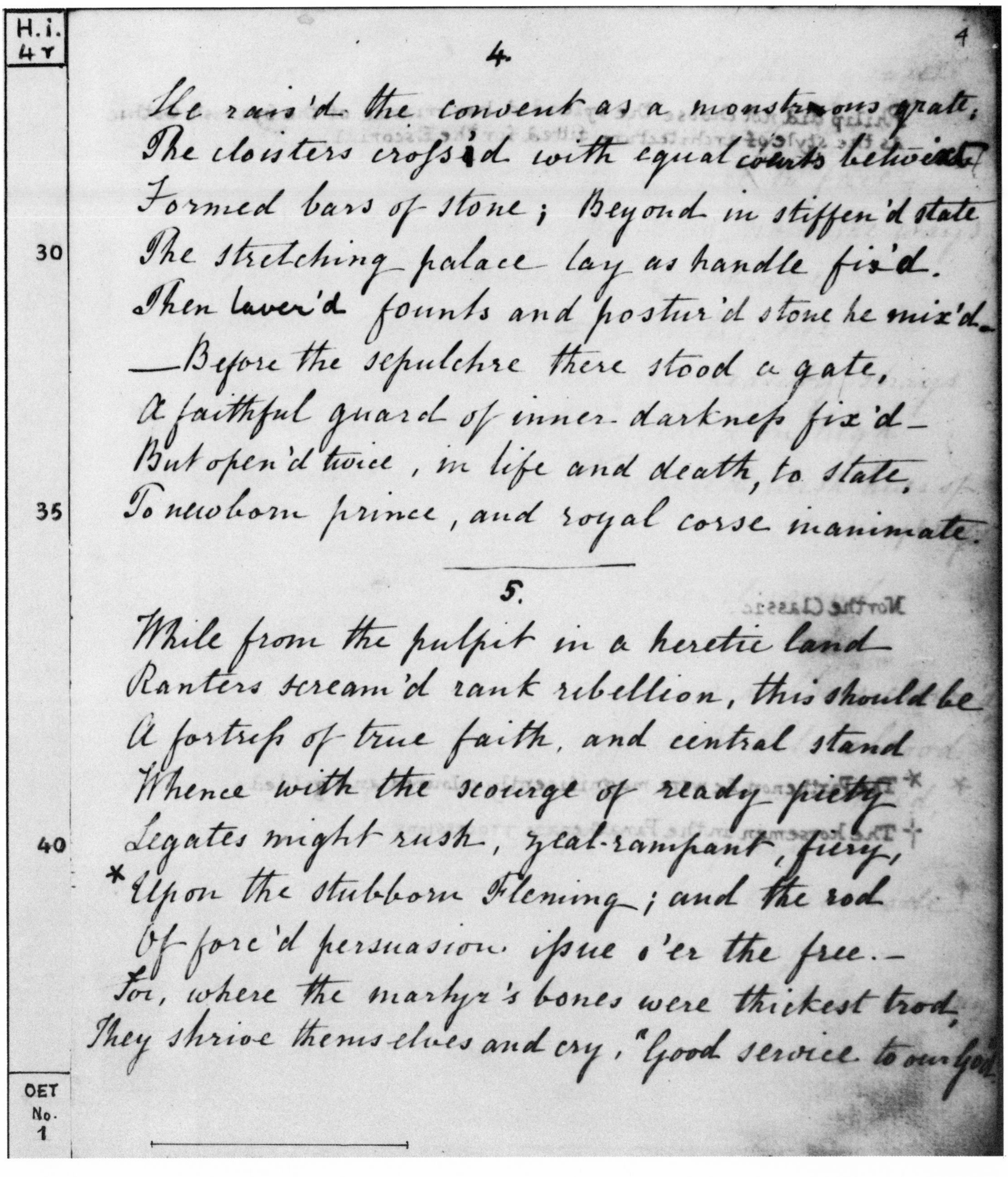

PLATE 7. OET 1. *The Escorial* • 57

4

4

He rais'd the convent as a monstrous gate,
The cloisters cross'd with equal courts between
30 Formed bars of stone; Beyond in stiffen'd state
The stretching palace lay as handle fix'd.
Then laver'd founts and postur'd stone he mix'd—
— Before the sepulchre there stood a gate,
A faithful guard of inner darkness fix'd—
But open'd twice, in life and death, to state,
35 To newborn prince, and royal corse inanimate.

———

5.

While from the pulpit in a heretic land
Ranters scream'd rank rebellion, this should be
A fortress of true faith, and central stand
Whence with the scourge of ready piety
40 Legates might rush, zeal-rampant, fiery,
* Upon the stubborn Fleming; and the rod
Of forc'd persuasion issue o'er the free.—
For, where the martyr's bones were thickest trod,
They shrive themselves and cry, "Good service to our God"

H.i.
4ᵛ

OET
No.
1

Plate 7   OET No.1: The Escorial (cont.)--MS.6
   H.i.4r. Changes and deletions include: 27 orig. "monstruous"   28 "between" mended to "betwixt"   29
orig. "stone."—period explains u.c. in "Beyond"   30 orig. "fixed"   31 "laver'd" added (in a different hand?)

H.i.
4 v

Philip did not choose the splendid luxuriance of the Spanish Gothic
as the style of architecture fitted for the Escorial,

Nor the Classic.

* The Parthenon &c were magnificently coloured and gilded.
† The horsemen in the Panathenaic processions.

PLATE 9. OET 1. *The Escorial* • 59

6.

No finish'd proof was this of Gothic grace
With flowing tracery engemming rays
Of colour in high casements face to face;
And foliag'd crownals (pointing how the ways
Of art best follow nature) in a maze
Of finish'd diapers, that fills the eye
And scarcely traces where one beauty strays
And melts amidst another; ciel'd on high
With blazoned groins, and crowned with hues of
                                        majesty.

_____

7.

This was no classic temple order'd round
With massy pillars of the Doric mood
Broad-fluted, nor with shafts acanthus-crown'd
Pourtray'd along the frieze with Titan's brood
That battled Gods for heaven; brilliant-hued, *
With golden fillets and rich blazonry,
Wherein beneath the cornice, horsemen rode
With form divine, a fiery chivalry —
Triumph of airy grace and perfect harmony.

H.i.
5v

✻ The Alhambra &c.

The Architect was Velasquez; the style Italian Classic, partly Ionic partly Doric. The whole is sombre in appearance, but grand, and imposing.

PLATE 11. OET 1. *The Escorial* • 61

H.i.
6r

6

8.

* Fair relics too the changeful Moor had left
Splendid with phantasies aërial,

65 Of mazy-shape and hue, but now bereft
By conqu'rors rude of honor; and not all
Unmindful of their grace, the Escorial
Arose in gloom, a solemn mockery

× Of those gilt webs that languish'd in a fall.

70 This to remotest ages was to be
The pride of faith, and home of sternest piety

9.

* * * * * * * * * * * *

OET
No.
1

Plate 11   OET No.1: The Escorial—MS.10
    H.i.6r. The pencil "X" before 69 may be a judge's query; "gilt webs" has been added in a different hand.
When the poem was transcribed st.9 may not have been ready. GMH later added a row of his five-pointed asterisks
in the space left for it. The lacuna after st.11 had been decided upon earlier.

H.i.
6 v

The interior was decorated with all the richest productions of art and nature. Pictures, statues, marble, fountains, tapestry &c (He refers to Philip.)

✗ In one of Raphael's pictures the Madonna and St Joseph play with their child in a wide meadow; behind is a palm-tree.

† Alluding to Raphael's "Lo Spasimo", which is, I believe, in the Escorial.

‡ Alluding to the dark colouring of landscapes to be seen in Rubens, Titian &c.

¶ A beautiful youth drowned in the Nile; the statue has the position described.

‖ Hyacinthus. § The Belvidere Apollo.

PLATE 13. OET 1. *The Escorial* • 63

H.i.
7r

7

10.

He rang'd long-corridors and cornic'd halls,
And damasqu'd arms and foliag'd carving piled.—
With painting gleam'd the rich pilaster'd walls—

75 * Here play'd the virgin mother with her Child
In some broad palmy mead, and saintly smiled,
And held a cross of flowers, in purple bloom;
+ He, where the crownals droop'd, himself reviled
And bleeding saw.— Thus hung from room to room
80 The skill of dreamy Claude, and Titian's mellow gloom.

11.

Here in some ‡ darken'd landscape Paris fair
Stretches the envied fruit with fatal smile
To golden-girdled Cypris;—Ceres there
Raves through Sicilian pastures many a mile;
85 ¶ But, hapless youth, Antinous the while
Gazes aslant his shoulder, viewing nigh
Where Phoebus weeps for him whom Zephyr's quill
Chang'd to a flower; and there, with placid eye
§ Apollo views the smitten Python writhe and die.

*∴ * * * * * * * * * * * * *

OET
No.
1

Plate 13   OET No.1: The Escorial—MS.12.
    H.i.7r. This page, less distinct in the MS, was misread in many places by Fr. G.F. Lahey (GMH, OUP, 1930,
10-11), and so too in Poems, 2nd and 3rd edns.; e.g. 72 "The rang'd" for "He..." (the reference in GMH's note to
"He" made no sense till I restored the text in Poems 4th. edn); also 75 and 81 "There" for "Here"; and 79 "There"
for "Thus"; and 84 "Roves" for "Raves" (corrected by 2nd edn)   In 82 "Stretches" was orig. "Reaches".

H.i.7v

*   *   *   *   *   *   *   *   *   *   *   *   *   *   *   *

The Escorial was adorned by succeding kings, until the Peninsular war, when the French as a piece of revenge for their defeats, sent a body of dragoons under La Houssaye, who entered the Escorial, ravaged and despoiled it of some of its greatest treasures, The monks then left the convent. Since that time it has been left desolate and uninhab. ited. The 12th stanza describes this.

* Alluding to the practise of arranging swords in circles, radiating from their hilts.

† The Escorial is often exposed to the attacks of the storms which sweep down from the mountains of Guadarrama.

PLATE 15. OET 1. *The Escorial* • 65

H.i.
8r

8

12

90 Then through the afternoon the summer-beam
Stop'd on the galleries; upon the wall
Rich Titians faded; in the straying-gleam
The motes in ceaseless eddy shine and fall
Into the cooling gloom; till slowly all
95 Dimm'd in the long-accumulated dust
Pendant in formal line from cornice tall
* Blades of Milan in circles rang'd, grew rust
And silver damasqu'd plates obscur'd in age's crust.

_____

13.

+ But from the mountain glens in autumn late
100 Adown the clattering gullies swept the rain;
The driving-storm at hour of vespers beat
Upon the mould'ring-terraces amain;
The Altar-tapers flar'd in gusts; in vain
Louder the monks dron'd out Gregorians slow;
105 Afar in corridors with painèd strain
Doors slamm'd to the blasts continually; more
low,
Then pass'd the wind, and sobb'd with mountain echo'd
woe.

_____

OET
No.
1

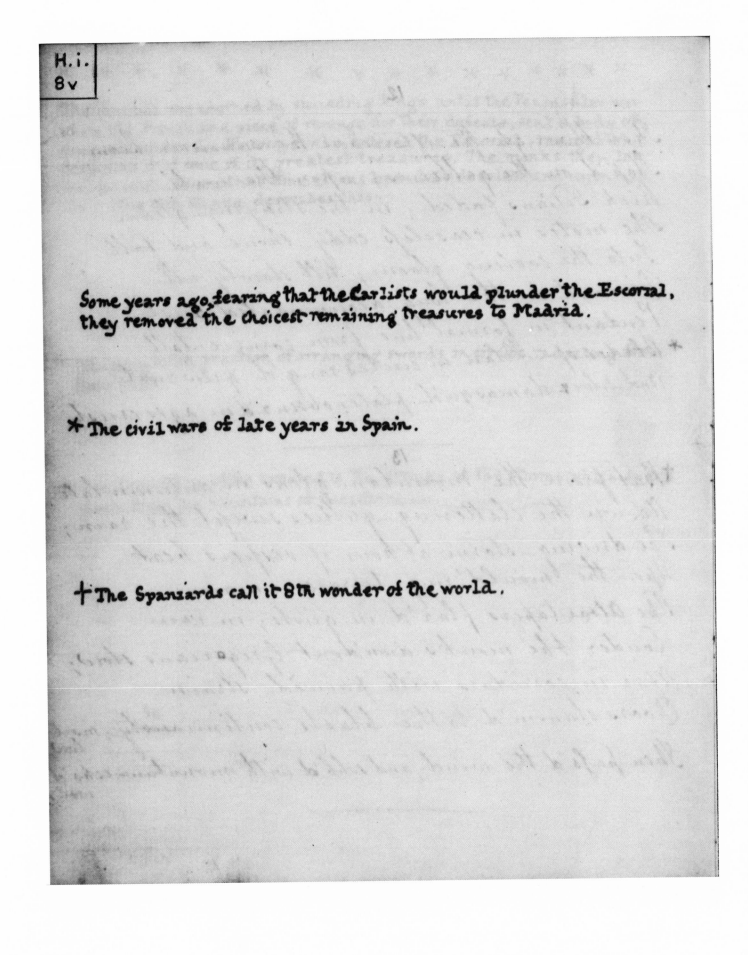

H.i.
8v

Some years ago, fearing that the Carlists would plunder the Escorial, they removed the choicest remaining treasures to Madrid.

* The civil wars of late years in Spain.

✝ The Spaniards call it 8th wonder of the world.

PLATE 17. OET 1. *The Escorial* • 67

H.i.
9r

14.

Next morn a peasant from the mountain side
Came midst the drizzle telling how last night

110 Two mazèd shepherds perish'd in the tide.;
But further down the valley, left and right,
(Down-splinter'd rocks crush'd cottages.—(Drear sight—
An endless round of dead'ning solitude:
Till, (fearing ravage worse than in his flight,

115 What time the baffled Frank swept back pursu'd
Fell on the palace, and the lust of rabble rude;)

15.

*Since trampled Spain by royal discord torn
Lay bleeding, to Madrid the last they bore,
The choicest remnants thence; — such home forlorn

120 The monks left long ago. Since which no more,
† ~~Eighth~~ Eighth wonder of the earth, in size, in store,
And art and beauty.: Fitte now too full—
More wondrous to have borne such hope before
It seems; for grandeur barren left and dull

125 Than changeful pomp of courts is aye more wonderful

Plates 16,17   OET No.1: The Escorial—MSS.15,16.
    H.i.8v. These notes were overlooked in Poems, 2nd. and 3rd. edns.
    9r. See Poems, 4th edn., 1iv, 1v, for the earlier misreading of the complicated parenthesis in 114-116.
An obscure comma follows "store" (121). In 122 "full" has been mended in ink to "null" (which rhymes with "dull"
but makes less sense).

BII 39r | Campion Hall 39

Prom. pp. 97, 112

Promêtheus Desmotês.

P. ἤτορ ἔξηῦρ᾽ ἐσ᾽ ἐμοί has found {and laid on me. / to lay on me. / in my case} ποιὰς ἀμπλα-

ἐμπλάκων τίνω penalties I pay for my transgressions.

88 – 124.   PROMÊTHEUS.

[ℓ. 88]
Divinity of air, fleet-breather'd gales,
Ye river-heads, thou billowy deep that laughst
A countless laughter, Earth mother of all,
Thou sun, all-seeing eyeball of the day,
5
Witness to me! look you I am a god,
And these are from the gods my penalties.
          Look with what unseemliness
          In thousand thousand years
          Must watch down with weariness
10
               Fallen from my peers.
The young chief of the bless'd of heaven
Hath devis'd new pains for me
[ℓ. 97]
               And hath given
This indignity of chains.
15
What is, and what is to be,
All alike is grief to me;
          Look all ways but only see
[ℓ. 100]
This drear dull burthen of unending pains.

          x x x x   x x x x   x x

[ℓ. 114]
               Ah well a day! —
20
What was that echo caught anigh me,
That scent from breezes breathing by me,
Sped of gods, or mortal sign,

---

f.40r | 40

Or half-human, half-divine?
To the world's end, to the last hill
25
Comes one to gaze upon my ill;
[ℓ. 118]
Be this thy quest or other, see
A god enchain'd of destiny,
Foe of Irus and hate of all
That wont to throng Irus' banquet-hall,
30
Sith I lov'd and lov'd too well
The race of man; and hence I fell.
Woe is me, what do I hear?
          Fledgèd things do rustle near;
          Whispers of the mid-air stirring
35
          With light pulse of pinions shirring,
[ℓ. 127]
And all that comes is fraught to me with fear.

118. ἢ τί δὴ θέλων or in short, if not that, with what intention?
(in exact but horrible English) 124 etc., it appears then that the
OET NO. 2 | Ukranid nymphs were winged. 126 – 140, σύθην without any.

PLATE 19. OET 2. *Aeschylus: Promêtheus Desmotes* • 69

L.iii.
p.6

the soliloquy in which it occurs as well as some beautiful lyric passages of which I give a specimen.

20   What was that echo brcaught a-
                    nigh me,   [me,
        That scent from breezes breathing by
        Sped of gods, or mortal sign,
        Or half-human half-this divine?
        To the world's end, to the last hill
25   Comes one to gaze upon my ill;
        Be this thy quest or other, see
        A god enchain'd of Destiny;

Foe of Zeus and foe of all   30
That wont to throng Zeus' banquet-hall,
Sith I loved and loved too well   →
The race of man; and hence I fell.
Woe is me, what do I hear?
Fledg'd things do rustle near;
Whispers of the mid-air stirring   35
With light pulse of pinions skirring,
And all that comes is brought to me
                    with fear.

OET
No.2

Univ. of
Texas

Plate 18 [opposite]   OET No.2: Aeschylus: Promêtheus Desmotês--MS.1.
    B II (Classics Note-book, Campion Hall, Oxford--see J.529), 39r,40r.--The autograph of this poetic translation
is embedded in working notes (including what he called "exact but horrible English"), made by GMH as he studied
Aeschylus in the summer of 1862, before he entered Oxford. To permit comparisons, line numbers from the Greek
are enclosed in square brackets, though the English and Greek do not always match line for line. GMH imitates
Aeschylus's variations in line length, showing this by indentation: thus 18, which should have matched 1-6 in length,
was begun two spaces too far from the margin, so the "Th" was deleted and rewritten. The translation omits
ll.101-113 of the Greek. Two additions are made in pencil: the apostrophe in "laugh'st" (2) and the comma after
"Look you" (5).

Plate 19 [above]   OET No.2: Promêtheus Desmotês--MS.2.
    L.iii.p.6 (autograph letter to E.H. Coleridge, 3-6 Sept.1862, now in the Harry Ransom Humanities Research
Center, Univ. of Texas at Austin). The "specimen" GMH copies is only 20 to the end, but this is in a slightly
revised form. Deletions include 20 "br[eathing?]"--perh. confused with line below.

L.iii.
pp.8-
10

Univ. of
Texas,
Austin

The best thing I have done
lately is <u>Il Mystico</u> in imitation of <u>Il Penseroso</u>, of which I send you
some extracts. It is not finished yet; write back whether you approve.

MS.
p.3

MS.
p.4

Hence sensual gross desires,
Right offspring of your grimy mo-
    ther Earth!
My Spirit hath a birth
Alien from yours as heaven from
    Nadir-fires:
    You rank and reeking things,
Scoop you from teeming filth some
    sickly hovel,
    And there for ever grovel
'Mid fever'd fumes and slime and
    cakèd dirt:
    But foul and cumber not
The shaken plumage of my spirit's
    wings.
    But come, thou balm to aching
    soul,
Of pointed wing and silver stole,
With heavenly cithern from high
    choir,
Tresses dipp'd in rainbow fire,
An olive-branch whence richly reek
Earthless dews on ancles sleek;
Be discover'd to my sight
From a haze of sapphire light,
Let incense hang across the room
And sober lustres take the gloom;
Come when night clings to what is
    hers   [stirs:
Closer because faint morning
When chill woods wake and
    think of morn,
But sleep again 'ere day be born;
When sick men turn, and lights are
    low,
And death falls gently as the snow,

5

10

15

20

25

When wholesome spirits rustle about,
And the tide of ill is out;
When waking hearts can pardon much
And hard men feel a softening touch;
When strangely loom all shapes that be,
And watches change upon the sea;
Silence holds breath upon her throne,
And the wakèd stars are all alone.
    Come because then most thinly lies
The veil that covers mysteries;
And soul is subtle and flesh weak
And pride is nerveless and hearts meek.
× × × × × × × ×
Touch me and purify, and shew
Some of the secrets I would know.
× × × × × × × ×
Grant that close-folded peace that clad
The seraph brows of Galahad,
Who knew the inner spirit that fills
Questioning winds above around the hills;
Who made conjecture nearest far
To what the chords of angels are;
And to the mystery of those Things
× × × × × × ×
Shewn to Ezekiel's open'd sight
On Chebar's banks, and why they went
Unswerving through the firmament;
Whose ken through amber of dark eyes
Went forth to compass mysteries;
Who knowing all the sins and sores
That nest within close-barrèd doors,
And that grief masters joy on Earth,
Yet found unstinted place for mirth;
Who could forgive without grudge after
Gross mind discharging foulèd laughter;
To whom the common earth and air
Were limn'd about with radiance rare
Most like those hues that in the prism

30

35

40

45

50

55

60

OET
No.3

Plate 20   OET No.3: Il Mystico—MS.1.
    L.iii.pp.8-10 (autograph letter, pp.3-4, to E.H. Coleridge, 3-6 Sept.1862, now in the Harry Ransom Humanities
Research Center, Univ. of Texas at Austin).—In 24 "'ere" should have no apostrophe.   44 "abov[e]" del.
"Earth" clearly has u.c. in 2, but not in 55,59 (cf. undoubted u.c. "E" in 16 and 48 and l.c. "eyes" in 51). Letter
continues on Plates 21,22.

PLATE 21. OET 3. *Il Mystico* • 71

L. iii.
PP. 10-
12

Melt as from a heavenly chrism;
Who could keep silence, tho' the smart
Yawn'd like long furrow in the heart;

   x   x   x   x   x

65   Or, like a lark to glide aloof
Under the cloud-festooned roof,
That with a turning of the wings
Light and darkness from him flings;
To drift in air, the circled earth
70 Spreading still its sunnèd girth;
To hear the sheep-bells dimly die
Till the lifted clouds were nigh,
In breezy belts of upper air
Melting into other lare; [won,
75 And when the silent height were
And all in lone air stood the sun,
To sing scarce heard, and singing
               fill
The airy empire at his will;
To hear his strain descend less loud
80 Onto ledges of grey cloud;
And fainter, finer, trickle far
To where the listening uplands are;
To pause – then from his gurgling bill
Let the warbled sweetness rill,
85 And down the welkin, gushing free,
Hark the molten melody;
In fits of music till sunset
Starting the silver riolet;
Sweetly then and of free act
90 To quench the fine-drawn cataract;
And in the dews beside his nest
To cool his plumy throbbing breast.
     Or, if a sudden silver shower
Has drench'd the molten sunset hour,
95 And with weeping cloud is spread

All the welkin overhead,
Save where the unvexèd west
Lies divinely still, at rest,
Where liquid heaven sapphire-pale
100 Does into amber splendours fail,
And fretted clouds with burnish'd rim,
Phoebus' loosen'd tresses, swim;
While the sun streams forth amain
On the tumblings of the rain,
105 When his mellow smile he sees
Caught on the dank-ytressèd trees,
When the rainbow arching high
Looks from the zenith round the sky,
Lit with exquisite tints seven
110 Caught from angels' wings in heaven,
Double, and higher than his wont,
The wrought rim of heaven's font, —
Then may I upwards gaze and see
The deepening intensity
115 O' the air-blended diadem,
All a sevenfold-single gem,
Each hue so rarely wrought that where
It melts, new lights arise as fair,
Sapphire, jacinth, chrysolite,
120 The rim with ruby fringes dight,
Ending in sweet uncertainty
Twixt real hue and phantasy.
Then while the rain-born arc glows higher
Westward on his sinking sire;
125 While the upgazing country seems
Touch'd from heaven in sweet dreams;
While a subtle spirit and rare
Breathes in the mysterious air;
While sheeny tears and sunlit mirth
130 Mix o'er the not unmovèd earth, —
Then would I fling me up to sip
Sweetness from the hour, and dip
Deeply in the archèd lustres,
And look abroad on sunny clusters

MS.
p 5

100

105

110

115

120

125

130

OET
No. 3

Plate 21   OET No.3: Il Mystico—MS.2.
    L.iii.pp.10-12 (autograph letter, pp.5-6, cont. from plate 20)—Changes include: 72,80 final semi-colons mended
to commas   86 "Hear" mended to "Hark"   117 "wer" mended to "where".   131 "an[d]" mended to "to". Slips:
75 "height were" prob. should be "heights were", as in orig. version mentioned in the P.S. (Plate 22, right): this
was squeezed in sideways at the beginning of the letter.

Plate 22   OET No.3: Il Mystico--MS.3.

L.iii.pp.12-13 (autograph letter, cont. from Plate 20) — MS.p.6. Col.b., Postscript, is from MS.p.1, where it is squeezed in sideways above the beginning of the letter. In 137 "leas" should have a comma, not period.

OET No.4: A windy day in summer.
Sole autograph. In ℓ. 7 "sapphire" was probably not meant to have u.c.. Cf. Postscript, ℓ. 6, "in-/Stead"

OET No.5: A fragment of anything you like. Sole autograph—the last of the three poems sent to Coleridge in the letter of Sept.1862.

L.iii.12
MS.p.6

OET No.3 cont.

Of wringing tree-tops, chalky lanes,
Wheatfields tumbled with the rains,
Streaks of shadow, thistled leas.
Whence spring the jewell'd harmonies
That meet in mid-air; and be so
140 Melted in the dizzy bow
That I may drink that ecstasy
Which to pure souls alone may be.
        Etc.   Etc.

The description at the beginning is founded on Milton's "The cherub Contemplation".

OET No.4

A windy day in summer.
The vex'd Elm-heads are pale with the
                view
Of a mastering heaven utterly blue;
Swoll'n is the wind that in argent billows
Rolls across the labouring willows;
5 The chestnut-fans are loosely flirting,
And bared is the aspen's silky skirting;
The sapphire pools are smit with white
And silver-shot with gusty light;
While the breeze by rank and measure
10 Paces the clouds on the swept azure.

OET No.5

A fragment of anything you like
Fair, but of fairness as a vision dream'd;
Dry were her sad eyes that would fain have
                stream'd;   I'd
She stood before a light not hers, and seem.

The lorn Moon, pale with piteous dismay,
5 Who rising late had miss'd her painful way
In wandering until broad light of day;

Then was discover'd in the pathless sky,
White-faced, as one in sad assay to fly
Who asks not life but only place to die.

P.S.   MS.p.

P.S. Do not read this till you have finished the letter. In "Il Mystico" I had formerly instead of the lines resembling them which I have put in the enclosed copy, "And when the silent heights were won, alone in air to face the sun". Now is that or is it not a plagiarism from Tennyson's Eagle "Close to the sun in lonely lands" (see the poem)? I am in that state that I want an unprejudiced decision. ₓ

Harry Ransom Humanities Research Center, Univ. of Texas at Austin

PLATE 23. OET 6. *A Vision of the Mermaids* • 73

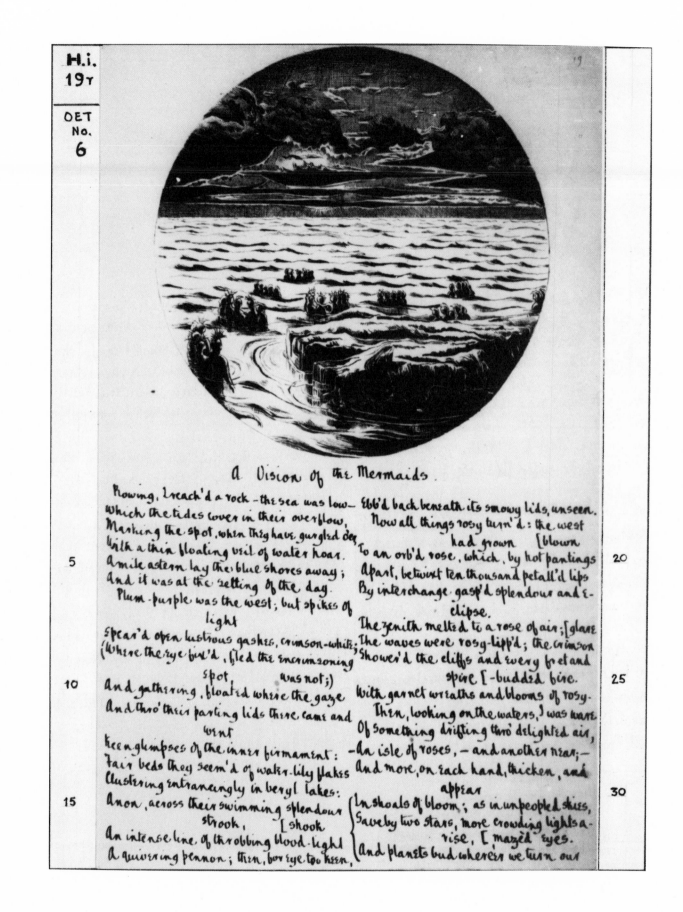

H.i. 19ᵀ

OET No. 6

A Vision of the Mermaids.

Rowing, I reach'd a rock — the sea was low —
Which the tides cover in their overflow,
Marking the spot, when they have gurgled o'er
With a thin floating veil of water hoar.
5   A mile astern lay the blue shores away;
And it was at the setting of the day.

Plum-purple was the west; but spikes of
          light
Spear'd open lustrous gashes, crimson-white;
(Where the eye fix'd, fled the encrimsoning
          spot,
          Was not;)
10 And gathering, floated where the gaze
And thro' their parting lids there came and
          went
Keen glimpses of the inner firmament:
Fair beds they seem'd of water-lily flakes
Clustering entrancingly in beryl lakes:
15 Anon, across their swimming splendour
          strook,   [shook
An intense line of throbbing blood-light
A quivering pennon; then, for eye too keen,

Ebb'd back beneath its snowy lids, unseen.
Now all things rosy turn'd: the west
          had grown   [blown
To an orb'd rose, which, by hot pantings
Apart, betwixt ten thousand petall'd lips
By interchange gasp'd splendour and e-
          clipse.
The zenith melted to a rose of air; [glare
The waves were rosy-lipp'd; the crimson
Shower'd the cliffs and every fret and
          spire [-budded fire.
25 With garnet wreaths and blooms of rosy-
Then, looking on the waters, I was ware
Of something drifting thro' delighted air,
— An isle of roses, — and another near; —
And more, on each hand, thicken, and
          appear
In shoals of bloom; as in unpeopled skies,
Save by two stars, more crowding lights a-
          rise, [mazèd eyes.
And planets bud where'er we turn our

20

25

30

Plate 23   OET No.6: A Vision of the Mermaids--MS.1.
     MS.H.i.19r--autograph faircopy, with a pen and ink sketch by GMH in a six-inch circle.   18 in "snowy",
"m" is mended to "n". Cont. in plates 24,25.

H.i. No.6
19v

35   I gazed unhinder'd: Mermaids six or seven,
Ris'n from the deeps to gaze on sun and heaven,
Cluster'd in troops and halo'd by the light,
Those Cyclads made that thicken'd on my
    sight.   [crest
  This was their manner: one translucent
Of tremulous film, more subtle than the vest
40 Of dewy gorse blurr'd with the gossamer fine,
From crown to tail-fin floating, fringed the
    spine,   [sway'd
Droop'd o'er the brows like Hector's casque, and
In silken undulation, spurr'd and ray'd
With spiked quills all of intensest hue;
45 And was as tho' some sapphire molten-blue
Were vein'd and streak'd with dusk-deep la-
    zuli,
Or tender pinks with bloody Tyrian dye.
From their white waists a silver skirt was spread
To mantle o'er the tail, such as is shed
50 Around the Water-Nymphs in fretted falls,
At red Pompeii on medallion'd walls.

A tinted fin on either shoulder hung;
Their pansy-dark or bronzen locks were strung
With coral, shells, thick-pearlèd cords, whate'er
The abysmal Ocean hoards of strange and rare. 55
Some trail'd the Nautilus; or on the swell
Tugg'd the boss'd, smooth-lipp'd, giant, Strom-
    bus-shell.   [head
Some carried the sea-fan; some round the
With lace of rosy weed were chapleted;
One bound o'er dripping gold a turquoise-gemm'd 60
Circlet of astral flowerets - diadem'd
Like an Assyrian prince, with buds unsheath'd
From flesh-flowers of the rock; but more were
    wreath'd   [gers
With the dainty-delicate fretted fringe of fin-
Of that jacinthine thing, that, where it lingers, 65
Broiders the nets with fans of amethyst
And silver films, beneath with pearly mist,
The Glaucus clepd; others small braids en-
    cluster'd
Of glassy-clear Aeolis, metal-lustred

Plate 24   OET No.6: A Vision of the Mermaids--MS.2.
    MS.H.i.19v--autograph faircopy, cont.. The upper half, the back of the sketch, was left blank so that ink penetrating the paper from either side would not spoil the text or the drawing. The blot at the beginning of 46 obscures "Were".

Plate 25 [opposite]   OET No.6: A Vision of the Mermaids--MS-3.
    H.i.20r,v--autograph faircopy, concl.. In Poems, 2nd and 3rd. edns., 73 was misread and deprived of its two verbs: "rubies" was foll. by an apostrophe and "hail" was read as "frail".   81 "One" looks like "Ane"   97 "f[loating?]" del. before "rosy"   121 "poets sings" final "s" del. in pencil   The date, "Christmas.1862", seems a later addition.

PLATE 25. OET 6, *A Vision of the Mermaids* • 75

H.i.
20 r

No. 6

20

70 With growths of myriad feelers, crystalline
To shew the crimson streams that inward shine,
Which, lightening o'er the body rosy-pale, [hail,
like shiver'd rubies dance, or sheen of sapphire
Then saw I sudden from the waters break
75 Far off a Nereid company, and shake [light
from wings swan-fledged a wheel of watery
Flickering with sunny spokes, and left and
right [tread
Plunge orb'd in rainbow arcs, and trample and
The satin-purfled smooth to foam, and spread
80 Slim-pointed sea-gull plumes, and droop be-
hind
One scarlet feather trailing to the wind;
Then, like a flock of sea-fowl mounting
higher, [into fire.
Thro' crimson-golden floods pass swallow'd
Soon—as when Summer of his sister
Spring
85 Crushes and tears the rare enjewelling,
And boasting "I have fairer things than these" "
Plashes amidst the billowy apple-trees
His lusty hands, in gusts of scented wind
Swirling out bloom till all the air is blind
90 With rosy foam and pelting blossom and
mists
Of dewy vermeil-rain; and, as he lists,
The dainty onyx-coronals deflowers, [-ers
A glorious wanton;—all the wrecks in show
Crowd down upon a stream, and jostling
thick
95 With bubbles bugle-eyed, struggle and stick
Ontangled shoals that bar the brook — a
crowd
Of filmy globes and frosy floating cloud:—
So those Mermaidens crowded to my rock,
And thicken'd, like that drifted bloom, the
block [Sea.
100 Sun-flush'd, until it seem'd their father
Had gotten him a wreath of sweet spring-
-broidery. [plash
Careless of me they sported. Some would
The languent smooth with dimpling drops,
and flash [there show'd
Their filmy tails adown whose length
105 An azure ridge; or clouds of violet glow'd
On pranked scale; or threads of carmine,
shot

Thro' silver, gloom'd to a blood-vivid clot,
Some, diving merrily, downward drove,
and gleam'd [l'd
106 With arm and fin; the argent bubbles stream
Airwards, disturb'd; and the scarce trou-
bled sea 110
Gurgled, where they had sunk, melodiously.
Others with fingers white would comb a-
mong
The drenched hair of slabby weeds that swung
Swimming, and languish'd green upon the
deep [long tresses weep. } 115
Down that dank rock o'er which their lush
But most in a half-circle watch'd the
sun;
And a sweet sadness dwelt on everyone;
I knew not why,—but know that sadness
dwells [knells
On Mermaids—whether that they ring the 120
Of seamen whelm'd in chasms of the mid-
-main,
As poets sing; or that it is a pain [sea,
To know the dusk depths of the ponderous
The miles profound of solid green, and be 125
With loath'd cold fishes, far from man—
or what;—
I know the sadness but the cause know not.
Then they, thus ranged, 'gan make full
plaintively
A piteous Siren sweetness on the sea,
With outen instrument, or conch, or bell,
Or stretch'd chords tuneable on turtle's shell;
Only with utterance of sweet breath they sung 130
An antique chaunt and in an unknown tongue.
Now melting upward thro' the sloping scale
Swell'd the sweet strain to a melodious wail;
Now ringing clarion-clear to whence it rose
Slumber'd at last in one sweet, deep, heart- 135
-broken close. [to
But when the sun had lapsed to Ocean,
A stealthy wind crept round seeking to blow,
linger'd, then raised the washing waves
and drench'd [quench'd
The floating blooms and with tide flowing
The rosy isles: so that I stole away 140
And gain'd thro' growing dusk the
stirless bay;

H.i. 20 verso

White loom'd my rock, the water gurgling o'er,
Whence oft I watch but see those Mermaids now no more.

The End.

OET
No. 6

Christmas. 1862.

he thou-
op."

1, at the
air man,
ould tell
ke, have

ok place
ighbour-
and in
ier and

with all
e imme-

valuable
ler sex ;
in equal
ombined
larly de-
will ask
finity of
those in
envious
er from
loes not
my from
rant her
nen are
if ever
u know
ether it
into an
ou must

ipetitive
ernment
itioning
o years,
ep, and
request
o ? He
no one
brush-
essed in
and an
if even

tells a
at least

norning
ur the
imper-
herself
s neces-

you will

hat you

i, "that
nt with
I am,
ie just-

ness of my actions ; I *must* know first what you
want."

The lady begged, prayed, wept, till the poor
man, wearied out, said, " Well, I promise," and
instantly regretted the words. " Monsieur,"
said the lady, calming down immediately, " I
have seen many delicious head-dresses which are
to be worn at the court *fête* next Monday ; I
much wish to surpass them, and have hit on the
idea of a garniture of parrots' feathers : I have
laid all my friends under contribution, and since
you have promised not to refuse me, I will trouble
you for six feathers from the tail of that remarkably fine Polly I have seen outside your balcony."

Has any fellow-sufferer from shyness and diffi-
dence read thus far in hopes of meeting with some
useful hints ? Alas, alas, I can give him none ;
the cheeky man, like the poet, is born, not made ;
he springs into the world like Minerva, armed in
a panoply of brass. For him are reserved the
front seats and liver wings of life ; he shoots the
game and rides the hunters of his neighbour, and
travels in cabs for the legitimate fare. For you
and me, my friend, let us take the drumsticks of
fowls, the back places of opera-boxes, the garrets
of country houses, and the extortions of cabmen
with smiling countenances. It is our Fate.

WINTER WITH THE GULF STREAM.

THE boughs, the boughs are bare enough,
But earth has not yet felt the snow.
Frost-fringed our ivies are, and rough

With spikèd rime the brambles show,
The hoarse leaves crawl on hissing ground,
What time the sighing wind is low.

But if the rain-blasts be unbound,
And from dank feathers wring the drops,
The clogg'd brook runs with choking sound,

Kneading the mounded mire that stops
His channel under clammy coats
Of foliage fallen in the copse.

A single passage of weak notes
Is all the winter bird dare try.
The moon, half-orb'd, ere sunset floats

So glassy-white about the sky,
So like a berg of hyaline,
Pencill'd with blue so daintily—

I never saw her so divine.
But thro' black branches—rarely drest
In streaming scarfs that smoothly shine,

Shot o'er with lights—the emblazon'd west,
Where yonder crimson fire-ball sets,
Trails forth a purfled-silken vest.

Long beds I see of violets
In beryl lakes which they reef o'er :
A Pactolean river frets

Against its tawny-golden shore :
All ways the molten colours run :
Till, sinking ever more and more

Into an azure mist, the sun
Drops down engulf'd, his journey done.

G. M. H.

THE HAMPDENS.
AN HISTORIETTE. BY HARRIET MARTINEAU

CHAPTER I. A HONEYMOON IN MERRY ENGLAND.

" Now you have seen the sea ! " said Richard
Knightley to his young bride, as they stood looking abroad from a point of the Cornish coast, at
sunset, one bright April evening of 1635. " Now
you have seen the sea at last ! "

" At last ! " repeated the young bride who, at
seventeen, felt as if she had been longing to see
the sea for an immeasurable length of years.
Aware that her husband looked to her for an
opinion on the spectacle, she observed :

" It is very beautiful ; but—"

" But not so grand as you had imagined. That
is what I felt when my father took me to the
coast, to see the company sail for the Plantations."

" That was from Plymouth."

" Yes ; but my father came hither on a visit
to Sir John Eliot ; and we saw much of the coast
as we travelled. I grew more afraid of the great
ocean as I saw more of it, in winds and on cloudy
days ; and, being little better than a child then, I
suffered under a torture of fear in hearing my
father and Sir John Eliot discourse of the lot of
those who went to the Plantations, and of the
expediency of others following, if the times should

grow too hard for honest men. Every night, after
hearing these discoursings, I made a venture to
pray that my father's mind might be turned from
carrying me away over the wide sea."

" I thank God that it was ! " the young wife
whispered. " I was but a young child then ; and
if you had gone away—"

" We might yet have been married," said
Richard Knightley, smiling. " If Sir Richard
Knightley and Sir John Eliot had emigrated, Mr.
Hampden would not have been left behind. You
and I should have understood each other on the
voyage, and have been betrothed and married in
some wild forest conventicle in Massachusetts ;
and we should now be looking forward to troubles
from Indian chiefs, instead of our headstrong
King. I should have been an office-bearer in the
nearest township ; and my Margaret would have
had to spend her days in the dairy and at the
spinning-wheel, instead of tending her flower
garden at Fawsley. How would you have liked
to entertain squaws, instead of the ladies of
Northamptonshire squires ? "

Margaret shuddered. She would have been
glad to be satisfied that her father would not

Once A Week Feb. 14 1863		WINTER WITH THE GULF STREAM.		
viii, (No.190) p. 210.	1	THE boughs, the boughs are bare enough, But earth has not yet felt the snow. Frost-fringed our ivies are, and rough	So glassy-white about the sky, So like a berg of hyaline, Pencill'd with blue so daintily—	16
	4	With spikèd rime the brambles show, The hoarse leaves crawl on hissing ground, What time the sighing wind is low.	I never saw her so divine. But thro' black branches—rarely drest In streaming scarfs that smoothly shine,	19
	7	But if the rain-blasts be unbound, And from dank feathers wring the drops, The clogg'd brook runs with choking sound,	Shot o'er with lights—the emblazon'd west, Where yonder crimson fire-ball sets, Trails forth a purfled-silken vest.	22
	10	Kneading the mounded mire that stops His channel under clammy coats Of foliage fallen in the copse.	Long beds I see of violets In beryl lakes which they reef o'er : A Pactolean river frets	25
OET No. 7.	13	A single passage of weak notes Is all the winter bird dare try. The moon, half-orb'd, ere sunset floats	Against its tawny-golden shore : All ways the molten colours run : Till, sinking ever more and more	28
			Into an azure mist, the sun Drops down engulf'd, his journey done. G. M. H.	31

PLATE 27. OET 7. *Winter with the Gulf Stream* • 77

Winter with the Gulf Stream.

The boughs, the boughs are bare enough
But winter has never felt the snow.
Frost-furred our ivies are and rough

With bills of rime the brambles shew.
The hoarse leaves crawl on hissing ground
Because the sighing wind is low.

But if the rain-blasts be unbound,
And from dank feathers wring the drops
The blogged brook runs with choking sound

Kneading the mounded mire that stops
His channel under clammy coats
Of foliage fallen in the copse.

A simple passage of weak notes
Is all the winter bird dare try.
The bugle moon by daylight floats

So glassy white about the sky,
So like a berg of hyaline,
And pencilled blue so daintily,

I never saw her so divine.
But through black branches, rarely drest
In scarves of silky shot and shine.

The webbed and the watery west,
Where yonder crimson fireball sits,
Looks laid for feasting and for rest.

I see long reefs of violets

In beryl-coloured fens so dim,
A gold-water Pactolus frets

Its brindled wharves and yellow brim,
The waxen colours weep and run,
And slendering to his burning rim

Into the flat blue mist the sun
Drops out and all our day is done.

N.B. In author's handwriting. Seminary (S.M. Hall)
August 1871

Originally printed in "Once a week" of which I
have a copy; preserved many years before I knew
G. M. H.
F.S.B.

printed. 1. stanza. "has never"   "not yet"
2. "   "Bills of rime"   " spiked rime
2. "   "Because"   "what time"
5. "   "the bugle moon"   "The moon, half orbed, ere sunset floats.
7. "   "of silky &c"   "In streaming scarfs that smoothly shine
8. 1st line   "Shot o'er with lights, the emblazon'd west
8. 3rd line   "Nails forth a purfled-silken vest.
9. 1st line   "Long beds I see of violets".
9. 2nd line   "In beryl lakes which they reef o'er".
9. 3rd.   "A Pactolean river frets
10. 1.   "Against its rawny-golden shore.
2.   " All ways the golden molten colours run
3.   "Till sinking ever more & more
11. stanza   "Into an azure mist the sun
"Drops down engulf'd: his journey done.
G. M. H.

Variations

OET No.7   Campion Hall MS. H.1.d

Plate 26 [opposite] OET No.7: Winter with the Gulf Stream—Published Text.
   Once a Week, Feb.14 1863, p.210. The poem was facing a drawing by Millais (whose sunset illustrated the beginning of a new serial by the popular Harriet Martineau); this was indeed an honour for GMH, who considered him "the greatest English painter, one of the greatest of the world" (letter to Baillie, 10 July 1863, L.iii.201). An enlarged copy of the printed poem, in two columns, is reproduced underneath.

Plate 27 [above] OET No.7: Winter with the Gulf Stream—MS.1.
   MS. at Campion Hall, H.1.d (see J.531)—transcript by Fr. Francis Bacon, SJ ("F.E.B"), of an autograph, now missing, made by GMH at St. Mary's Hall, Stonyhurst, Aug.1871. Bacon adds an (incomplete) list of variants found in the early printed version. In 11 "clammy" was misread as "damming" by Fr. Lahey and so published in Poems, 2nd edn., 143. The initials "G.M.H." at the end refer to the authorship of the poem (both versions).

H.i. 26r

SPRING AND DEATH.

26

I had a dream. A wondrous thing:
It seem'd an evening in the spring;
– A little sickness in the air
From too much fragrance everywhere:–
5 As I walk'd a stilly wood,
Sudden, Death before me stood:
In a hollow lush and damp,
He seem'd a dismal mirky stamp
On the flowers that were seen
10 His charnelhouse-grate ribs between,
And with coffin-black he barr'd the
green.

"Death", said I "what do you here
At this spring season of the year?"
"I mark the flowers ere the prime
15 Which I may tell at autumn-time".
Ere I had further question made
Death was vanish'd from the glade.
Then I saw that he had bound
Many trees and flowers round

H.i. 26v

20 With a subtle web of black,
And that such a sable track
Lay along the grasses green
From the spot where he had been.
But the spring-tide pass'd the same;
25 Summer was as full of flame;
Autumn-time no earlier came.
And the flowers that he had tied,
As I mark'd, not always died
Sooner than their mates; and yet
30 Their fall was fuller of regret:
It seem'd so hard and dismal thing,
Death, to mark them in the spring.

OET No. 8

Plate 28   OET No.8: Spring and Death
   H.i.26r,v—sole autograph. At the
end of 2 the dash was smudged and partly
erased: in the MS. it is very faint.

PLATE 29. Early Note-book C.i. • 79

FIRST EARLY NOTE-BOOK -- Campion Hall MS. C.i.

Plate 29: Flyleaf and pp.13,14. The tiny Note-book which begins here runs through in unbroken sequence to Plate 77. It is reproduced in its entirety. The first page numbered by GMH is 15: of previous leaves cut out, prob. by GMH himself, the only survivor is this half leaf (lower part of pp.13 and 14), kept in a pocket at the end of the volume. We now lack the beginning and ending of the paragraph on words implying growth and ripeness, though the missing top half of 14 must have completed the free quotation from Ps.144:12 as found in the Anglican Book of Common Prayer (30th day, Morning Prayer): "That our sons may grow up as the young plants." These entries were first made in pencil, then rewritten in ink which sometimes caused blots on the other side: thus the illegible line above "Horn" on p.14 is simply the top line of p.13 showing through, "growth...vigorous--," leaving only the pencilled end of the lost para, "convenit," clearly legible. In p.13, ℓ.3 "fruit" is blotted by p.14, ℓ.2, "lights." The pencil (where still legible) sometimes differs from the ink revision. In 13 ℓ.2 the pencil has "but not yet producing fruit." Though the ink began "not" it probably intended "but yet producing no fruit". The "not" (or "no") is omitted in ℓ.4, reversing the sense. In p.13, ℓ.5, the ink abbreviates the pencil "of" to the shorthand ∪, and in 13, ℓ.7 "root" (pencil) becomes "rt." (ink). After p.14, ℓ.7 the writing is in pencil until p.18. The shorthand signs used are

    ∪   of
    ⌢   and
    θ   th or the

GMH takes little trouble to differentiate u.c. theta from l.c. Each page is approximately 7 cm. wide x 12 cm. No scale line is needed. References have been compressed: "15.8" means "C.i.page 15, line 8."

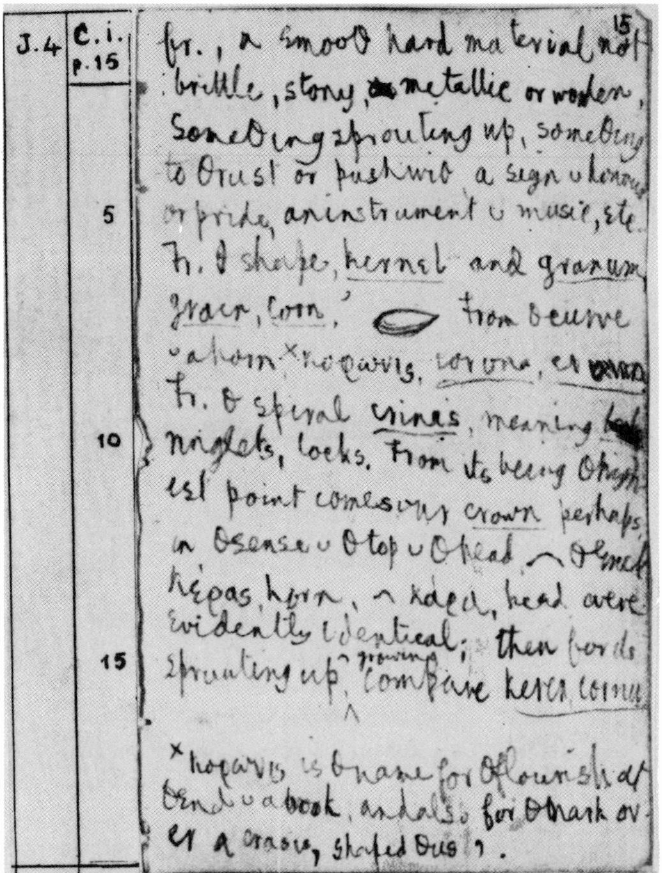

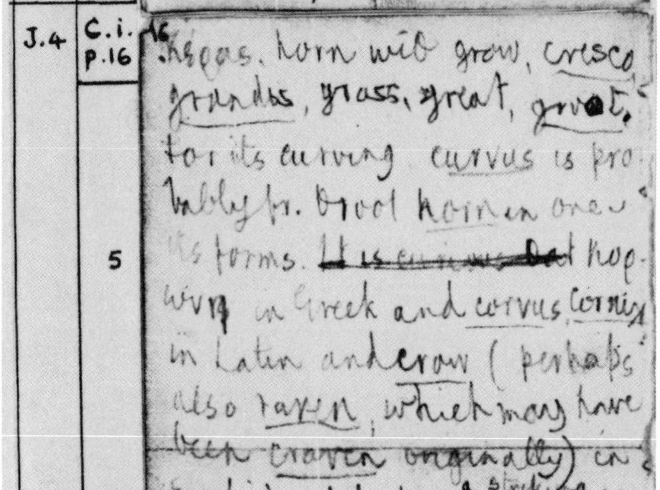

J.4	C.i. p.15

[handwritten notebook page, C.i. p.15:]

fr., a smooth hard material, not brittle, stony, ~~metallic~~ or wooden, something sprouting up, something to thrust or push with, a sign of honour or pride, an instrument of music, etc. Th. ø shape, kernel and granum grain, corn, ◠ from θεύρω ·a horn ×κέρας, corona, et ... Th. ø spiral vines, meaning ... ringlets, locks. From its being the highest point comes ... crown perhaps in θ sense ø top ø head ... κέρας, horn, ... head, head were evidently identical; then [words] sprouting up, growing, compare κέρας cornu ...

×κέρας is ø name for ø flourish at end of a book, and also for ø mark over et a comma shaped thus .

J.4	C.i. p.16

[handwritten notebook page, C.i. p.16:]

κέρας, horn with grow, cresco grandis, grass, great, grout, for its curving curvus is probably fr. ø root horn in one of its forms. It is ~~curious but~~ κέρας in Greek and corvus, cornix in Latin and crow (perhaps also raven, which may have been craven originally) in English ... bear a striking resemblance to cornu, curvus. So also γέρανος, crane, heron herne. Why these birds should derive their names fr. horn I cannot presume to say. ø tree cornel, Latin cornus is said to derive its name fr. ø hard horn.

[printed editorial notes, right column:]

Plate 30   C.i.15—in 15.8 crinis is mended to crown; in 15.9 "locks" is del.

C.i.16—deletions: 16.5 "It is curious that"; 16.10 "shd." (should); "such". The line across 16.9 is not a deletion.

C.i.17--The page begins with a dot meant for a hyphen (cf. 17.15), "horn-like". 17.9 "like horns" del.

Plate 31 [opposite] C.i.18—ink on mostly illegible pencil. GMH's ink corrects some slips: 18.4 in pencil quoted Luke 1:69 (AV) incorrectly, "He hath raised us up a horn of salvation"; and the pencilled "High Holborn" (for "Holborn", 18.14) can be read above "fash yourself" (18.18).

C.i.21—a leaf was removed after p.18, but there is no gap in the sense. This, the next page, though unnumbered, must be 21 since its verso is 22. A folded corner of paper obscures "lick" (21.1) and the end of "tactus" (21.2), but these are legible in pencil below (21.14-15). The ink passage ends in the middle of 21.6, cont. 22.1. The smudged pencil below it in 21.7 to 21.9 (ending "other states?") is not repeated in ink; but 21.10 to 21.19 represents the ink from 18.18 to 21.6.

C.i.22—22.1 cont. from 21.6, ink over pencil, down to 22.17. The pencil of 22.18-20 is repeated in ink 22.15-17. In 22.13 the ink "possible" is a slip for "possibly" (faintly pencilled below "together" in 22.15).

C.i.23--ink on pencil to 23.17 (cont. 24.1). The pencil in 23.18 to 21 is repeated above it in ink (15 to 17), but pencil has "tenden" for "tendon" and "description" for "sort".

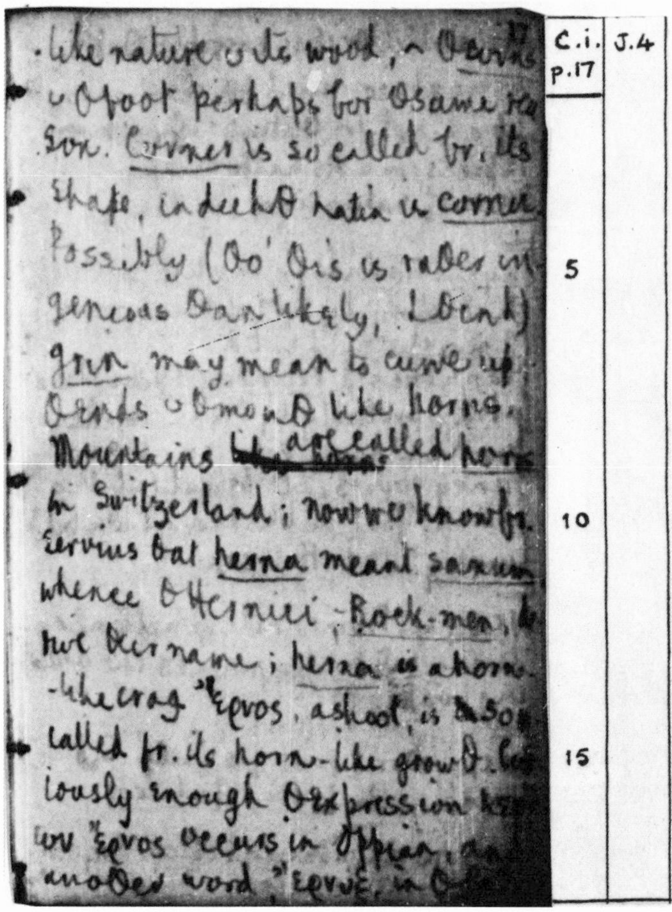

[handwritten notebook page, C.i. p.17:]

... like nature of its wood, ~ θ ... ø foot perhaps for ø same reason. Corner is so called fr. its shape, indeed Latin ... corner possibly (θθ' θis is rather ingenious than likely, I think). γ... may mean to curve up θ ends ø ... like horns. Mountains ~~are called~~ horns in Switzerland; now we know fr. cervus that herna meant same whence ø Hernici, Rock-men ... their name; herna is a horn-like crag. ἔρνος, a shoot, is also called fr. its horn-like growth. Curiously enough ø expression ... ἔρνος occurs in Oppian, another word ἔρνοξ in ...

C.i. p.17	J.4

PLATE 31. C.i. pp 18,21,22,23   •   *81*

C.i. p.18 (J.4 / J.5)

Aristotle. Or it is possible that εξ-
ρος may be so called fr. its shooting
up as, not in σ shape of, a horn.
Sapressions. He hath raised up a
horn of salvation for us.

Lays & Ballads fr. English, Scottish
etc history, by S.M. (Miss Smedley)
12 mo, cloth, 2s. 6d.
Manzoni's Is Promessi Sposi, translated (probably by Miss Smedley.)
Two handsome vols., small 8vo,
fancy covers, 60 beautiful Vig-
nettes, 7s. (published at 10s. 6d)
Lumley, 126, Holborn

Westley, Promenade, Cheltenham
is the man who makes the drawing books.

Fash. Don't fash yourself. Scotch.
Connate with λεσσω, fatisco
N before a consonant often dropped.
Grind — gride, gird. Lingers —

C.i. p.21 (J.5)

, λειχειν, tangere — touch, tac-
as. fingers — factus, λαγχανειν
λαχειν, tangere — pactus, etc. sic
see horn above. On the other hand
the derivation may of granum,
grain may be

other states?

Fash. To trouble. Don't fash yourself...

lick, λειχειν; tangere —
touch pactus; tangere—factus;
λαγχανειν — λαχειν; tangere

On the
derivation of granum

C.i. p.22 (J.5)

referred to & read
Grind, gride, gird, grit, groat,
grate, greet, & κρουειν, crush,
crash, κροτειν etc.
Orig meaning to strike, rub
particularly together. Such ph. is
produced by such means is e
grit, & groat, i.e crumbs, likeel
frequentem fr. frangere, but to
bite, crumb, crumble, etc. akin
to greet, to strike & hands together
(?). Greet, grief, meaning, the
ulation. Grief possibler connected.
Grief, with a sound as of 2 things
rubbing together. I believe these
wds. to be onomatopoetic. Gr
common to them all, expressing
rubbing together. I believe these

C.i. p.23 (J.5)

a particular sound. In fact I
think the onomatopoetic theory has
not had a fair chance. Cf. creak
creak, croak, crake, graculus,
crackle. These must be onomatopoetic.

Crook, crank, kranke, crick crany
Orig. meaning crooked, not straight
or right, wrong, awry. A crank
in England is a piece of mechan-
ism wh. turns a wheel or shaft
at one end, at the other receiving a
rectilinear force. Knife-grinders
velocipedes, steam-engines etc.
have them. Crick in the neck is
when some muscle tendon or something in the neck is twisted or goes wrong in some way.

ten or some thing
that deserib
or in the neck
is twisted or goes wrong

[C.i. p.24]

way. Cranky, provincial, out of sorts, wrong, the original meaning being crooked, cf. curvus — for derivation see under horn.

The legend of the Rape of the Scout, related in the manner of Arnold and Liddell.

[This legend bears a close resemblance to that of the Rape of Lucrece, with w it no doubt had an identical origin. It is curious however that while in the Latin legend it is the people of Rome who besiege the Volscian town, in the English the people of Ballioli (a name wit w cf. Corioli etc.) "sit down at the room of Woolcombe" (Romam Volscam). But

[C.i. p.25]

see hereafter.]

It chanced that once while the youngmen of Ballioli were sitting over their wine, being already, so runs the tale, heated with their cups, the discussion ran high on the respective excellences of their several scouts.× Each gentleman

× Scout. the word in "legenda Oxoniana" is used as = servant, slave. It is not however found in ancient english, in any other place in this sense, but means outcast. (See however Litius Candens de Arte Crit. sub vo. scout.) Some derive it fr. σκευοφόρος, (v. Aristoph. Frogs, 15), σκευηφορεω, σκευη. But the real sense was first established in Müddler's Scotians.

[C.i. p.26]

maintaining that the good fellow who that writer shews that a large part of the population of Ballioli was Scottish. This is proved by the frequent recurrence of Scotch names in the legends, and the fact that the eponymous hero of the college was (John Balliol) is called a Scotchman. He believes that the original population was Scotch, but that it was reduced to subjection by a body the arrival of the English, and the Scots became slaves or attendants of the conquerors Hence the name Scot or Scout became synonymous per servant, as Geta was a common name for a slave at Rome, and Slave comes fr. the Slavonians or slaves, ~ Brutus, an old word for a runaway slave from the Bruttii.

[C.i. p.27]

served. him, surpassed all others.

this view is ably combated by Madler in his Excursus on the subject. He shews incontrovertibly that the Scots in Ballioli were (as everywhere) the dominant element; ~ that at the days, when the events of the legend were supposed to take place Robert the Scot was alleged to have held the chief magistracy. He asserts that Scout must be compared with scuttle — one who attends to the coals etc. Püzler compares it with to scuttle, skulk, skunk. At some public lin schools he says the fags were called Skunks. Doltz in his Animadversions against Püzler compares it with scathe, scot-free, so that it means a maimed or ill-used wretch. Muffer ~ Muller in their Lexicon Anglo-Neozelandicum make it fr. scutiger, scutifer, armour-bearer. m

PLATE 33. C.i. pp 28,29 • 83

[Manuscript pages 28 and 29, in Hopkins's hand:]

p. 28

Then, quod one, what, sirs, if we put our scouts to [the] proof. Let us plot to surprise [the]m when [the]y wot not we are near. ~ he whose serf is found most trusty he shall win [the] mead & glory and his cate-cheties shall be written for him for [the] term. And to [thi]s [the]y agreed. So when [the]y were sitting down at [the] room & Woolcombe×, and were

× the Medicean reads '[the] room & Woolks'. But omn. cod. hab. [the] room & [the] Critical editors omit [the], ~ under-stand Roman Volscôm or home & Volees, wh. is another form & Vols-cians, as in Shakspere, flattered [the] Volees in Corioli.

fact as [the] great Bentleius long ago remarked, [the] whole subject is wrap-ped in Chaos.

p. 29

now tired with [the] long & [the] siege×, feigning a sudden message from [the] Master & [the] Horse. [The]y got sud-denly on foot ~ came to [the]ir rooms, then one scout was found making away with coffee-cups [tha]t his master might get more & Hopkins ~ he have a percentage, and o[the]r was decanting port in such wise [tha]t [the] decanter was but one 3rd full. ~ ano[the]r, who was a clerk was reading Bohn's literal translations of [the] poet Ovid Naso's Art & Love on his master shelves, ~ ano[the]r used his master's [coo] [the] brush ~ yet ano[the]r was idling his time in unseemly dalliance with [the] washer-woman, ~ yet one more was quarelling with his wife whe[the]r it were safe to take [the] fift pot & apri-cot marmalade. But only one was

× Siege, it sh[oul]d. be remembered ~ wa[s]

<u>Plate 32,33</u>: <u>C.i.24</u>--in pencil, as are the rest of the pages, except four lines on p.33, a few rewritten at the bottoms of pp. (eg. 42-3, 46-7), and two pages near the end.   24.1 "way" repeated with the turn of the page.   24.16 "besiege the" del..   24.18 "Volscôm" orig. "Volscam" (? GMH's <u>a</u> often like <u>u</u>)

    <u>C.i.25-28</u>--GMH makes his burlesque note on "Scout" so exhaustively erudite that it overflows p.25 onto pp.26 and 27, leaving room (as in some editions of the classics) for only a single line of text on each page. It is completed p.28, *ll*.18 to 20. The pin used to fasten down a page while it was being photographed sometimes appears in the bot. left or right corner (e.g. p.26). <u>Changes</u>: p.26.7 "was" del.   26.12 "a body" del.   26.14 "conquerors" orig. "new" (?)   27.8 "is" orig. "was"   27.21 "as one who" del.

C.i. p 30 [J.7]

found faithful, for he was not
in grooms at all, but all things
wise set forth ~ he was within
call, and O young gentlemen
straightway adjudged that he
had the prize whose scout was
not in, yet within call, and he
being an exhibitioner Dey had
him excused from paying for
Cameron party. Now one of
young gentlemen was seized
with a guilty desire to have that
trusty scout upon his own stair-
case, So one day whenas it
chanced his master was out
he went to his rooms ~ having
there found the good scout
tried him first with persuasi-
ons that he shd leave that stair-
seat ~ beleaguerment.

[J.7 n.] [Cont. from bot. 29]

C.i. p 31 [J.7] [Cont. 31·14]

case and come to his And thus
to be continued.

See grind &c.
Grando meaning splinters, fragments, little pieces detached in
grinding, hence applied to hail.
Grunt: & is wd gruff.

Foot, pes (ped - is), πoυs (πo-δo
pada, pad, pat &c.

Origin onomatopoetic, describing
sound ~ foot-fall. Foot-pad,
only one meaning in both parts
~ composition.

Continued fr. last page.
He said thou mayest con-
trive it. Say that the work on
this stair is too much for

[(cont. from C.1)] [22·3]

C.i. p 32 [J.7]

thee and pray to be allowed
to exchange with the scout
on mine. Say to him the pay
of the gentlemen is good
and thou mayest freely steal
no man forbidding, but the
work is hard: Now on these
both the pay and the work is
light. And when he constantly refused, he said So be it then
and I will tell thy master that
I have found out that thou
hast agreed for a piece of
gold to cut thy master's sofas
in order that so the valuation
may be less and he that com-
eth after may gain the advantage and for this he pays thee.
So he was compelled and did.
See p. 39.

Macbeth, Act V, Sc. V [C.i. p 33] [J.8]

till famine cling thee. There is
a North Country word claw or clem,
meaning starve; and there was at
the time of the battle ~ Bosworth field
a prophet, I think in Norfolk or Suf-
folk, who prophesied, or rather
described in his idiotic ramblings, the

Eustace Kivington, 58, Harley
St. W.

result of the battle. He was heard
to say "Now Dick! now Harry! run
Dick! run Harry! Harry has the
day." which was interpreted of the
Richard III and Henry Duke of
Lankaster, at that time, it was
said, engaged in the battle. Being
brought to see the king Henry VII
called him an idiot knave but
appointed him a maintenance in

[Cont. 33·11] [20 Lcont. 35·5]

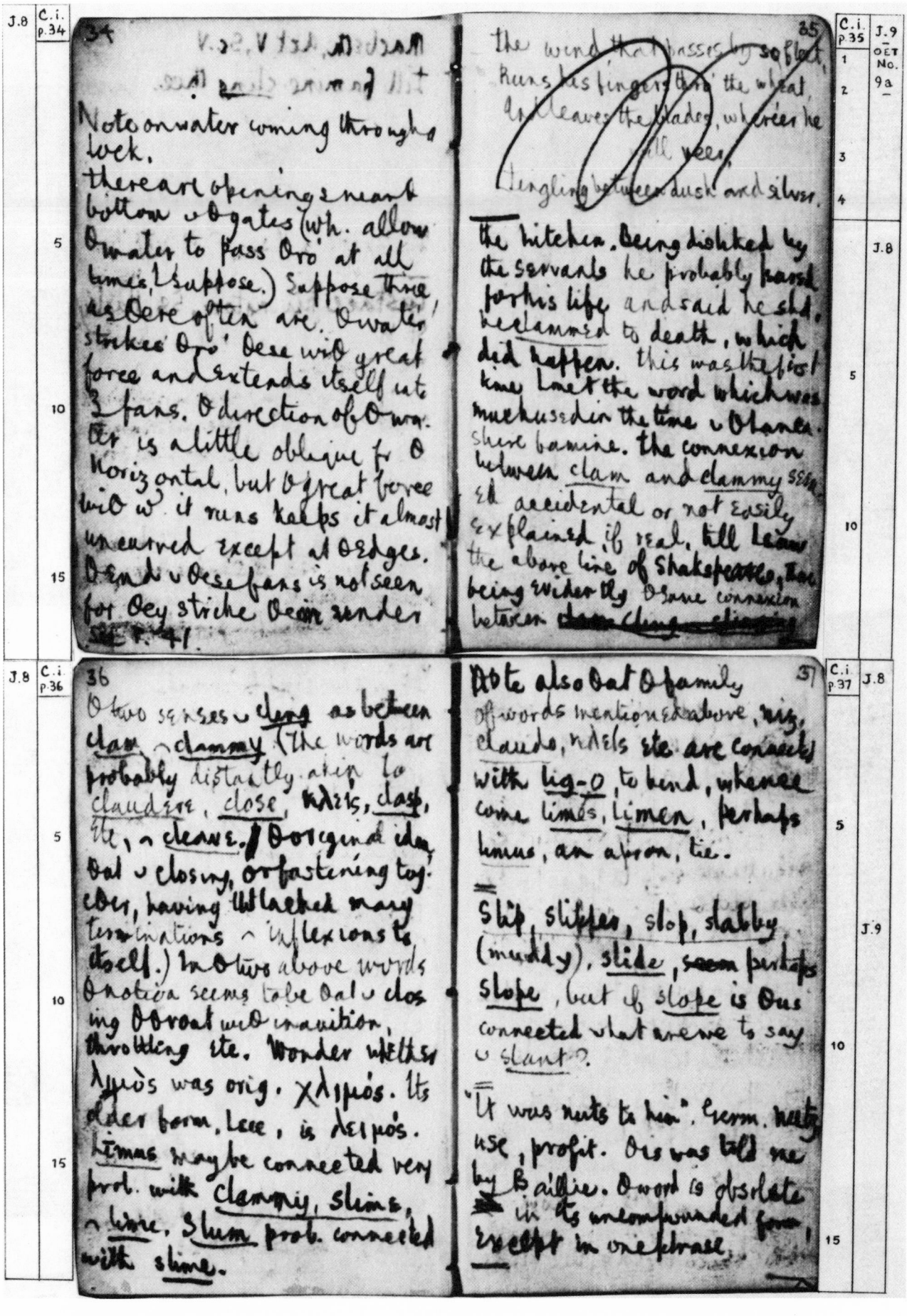

Plates 34,35: Deletions include p.31.15 "yo[u]" p.38.8 "his" p.33.14 "the" p.35.1 to 4, del. presumably by GMH p.37.8 "seem" p.33, ℓℓ .1,2,9,10 are in ink; blots spoil top of p.34, which GMH therefore left unused. Note spelling of "Lankaster" p.33.16 (contr. "Lancashire" 35.11). p.34.16 "them" (orig. "their") superfluous? 35.14 "clam" del. then "cling and clinging" also del.

[C.i. p 38]

Earwig. I had imagined this
word might be same as from Ex-
winger, throttler, but I find
from for earwig is ohrwurm,
i.e. ear-worm, which wd. shew
O syllable Ear to be not a par-
ticle but O same as O word
Ear. It is said that earwig

"Purpurea intexti tollant aulaea
Britanni ':
translated by Reiss, Dec. 1863,
How the Britons clad in purple
strike up the flute.

Aneotts.
Hackthorn Hall, Lincoln.

shd. be Earwing, the wing.

[C.i. p 39]

cases resembling Ears. This is
not likely I think. As far as
I know to give one a wiggling
means a shaking and is prob.
connected with wag, waggle,
perh. weak (shaky).

as he was commanded, and
was greatly distressed and
wrote a letter to his master
which he left on his table
praying for revenge and that
he wd. have pity on his fam
ily, and then, as the manner
of scouts is, went to Gurney's
old rooms and there hanged
himself. When these things
were known there was great
indignation in Balliol and

[C.i. p 40]

they drove out the wicked
man, and he went to the
Alban Hall*, and stirred
up the minor colleges against
Balliol. Such is the legend.

Mem.
Maps to be taken up to Oxford
and coloured sketch by Clara
Lane.
Portraits v Raphael, Tennyson,
Shelley, Keats, Shakspere – Mil-
ton, Dante, Albrecht Dürer.

*So the MSS. But the Alban
Hall shd. probably be read.

[C.i. p 41]

Mrs. Chapple
16g, Chester St. (or perhaps td)
the Birkenhead.

a mass of yellowish boiling
foam wh. runs down between
O fans, and meeting covers
O whole space of O lock-en
trance. Being heaped up in
globes – bosses – round masses
O fans disappear under it.
this turbid mass smooths itself
as O distance increases fr. O
lock, But O current is strong
and if O basin into which it runs
has curving banks it strikes O em
and O confusion v O already
folded and doubled lines of foam
is worse confounded.

PLATE 37. C.i. pp 42,43,44,45 • 87

C.i. p.42 | J.9

Twelfth Night. Act 1, Sc. III. Sir
Toby. My niece ̶ ̶ . . .
Maria . . . Your cousin.
Niece and cousin "Cousin" is used
for "niece."
Sc.1. — So full of shapes is fancy,
Out it alone is high-fantastical.
Why alone?
How will she love, . . . [or heart,
. . . . . . — when liver, brain,
Those sovereign thrones, are all supplied,
fill'd, [king?
(Her sweet perfections,) with one self
Meaning? Knight says her loving
or marrying will fill them with one
lord, and this will constitute her per-
fection, comparing Froissart, a woman
being not complete till married. This

C.i. p.43 | J.10

I do not believe.
III. "As tall a man as any's in Illyria."
tall is here said to = stout - bold.
So Amurican use of the word seems
to have developed fr. some such use
as this. — "Gust", taste, ×cf. gusti×
— "Subtractors", detractors. — "Coys-
tril", what? — "What wench? —
Castiliano - vulgo; for here comes
Sir Andrew Ague - cheek. "Meaning?"
— Sir A. A.'s name applies to the
mulous hue of his cheeks, hanging
down and shaking with his motions.
Sir Toby Belch may be noticed as
Eng. equiv. for such Sir. names as
B. Sedundiew etc.
For Castiliano - v
Steevens) reads ((or

× Derived straig
fr. Fr. goût (Fre

C.i. p.44 | J.10

put on a Castilian, Spanish,
grave face. — The Spaniards being
distinguished for their grave dig-
nity — and for their courtesy
which wd. suit the drift of the passage as well :— be on your best behaviour. But how is this got out of the
words?
Above, for "perfections" Knight wd.
read "perfection". But I believe the
meaning to be that "liver, brain,
and heart" are the parts of the
body in which all the qualities
of the mind and soul reside. They
make up the whole immaterial
part of man, they are his "perfections." However Knight's explanation
is perhaps good. Qy. How far is
the classical view of the func-
tions of Oliver to be found in Shs.
poetry. It is in Eng. poetry generally
allowed to be the seat of envy, I think.

C.i. p.45 | J.10

It was Dr. Ogne, I think, who
suggested an ingenious, I do not
think it can be new, explanation
of premises. He said it arose fr. a
mistaken reading of half legal documents where, in treating of the estate, of houses, estates etc., instead
of specifying the subject of the document repeatedly the word prae-
missa — the said, the aforesaid —
was used. and translated into the
Eng. premisses (as used in logic)
in same sense as in Lat. but which
has since been spelt premises and
lost its meaning.
Drill, trill, thrill, nostril, reso-
thirl (Wiclif etc.)
Common
The early idea piercing, to drill,
in sense of discipline, is to wear
down, work upon. Cf. to bore in
slang sense, wear, grind.

Plates 36,37: Deletions include: 41.3 "Che[shire]"   42.2 "x x x"   42.4 "Niece and cousin"   43.6 "gu[sto]"   44.19 "old"   45.18 "Primary". In 41.13 "lock. But" orig. "lock, but"   44.6 "be", "Be" superimposed
Bot. two lines of 42 and 43 are in ink. 43, ℓℓ.19,20 (footnote on gusto) read: "Derived straight from Latin gustus, not from French goût (earlier however goust)." 43, ℓℓ.17,18: "For Castiliano-vulgo Malone (or Steevens) reads Castiliano volto--" (cont. top. p.44).

46

...are connected with *lavo*.

Gk. inscription on fount, reading both ways (Jeremy Taylor) —

NIΨON ANOMHMA , MH MON
AN OΨIN .

Πέταλον. Ωκεανοῦ πέταλα . springs.
Pind. Fragments, 220. πέταλα κορίνα
the stars, for wh. cf. "See how the floor
of heaven
Is thick inlaid with patines of bright gold".
Merchant of Venice. I shd. like to see how
this occurs for it is given as Plutarch's —
II, 889 A, whatever that reference may
mean; or is "Plut." for Aristophanes' Plu-
tus, or a misprint for "Plat" (Plato)?
It is not to be found in 889 of the Plu-
tus and Aristoph. that play. it says in
L. and S.'s list of abbreviations, is
indicated by "Ar. Plut."

~~By connection between lather and lavo~~

47

flick, fillip, flap, fleck, flake.
Flick means to touch or strike lightly
as with the end of a whip, a finger etc. To
fleck is the next tone above flick, still
meaning to touch or strike lightly
(and leave a mark of the touch or stroke)
but in a broader less slight manner.
Hence substantively a fleck is a piece
of light, colour, substance etc. looking
as though shaped or produced by such
touches. Flake is a broad and decided
fleck, a thin plate of something, the
tone above it. Their connection is
more clearly seen in the applications
of the words to natural objects than in
explanations. It wd. seem that fillip
generally pronounced flip is a variation
of flick, which however seems connected with fly, flee, flit, meaning to
make fly off. The keybo meaning of flick,
fleck and flake is that of sticking or
cutting off the surface of a thing, in flick
(as to flick off a fly) something little

48

or light from the surface, while flake
is a thin scale of surface. Flay is
therefore connected, perhaps flitch.

No great difference can be shown, in spite
of the points, to exist between the verbs to
fly and to flee. Originally they were
just the same, but there is a difference in
their inflexions. Fly and flee are both
used as = fug-ere, but flew is the past
of fly ~~flee flet of flee~~ (volare), fled
of flee (fug-ere), ~~whereas~~ flown the
partic. of fly (vol-are), fled of flee
(fug-ere). Flee and fly have only the
difference of pronunciation wh. wd.
be between Eng. and Lowland Scotch.
Flit, vol-are, volit-are, fleet, to
fleet, flight, flutter, flitter, etc. are
variations.
Fluster variation of fluster. Fluster
prob. to fan with applause, to fluster
up — or else to inflate, blow out.

49

Original connection with flow,
blow, flare, flamma, φλόξ, fluere,
fluo, πλέω, float, flute (wind instrument), plovámi, etc.

Flag (droop etc.), flaccère, notion
that of waving instead of rigidity,
flowing (as we say of drapery) —
Hence flag the substantive. Fledge
to furnish with wings with w. compare
fly, fled etc. above.
With fillip, flip cf. flap, flob.
Cf. the connection between flag and
flabby with that between flick and
flip, flog and flap, flop

The meaning of hernshaw is disputed
about. It is variously said to mean the
heron, heronry and heron, the latter
prob. being the sense in "I know a hawk..."

Plates 38,39: 46.17 "Arist.'s" del.   46.20-21 (ink over pencil) "Query connection between <u>lather</u> and <u>lavo</u>, λούω ?"
47.22,23 (ink over pencil) "in <u>flick</u> (as to flick off a fly) something little" (pencil differs)   48.5 "verbs
to" orig. "verb to"   48.10 "<u>fled</u> of <u>flee</u>" del.   48.11 "whereas" del.   49.6 "drooping" del.   50.4 "orig"
del.   50.5 para. dividing-line del. (also at 52.18)   52.11 "for" del.   52.13 "to" orig. "with"

PLATE 39. C.i. pp 50,51,52,53 • 89

[C.i. p.50 — J.12]

50

fr. a hernshaw", but there is no
doubt that shaw is sometimes added
to words in sense ~ sham without.
It prob. is connected. the orig. meaning may have been concealment,
cover, pretence, shield etc. fr.
original sense ~ shade. Hence
hernshaw may also mean a heron
by â heron's shelter, shade, cover.
Shaw in old Eng. means shade ~
trees, cover, underwood etc. With
it are connected shadow, shade,
shed, shelter, shield.

I do not believe school is fr. schola,
viz. σχολή, but a Teuton word
meaning assemblage, collection,
as shoal, a school of whales
shell (in a school ~ a form).

Skim, scum, squama, scale,
keel (i.e. skeel) ~ squama ~

[C.i. p.51 — J.12]

51

scale being the topmost flake what may
be skimmed fr. surface ~ a being.

Hollow, hull (~ ships ~ plants),
κοῖλος, skull (as κεφαλή ~ caput
that wh. holds, contains), hole, hall,
etc. Hell.

I believe both caelum and caena
or cena to be fr. κοῖλον and κοινή.

Skip. ~ escape.

Revd. Edwin Palmer. 12, Southwood
Lane, Highgate.

Hale (seize). haul.

Hold, hilt. Halt (lame) = held
as captus oculis etc.??

Heal, hale.

Shear, shred, potsherd, shard.
The ploughshare that which divid-

[C.i. p.52 — J.12 / J.13]

52

es the soil. Share prob. = divide.
Shred also, wh. is same as shred.
Shire, a division of land? Shore,
where the land is cut by the water?
Shower. cf. shred, a fall of water
in little shreds or divisions? Short,
cut off, curtailed.

In Attic λίτρον πλείονων are for
νίτρον πνεύμων. L. and S. cf. λήψ
αδνίξ. Ἐν Δωριε ἦλθον φίλτατος
ηθον φίνταχος. So no doubt
πνεῦμα is for πλεῦμα connected
with πλέειν, flare, blow, two owl. wds.
above plume that with wh. birds fly.

Flos, flower, blow, bloom, blossom.
Orig. meaning to be inflated. to
swell as the bud does into the flower
Also φλέω (abundo) and flaw
(storm), flaw (Eng. not Lat.)

[C.i. p.53 — J.456 Fig.1]

53

C.i. p.54

J.13

54

Note. there is now going on what has no parl. but I know of in history of art. Byzantine or Romanesque Architecture star- ted fr. ruins v Ro- man became itself beautiful style and died as Ruskin says, only in growing bird to another more beautiful than itself. Gothic. O Renaissance Die O Renaissan appears now to be in Pro ass v being succeeded by spontaneous Byzantinesque style, retaining still some v bad features (such as pilasters, rus- tic-work etc) v O Renaissance, these it will throw aside. Its ca.

C.i. p.55

J.13

55

pitals are already, as in Roman- esque art, most beautiful. Whether Oen modern Gothic or Ois sponta- ous style conquer does not so much matter, for it is only natural for latter to lead to a modern spontan- eous Gothic as in middle ages, on- ly that O latter is putting off what be might've or rather are doing now Or O two may coalesce

γάλα (γάλακτος), γλαγος, Lac (lactis), leghen (pail) milk. v.C. mlik.

Neatherd = cowherd. Neats' feet = or something like calves' feet, ox-foot. Neat's leather, ox-hide or cow-hide. Deriv. v orig. meaning v Neat?

Naus (S), ναῦς, navis, vew, no, newt (?)

C.i. p.56

J.13

56

than in Macmillan's careful reprint v Bacon's Essay written then, while then in old ballads etc written than. Words identical "I had ra- ther die than do it" - "I had rather die, then, next after that, I would do it". Nor is better nor that is old English, for ne were and is written in old ballads etc sometimes nor.

(See J. 456 Fig. 2)

Kirkham Abbey, Yorkshire.

C.i. p.57

57

(See J. 456 Fig. 3)

Norman stairs Canterbury Cathedral. the same arrangement of arches and pillars I have seen in a modern building unconscious repeti- tion of form. See ∴ 54. the doorway and stairs in which above piece occurs are unique.

Transoms in Decorated and early Eng. In former not unfrequently found, for O purpose wh. they were intended to answer, before they became in Perpend only ornamental, viz. to give strength to mullions v tall windows. So also to Dec. where they are quite common in

J.14

See P. 60.

I cont 60.4

PLATE 41. C.i. pp 58,59,60,61 • 91

(See J. 456 Fig. 5)

C.i. p 58

58

J.14

Whitby abbey. I have not seen any parallel to this kind of tracery in French or Ital. Gothic. This style did not last long I think and seems to me to have been more capable of grand development than any others. The bars, split at the ends, which connect O lights

C.i. p 59

59

J.14

or recesses & of fourside openings with other plates & of tracery are at a distance and in effect, straightly and yet harmonize completely. This is O only successful manner & introducing Oem in Decorated windows Oat I know, for Oose in early geometrical are poor and O instance in Merton choir erected in finest style and in company with other windows of exquisite tracery is quite unworthy of O Oers and a failure. O above window I have restored as far as possible to a photograph by Uncle George. There was probably no circle or O other opening with in O four-sided ones. O mouldings I have not given. O whole rough.

(See J. 456 Fig. 6)

What has I try Cathedral by themselves.

C.i. p 60

60

(See J. 456 Fig. 4)

J.14

Decorated transom in domestic architecture Archbp's palace, Mayfield, Sussex Fr. photograph by Uncle G.

domestic architecture, but very rare in ecclesiastical, O necessary positions two examples. In long wind-

C.i. p 61

61

J.14

Ref. to Jan. 1864

ows however as in towers (e.g. St. Mary's, Oxford) they are not uncommon. Oeir evidently deliberate rejection in ordinarily proportioned windows by O Dec. architect ought to be decisive against Oem.

Names & Yorkshire rivers taken fr. Cornhill for Jan 1864

Aire. British and Gaelic – Rapid stream.
Calder. British Erse – Woody water
Douglas. British – Blue water.
Eden. – Gliding stream
Humber Gaelic Confluence & 2 waters
Ribble. British – tumultuous.
Oun. ____ Erse. Dusky.
Derwent. ____ Fair water.
Dove. ____ Erse – Black.
Greta. ____ Swift.
Aid. ____ that which is.
Wharfe. Gaelic British – Rough.

Dhu in one or more & O Celt languages is black – Gaelic e.g. Donuil Dhu – Donuil O Black. I as above.

[C.i. p 62 / J.15]

62

names it enter into Dun & Dove,
perhaps Douglas, Dou- being
blue, orig. black. But perhaps
-glas is blue, ~ we may may compare glastum or glassum or glessum
Latin — or rather prob. latinising
~ native word. for ꝺ blue-dye pro
ducing plant, woad. Humber always supposed to be fr. ꝺ lymow.
Wharfe and rough (rough orig)
are identical. Dun, dusky, dull
prob. fr. or connected wꝺ dhee, perhaps tawny. Ribble perh. connected wꝺ revel, rave. — Went, Gwend
(Gwendolen), Gwin (Guinevere)
mean white or fair. Aras whe
Gunggung (Ganges) means litera
ly flow-flow — As. as. Ouse, Ar &c.
fr. ii ele ete to run, flow, go.

[C.i. p 63 / J.15]

63

Duffer in Cumberland means ass (literally; in slang parlance metaphorical
lazy, lassus?

Clarty, North country — sticky. See
pp 33, 35, 36. Clay perhaps may have
same ʼt fr. its clammy clinging
nature.

"Virginibus puerisque canto"
Ising to ꝺ virginals and hautboys.
Hawk. is sell about ꝺ streets. I had
imagined ꝺis to be derived from ꝺ
bawling or screeching ꝺ hawkers
made in proclaiming their wares,
to hawk meaning to make a noise
in ꝺ throat, as before spitting. But
Kingsley uses a word to "hawk
~ birds in sense ~ to move up and
down in a place, to haunt. ꝺ
above sense may be derived fr.

[C.i. p 64 / J.15 / J.16]

64

ꝺis. He also uses a verb to hawk
in sense ~ to harry ~ "ꝺ ꝺis perhaps is connected ꝺ bird hawk.
In Isle ~ White dialect to gally
is to harry, annoy, and Shaks
pere has gallow in same sense.

Spuere, spit, spuma, spume,
spoom, spawn, spittle, spatter, spot
sputter.

Mucus, muck.

Almost all, probably all, slang
is ꝺ application ~ a provincial term
a metaphorical or whimsical sense,
or adoption of a provincial one,
excepting indeed words like chouse.

Twelfth Night Act II, Sc. II.
"ꝺ pregnant enemy".
"Disguise, I see, ꝺ art ~ wickedness,

[C.i. p 65 / J.16]

65

wherein ꝺ pregnant enemy does much
Chalmers says i.e. enemy ~ mank-
ind, emphasizing pregnant. Of course
it means ꝺ devil but if he draws
any meaning ~ ꝺis kind fr. ꝺ word itself he is wrong. ꝺ meaning must be
Disguise is a wicked ꝺing in which
crime is conceived (pregnant) and
brought to birth by ꝺ devil's means,
i.e. brought to commission.
"How will ꝺis fadge?" "to fadge is
to suit, to fit" Chalmers.

to fond on, to be fond of, to
dote on.

Monday. Odyssey, Riddell. 11. R.R.
Virgil. Palmer. 12. N.R.
Tuesday. Jowett. 8.30 A.M. Repeti-
tion. Woolcombe. Gospel of S John.
11. Palmer. Demosthenes 12 J.R.
Jowett. Ajax. T. Hall.
Wednesday. Palmer ~ Virgil. 12

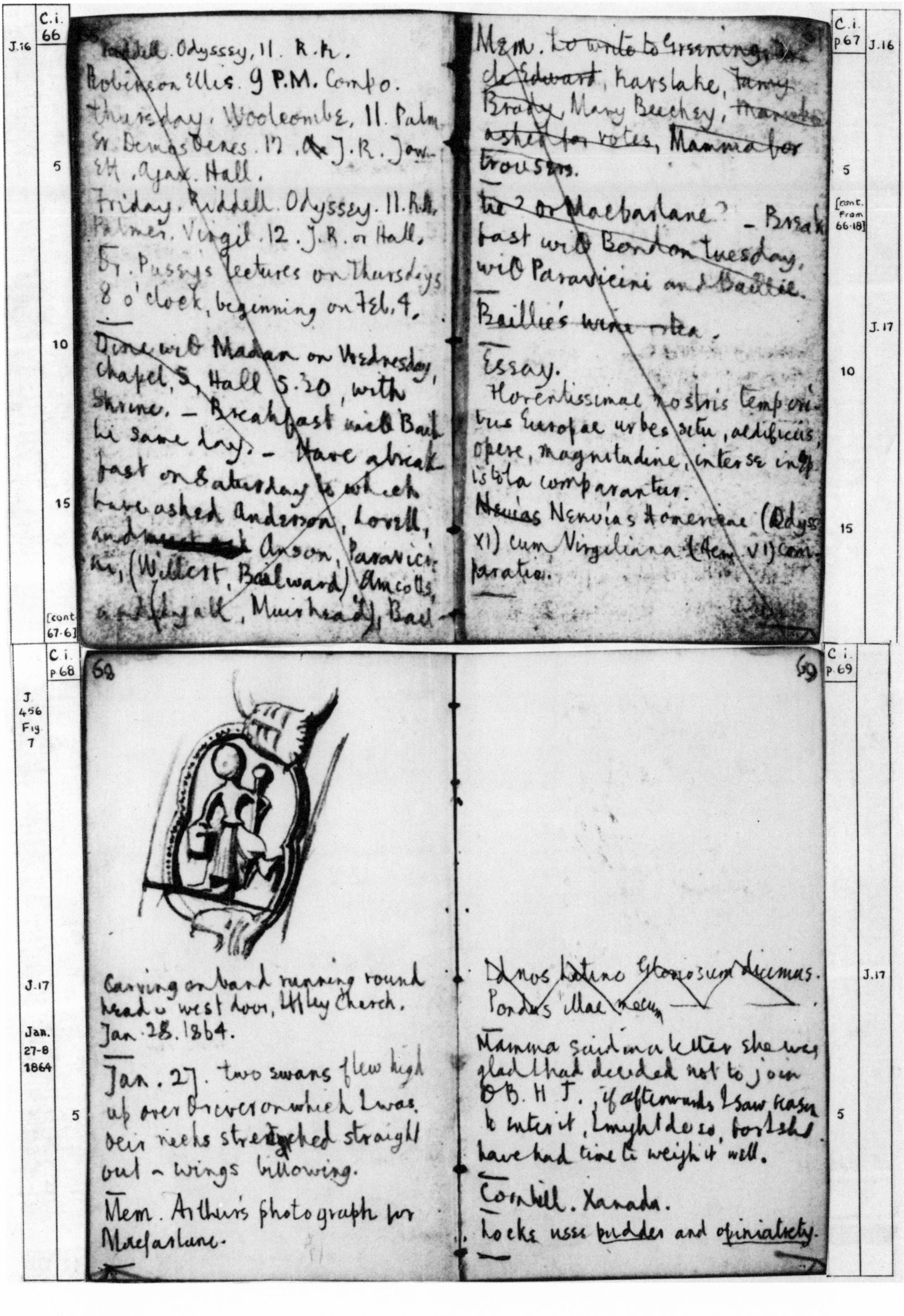

PLATE 43. C.i. pp 66,67,68,69 • 93

C.i. p.70 — J.17 — OET No. 9(a) — [cont. p 90] — J.18

70

Sketches Fir-grove on top of Hill past
Bagley Wood. Hill towards Cumnor.
Views beyond Ovillage where Church
is being restored on leftside & Heading-
ton Hill road. Lane(overarched) on
left before entering Marston. Iffley &c.
Till in Oeastward seas there rise the
lustrous (or splendid) sails & dawn;
Oseas being Osky, not literal.
Osun coming wth pennons & cloud,
cloud-bannerets, an oriflamme, a
"plump" or something & Osort &
spearlike rays.
The sluiced sunrise.
Oshields & heaven covered wth Eye-
brights. — White. diapered wth Ostars.

Ajax soliloquizes. Creeps towards O
Scamander. His sides washed in blood,
cheeks painted wth mud. The cheeks
& his flesh are lined in blood. His
ground rough-edged. Blades & grass-
bro' it as he moves.

C.i. P.71 — J.18 — OET No. 9(b)

71

Water dangerous.

Odysseus might meet wth one
& those dangerous Trojan or Lycian
heroes who are not Oless noble because
they are never named wth Oour best
whose braggart 'scutcheon, whose complaisant crest [praise.
Catch sunlight and one strain & stupid
Then when he was wounded and on
Opt. of being overcome I would rescue him, assist him home, nay carry
him wth cruel carefulness, avenging
myself by praises & his head & wisdom in council. but hinting O hand
could not be equal to O head, all owing
Ed him superior in Oatete. and praise
his courage and tell him I old do so
about O camp. — But no he won Oarms
fr. me . . . . . I hate his complaisant
goodnature about it. his forgiveness
& my rancour wh. I will not forgive
often in Opassages & Otents

C.i. p.72 — J.18 — OET No. 9(b)

72

strike his cheeks. — Ah! but it wd.
set me Ocontempt & ridicule & O
Greeks. O sullen sheepish Ajax &c!
I grip myself. — How I remember
when Oshameless hard-eyed
Athene betrayed me into unwarrior-
-like disgrace, my clumsy fall, my
muck'd cheeks, then now in a mist
& raging shame I could discern
but not see Oinnumerable faces
like lights and heard Olaughter
like Owind flaps flapping Oou-
sands & coarse fig-leaves. And when
lately I tried for O — who pitied
me, yet I pitied Oem & loved Oem,
seeing all Oeir case.
Ovillain shepherds & misguided flock.

— Ah! flock! how my Ooughts run
towards my shame, — my shame
blazoned in Olane's own colours

C.i. P.73 — J.18 — [cont. 74-14] — J.19

73

blood!. I remember when I came to
myself I saw Oopposite in Opolished
shield I got fr. (some Trojan) my
wild white face!. fifty times Ajax
and one great round drop & blood
has sunk in my hair like Ored
sun fallen into tangled golden
mists. sheep's blood. see P. 74

Do Oancients appear to have possessed a sense & O Picturesque in
external nature?
or.
Estimate Onature & Oehate to Oyland.

Od. V, . Odysseus Oere says O
he was in great danger when
O Trojans Orew Oeir
darts at him, while Ajax bore off
O body & Peleion.
Locke. Conduct & OUnderstanding
§ XX. "Who fair and softly goes

Plate 44: 70.6 ref. to [p.] 90 after "Iffley"   70.8 "dawn" del   70.19 "chinks" rewritten above a confused
entry   70.22 "drawn thro'" smudged   71.21 "I long to" smudged   72.12 "flaps...coa[rse]" del.   73.1
"blood" exclamation del.   73.4 "face" orig. "faces"   73.15 'round[?] the body of "Peleion"' del. 73.17 "of"
for "off"

PLATE 45. C.i. pp 74,75,76,77 • 95

p. 74

steadily forward in a course oak
pts. right." In same & "mig maze".
~~Parallellis~~ Parallelisms. Miss
Ingelow in first poem says "worlds
v hea Oes." Browning in Old Pictures
in Florence. stanza 1. "Wash'd
by O morning's water-gold" That in
Shelley, O Pine-grove near O Casci.
he or something v O sort, where O
lines describing O twinkling v O sun
thro' O leaves at morning occurs. Here
v elsewhere, also, O leaves in reflec-
tions etc
Fr. p. 73. If he be allowed to lie
here — for of course they will not
burn his body with funeral honours
— perhaps some one may bury his
bones, scattering dust on Oem or
digging a hole. But 2y. Is Ois a
Gk. custom? Oen on summer days,

p. 75

after Troy is taken, his soul will
feel O roots v O grass warm, ~ &
while (brilliant air waits on O capes
~ headlands and O skies swim blue-
ly ~ O gulfs are bare are bare, he
will be double-sighted ~ see O
~~stan~~ sails standing in O sea off
Tenedos and O Gks. sailing home.
But no. he will not have this, he
cares not for Oem, he prefers visions v O plain v Elysium.
Aulus Gellius says de id genus
hominibus, cf. "Oose sort v men"

Ite domum saturae, venit Hesper-
us, ite capellae.
"Go one home on Saturday, the
Evening comes on, go to ~~even~~ chapel."
A. E. Hardy.

Apoll. Rhod. IV, 771. τέρυειν (absolute)

p. 76

to ~~cut~~ go, "cut.) See L. ~ S. sub v.
τέρυειν. Prob. O Sov understood.

(See J. 456 Fig 8)

Lasher, h. canal at Woolver-
cote. the water running down O
lasher violently swells in a massy
wave against O opposite bank
wh. to resist its force is defended
by a piece v brick wall. O shape
v wave v course bossy, smooth v
globy. full v bubble ~ air, very
liquid. — for O rest v O lasher, all
except O shoulders where [See next pag]

p. 77

it first sweeps over it is covered with
a hind v silver links. Running like a
wind or element at O shoulder.
Pregnant phrases in English. Putting
O stone ~ the good ship. — To put things,
i.e. represent Oem.

[p. 78] *(margin: C.i. p.78; J.19)*

the new names are Daniel, Worcester; Baker, S. John's; Madan, Fellow of Queen's; Copeman, Ch.Ch.; Plummer, Exeter; Towgood, S. John's; O-gle, Magdalen. Suggested Stafford, New Coll., but prob. objectionable.

[p. 79] *(margin: C.i. p.79; J.20)*

Newdigate to be sent in March 31, under sealed cover with cover and another sealed cover containing name and motto outside. to ye Registrar.

Note on green wheat. ye difference between ye green — Oat v long grass is ye first suggests silver, latter azure. Former more opacity, body, smoothness. It is ye exact complement v carnation. Nearest to emerald v any green I know, ye real emerald stone. It is lucent. Perhaps it has a chrysoprase bloom. Bob blue greens.

There was neither rain nor snow, it was cold but not frosty: it had been a gloomy day with all ye monotonous ye painful dreariness wh December rain wears over Clapham. M.C. came in. a little warmed by her walk she had made a call, she had met ye Miss Finlaysons, she...

[p. 80] *(margin: C.i. p.80; J.20; Not in J.20 see L.iii 208f.)*

done some shopping, she had been round half the place and seen ye nakedness v ye land, and now it struck her how utterly hateful was Clapham. Especially she abominated ye Berlin-wool shop, where Mrs. Vandeleur and her daughter called her "Miss" — Here was a continual sound v sliding glass panels v a smell v Berlin wool.

A Morall Essaye by Francis Lo. Verulam, Viscount St. Alban.

It was a good saying of Petronius Gallus when Augustus Caesar wd. have him to sign ye thirty-nine articles, that he wd. do that very willingly for that oft times the food of a fool must be a wise man's physick. So I think also is Seneca —

[p. 81] *(margin: C.i. p81; Not in J.20)*

to be understanded Quot corpora, tot capita. Every woman has a bodice, but not every one stays. There is a toye in Hungary ye which I set down for the better memory of it & which they use of one that hath drunk deep and then afterwards hath suffered, yat such come in wid ye high tide and out again wid ye ebbe. Which I would not affirm to be true, but this I say that it hath been an opinion that many pass a high matter wid secresy and yet are but cormorants at the heart. And yet the old proverb doth hold Better a blind man that may reach one apple ban fifty eyes yat look and reache not. So Plautus Susanna said of Silvius Pellicus;

PLATE 47. C.i. pp 82,83,84,85 • 97

C.i. p 82	**82**
Not in J.20	

Exerpe laedo, juvo et guberno quae
requnt accusaturum ; the Devyll
is a cold anvil but a good accuser.
But that may be more verbal, I
have known ~~some~~ one who would give
away pretty sum as it were by Mer-
chandizing or Purchasing to get that
he might have for Nothing, and
another would use any triviall
or poor conceit to fetch a great
burthen. And of a truth though
You shall see it said tho I Wise-
hone is to be searched keenly you
shall never find Oat is to be
discovered in ferret's holes. But
Enough. Oese toyes 83.
the rest was not finisht.

A. Westenholz, 2b, Mark-Lane 83

(J.20) (see 83.18)

C.i. P.83	**83**
[cont. from 82.15]	
Not in J.20	

Not to be held in any confirmation
or extravagancy etc. the which
albeit they are but conceited devis-
ings of man's wit yet tho' sith they
are not to be held etc.

March 19. Saturday, 1864, walked to Edgware br. Hampstead
homely Hendon, stopping at Kingsbury water aquarter of an hour or
so. Saw what was prob. a heron.
Frederika's photograph.

It settled on a distant elm, was
driven away by two rooks settled
on a still more distant. Osame being
happened, Drooks pursuing it. At Oen
flew across Owater, circled about
flew Hampsteadwards away. 84

Danish Soldiers' Sailors' sick
wounded Relief fund. Subscrip(t)

J 20 March 19 1864
10 [cont 83.12]
15 [cont 84.9]

C.i. P 84	**84**
J 20	

tions to be paid to Messrs. Ransom
Bouverie Co, I Pall-Mall east;
Messrs Robarts, Lubbock, Co, Lom-
bard-street.

Hislop Clarke, Bank of Aus-
tralasia, Melbourne, Victoria. To be forwarded.

Ti. page 83.

          The sparky air
leaps up before my vision,—thou art
gone.

Speke says "O language Ois people"
i.e. that between Zanguebar and
Lake N'yanza" ... , is based on En-
phony. fr. wh. cause it is very com-
plex, Omore especially so as t u

J 21 5
(cont from 83.17)
OET No. 9(c)
10
15

C.i. P 85	**85**
J.21	

quires one to be possessed of any'ro's
turn of mind to appreciate Osys.
tem, unravel Ossecret its Eu-
phonic concord. I shall ∴ put
down some notes on Oeuphony.
U-sa-Gara, U-za-Ramo,
Dégé la Mhora; U-ra-guru,
Maji ya Whita, Juwa la Mhoa,
U-n-ya-muezi,

Note Oat O Wabembé (W. Tangan-
yika lake) "O Masai, Oeis
Cognates, O Wahümba" (N. Ugogo)
Watatürü," (N. Mgünda-Mkhs)

5
10

Plates 46,47: 79.17 "montonous" del. 79.19 "N" (?) mended to "M"   80.3 "c" del. in "nakedness". 80.11 "Mr." (?)
81.4 and 6 "the" del. twice before "which"   81.15 "it is true" del.   82.5 "some" changed to one because
of "sum" in 82.6   85.11 "W" del.

[p. 86]

(i) "Wahasange," (where?) "Wa-
nyarambá" (where?) ~ Even ô
Wagozo ~ Wahimbú," (where?)
Circumcise".

ô woman's dish worn among ô
Waganda is the ô ancient E-
gyptian.

Coincidences the ô Usagari is
in Unyamuězi (between
Unyanyembé ~ Unyambewa).
Cf. wô Usagara.

Lionel said (Good Friday, 1864)
to Cyril, on walking to Kingsbury,
that this year he had been more
about the country than ever before
in his life. - the next day he ___
the hairdresser for a razor

[March 25] 1864

[p. 87]

to remove ô down on his upper
lip. Age just 16. Mr. Kayne suggested butter on ôat quarter to be
licked off by ô cat which wd. remove it.

NB. Münster Church or Cathedral.

Cyril's declension ~ imperfect
~ τύπτειν. - ετυψα, ετυψαστι
ετυψαι.

New College Chapel.
Gardens.
Trinity,
S. John's
Wadham
the Radclyffe.
Bodleian
Christ Church Meadows.
the Barges.
Law Kath.
Merton new buildings
Ch. ch.

[p. 88]

The Botanical Gardens
- Museum.

The other day I heard a crow sitting
in a tree in a field on my left croak-
ing dolefully. at West End, Hampstead.

1269 - 1270. Aristoph. Frogs. ô scholiast
on this line. a quotat. fr. Aeschylus
says "Αρίσταρχος και Απολλώνιος ἐπίσαν
κέφαλος, πότερ εἰσι"; - Query. Whence
use these ô words? this is note worthy,
first as ô Gr. for our express. Query,
secondly as shewing how ô set. goes on
to say that Timakhidas ô said Oynca
fr. Aesch's. Telephos. Asklebiades fr. his
Iphigeneia, ô ignorance possible in
ôsch's time, which perhaps implies
ô loss or extreme rarity of some of
Aesch's plays.

Locke says "when as".

[p. 89]

C. J. Bloxam 16 Bedford
Place, Russell Sq. W.C.

Monday. 12 Logic. - 8.40. P.M.
Comp.
Tuesday. 10. the Gospels. - 12. Trans-
lation.
Wednesday. 12. Logic. - 1. Sophocles.
- 8.40 P.M Comp.
Thursday. 12. translation
Friday. 12. Logic. - 8.40 P.M. Comp.
Saturday. 10. the Gospels. - 12.
Grammar. - 1. Sophocles.

Sunday 10 in April. Walking into
Addis in ôfields fr. Cumnor to ô
Witney Rd., saw a snake glide
thro' a hedge, thus -

ô ... curves being appa-
rently formed by twigs
etc road. wh. he drew

April 10 1864

(J. 456 Fig 9)

Plate 48: 86.8 "Coincidences the" del.   86.16,17 "Said to" del.   87.2 "Kayne" (?)--J. has "Payne"   89.17 "sinu[ous?]"

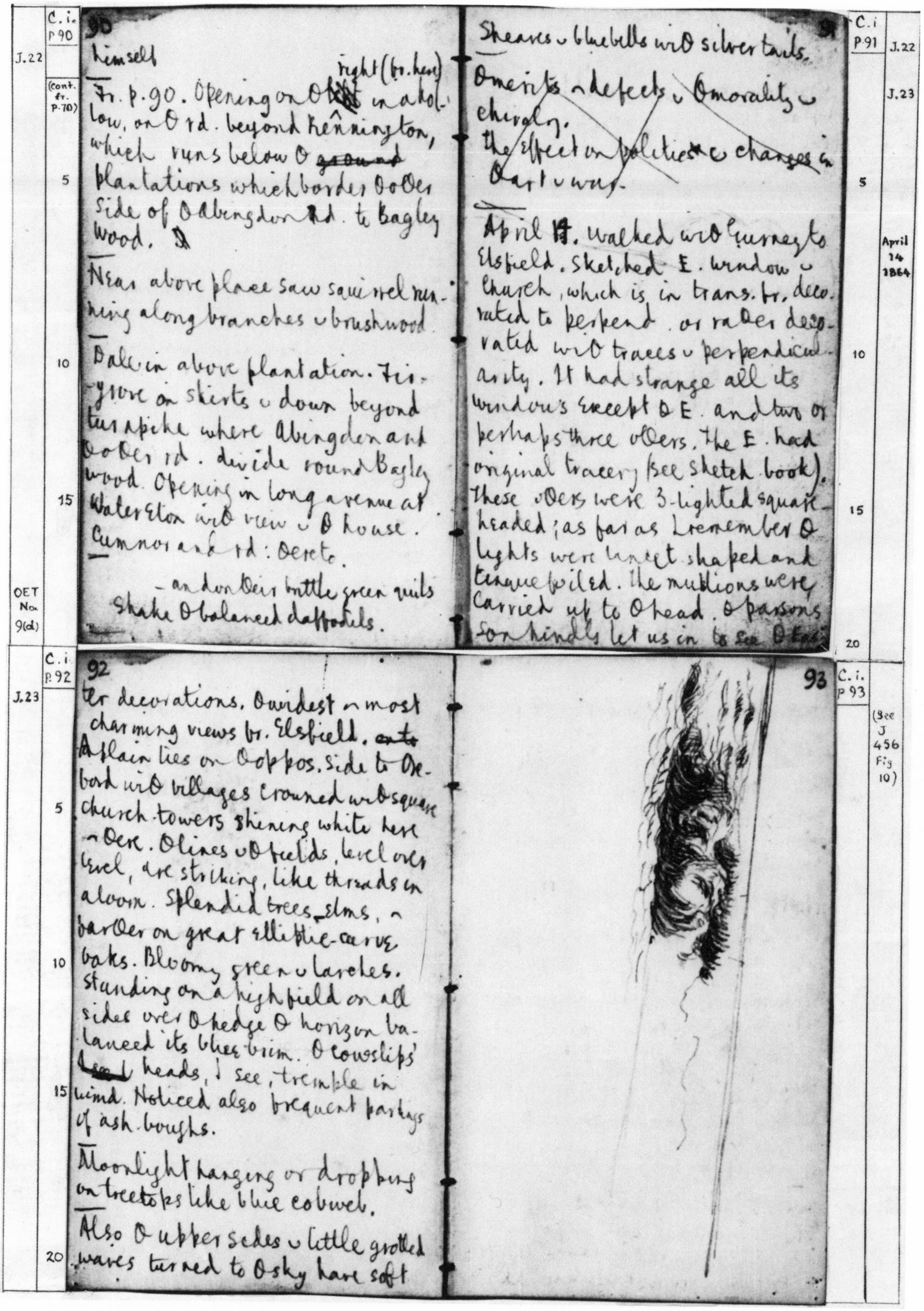

PLATE 49. C.i pp 90,91,92,93 • 99

C.i p 90 J.22

90

himself

Fr. p. 90. Opening on O~~left~~ right (fr.here) in a hollow, on O rd. beyond Kennington, which runs below O ~~ground~~ plantations which border O Oer side of O Abingdon Rd. to Bagley Wood. ~~I~~

Near above place saw squirrel running along branches ~ brushwood.

Dale in above plantation. Fir-grove on skirts ~ down beyond turnpike where Abingdon and O Oer rd. divide round Bagley wood. Opening in long avenue at Water Eton w O view ~ O house. Cumnor and rd: O etc.

— an don Oers brittle green quills shake O balanced daffodils.

(cont. fr. p.70)

OET No 9(d)

C.i P.91 J.22 J.23

Sheaves ~ bluebells w O silver tails.

~~O merits ~ defects ~ O morality ~ chivalry.~~
~~the effect on politics ~ changes in O art ~ way.~~

April 13. walked w O Currey to Elsfield. Sketched E. window ~ church, which is in trans. fr. decorated to perpend. or rather decorated w O traces ~ perpendicularity. It had strange all its windows except O E. and two or perhaps three oOers. The E. had original tracery (see sketch book). these oOers were 3-lighted square-headed; as far as I remember O lights were uncet shaped and trefoil foiled. the mullions were carried up to O head. O parson's son kindly let us in to see O Eas.

April 14 1864

C.i P.92 J.23

92

Oer decorations. O widest ~ most charming views fr. Elsfield. ~~onto~~ A plain lies on O oppos. side to Oxford w O villages crowned w O square church towers shining white here ~ Oer. O lines ~ O fields, level over level, are striking, like threads in a loom. Splendid trees, elms, ~ barOer on great elliptic curve oaks. Bloomy green ~ larches. Standing on a high field on all sides over O hedge O horizon balanced its sheer brim. O cowslips' ~~bent~~ heads, I see, tremble in wind. Noticed also frequent partings of ash boughs.

Moonlight hanging or dropping on treetops like blue cobweb.

Also O upper sides ~ little grotted waves turned to O sky have soft

---

C.i P 93

93

(see J 456 Fig 10)

[p. 94]

pale-coloured cobwebs on them, the under sides is green.

Note. That the beaded oar, dripping, powders or sows the mould with dry silver drops.

Poetry at Oxford.

It is a happy thing that there is no royal road to poetry. The world shd. know by this time that one cannot reach Parnassus except by flying thither. Yet fr. time to time more men go up and either perish in its gullies fluttering excelsior flags or else come down again with full folios and blank countenances. Every age has its. Yet the old fallacy keeps its ground. Every age has its false alarms

May 3. Walked with Addis to Staunton Harcourt. The church is cruciform - rather large, with a Norman door and several

[p. 95]

windows etc, Early English E. end over windows, windows in tower (prob.) Decorated, a Decorated or more prob. Perpendicular parapet, Perp. windows. O.E.E. is certainly unattractive, however the church is evidently in Egypt, churchwardenship. We did not go into it, nor into the tower (close to the church, in Perpend. rather shorter than that of the church,) in the top storey of wh. Pope finished his 5th vol. of Homer, or of the Iliad, nor into the Octagon-roofed kitchen, which except one at Glastonbury is unparalleled in England, nor into the chapel, wh. with the tower the kitchen belonged to ~~Harcourt~~ Stanton Harcourt

[p. 96]

Manor-house, I believe, Pope lived here two years, Gay some time. We saw to our great surprise the tablet (on church wall) raised to William (or John) Hewett & Sarah Drew, affianced lovers, killed by lightning; one of Pope's epitaphs is on the tablet. Vide the account, writings wh. rose on subject. Charming place, rather of my ideal Stratford on-Avon kind; willows, lovely elms. Pool of inky black water with leaves in it. Vertical shortish grass. Orchards with trunks & trees smeared over with the common white mixture, whatever it is, rather pretty otherwise. Primroses, large, in wet, cool, shady places. — on

[p. 97]

way, fields yellow with cowslips, dandelions. Found purple orchis wh. opens flowers fr. ground, then rises the stem pushing upward. Crossed Isis at Skinner's weir, or, as people about call it, Wire. Beautiful effect of cloud. Wild apple(?) beautiful in blossom. Caddis-flies on stones in clear stream, water-snails, leeches, round-looking glossy black field-mouse or some kind of water-rat in ditch on Witney Rd. Cuckoo. Peewits wheeling, tumbling, just as they are said to do, as if with a broken wing. They pronounce peewit pretty distinctly, sometimes querulously, with a slight metallic tone like a bat's cry. Their wings are not pointed to the eye, when flying, but broad, white, the black or

PLATE 51. C.i. pp 98,99,100,101   •   *101*

Plates 50,51: in C.i.pp.94-99 all deletions are plainly legible. C.i.100 introduces   OET No.10: Pilate
Drafts occur on C.i.pp.100 to 108, and C.ii.pp.28-29 (see Plate 91). Only 5 sts. are numbered, so the sequence
is not certain. Humphry House chose "The pang of Tartarus" as the opening, pp.102-3: no other st. seems more
suitable. The incomplete rev. of st.2 on p.108, perhaps meant to convert it into a suitable opening st., would
have led to changes in ℓℓ.12 to 14 and st.3: it cannot therefore form part of the final text. See Note-books and
Papers, ed. HH, 12-15. In 100.10a there is an apostrophe in "blade's", not comma after "heat"   11b "burs" mended
to "burns". Line 15 abbrev. for "and" where "of" seems needed (GMH confuses these signs quite often).   101.20
"icy" (a crux which N.12 had to leave blank--cf. "ice", 105.83). 101.23b "air--" I overlooked this obscure dash
in the 1970 revision of Poems 4th edn.

Plate 52: 102.28 "hamlets round" (dittography) del.   29a "More oft loud" del.   32 "Yea" del., foll. by either "O" (but contr. *l*.72 [below] and 47 [Pl.53]),or theta for "The" (no cross-bar visible, but cf. *l*.53)   33 orig. "nerves"   102.2 "cast" del.   3 "where I...this [?]" del.
103.7 after "keep", "me" seems needed for sense and metre   52 "gather to me" del.   55 "Because" del.   58 "part" del.   105.80a to 106.97a lines crossed through (unpublished 1st draft)   For 76-79 see C.ii.29 and for 85-86 see C.ii.28 (both Plate 91). 105.84a "frey" (slip for "fray")..."a precipice" mended to "the..." 105.88a orig. "there to stand", rev. "and there I stand."   89a orig. "part the bones", rev. "part my feet"

PLATE 53. C.i. pp 106,107,108,123 • 103

106

... dark band
To hold me quite fix'd in Oself.
        same plight.
And thus I will thrust in my right.

I'll take in hand O lady stone,
& to my palm Opoint apply.
And drive it down, on either side above,
W/i hope, w/o shut eyes, fixedly,

Wade, waddle, vadex, vadum.
Wade : waddle = stride :
straddle = swathe : swaddle =
ming (mix) : mingle etc.

Newton Hall is quite a mistaken way of writing Oname.

107

It std be Newing Hall. Newing
must be Opartieiple v an obs.
verb to new (p. w/ renew) intran-
sitive. Cf. Stoke Newington,
& Newingate, meaning ONew
Gate v some town Iforget what,
wh. I saw Oo Oer day. Cf. also
Newnham bor Newinham or
Newingham.

renew (see above) is verb. br.
renovare v took its English form
br. Oanalogy v new.

Whatever time Ovapourous roof,
Oscreen v my captivity,
Folds olt aloof, Oat signal is v proof
Not v clearskies, but storm to be,
But Oey I make an eager shift to see
Houses Oat make abode beside Olake,
And Oea my heart goes near to break

108

Oen clouds come, like ill-balanced Crags,
Shouldering. Down valleys smokes Ogloom.
O Ounder Crags, in joints v sparkling
        Jags
Olightnings leap. Oheday v doom!
Eny O rocks v mountain make me
        room
And yet I know it be better so.
Ay, sweet to taste beside Ois use

Betwixt Omorsels v Osnow,
Under Obrightening blue black heat,
— — mastering blue black heat,
When Ou winks blow, when strong rains
        twist v flow
Along my face v hands v feet

Some Oing, upper Seymour
Street, Oxford Street. Bow-
ditch.

123

with φλιάξειν. O scoff is with
σκώπτειν.

Gulf, golf. Is Ous game has its
name fr. Oholes into w/ Oball is put
Oey may be connected, v O being br.
Oorig. root meaning hollow. Gulf
gula, hollow, hold, hilt, κοιλός,
caelare (to make hollow, to make
grooves on, to grave), caelum wh.
is .: same as Oo' it were what it
once was supposed to be a translation
v κοιλόν, hole, hell ("O hollow heel)
skull, shell, hull (v ships v
beans).

Skull, orig. I believe to divide,
discriminate. Fr. same wd. or st.
shell (in a school), Oshilling
(division v a pound), v Oey say
school (vw v boys v whales),

Plate 53: 106.92a to 97a first draft (unpubl.) del.   Philology notes intervene before the poem returns, bot.
of 107   107.36 "the" rev. to "this"   38 "Folds" (not "Holds": cf. "Houses", 107.41), mended from an uncompleted
word, prob. beginning "Fli[es?]"   40 "then" orig. "yet"   108.44 "valleis (?)" mended to "valleys"   46
orig. "lightning leaps"   108.8c to 11c uncompleted revision, comma in 11c del.   Further drafts may have been
among pp.109 to 122, torn out of C.i, prob. by GMH.   The next sts. extant are in C.ii.28,29.   C.i.123 and 124
is the only leaf preserved (loose) out of twelve cut out between p.108 and p.133.   123.1 begins in middle of
a note. 123.6 "orig." del.   17 "schilling" (old spelling) mended to "shilling"

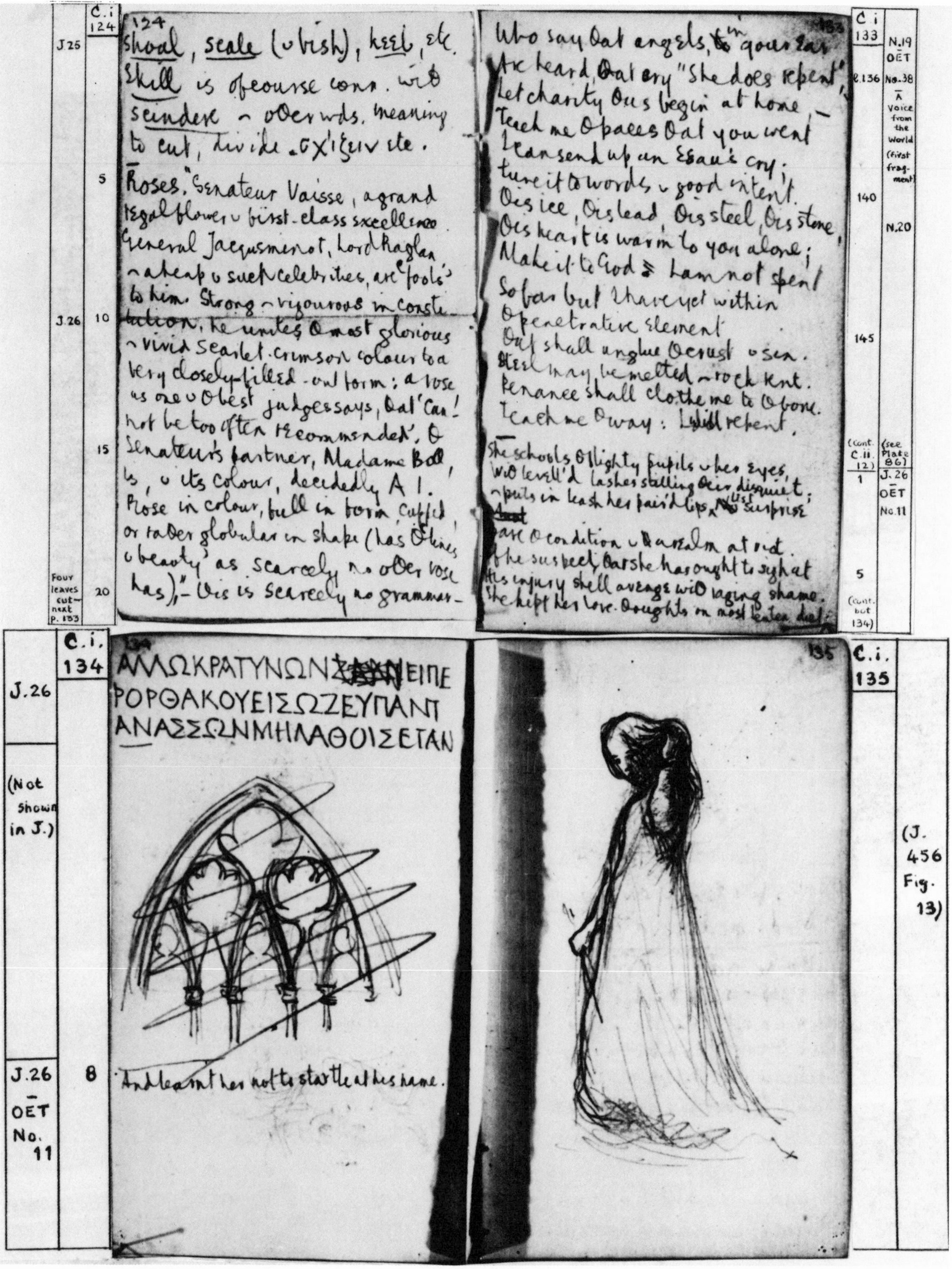

ΑΛΛΩΚΡΑΤΥΝΩΝ~~ΤΑΝ~~ΕΙΠΕ
ΡΟΡΘΑΚΟΥΕΙΣΩΖΕΥΠΑΝΤ
ΑΝΑΣΣΩΝΜΗΛΑΘΟΙΣΕΤΑΝ

Plate 54: the four leaves cut out between pp.124 and 133 deprive us of the rest of GMH's quotation from a flowery description of roses (culled from a nurseryman's advertisement?), and from a poem in answer to Christina Rossetti's "The Convent Threshold" (L.iii.213,36). A fifteen line fragment is the only remaining early portion of

No.38: A Voice from the World (MS.1)

C.i.133 begins in mid-sentence, with line 135: traces of "which say [?]" lie beneath "that cry"   142 "alone;" mended to "alone:" or v.v.?   143 "God:" rev. to "God."   149 "do" mended to "will"   Next drafts in C.ii.12, etc. (Plate 86).

No.11: "She schools the flighty pupils"

C.i.133, with one line bot.134 (del. in error along with the drawing above it)   Lines 3 and 4 "lips. No surprise/Must" rev. to "lips list [for lest] surprise/Bare"   133.4 "the" rev. to "a"   134 Greek:the del. letters anticipate the line below. Below the sketch of window-head (del., one line crossing through "learnt" in error) is a faint sketch of a girl's face, erased.

PLATE 55. C.i. pp 136,137,138,139 • 105

C.i. 136 J.26

to Grandmamma 9s. 6d.

Ticket to Victoria . 1s. 4d.

£2 8s. 1d.

11s. 4d.

£1 16s. 9d.

—

Notes for essay on some aspects
v Mod. mediaevalism .

Title not such as might be worded,
but represents pictorially what
is meant. May be objected
0at 0various movements v 0
Century wh. have mediaeval
Externals deeper 0an a mere return to middle age forms. Very
true. But no 0er title conveys
so much v what I mean .
Subject treated not 0ro' all its

C.i. 137 J.26

bearings but remarks on various
pts. to be made.
Historical remarks . .
German movement. Tieck etc. Orig.
I must get up. v Schlegels. Goethe,
whose balanced mind must not
be considered as 0 ideal v 0 century. Representing 0 most desired
union v 0 classical ~ mediaeval .

Note. Curious inst. v early application v local colour. In Byzantine school casket v ivory (preserved in Cathedral v Sens, a facsimile v wh. is in possess. v Arun-
del society) has a representation
v Joseph in Egyptian dress, head-
dress in particular.

He was a shepherd v 0 Arcadian mood,
0at not Arcadia knew no Harmony.
Affined to 0 earnest solitude,

Glistening downs ~ breezes seemed he.
0 downs ~ listening downs he seemed to be.

J.27

OET No.44 (a) Richard
1 2 3 4a 4b

C.i. 138

(J.456 Fig.14)

J.27 OET No.44a

(J.456 Fig.15)

5 6 7

He went into restless strides, disorderedly .
And vanished v 0 dry temples v his sleep
v th piping unexpected melody

8a his absent looks inspired as one
drunk deep

C.i. 139

(J.456 Fig.16)

J.27 OET No. 44a — Richard

(rev. C.ii plate 92)

In
was
Greater bliss v 0ro' 0 v my leaves
v sleep

9a

He sat rested on 0 frontal v 0 down
forehead

10

Shaping his outlines on a field v cloud

11

as drinking deep 8b

True nectar etc [crown 9b

His sheep seem'd to step v it, past 0
v 0 still grazing: 12 13

Plate 55: C.i.136-137. Summer vacation notes, prob. June 1864.
No. 44(a). Richard

C.i.137-139: early draft in Spenserian stanzas, with alternatives and revisions. Title preserved in L.iii.214
(July/Aug. 1864). No break is intended between lines 4 and 5, but 9 ends the stanza. 138.8a "one" orig. "d...(?)",
rev. 139.8b "as drinking deep"   139.10 "sat" del.   The poem was resumed in heroic couplets, C.ii.33-34, 83-84.
See plates 92-3, 123-4.

140

Different cloud floating over

June 30.
On this day ⊙ clouds were lovely. Opposite ⊙ sun between 10 and 11 was ⊙ disshevelled cloud on page opposite. ⊙ clouds were repeatedly formed in horizontal ribs. At a distance their straightness & line was wonderful. In passing overhead they were something

141

Good blue

Red-grey shapeless clouds, pale and not strongly marked in reality.

Grey

Horizon.

Sun opposite.
June 30.

As in the (now) opposite page, ⊙ ribs granulated delicately ⊙ splits fretted with lacy curves & honeycomb work, ⊙ laws & wh. were exquisitely traced. They

142

in ⊙ zenith thus. There were squared odd disconnected pieces ⊙ cloud now and then seen thus, as if cut out for a lost. whole. ⊙ blue & ⊙ sky was very good. A web & ⊙ finnest lacy cloud near ⊙ sun had films & colour chiefly rose (pale) and greenish blue in broad bars & caught on its tissue. Torn wisps & cloud prevailed later in ⊙ day like this.

and so on. Plots & blue sky. Tendrils and wisps & cloud

143

Damask clouds.

PLATE 57. C.i. pp 144,145,146,147 • 107

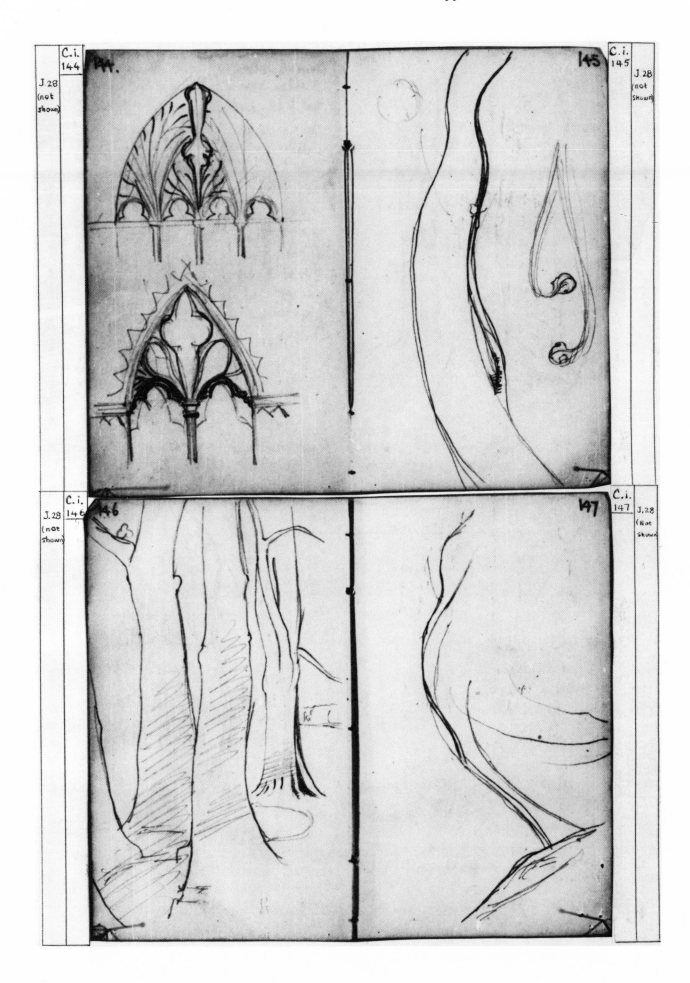

tito télémaque terzio
3io themistoclès théo-
phile Paliardeni,
wh. in Ois form
is half ~~french~~, half
Italian. perhaps

One shd. read tito telemacho te-
1snzio temistocle teofilo or
however it is in Italian. I met
~~all but~~ at Miss Vatnan's on
July 9, 1864.

Two weather clouds. Sun above. July 11.
Hampstead.

He feeds men w Ois manna every day:
My soul does loathe it ~ my spirit fails.

C.i. 150

A press u wingèd Oings along Ogates!
O gross Oock call Oem fails

A press u wingèd Oings comes down Ois
way:

O gross Oock call Oem quails.
Into my hand he gives a host for prey,
Come up, Arise ~ slay.

Who w. drink water br. a stony rock?
O for O wells u Elim, ~~Oe~~ sweet calms!
Are manna-lashes shelter for Ois flock?
Behold O seventy palms!
Dig not wid staves, ye princes; sing no
psalms.
Here are u O myrrh ~ balms.

Egypt, O valley u our pleasance here!
Most wide ye ar who call Ois gust Sim-
oom.

C.i. 151

Your parchèd nostrils snuff Egyptian air,
O comfortable gloom
After O sandfield ~ O unreinèd glen!
Oposhen is green ~ bare.

Not Goshen. Wasteful wide huge-
~~8~~ is thèd Nile [blesh.
Shall cool our shoulders ~ unbake our
{Unbakes my pores, ~ streams, ~ makes
all bresh.

I gather points u lote, I lower from an
isle
u leaves u greenest flesh.
Are you sand blind?
Ye sandblind! Slabs u light Ois many
a mile
Blaze him all Ois white.
In beds, in gardens, in thick plots

Plate 58. OET No.12—[SOLILOQUY OF ONE OF THE SPIES]
 Drafts, which begin bot. C.i.148, are spread over 150 to 157, 161, 193 (with one line 203). The title has been made from the description in L.iii.213. In the OET the sts. have been rearranged in MS. sequence: the sts. placed first and second by H. House in N.23-24, and WHG in 3rd. ed. of Poems, and (with a rev. text) in our 4th. edn., occur in the MSS. and OET as 8th and 9th.
 C.i.150—the del. sketch of a girl extended to the lower half of the page (running through "the sweet calms"). The del. lines 3a and 4a would have made a st. with three b rhymes together: "fails" is repeated in error from 2 (slip for "quails") Stanza 2 appears in four different versions (150,156,161,193 with last line on 203), and the earlier ones cannot be given line numbers. 151.17 "unreinèd" till 4th edn. reissue of 1984 printed "unveinèd"
 "Goshen" orig. "Groshen" 23a line unfinished 24 orig. "Blaze from him" [the personified Nile], then "from" entirely del. and rev. to "on," not "for" as I once thought. 25 "green" del.

PLATE 59. C.i. pp 152,153,154,155 • *109*

Plate 59: No. 12 [Soliloquy of One of the Spies]—Plate 2

C.i.152—29 "The ease" del.   30 "your" orig. "my"   32 "w" mended to "law"   36 "nor" del.
C.i.153—41a "wet. We love" del.   43 w in "who [did del.]" much smaller than in "Who is"—GMH often uses l.c.
after a mid-line query. 44 abbrev. for "of" rev. to "and" (abbrev.)

C.i.154—The lines in this first version of st.9 correspond only roughly with those in the final version:
the nos. assigned are mainly for reference purposes.   Line 54a "rul[ers]" del.   49b "Are" mended to "Your"
50a "of" (abbrev.) mended from "and" (abbrev.)—"threatens you" mended from some other words   "we", "us",
"our" are mended to "you", "your" in various places, e.g. 51b orig. "pots [we del.]: we will"   54b orig. "That
will not make you plod."   C.i.155—49c "are tire[d]" del.

C.i. 156

J.28
OET No. 12 cont.
J.29
St.2b
Soliloquy cont.
(rev. p 161)
N.24

i
54 j
K

less sod,
{ serve a grateful god .
{ for a more — — .
{ To - — — —.

O for O wells o Elim, O sweet
calms! [rock?
who ud. drink water fr. a stony
Scant is O manna-bush.
— ash. — — -trees. O seventy
palms
Are shelter for O is flock.
Dig not wid staves, ye princes;
Sing no psalms.
Here are boo myrrh n balms.
—

55 Go Ben: I am contented here to lie
56 take Canaar wid your sword n wid
     your bow.

C.i. 157

OET No. 12 cont. N.24
Soliloquy cont. p.161

57 a
57 b
58
59
60

Match yourselves
Rise: match your streng O ur O mon-
strous talmai,
At Kirjath Arba; 80. —
Sure, O is is Nile: I sicken, I know
not why.
And faint as O o' to die.

OET No. **13 a** — The Lover's Stars —
J.29

1 a
2 b a c
3 a
4 a
5 a
6 a
7 a
8 a (cont. bot.158)

The destined lover, whom his stars,
More golden O an O er kindred lights,
thro' ~~~~ passes bleak, O ro' raging
bars
o rivers, lead, O ro' storms n nights,
Or if he leave O West behind,
Or fader'd by O sunder' d south
Shall, when his star is zenith'd, find
Acceptance round O lady's mouth,

C.i. 158

(J. 456 Fig. 19)

July 16 1864

OET No.13 (a) cont.
J.29

1
2
9
10
11
12

July 16.
Caen Wood.

Altho' unchallenged, where she sits,
Three rivals O ron her garden chair,
O o' O silver o' seed O at flits,
Above O em, down O draught o air,

C.i. 159

OET No. **13 a** cont.
J.29 — The Lover's Stars —

13 a
b
14 a
15 a
16 a
13 c d
14 b
15 b
16 b
17
18
19
20 a b
21
22
23

And his
Travel all day n bag O sea
And lighting on O downs o France,
leave
Eight thousand furlongs in advance.
And holds { O breeze n clears O seas
     keeps {
And tangles on O down o France
Yet leaves him in ungirdled ease
8000 furlongs in advance

But in O o ther's horoscope
Bad Saturn wid a swart aspect
Fronts Venus. — His ill launched hope
{ In unemperill'd roads is wreck'd
—   haven. —
He meets her, stintless o her smile,
Her choice n roses knows by heart,
Has danced wid O her; n all O white

Plate 60: No. 12 [Soliloquy of One of the Spies]--Plate 3
C.i.156--variants include the second of four versions of st.2 (others on pp.161, 193).
C.i.157--No. 13. **The Lover's Stars**--Plate 1. Drafts occur on pp.157 to 161. The title is found in L.iii.213. The first draft of st.1 is fitted round a del. face. 2b and 2c need "of" before "lights" for sense and metre (supplied p.160).   5a "west" mended to "West"   158.2 "Lord !" [beg. of "Mansfield", who owned Caen Wood--see J.314]   159.18 "malign aspects" rev. to "a swart aspect"   20a orig. "unemperill'd"   22 orig. "He knows"

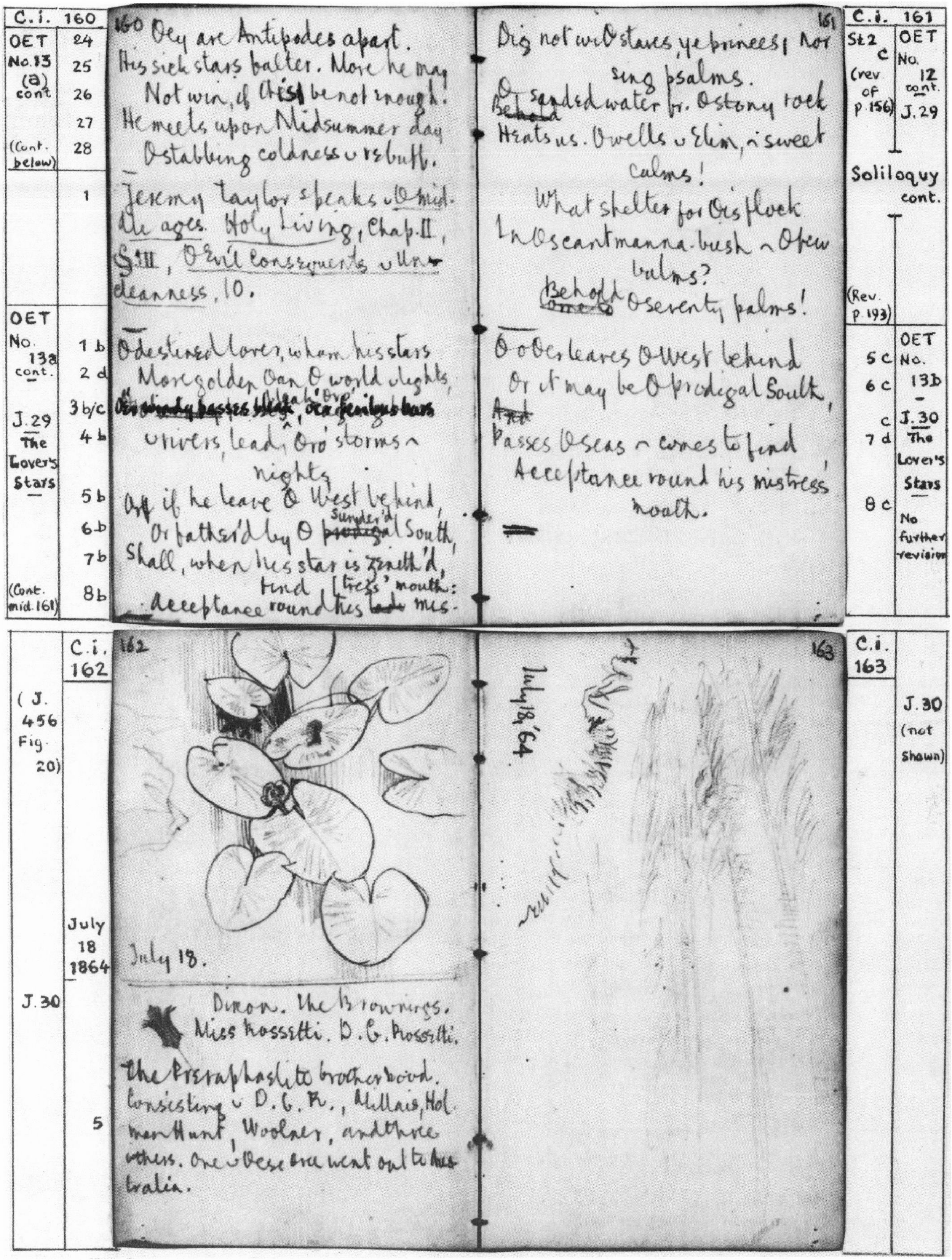

PLATE 61. C.i. pp 160,161,162,163 • *111*

The page reproduces four facsimile notebook pages (C.i. 160, 161, 162, 163) containing handwritten draft verse and sketches, with printed marginal index columns.

C.i. 160 (left margins):

OET No.13 (a) cont	24 25 26 27
(Cont. below)	28 1
OET No. 13a cont	1 b 2 d 3 b/c 4 b
J.29 The Lover's Stars	5 b 6 b 7 b
(Cont. mid.161)	8 b

C.i. 161 (right margins):

St.2 c (rev of P.156)	OET No. 12 cont J.29
Soliloquy cont.	
(Rev. P.193)	
	OET No. 13 b J.30 The Lover's Stars
5 c 6 c c 7 d 8 c	No further revision

C.i. 162 (left margin):

(J. 456 Fig. 20)

July 18 1864

J.30

C.i. 163 (right margin):

J.30 (not shown)

Pencil sketch of water-lily leaves and flower, dated "July 18."

Pencil sketch of grasses, dated "July 18, '64."

Plate 61: No.13: The Lover's Stars--Plate 2

    C.i.160.26 "these" mended to "this"   3b orig. in pencil "Thro' [windy del.] passes, [bleak,thro' added above] raging bars" rev. in ink to "O'er [windy del.] passes bleak, o'er perilous bars"   5b orig. "Ore" 6b "prodigal" del.   8b "lad[y's]" del.   C.i.161 (bot. half)--rev. of st.2 (5c to 8c), incompatible with the rest of the poem.

No.12: [Soliloquy of One of the Spies]--Plate 4

C.i.161 (top half)--third rev. of st.2. Final version pp.193,203 (Plates 68,71).

C.i. 164 · 164

(J. 456 Fig. 21)

J.30 – OET No. 14

1 During o'ercasting v untainted morns,
2 In b'ascendancy v rainbow's horns,
3 In O'erist signals v o several drops
4 Oat lick o shelly leaves w. flowy dewbe,
5 In O'er fragrance v trolling pines,
6 Under O'cloister-light v green-house haus,

— — till

OET No. 30a – J.31

2 Heaven v every field, are still
3 a As a self-embraced sweet thought.
3 b — — caressèd —
4 a And O thin stars tremble not,
4 b — — lessen'd stars v ray — .

C.i. 165 · 165

(J. 456 Fig. 22)

July 22 1864

J.31

July 22. '64

ἄττελεφθαλμος, beast-eyed, = bee-faced. Eubulus, I, 10.

C.i. 166 · 166

OET No. 30b J.31

OET No. 15a

Distance
Dappled w/O diminish'd trees
Spann'd w/O shadow every one.

O peacock's eye
1 Winks away its azure sheen
2 Barter'd for a ring v green.
3 O bean-shaped pupil v moist jet
4 Is O silkiest violet.
5

No. 15b — The peacock's eye —

1 Mark you how O pea-cock's eye
2 Winks away its ring v green,
3 Barter'd for an azure dye,
4 And O bean Oat's like a bean.
5 O pupil, plays its liquid jet
6 To win a look v violet.

Overclouded, apparently

OET No. 16

1 Love preparing to fly
He play'd his wings as bo' for flight;

C.i. 167 · 167

2 Oey webb'd O sky v O glassy light.
3 His body sway'd upon tiptoes,
4 Like a wind-perplexed rose.
5 In eddies v ound he went
6 At last up O blue element.

Mem. To ask Mr. Burton about picture-frames, price of models, whether the pictures by W. S. Burton in the Academy are his, about the Presaphaelite Brotherhood, O French Presaphaelites, O Düsseldorf school etc.

Skill etc. Primary meaning, to divide, cut apart. Skill, discomment. to keel, to skin. keel, Oat part v ash of w. cuts away O w' O water. Skull, an oat.

OET No. 16 cont.

J.31

(J. 456 Fig. 23)

PLATE 63. C.i. pp 168,169   •   *113*

Plate 62: OET No.14: "During the eastering of untainted morns"

C.i.164--sole draft. 2 "horns" smudged to "korns"   4 "shelly leaves" prob. not hyphenated; contr. five undoubted hyphens on 164-165. "floor[of" del.--slip for the]   5 orig. "fresh fragrance of the"

OET 30, Fragments II--July to Sept.1864:a "Hill/Heaven..." 3b orig. "caressed"   4b a different "r" del. before "ray"
165.2 "locust" (not "beast")

C.i.166 OET No.15: The peacock's eye. In the first version "The peacock's eye" is both title and first line (cf. title of No.16 below); 166.2 "au" mended to "azure";   3 "from" del. No.15b avoids writing on the back of the lovely sketch on p.165. 4 stop after "bean", an undoubted period, is undoubtedly meant for a comma.

C.i.167--No.16, ℓ.2 "skies" mended to "sky with"   5 "a" mended to "he"   6 "element" not del. in MS.

Plate 63. 168.3 abbrev. for "of" after "School" (slip for "and").
C.i.168-170   OET No.17: Barnfloor and Winepress--MS.1 This is the earliest draft and only autograph. For two transcripts of rev. versions and the text publ.1865, see Plates 78-79. Line 1a "Thou whom thy taskmaster Si[n]" del.   3 and 4 "are" rev. to "was"; "first" l.c. mended to u.c.   5a "For us are/was" del.; "bruis'd" mended to "bruised" (two syllables).

169.18a "Was wr" del.   18b "wrecked" mended to "wracked"   19 "on" mended to "in"
20,22 "vintage", "vine" l.c. mended to u.c.   23 "On" mended from "At" or "That" [?].

C.i.168 to 171 are repeated on Plate 80A (from a different reproduction) to facilitate a comparison with later versions of "Barnfloor and Winepress" and of "New Readings".

C.i. 170 / OET No. 17 cont. N.25

25 Soon O whole world is overspread.
26a Come ye
26b Ye weary, come into O shade.
29 So he has bound us in this sheaf,
30 He has made us bear his leaf.
31 We scarcely call Oat banquet food,
32 But even our Saviour's ~ our blood
33 When we are grafted on his wood.

Barnfloor and Winepress —

N.26 See Plates 78-9 (other mss.)

27 Perhaps to be put in somewhere
O field where He has planted us
28 shall shake her fruit as Libanus.

OET No. 18a — N.26 - J.32 New Readings —

NEW READINGS.

1 Altho' God's word has said [gather,
2 On thistles that men look not grapes to
3 I read O story rather
4a How soldiers matted
4b plaited O thistles round his head
5 Where fruit ~ precious wine was shortly
shed.
6a Tho' when O sower sowed.
6b

C.i. 171 7a

Some whe

7a O winged bowls eat part, part fell
7b on O born,
~ never grew to corn.
8 Part could not spring upon O flinty
9 road, O hath shew'd
10 Yet at all hazards Christ his fruit

11 Hard ways, rough wanderings
12 Made him not fruitless; and O born's he shed
13 Grains from his drooping head
14 And would not have Oat legion ~ wing'd
things
15 Bear him to heaven upon easeful wings.

OET No. 19 N.26 "He hath abolish'd the old drouth"

1 He hath abolish'd O old drouth,
2 And streams run when all was dry,
3 O field is soft'd with merciful dew.
4 He hath put a new song in my mouth,
6 And taught my lips to quote O's word
7 That I shall live, I shall not die,
8 That I shall when O stocks are stirr'd

C.i. 172 / OET No. 19 cont. N 26

9 See O salvation ~ O Lord.
10 We meet together, you ~ I,
11 Meet in one acre ~ one land,
12 And I shall turn my locks to you
13 ~ you shall meet me with reply,
14 We shall be sheaved with one band
15 In harvest ~ in garnering,
16 When heavenly vales so rich
shall stand [sing.
17 Und O corn Out they shall laugh.

5 O words. ~ old, O purport new.

J.32
1 Barbe, O adrant.
Fanz Anatomie.
F. Madox Brown.
Seddon.
5 Cornelius, Overbeck ~ some one
else (Rethel?) founders ~

C.i. 173 / J.32 / J.33

German medievalism. Cornelius
used to draw his smallest figures
in charcoal.
Rethel a man ~ real genius would
5 have been O master ~ O school
but died young
Düsseldorf school, a poor affair.
Now split into sects. Chiefly imitates O French.
Belgian school. Has one great medi-
10 evalist Henri Leys. His follow-
ers feeble.
Sort ~ French Preraphaelitism,
but very little medievalism in
feeling Oo' medieval subjects.
15

Plate 64: OET No.17: Barnfloor and Winepress (cont.)

C.i.170. After 26b a marginal X is del., and rewritten after 30 to indicate where 27 and 28 (added at end) could
be inserted. 29 "he" mended to "He" 30 "bare" mended to "bear" 33 "wood"

C.i.170-71—OET No.18a: New Readings—(MS.1) Sole autograph. See Plate 80 for transcript by V.S.S. Coles of a
rev. autograph (now missing). 2 "men" mended to "that" and "men" rewritten 5 "gra" mended to "fruit" 6a
"Alth" del. C.i.171 7a "Some whe" del. 11 "He" mended to "Hard" 12 "him" l.c. mended to u.c.... "on"
mended to "in" 14 "Legion", u.c. because it refers to angels. If this was also in the missing rev. autograph,
Coles did not notice it: see Plate 80. Note cont. on opposite page.

PLATE 65. C.i. pp 174,175,176,177 • *115*

C.i. 174

C.i. 175   J.33

July 25 1864

C.i. 176

(J.456 Fig. 24)

C.i. 177

(J.456 Fig. 25)

C.171-172--OET No.19: "He hath abolish'd the old drouth". Sole MS. For 5 (here marked with a marginal X between 4 and 6) see end of poem, p.172.   8 "But I shall when the shooks are stored"   172.10 No clear comma after "together"   172.17 "laugh and sing."   172.12 "shall" del.

    Notes on Painters: GMH had difficulty spelling various artists' names, e.g., "Madox" (3), "Rechel" (6), corrected to "Rethel" (173.4), 173.11 "Lluys" (written like "Huys", through insertion of second "l"--should be "Leys")   173.14 "no" mended to "very" In 172.1 the name (or instrument) after "Barbe" has been mended, creating uncertainty.

Plate 65: C.i.175.4 "appear to" del.

REST.

I have desired to go
Where springs not fail;
to fields where flies not any brindled hail,
~ a few lilies blow

I have desired to be
Where havens are dumb; [come,
Where the green waterheads may never
As in Our loved sea,

or

I have desired to be
where gales not come;
Where the green swell is in the havens dumb
~ sunder' dwr. Osea

I must hunt down the prize
Where my heart lists.
Must see the eagle's bulk, render'd in mists,
Hang of a toble size.

Must see the waters roll
where the grasses set

Towards wastes where round the ice-blocks
tilt ~ wet
Not so far to the pole.

Must see the green sees roll
Where waters set tilt ~ fret,
Towards Ouse wastes where the ice-blocks
Not so far to the pole.

Mem.

Miss Yatman. Tourists book.
Bond's books. Ticket Money
Hair to be cut,

Cerente. designed windows at All Saints
except those in the clerestory, which are by
O'Connor.
A Majesty.
5, Orwell Terrace, Dovercourt, Essex.

fr. Papa & 5. Umbrella & [.

Book for Hardy. 4s. Hair cutting.
6d. Cab. 3s. 6d. Ticket £2 10s.
Omnibus to Llangollen station.
4d. Bill at Llangollen. £8 9.
Coachman. 1s. Porter
6d.

Written on flags below the words "Suc-
cess to Savin".
Hir oes allwydd i'r ddau brawd Sav.
in, - diehon
Gor fo byth i'w dylyn;
A bhan ddaw terfyn i'w hoes brau,
Y rhoedd byddo cartre'r ddau.

Why shd. the foolish bands, their hopeless hearses
blot the perpetual festival ~ day?
Ravens, for prosperously-boded cursss
Returning thanks, might offer such ar-
ray. [away
Heaven comfort sends, but harry it
Crake the sooty plumage to time's wrong
the dead
~ the poor corse impale
Impale the poor corse with the old
and
bray
far the its head an angels' covering
If so it be,
And count their rosy cross with damn'd
disastrous things.

Why if it beso, the dism
at the dismal morn
Unto his hollow'd palm
Why if it beso, for the dismal morn
Into his hollow'd palm sh. moan the

Plate 66   OET No.20a: Heaven-Haven (MS.1)
C.i.178: "Rest", the first of four titles given this poem, of which this is the earliest draft. For other MSS.
see plate 81: this MS. is repeated as Plate 81[A]. In lines 1,2 and 5a changes rectify the identation. No stop ends
4 or 8b.

OET No.21: "I must hunt down the prize" (sole MS.)
178.5a "Must" and "I Must" both mended to "Must" (with corrected indentation).   179.5b "I" mended to "green",
"long" del., replaced by "sees" (sic.).   Between pp.180 and 183 a leaf was cut out (by GMH?).   Note cont. opposite.

PLATE 67. C.i. pp 184,187,188,189 • *117*

C.i. 184		
OET NO.	3	blast; [still born:
23 cont.	4	And in grey bands & sun shd . lie
N.28		And straight showers parallel shd.
	5	follow fast; [cast
	6	And, swayter still, O rolling pines shd. their heads together in a stormy blot.

(Not shown in J.)

	C.i. 187
	(Not shown in J.)

J.34	C.i. 188

John Price.
Caeswern.
Carnarvon.

	5	κοτύλη.	χοῖνιξ.	ἑκτεύς.	μέδιμνος
		4	1		
		32	8	1	
		192	48	6	1

	10	μέδιμνος = 12 gallons = 6 modii.
		Modius = 2 gallons.
		ἑκτεύς = modius = 2 gallons.
		χοῖνιξ = a quart.
	15	κοτύλη = half a pint.

μύστρον.	κόγχη.	κοτύλη.
2	1	
4	2	1
½ gill.	1 gill.	½ pint.

κοχλιάριον (spoon) μύστρον or μύστ-ριον (spoon)

| | C.i. 189 | (Not in J.) |

[opposite] OET No.22: "Why should their foolish bands" (sole MS.)
183.7a (del.) "Impale the poor corse with them, set and [abbrev.]" (?) del. rev. to end "with it and fray". An erased drawing (of trees or perhaps funeral plumes) occupied the lower half of 183.
OET. No.23: "Why if it be so" (sole MS.)
183.1a "the dismallest" (del.)   1b "at that dismal morn"   2b "Unto" mended to "Into".

Plate 67—The pagination jumps from 184 to 187, though no leaf may be missing. 188.4 "Merio[neth]" del.   5 "4" del.

The upper-left notebook leaf is labelled in the margins: J.34 / C.i. 190 / OET No. 30c – J.34 / OET No. 24 – N.28, with handwritten verse. The upper-right leaf is labelled C.i. 191 / (J.456 Fig 27) / Aug. 14 1864 – J.34, with a sketch.

Caption beneath sketch: *Gerard Hopkins, reflected in a lake. Aug. 14.*

The lower-left leaf is labelled C.i. 192 / OET No. 25 – J.35 / OET No. 30d – J.35. The lower-right leaf is labelled C.i. 193 / OET No. 30e – J.35 / OET No.12 (cont. from C.i. 161) (Not published) – Soliloquy – N.23 (cont. 203), with marginal line numbers.

Plate 68: OET No.30c: "Or else their cooings" (sole MS.)   No.30 contains fragments composed July-Sept.1864.
190.3 orig. "waters".

OET No.24: "It was a hard thing to undo this knot"   C.i.190--sole MS. The top half of the leaf 191-92 was
cut out because of the sketch showing GMH reflected in a lake. It was restored to Campion Hall through
Fr. Bischoff's exertions.

OET No.25: "Glimmer'd along the square-cut steep" (sole MS.)   192.1 "steep" first e dotted in error?   192.3a
"You saw" del. 3b "The" mended to "Their"; abbrev. for "of" rev. to one for "and"   10 (impaired by the cutting
of the leaf): "Which with its lined and creased flank"   13 "Like" rev. to "As"..."embers" del.

OET No.30d: "Late I fell in the ecstacy"   192. Space left after this fragment for its continuation.   192.1
comma del. after "Late".

C.i.193   OET No.30e: "Think of an opening page"   2 "With thready azure" (misread till Jan.1989 as "With
the ready")   "with" and "streak" del.   3 orig. "diaper'd" (apostrophe del.)   4 orig. "and not with"

PLATE 69. C.i. pp 194,195,196,197 • *119*

C.i. 194

C.i. 195
1
2
3
4 a
4 b
OET No. 26 – N.28

C.i. 196
OET No. 27 – Miss Story's character
3 a
4 a
5 a
6 a
7 a
8 a
9 a
10 a
11 a
12 a
13 a

C.i. 197
OET No. 27 cont.
14 a
15 a
16 a
17 a
18 a
24 a
23 a
25 a
26 a
31 a
32 a (cont. bot. 198)
Miss Story's character

OET No.12: [Soliloquy of One of the Spies] (cont. from plate 61) 4th and 5th revs. of st.2 (last line top C.i.203). In 11a "the" should also have been del. before "wells of Elim"

Plate 69: C.i.195—OET No.26: "Of virtues I most warmly bless" (sole MS.).   1 orig. "The virtue"   2 orig. "seen, unselfishness"--the heavy V, (perhaps accentuated by the jolting van) deletes n and a comma.   3 orig. "My favourite vice I think is pride."   OET No.27: "Miss Story's character"—drafts run from 196 to 202. First draft (pp.196-97) has only 22 lines, omitting drafts of 1,2,19 to 22, 27 to 30. C.i.196 is made difficult to read by the inked sketch of window tracery showing through from p.195.   11a,12a "And hide it as she [will del.] does one can divine/She nourishes a [strong del.] great desire to shine."   13a "capable" del. 15a "women" del. 18a "And loves—a fatal fault—to patronize."   24a "scarcely can" del. rev. to "wise will"   26a "rather" del.   32a "But single lead a misdirected life."

J.35	C.i. 198	

198

Miss Louisa May
Sidmouth House
Reading

OET No 28	1	Her prime of life — cut down too soon
	2	By death — as th' morning flower at noon: [love:
	3	Her loving husband lives to dep.
	4	Yet hopes she'll flourish evermore.

Jane Green.
Wife of Jonathan Green, of this
Parish, Baker.

20th 1848.

Aged 52 yrs.,

| No. 27 Cont. from p.197 | 27a | Her character she does not real |

iʒe

~cannot see at all in'd others' eyes

Has wit enough but less than female

ca ct.   [act.

Sees bright thing to do — does not

too sensitive.   [sive.

Talks of self-sacrifice, yet can't bor-
Train or. farm to
Crawdon.

Is fond of flattery, as any she,
But has not learnt to take it gracefully.

Miss Story's character.
too much you
task!

When 'tis the confidante that sets to task.
How dare I paint Miss Story to Miss May.
And what she.
what if my subject seeing this is resent
What were she.
No: shewn to her it cannot but

	C.i. 199	
28a	OET No. 27 Cont.	
19a		
20a		
21a		
22a		Miss Story's character
15b		
16b		
1a		
1c b		
2a		
3b		
4b		
5b		
6b		
7b		

	C.i. 200	
OET No. 27 cont.	8b	But candour never hurt o dearest friend.
	1d	Miss Story's character: too much You ask, [the task.
	2b	When 'tis the confidante that sets
	3c	How dare I paint Miss Story to Miss Story May?
	4c	And what if she my confidence betray! [sent
Miss Story's character	5c	what if my subject, seeing this, is
	6c	What were worth nothing if all complement? [fend;
	7c	No: shewn to her it cannot but of,
	8c	But candour never hurt the dear est friend. [I will,
	9b	Miss story has a moderate power
	10b	But, that believes it greater still
	11b	And hide at she does, one may divine

She only nourishes a wish to shine,
Is very capable of strong affection
tho' apt to throw it in a strange di-
~rection;
Is fond of flattery, as any she,
But has not learnt to take it grace-
bully; [despise,
things that she likes seems often to
And loves — a fatal fault — to patron-
ize;   [tact,
Has wit enough, but less than female
Sees the right thing to do and does
not act;
About herself she is most sensitive,
Talks of self-sacrifice, yet can't
forgive;
She's framed to triumph in adversity,
Prudence she has, but wise she'll
never be;
Her character she does not realise,
And cannot see at all with others' eyes.

	C.i. 201	
12b	OET No. 27 cont.	
13b		
14b		
15c		
16c		
17b		
18b		Miss Story's character
19b		
20b		
21b		
22b		
23b		
24b		
27b		
28b		

PLATE 71. C.i. pp 202,203 • *121*

Plate 70: C.i.198 Miss May's address and (no doubt) handwriting.   OET No.28: "Her prime of life"--quite possibly an epitaph invented by GMH, rather than one he simply copied (cf. J.317).

OET No.27: "Miss Story's character" cont. 199.1a "Invidious task" rev. to "Too dangerous task!" then "Too much you ask!" [GMH's pagination ends here, mine begins.] C.i.200, line 3c "Story" del.   10b orig. reading obscure   11b orig. "hide as as" rev. to "hide it though"   201.13b "ca[pable]" mended to "very"   14b "r" in "dir-" del. before hyphen.   19b "tact," dash is from p.202   In 20b the X below sees refers to rev. of 19,20 on p.202.

24b "X" below "Prudence" seems to mark the place for insertion of 25b, 26b (p.202; cf. p.197) which are in otherwise inexplicable parentheses.

Plate 71:   OET No.27: "Miss Story's character" concl. C.i.202   25b is smudged: "(And well supplied...Whole," [u.c. must surely be a slip].   The parentheses round 25b and 26b indicate the need to reposition them.   20c "often" del.   Lowest third of p.202 and all p.203 is ink on pencil, usually confirming the pencil text where visible.   [Another leaf is missing after p.202, perhaps with the "bad verse" mentioned in No.29: I have ignored this in my pagination.]

OET No.29: "Did Helen steal my love from me?" The ink ignores the pencilled line 3b: "Or was it Jane? She is too plain,"; but "A bad verse in the middle, then" occurs only in ink.

OET No.31(c): Floris in Italy. Drafts of this play, begun in narrative stanzas now lost, are scattered in disorder, mainly through the last 18pp. of C.i and the first 13pp. of C.ii, with others in C.ii.24-25, 95-7.   Further surviving poems and fragments may have been meant for it.

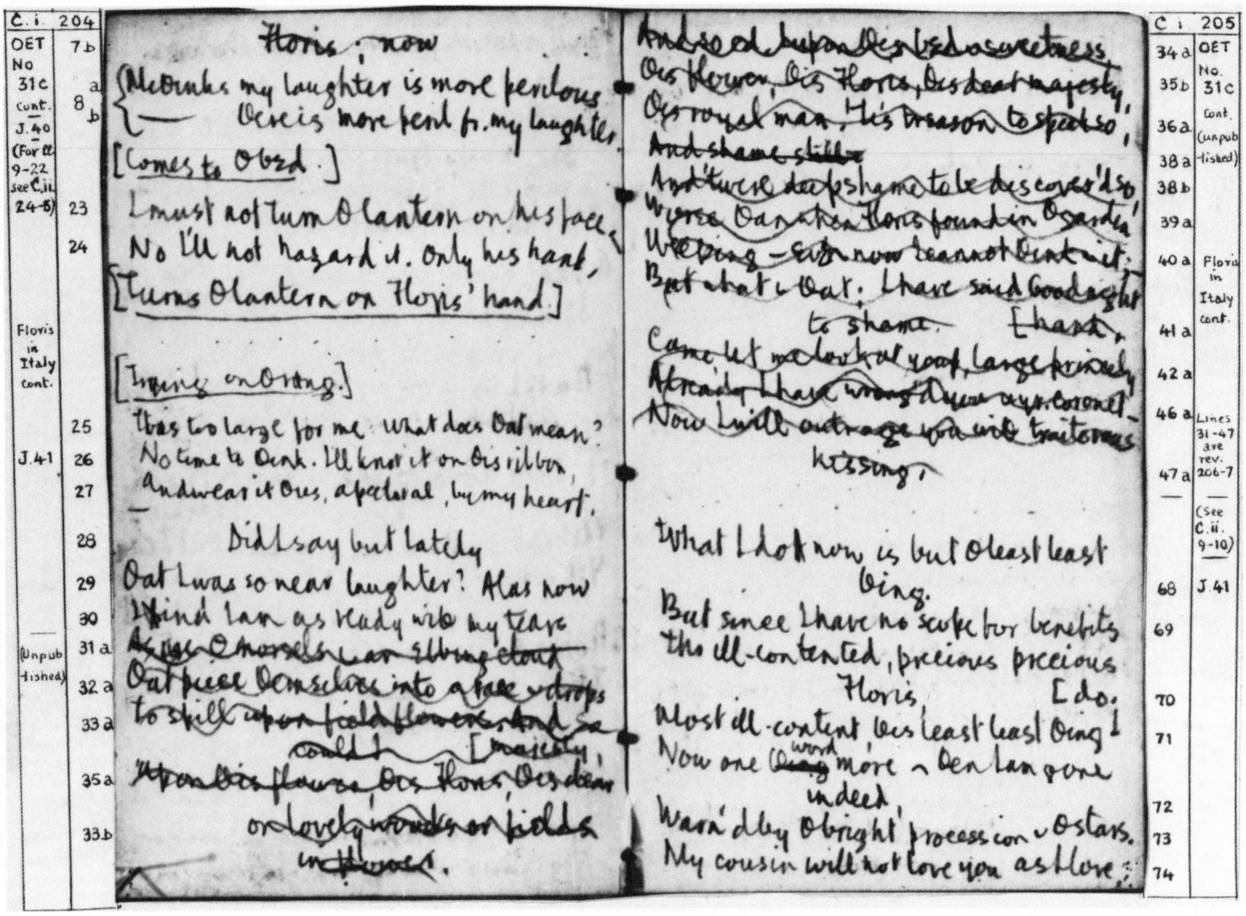

C.i	204	
OET No 31c cont. J.40 (For ll 9-22 see C.ii 24-5)	7b / a / 8 / b	

Floris, now
{ Methinks my laughter is more perilous
[— Yours is more perilous than my laughter

[Comes to Obed.]

23 I must not turn O lantern on his face
24 No I'll not hazard it. Only his hand,
[Turns O lantern on Floris' hand.]

[Trying on O ring.]

25 'tis too large for me. what does O'at mean?
26 No time to think. I'll knot it on O'is ribbon,
27 And wear it O'es, a pectoral, by my heart.

28   Did I say but lately
29 O'at I was so near laughter? Alas now
30 I find I am as ready with my tears
31a ~~As are O morsels... an ebbing cloud~~
32a O'at piece O'emselves into a face o'drops
33a to still upon field flowers, and
    could [majesty]
35a ~~Upon O'is flower O'is Floris O'is dear~~
33b on lovely woods or fields
    in flower.

34a And so cd. I upon O'is bed o'sweetness
35b O'is flower, O'is Floris, O'is dear majesty,
36a O'is royal man, 'tis treason to speak so,
38a And shame still
38b And these deep shame to be discover'd so
39a ~~Or else O'at... Floris found in O garden~~
40a Weeping — ev'n now I cannot find it.
41a But what o'at. I have said goodnight
    to shame. I have
42a Come let me look at your large princely,
46a Already I have wrong'd O'ese your coronet
47a Now I will outrage you with traitorous
    kissing.

68 What I look now is but O least least
    O'ing.
69 But since I have no scope for benefits
70 O'is ill-contented, precious precious
    Floris,   [I do.
71 Most ill-content O'is least least O'ing I
72 Now one word more ~ O'en I am gone
    indeed.
73 Warn'd by O bright procession ~ O stars.
74 My cousin will not love you as I love;

C.i	205	
34a	35b	36a
38a	38b	39a
40a	41a	42a
46a	47a	68 69 70 71 72 73 74

OET No 31c cont (unpublished) — Floris in Italy cont. — Lines 31-47 are rev. 206-7 (See C.ii 9-10) — J 41

Plate 72: OET No.31c: Floris in Italy cont.
C.i.204 (before 25) "Trying" mended from "Trie[s?]"   25 "Wa[s?]" mended to "It is"   30 "find" del. of _f_ an error.   31a to 47a all del., replaced on pp.206-07.   31a orig. "As is" mended to "As are the morsels of an ebbing cloud"   33b ["To spill] on lovely woods or fields in flower."
    C.i.205—34a "And so cd. I upon this bed of sweetness,"   39a "me" is needed after "found" for sense and rhythm (as in 206.39b).   40a "ev'n" mended to "even"   42a "your" rev. to "you,"   After ll .31-48 (as rev. pp.206-07) in the OET I insert "I am like a slip of comet" from C.ii.9-10, which seems to fit the lacuna perfectly (Giulia's missing speech, promised in line 48)--see Plates 84-85.

PLATE 73. C.i. pp 206,207 • *123*

C.i. 206		
OET No. 31c Cont.	75	Floris; she will *not* ~~love~~ *by* sum ~~wood~~
J.41	76	Our jacinD; nor have shall v all by virtues,
	77	Floris, Our late-found All - heal;
Floris in Italy cont.		
	31 b	As ~~are~~ O fine morssels v dwindling cloud
	32 b	Out piece Oer selves into a race v drops
	33 b	To spill o'er fields v lilies. So ed. I
	34	So waste in tears over Ois bed v sweetness
	35 c	Ois flower, Ois Floris, Ois dear majesty,
	36 b	Ois royal manhood, - 'tis in me rebellion
	37	to speak so, yet I'll speak it for Ois once
	38 c	Deep shame it were to be discover'd so
	39 b	Worse. Oan when Floris found me in O garden
	40 b	Weeping, - evm now I curse my self remem.
		wrong; - [shame.
	41 b	No, let Oat go; I have said Good-night to
	42 b	Now let me see you, you large princely
		hand
	43	Since ~~on~~ O face it is unsafe to look:
	44	Yet O is ed. be no other's hand Oan his,
	45 a	'tis so conceived in his lineament.

		C.i. 207
[Or 'tis so conceived in his true lineament.]	45 b	OET No. 31c
I have wrong'd it v its coronet, - now	46 b	J.41
I outrage it wrD treasonable kissing.	47 b	(Floris Cont. P 216)
Ah Floris, Floris, let me speak Ois little	48 (see Pl 84)	
. . .		OET No. 30f J.36
- O shallow folds v O wood	1	
We found were ~~dabbled~~ dabbled wiD a colouring		
snow, [roses.	2	
In lakes v bluebells, pieced wiD O prim	3	
		OET No 30g J.36
In O green spots v Oat wood	1	
Were eyes v central primrose: blue.		
bells ran	2	
In shrins about O brakes.	3	
		OET No. 30h
Like shuttles fleet O clouds, v after	1 a	
A drop v shade sweeps instan rock	2 a	
the wind comes here v there v laughs	3 a	
on;		
O violet moves v copses rock	4 a	
Likes shuttles fleet O clouds, v after	1 b	J.36
A drop v shade rolls over field v block.	2 b	

Plate 73: OET No.31c: "Floris in Italy" (cont.)
     C.i.206--31b "are" del. 37,38c Note "so" written like "eo"   38c "do" mended to "to"   40b "ev'n" (l.c.
prob. intended after comma) mended to "even"   43 "at" mended to "on"
     C.i.207--47b "It" rev. to "I".   The fragments which follow seem unconnected with "Floris", until p.216.
     OET No.30f. 2 "dabbled"--orig. reading obscure--"dainty"??
     OET No.30h. 4a orig. "moves, and the"   1b "Likes" slip for "Like" 2b "th" del. after "drop" (wrong
abbreviated form used—theta for "of" sign).

C.i. 208				C.i 209	
OET No. 30h (cont.)	3b 4b	O wind comes, here ~ here ~ there with laughter; / O violet moves ~ copses rock.	On a dunce who had not a word to / say for himself.	OET No. 32b J.37	
	5	When O wind drops you hear O skylarks / sing;	He's all that's bad, I know; a knave after that, / Book ~ or ~ at least he has not come to that.		1 2a
	6 7	At Oxford comes O throng ~ hum o bells / Breathing O . . . . air o spring.	But his effrontery's not come to that. / By Mrs. Hopley.		2b
J.36	5 10	In Slavonic bugti ~ terreo. Cf. Bug-bear / boggle (Norse country name for ghost), / bogy, bug. Liddell ~ Scott connect Gr. / φεύγω, φυγεῖν with Sanskr. bhaj, bhujāmi / (flects); Goth. biuga (biege); Slav. bega / (fugio), bugti (terreo); Lat. fugis. they / might have added our budge which is al- / most identical in sound with O Sansk. / bhuj, i.e. bhuj. And perhaps goblin / is for boglin but o this I have no certain- / ty.	He's wedded to his Deary, they say. / If that were true, it cd not live a day. / And did he on O children ~ his brains / Bestow but half O . . . . pains / the children ~ his loins receive in- / stead [head. / there wd not be a whole place in his / Or And did O children ~ his brains enjoy / But half O pains he spends upon his bry. / You may depend on't are a week wasted, / there etc.	OET No. 32c J.37 By Mrs Hopley	1 2 3a 4a 5a 6a 3b 4b 5b 6b
OET No. 32a (rev. bot. 210)	1a 2a	Why can't Clarissa hold her tongue? / She fears to get her fingers stung.	On seeing her children say Goodnight / to their father. / Bid your Papa Goodnight! sweet exhi- / bition!		7

C.i. 210				C.i. 211	
	8	they kiss O rod with filial submission.	Houpel's flattering account o his / crimes	J.37	
OET No. 32d N.29	1 2a 2b	Modern Poets. / Our swans are now o such remorse- / less quill, [kill. / They ~ / themselves live singing ~ their hearers	A candied confession. / He thinks O pretty chatterings / lovers shd. be called Jargonelle / Pairs, they are so sweet in O mouth.		5
OET No. 32e J.37	1 2	By one of O old school who was / bid to follow Mr. Browning's flights / To rise you bid me and O lark / with me 'tis rising in O dark.	On one who borrowed his sermons. / He thinks preaching I'll no longer / hear: [O year. / they're out o date ~ lent sermons all	OET No. 32g N.29	1 2
OET No. 32f N.29	1 2 3 4	On a poetess. / Miss M.'s a nightingale. 'tis well / Your simile I keep. / It is O way with Philomel / to sing while others sleep.	Fast days I have & slow days; you / do not know how long short com- / mons will last	J.37	7
OET No. 32a (rev. from bot. 208)	1b 2b	You ask why can't Clarissa hold her / tongue [stung. / Because she fears / her fingers will be	Reflection o stars in water. ~ Pointed / golden drops. Gold tails. / Church times. / There is a proverb that a watched / pot never boils. / Necktie.	J.38	10 15
N.29					

Plate 74: prose line 7 "with" slip for "which"
    OET No.32: [Epigrams]
    C.i.208: OET No.32a. 1a "can't" above "Wh[y]" del.
    OET No.32b--C.i.209, line 1 orig. "I know. A fool,"
    OET No. 32c. 1 "his" orig. "a" (?)   2 orig. "If this...it wd." rev. "If that...it cd. [could] not live"
5 a "receive"   6a "were" (?) mended to "wd."   5b "before" del.   The whole first draft is crossed out,
but only 3-5 are revised.   Note cont. on opposite page.

PLATE 75. C.i. pp 212,213,214,215 • *125*

C.i. 212

Epitaph on O last ~ many husbands
buried by one enduring wife.
　　Numbered wt O dead.

The poetical language lowest. to use
Oat, wh. poetasters, ~ indeed almost
everyone can do, is no more necessan-
ly to be uttering poetry than striking
O keys upiano is playing a tune but-
ly, when O tune is played it is on O
keys. So when poetry is utteredit is
in Ois language. Next, Parnassian. Can only be used by real poets.
Can be written without inspiration
Good instance in Enoch Arden's island. Common in professedly descriptive pieces. Much v it in Paradise
Lost ~ Regained. Nearly all O Fairy
Queen. It is O effect v fine age to ena-
the ordinary people to write something
very near it. — Third ~ highest, poetry proper, language v inspiration.
Explain inspiration. On first reading a strange poet his merest Parnassian seems inspired. Ois is because
Oen first we perceive genius. But when

C.i. 213

we have read him ~ ... are accustomed
genius we shall see distinctly O ins-
pirations ~ much Oat wd have struck
us wt great pleasure at first loses
much v its charm ~ becomes Parnassian. ~ Castalian, highest sort v Parnassian. E. g "Yet despair touches me
not, Go pensive as a bird whose ver-
nal coverts winter haO laid bare." Or
"Oh roses for O flush v yout Etc." Real Parnassian only written by poets
~ as is impossible for oOers as poetry,
As practically it is as hard to reach
O moor as Ostars but some Oing very
like it may be. Much Parnassian
takes down a poet's reputation, lowers
his average, as it were, Pope ~ all
artificial schools great writers v
Parnassian, Ois is O real meaning
van artificial poet. — O poetical language may be called language v Osa-
cred Plain, Delphic Oervis seemingly
much Parnassian music. Same Oing
no doubt exists in painting.

Io.
Forwardshe leans wt hollowing back, stock-still.

C.i. 214 — OET No. 33 (Io)

Her white weed-bathed knees are Ok shut together,
Her silky coat is sheeny, like a hill
Gem-fleeced at morn, so brilliant is O weather.
Her nostril glistens; fm O dazzling sky
　　~ her wt black eye
She kils half-meshing b. O too-bright
Her lids half-meshing shelter b. O sky.

Her finger-long new horns are capp'd wit black;
O shadow clings in hollows v her form;
Her milk 3white Ooat ~ folded dewlap slack
Are still; her neck is creased in closs-ply rings;
Her hue's a various brown wit creamy lakes
Like a cupp'd chestnut damask'd in O dark
　　breaks,

Thick-fleeced
Out-fleeced　bushes like O... ear.
　　　　spaniels

New trees, like ears, in hedges.

Oeres an island, wester'd in O main,
Around it balances O level sea.
Winds housing in trees.

O time was late ~ O wet yellow woods
Told off Oeir leaves along O piercing gale,
Stars
　float fr. O border v O main

C.i. 215

Olympian. E. g. Blessed Damozel, Mil-
man.

Backward are laid her pretty black-fleeced
　　ears;
The knot of feOery locks upon O her head
　　— feOery knot —
Plays to O breeze; where now are fled her
　　fears?
Her sailor wit O his vigil-organ dead?
Day brings not back his basilisk king'star,
Nor night beholds a single flame-ring
　　　one flame-ring left to
　　　flare.

Night is not blown wit flame-ring every...
Nor day new-basilisks his tireless star...
Or
Morn does not now new-basilisk his star
Nor night is blown wit flame-rings every-
　　where.

　　　　... in her cheeks Oat dwell
Centred like meteors, bright like pimpernel.

C.i.210. OET No.32e title orig. "follows" 1 "Lark"(u.c.) OET No.32f. 3 orig. "'Tis" OET No.32a (rev). 2b orig. "fears that it w[d]"

　　C.i.211. 5 "lovers" orig. prob. "Woers" (intended for "Floris in Italy"?)

Plate 75.　　OET No.33: Io
C.i.214: 2 "Io" del.　5a "from the dazzling sky" del.　6a "Her lids" del.　6b "dazzl." del.　8 the numbers "1" and "2" below the lines enclosing the two halves indicate that they are to be transposed
　　C.i.215. 14a "the" del.　14b in error the sign for "and" (not "of") follows "knot"　15 final query del.　16 "the" del., rev. to "his"

OET No. 30m – J.39	C.i. 216		C.i. 217

A brittle sheen, runs upward like a cliff,
Flying a bow.

Gatherd pansies. etc. Favours.

Orainbright.

See on one hand

He drops its bright roots in ounter'd sand,
– rosing part, on part dispenses green;
but wiô his oôer boot ôsee miles beyond;
He rises br.ô flocks – villages
ôat bead ô plain;
did Ever Havering church.
– tower

Breaôe in such sôes? or ô Quickly elms
Wiô such a violet slight ôeir distanced green
Slight wiô such violet ôeir bright-mask'd
green?
or such
Mask'd wiô violet disallow ôeir green?

Wiô what ôold grace
ôis sweet Deserter lists herself anew

E.S.R. po. Jan. 6. – 11. – 14 or 15,
or 15 or 16, for I cannot recollect
exactly, but I remember being
doubtful at ô time whether
noste
Et diei quo maculas
notavi praecedente an priori
accidisset. Sed priore potius
accidisse id arbitror. And now
I think it must have been on 14
or 15 not 15 or 16, and therefore
probably 14. Aegrotabam eo tempore
et quod vix anquam mihi prius
acciderat, ignoranti accidit.
Itaque ignorabam nocte post
17, aegrotans. – Again about
19 or 20 or 21. – Feb. 19 or 20,
19 prob. – March 1. – 19 – 29. – April
2. Aegrotabam iis diebus. – Circa
18? – Oneoccasion prob. occur

Floris in Italy cont.	C.i. 218		C.i. 219

red taler in ô mon ô. – Early in
May. – July 7. – July 20. Pache
ignorabam. – July 29 Aegrotabam.
Aug. 22. Ignorabam. – Sept. 26 ig-
norabam. Versor ne b's acciderit. – Oct. 1
October 12. – Oct. two days running some
these about 16 or 18 or so. – Nov. 29 –
Giulia writing. Tool jumps up ~ seats
himself in window.
T. Madam.
G. You startled me.
T. Madam, what are you doing?
G. Tool, writing a letter.
T. I thought it was your will. I approve
your care; but indeed it is better to have
a lawer at once. For my part I never send
a love-letter without an attorney. I wd
not bid any one to dinner without taking
legal opinion.
G. This is not a love-letter nor an invita-
tion. It is to my cousin. Hear make nothing of it. Dictate me now, Tool.
T. Truth or untruth?
G. Truth.

Irking – tanking in our ruder files
Enroll'd –
– marching false colours! ôose few
strokes

ôat forge her title – inheritance
to manhood, on ô upper lip, – ôey look'd
Most like ô tuft of plighted silver round
plighted tuft
silver plighted tuft about
ô moulded centre – a violet.

Sept. 7, Saw a violet, near Caterham June-
tion station on ô down, in a brake.
This – Autumn crocus melancholy.

– Yes for a time ôey held as well
togeôer, as ô criss-cross'd shelly cup
Sucks close ô acorn; as ô hand ~ glove;
As water moulded to ô duct it runs in;
As heel looks close to heel so –
Let me now
Now, you mean
stroke – ungluess't your mortiess metaphors
ô hand draws off ô glove; ô acorn – cup

PLATE 77. C.i. pp 220,221 • *127*

C.i. 220 | OET No. 31d concl. - J.40 | 8c 9 10

Drops of fruit out; & duct runs dry or breaks.
& stranded keel - kelson warps apart;
And your two sie.

OET No 31b (cont. from p.218) - J.42

7. And will you set down whatever I read to you?
G. Why, truth they say, is not expedient to speak at all times
7. Do you defend lying, Madam?
G. You know what I mean. It is better to conceal at times.
7. There are some ladies who conceal all things at all times. Crystal sincerity had found no shelter but in a fool's cap; I have long found it so. It loves the innocent tinkle of the bells, and only speaks by amounts & men & my profession. But to settle whether when it is set down you will read it or no, you shall decide. If you do not read it, I shall despair of your judgment but it shall be as you will. Now will you promise to set down what I read you?
G. If it be truth.

Floris in Italy cont.

(lines 20, 25, 30, 35)

C.i 221 | OET No 31b - J.42

7. You must forfeit a gold piece, if you refuse.
G. Very well, I will forfeit a gold piece.
7. Lay it down on the table.
G. Can you not trust me?
7. No, Madam, not a woman; least of all in matters of money.
G. Then you shall not have it at all.
7. I said so. Madam, you stand convicted. You must even pack with your sex.
G. Then there it is (laying it down.)
7. A hostage. Now, truth, you say?
G. Why wd. you have me write lies?
7. Madam, if you follow me, I will take care it be nothing but truth. If at any place you refuse to write you forfeit. Is it agreed?
G. As long as you keep to truth, it is
7. Thus then. Cousin, —
G. Why what a boorish opening is that!
... a peremptory salutation do you...

Floris in Italy cont. — J.43

(lines 40, 45, 50, 55)

End of C.i | Cont. C.ii p.1

[opposite page] Plate 76.   C.i.216: OET No.34. Title orig. "The rainbows", plural del.   2 "It" mended to "He" but "its" not rev. to "his".   6a "never" separately del. and trans. to after "Havering church-tower"   In 8c "Slight" is written on top of a little division line marking the end of a piece; "masked" rev. to "mask'd"
OET No.31, Floris in Italy. Further snatches of the play occur, No.31f at bot. of 216 (in 1 "a" rev. to "bold grace"), cont. p.219 (ℓ.5 after "title" the sign for "and" is prob. slip for "of").
    Private Notes C.i.217 to 218 ℓ.7, then cont. Plate 151. For GMH's scrupulous fears that wet dreams, which began about this time, were sinful, see Introd.   See esp. "Medical Commentary"   ; also Plates 103, left, ℓ.18; 143, ℓ.19.
    C.i.217, ℓ.1 "E.s.n.po. Jan.6" (cf. ℓ.14, "nocte post 17"), perhaps "Emissio seminis nocte post Jan.6 [1864]," a wet dream on the night following Jan.6.   ℓℓ .3-8 "being doubtful...whether it happened on the night preceding the day when I noticed the stains, or earlier; but I consider it happened earlier."   ℓ.11 "I was unwell at that time, and since it had scarcely ever happened to me before, it happened to me unawares. In like manner I was unaware on the night after the 17, when I was unwell." ℓ.18 "I was unwell on those days."
    C.i.218 ℓℓ2,3 "July 20. I was more or less unaware.—July 29. I was unwell.—Aug.22. I was unaware.—Sept.26. I was unaware. I'm afraid it happened twice."
    C.i.218: OET No.31b--Floris in Italy: Giulia writing. Cont. p.220.
    C.i.219 (bot. third of page): OET No.31d--Floris in Italy: "Yes for a time".... ℓ.1 "tog[ether]" del. 5a "Now, you mean,--" del.   6a "Let me unwind, unglue" del.   8a "Lets the fruit drops" (sic) rev. to 8b "Drops out the fruit" both del.

[above] Plate 77—C.i.220. OET No.31b (cont.): Floris in Italy.   19 "to" mended from "a[t?]"   33 "ill" del.
C.i.221—Line 46 It is sometimes hard to distinguish GMH's final "n" and "r": here I read "even", not "ever" [cf "con-" in line above; "can" (218.12);   "moon" (213.14), "only"/"written" (212.12,13)] 50 "I" mended to "you"
    58,59 "Why" separately deleted "What a martial opening/assault/salutation/and peremptory salutation do you" all del.   The scene is continued in the second Early Note-book, C.ii.1 (Plate 82).
                THIS IS THE END OF EARLY NOTE-BOOK C.i.

H.i.
21r

OET No. 17

Barnfloor and Winepress.

"And he said, if the LORD do not help thee, whence shall I help thee? Out of the barnfloor, or out of the Winepress?"

2 Kings vii. 27.

1 Thou that on sin's wages starvest
2 Behold we have the joy in Harvest:
3 For us was gathered the first-fruits
4 For us was lifted from the roots,
5 Sheaved in cruel bands, bruised sore,
6 Scourged upon the threshing-floor;
7 Where the upper mill-stone roof'd His Head,
8 At morn we found the Heavenly Bread,
9 And on a thousand Altars laid,
10 Christ our Sacrifice is made.

11 Thou whose dry plot for moisture gapes,
12 We shout with them that tread the grapes:
13 For us the Vine was fenced with thorn,
14 Five ways the precious branches torn;
15 Terrible fruit was on the tree
16 In the acre of Gethsemane;
17 For us by Calvary's distress
18 The wine was racked from the press;
19 Now in our Altar vessels stand
20 Is the sweet Vintage of our LORD.

H.i.
22r

21 In Joseph's garden they threw by
22 The riv'n Vine, leafless, lifeless, dry:
23 On Easter morn the Tree was forth,
24 In forty days reach'd Heaven from earth,
25 Soon the whole world is overspread;
26 Ye weary come into the shade.

27 The field where He has planted us
28 Shall shake his boughs as Libanus,
29 When He has sheaved us in His Sheaf,
30 When He has made us bear His leaf.—
31 We scarcely call that Banquet food,
32 But even our Saviour's and our blood,
33 We are so grafted on His Wood.

G. M. H. 1865.

Union Review, iii

P. 579
Sept./Oct 1865

1
2
3
4
5
6
7
8
9
10
11
12
13
14

P. 580

15
16
17
18
19
20

21
22
23
24
25
26

27
28
29
30
31
32
33

OET No. 17

BARNFLOOR AND WINEPRESS.

And he said, if the Lord do not help thee, whence shall I help thee? out of the barnfloor, or out of the winepress?—2 Kings vii. 27.

Thou that on sin's wages starvest,
Behold we have the joy in harvest:
For us was gather'd the first fruits,
For us was lifted from the roots,
Sheaved in cruel bands, bruised sore,
Scourged upon the thrashing floor;
Where the upper mill-stone roof'd this head
At morn we found the heavenly Bread,
And, on a thousand altars laid,
Christ our Sacrifice is made!

Thou whose dry plot for moisture gapes,
We shout with them that tread the grapes:
For us the Vine was pierced with thorn,
Five ways the precious branches torn;

580   *Original Poetry.*

Terrible fruit was on the tree
In the acre of Gethsemane;
For us by Calvary's distress
The wine was rackèd from the press;
Now in our altar-vessels stored
Is the sweet Vintage of our Lord.

In Joseph's garden they threw by
The riv'n Vine, leafless, lifeless, dry:
On Easter morn the Tree was forth,
In forty days reach'd heaven from earth;
Soon the whole world is overspread;
Ye weary, come into the shade.

The field where He has planted us
Shall shake her fruit as Libanus,
When He has sheaved us in His sheaf,
When He has made us bear His leaf.—
We scarcely call that banquet food,
But even our Saviour's and our blood,
We are so grafted on His wood.

G. M. H.

Plate 78. No.17 Barnfloor and Winepress— (MS.2) [For MS.1 (July 1864) see Plates 63-4, repeated Pl. 80ᴬ.] H.i.21r,22r. Transcript in an unknown hand of a missing revised autograph; dated "G.M.H. 1865". The writer's small "w" (e.g., in the epigraph, and 25) is sometimes hard to distinguish from the capital "W" (7,12,30,31, end of 33).

- - - - - - - - - - - -

Union Review: A Magazine of [Anglo-] Catholic Literature and Art, London, vol.iii, pp.579-80, Sept./Oct.1865. The editor is believed to have quietly "corrected" contributors' punctuation, capital letters and even words; but misreading the autograph probably accounts for 7 "this head", and perhaps 13 "pierced with thorn".

PLATE 79. OET 17. *Barnfloor and Winepress* • 129

Barnfloor and Winepress.

If the Lord do not help thee, whence shall I help thee? or barn-floor, or out of the wine-press? II Kings. vi.27.

Thou, who on sin's wages starvest,
Behold we have the joy of harvest:
For us was gathered the firstfruits,
For us was lifted from the roots,
Sheared in cruel bands, bruised sore,
Scourged upon the threshing-floor.
Where the upper mill-stone roofed His Head,
At morn we found the Heavenly Bread,
And, on a thousand altars laid,
CHRIST our Sacrifice is made.

Thou, whose dry plot for moisture gapes,
We shout with them that tread the grapes:
For us the Vine was fenced with thorn,
Five ways the precious branches torn;
Terrible fruit was on the tree
In the acre of Gethsemane:
For us by Calvary's distress
The wine was racked from the press;
Now in our altar-vessels stored,
Lo the sweet Vintage of the Lord.

In Joseph's garden they threw by
The riven Vine, leafless, lifeless, dry:
On Easter morn the Tree was forth,
In forty days reached Heaven from earth,
Soon the whole world is overspread;
Ye weary, come into the Shade.

The field where He hath planted
Shall shake her fruit as Libanus.

When He has sheared us in His sheaf,
When He has made us bear His leaf.
— We scarcely call that banquet food,
But even our Saviour's and our blood,
We are so grafted on His wood.

— GMH. 1865 this date &
collation of a copy in family.

Plate 79 No.17 cont.—Barnfloor and Winepress (MS.3). MS.A.pp.144-6. These form part of two leaves guarded into album A, containing transcripts of three Hopkins poems by V.S.S. Coles. Above No.17 comes "The Convent" (version of "Heaven-Haven", No.20—see plate 81, right top) and after it "New Readings," No.18. The autograph of No.17 copied here is missing. A few words on pp.144,145 have been cropped off or lost in the hinge. The epigraph reads "...shall I help thee? out of the barn-floor,...". The ends of obscured lines run: 11 "gapes," 12 "grapes:" 24 "earth" [punct.?] 25 "oer" mended to "overspread" [punct.?] 27 "us" [,?] 28 "Libanus" [punct.?]

Coles is an unreliable guide to capitalisation in the missing autograph: in 26 he seems to intend "come into the Shade" [i.e., "come to Christ"], but in 28 "shake" has almost as large an "S", surely not meant as u.c., though far larger than initial "s" in 29-33.

Annotations in pencil by RB. His end note explains: "GMH. 1865..this date & collation [i.e. variants] of a <u>copy</u> in family" [H.i.21r,22r]. RB notes: 1 "that" (for "who") 3 "sic" after "Firstfruits,"--either because one word seemed intended, or because of the u.c.) 28 "his boughs"

A. P. 146 OET No. 18b	New Readings.
1	Although the letter said
2	On thistles that men look not grapes to gather,
3	read the story rather
4	How. soldiers plaiting thorns around CHRIST's Head
5	Grapes grew & drops of wine were shed.) *
	(* see note overleaf)
6	W Though when the sower sowed
7	'the winged fowls took part. part fell in thorn
8	And never turned to corn,
9	Part found no root upon the flinty road,—
10	CHRIST at all hazards fruit hath shewed,

A. P. 147	
11	From wastes of rock He brings
12	food for five thousand : on the thorns He shed
13	Grains from His drooping Head ;
14	And would not have that legion of winged things
15	Bear Him to Heaven on careful wings.

Written at Ball Coll: 1867 (?)

Copied S. V S S Coles

* This conceit of the grapes & thorns is not a "new reading". No doubt it must
have occurred to the allegorisers but Geo Herbert pushes it ingeniously to include the
"thorns also & thistles" of Genesis & the vine of the Psalmist

Plate 80. No.18: New Readings (MS.2)

[For MS.1, C.i.pp.170-71, on Plate 64 above, see Plate 80^A opposite (the text of No. 18a)]

A.pp.146-7 (see introductory note on plate 79): transcript by V.S.S. Coles of an autograph now missing—the text of No.18(b). In 5 Coles probably misread GMH's "sped" (the reading of C.i—see Plate 64) as "shed": the poet was unlikely to repeat the rhyme in 12. Coles' writing shows signs of haste.

RB's pencil notes at the end "Written at Ball Coll: [1868? mended to] 1867/Copied by V.S.S. Coles". An asterisk in black ink at the end of 5 refers to his footnote in ink: "This conceit of the grapes of thorns is not a 'new reading'. No doubt it must have occurred to the allegorisers but Geo Herbert pushes it ingeniously to include the 'thorns also & thistles of Genesis [3:18] & the vine of the Psalmist". RB then quotes Herbert's "The Sacrifice", 161-168 [not included in this plate].

Plate 80^A   OET No. 17: Barnfloor and Winepress--MS.1. This, the earliest draft and only autograph , is reproduced again here from Plates 63, 64, to facilitate comparison with Plates 78, 79 (transcripts of rev. versions).

C.i.168. Line 1a "Thou whom thy taskmaster Si[n]" del.   3 and 4 "are" rev. to "was"; "first" l.c. mended to u.c.   5a "For us are/was" del.; "bruis'd" mended to "bruised" (two syllables).   See oppos. for notes on C.i.169 to 171.

Barnfloor and Winepress

(facsimile of manuscript pages C.i.168–171, with handwritten draft of the poems "Barnfloor and Winepress" and "New Readings")

OET No. 17 (See Plate 63) — N.24 -25	C.i. 168		C.i.169	OET No. 17 Cont.
	1a		9	
	1b		10	
	2		11	
	3		12	
	4		13	
	5b		14 a/b	
	5a		17	
	6		18 a/b	
	7 {		15	
Cont. p.169	8		16	
			19	
			20	
			21	
			22	
			23	
			24	cont. p.170

OET No. 17 concl. (See Plate 64) — N.25- 26	C.i.170		C.i.171	OET No. 18a cont.
	25		7a	
	26 a/b		7b	
	29		8	
	30		9	
	31		10	
	32		11	
	33		12	
	27		13	
	28		14	
OET No. 18a			15	
	1			OET No. 19 — see Plates 64, 65
	2			
	3			
	4 a/b			
	5			
Cont. p.171	6 a/b			

NEW READINGS.

OET No.17: Barnfloor and Winepress, cont. from opposite

C.i.169   18a "Was wr" del.   18b "wrecked" mended to "wracked"–19 "on" mended to "in"–20,22 "vintage", "vine" l.c. mended to u.c.   23 "On" mended from "At" or "That" [?].

C.i.170   After 26b a marginal X is del., and rewritten after 30 to indicate where 27 and 28 (added at end) could be inserted.   29 "he" mended to "He"–30 "bare" mended to "bear"

C.i.170-71. OET No. 18a: New Readings--MS.1 (Plate 64, reproduced again here for comparison with Plate 80). Sole autograph.   2 "men" mended to "that" and "men" rewritten   5 "gra" mended to "fruit"   6a "Alth" del. C.i.171 7a "Some whe" del.   11 "He" mended to "Hard"   12 "him" l.c. mended to u.c. ... "on" mended to "in"

**H.i.
25v**

Fair Havens.—The Nunnery.

1 I have desired to go
        Where springs not fail,
3 To fields where flies not the unbridled
        hail,
    And a few lilies blow,

5 I have desired to be
        Where havens are dumb,
7 Where the great water-heads may never
        come
    As in the unloved sea,

**OET
No.
20a**

**Dolben
D(F)2**

Fair Havens, or The Convent.

—

1 I have desired to go
    Where springs not fail;
3 To fields where flies not the unbridled hail;
    And a few lilies blow.

—

5 I have desired to be
    Where havens are dumb;
7 Where the green waterheads may never come,
    As in the unloved Sea.

—
                                G.M.H.

**OET
No.
20a**

MS.A.p.144 OET No.20a: Heaven-Haven (here "The Convent")

1 I have desired to go
        Where springs not fail,
3 To fields where flies not the unbridled hail,
        And a few lilies blow.

5 I have desired to be
        Where havens are dumb.
7 Where the green water-heads may never come,
        As in the unloved sea.

The Convent
see p

MS.A.p.64

*HEAVEN — HAVEN
(a nun takes the veil.)*

1 I have desired to go
        Where springs not fail,
3 To fields where flies no sharp and sided hail
        And a few lilies blow.

5 And I have asked to be
        Where no storms come,
7 Where the green swell is in the havens dumb,
        And out of the swing of the sea.

**OET
No.
20b**

Plate 81. No.20: Heaven-Haven [For MS.1, C.i.178, see above, plate 66: title "Rest"; reprinted as Plate 81^A]
MS.2—H.i.25v—"Fair Havens.—The Nunnery": autograph faircopy (following "For a picture of St. Dorothea," No.42).
6 orig. "dumbs". An ink smudge runs through 8. Handwriting suggests 1865.
MS.3—A¹ (A.p.144)—"The Convent": transcript by V.S.S. Coles—see note on plate 79. The title (cut from the MS.?)
is added in a corner by RB, with an uncompleted cross-ref. to A.p.64 (A²). Grave accent intended on "unloved" (8).
MS.4—Dolben MSS. D(F)²—"Fair Havens, or The Convent" (Northants. Record Office, Delapre Abbey): transcript by
Digby Dolben (who died June 1867). 3 ends with a semi-colon.
MS.5—A² (A.p.64)—"Heaven-Haven": autograph faircopy, made c.1867-68, selecting and revising the alternative st.2
in MS.1, plate 66. This is the text of No.20(b)

OET No.	C.i 178	178			C.i. 179	OET No.
20a — N.27 — J.33	1		REST.	*179* Towards wastes where round O ice-floes tilt ~ fret	7a	21 cont. N.27
	2	I have desired to go where springs not fail;		Not so far h. O pole.	8a	
	3	to fields where flies not O sharp-brindled hail		α		
	4	~ a few lilies blow		Must see O green ~~sees~~ roll where waters set (tilt ~ fret,	5b	
	5a	I have desired to be			6b	
	6a	where havens are dumb; [Come,		towards O ose wastes where O ice-floes	7b	(see Plate 66)
	7a	where O green waterheads may never		Not so far h. O pole.	8b	
	8a	As in O unloved sea,				
	5b	by I have desired to be				
	6b	where gales not come;				
(See Plate 66)	7b	where O green swell is in the havens dead				
	8b	~ reader' d h. O sea				
OET No. 21	1	I must hunt down O prize				
	2	where my heart lists.				
	3	Must see O eagle's bulk, render'd in mists,				
	4	Hung of a huge size.				
	5a	Must see O waters roll				
	6a	where O seas set				

Plate 81[A]   OET No.20a: [Heaven-Haven] here entitled REST--MS.1 C.i.178--from Plate 66 above; reproduced again (with its contrasting companion-piece "I must hunt down the prize") to facilitate comparison with the four versions on Plate 81. In lines 1, 2, and 5a changes rectify the indentation. No stop ends 4 or 8b.

OET No.21: "I must hunt down the prize" (sole MS.)
178.5a "Must" and "I Must" both mended to "Must" (with corrected indentation). . 179.5b "l" mended to "green", "long" del., replaced by "sees" (sic.). Between pp.180 and 183 a leaf was cut out (by GMH?).

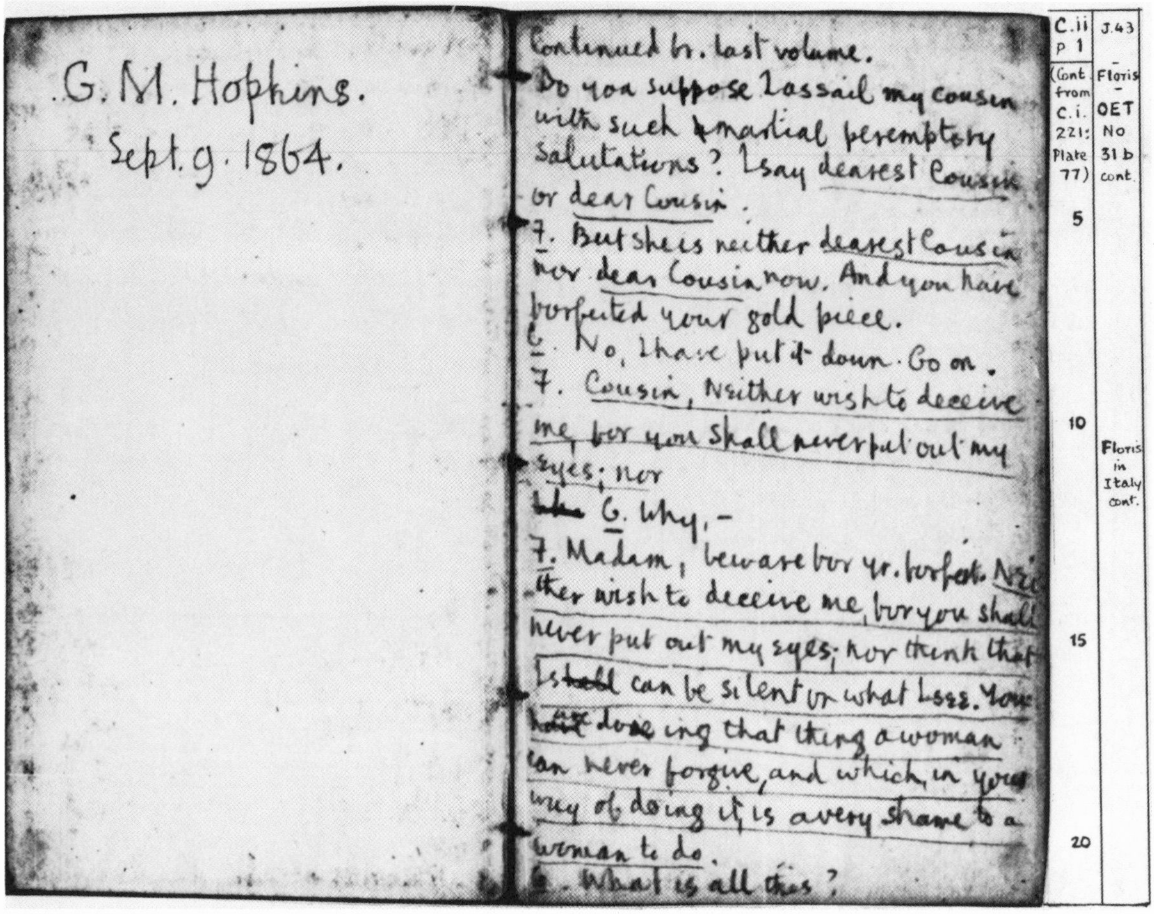
G. M. Hopkins.
Sept. 9. 1864.
Continued fr. last volume.
Do you suppose I assail my cousin
with such martial peremptory
salutations? I say dearest Cousin
or dear Cousin.
7. But she is neither dearest Cousin
nor dear Cousin now. And you have
forfeited your gold piece.
G. No, I have put it down. Go on.
7. Cousin, Neither wish to deceive
me, for you shall never put out my
eyes; nor
G. Why, -
7. Madam, beware for yr. forfeit. Neither wish to deceive me, for you shall
never put out my eyes; nor think that
I shall can be silent on what I see. You
have done ing that thing a woman
can never forgive, and which, in your
way of doing it, is a very shame to a
woman to do.
G. What is all this?
C.ii p 1
(Cont from C.i. 221: Plate 77)
J.43
Floris
OET No 31 b cont.
Floris in Italy cont.

SECOND EARLY NOTE-BOOK--CAMPION HALL MS.C.ii

This note-book is reproduced in its entirety, for the first time, in plates 82 to 151. When other MSS. exist of poems which are found here in draft form, these revisions are postponed till later plates.

Plates 82,83. No.31(b): Floris in Italy cont. [Note: References to this play are put in the outer margins for clarity.] C.ii.pp.1-2--This continues the scene between Giulia and her Fool which ended the first Note-book (C.i.221). Deletions are easy to read. Note the imperfect del. of "shall" and "have" in C.ii.1.17 and 18. The scene ends at p.2.8. In the next scene (No.31e), bot. p.2, "B" is del. before "C". On p.4.10 "one" orig. "one's".

GMH's visit to Croydon (see sketch p.3) where his grandfather owned a large estate (see J.349-50, 362-3) explains the brilliant night skies: star images (from C.ii.4 to 30, with one from C.i.214) are gathered in OET No.37.

The philological notes on C.ii.p.5 remind us that GMH's Part I exams at Oxford ("Moderations") were to begin in ten weeks (20 Nov.). If the second "u" in "quantity" (p.5, end line 2) is a badly formed "a", the word above it may be meant for the correct "conveniant" (cf. five lines from the bot., "ush", i.e. "ask").

PLATE 83.   C.ii. pp 2,3,4,5   •   135

C.ii p.2

(margin: J.43 / OET No. 31b Cont. / Floris in Italy cont. / Floris cont. bot. of p. (31e))

7. Madam! that I love desperate-²
ly you know well: that you love
at all I much doubt: that I am
not loved is my misery: that you
are loved is the fear that graces my
fenton of loveless ness with the diet
of gall and bitterness O mortifying
& tears. You are not writing.

(OET No. 30n)

They came
Went to meadows abundant pierced with
flowers,
With sulphur-colour'd dikes, brittle in stalk,
And seals & red carnation wh. had such
Two tongues like butterflies.

(OET No. 37b)

O vast & heaven stung with brilliant stars. Above

(OET No. 31e)

A. What is yr. name, boy?
B. George, please Sir if you please Sir.
A. why it doesn't please me at all.)
think George is a fustian name.
C. fustian, what a word! why la-

C.ii p.3   3

See J.43 (not shown)

(faint pencil notes)

Sept. 10. 1864. Croydon.

Sept. 10 1864

C.ii p.4   4

(margin: OET No 31e (Cont. from p.2) – J.44 / Floris in Italy cont.)

trousers' jackets are made of fustian.⁴
(aside.)
A. You see it isn't how it pleases me,
but how it pleased your godfathers &
godmothers – how many years ago?
B. What, Sir?
A. Why, how old are you?
B. Fourteen.
A. Fourteen? A pretty age.
C. How can one of age be prettier than
another? You might as well say half
past nine was a very handsome time of
day. (Aside.)

(OET No. 37c)

How looks to-night? There does not miss a star.
O million sorts & unaccounted notes
Now quicken, sheathed in O yellow galaxy.
Here is no parting or black bare interstice
where & stint compass & a skylarks wings
Cd. not put out some tiny golden centre.

(No. 37d)

Stars waving their indivisible rays.
Sky fleeced with O milky way.

(No. 37e)

night's lantern
Painted with pierced lights, & breaks & rays
Discover'd everywhere.

C.ii p.5   5   J.44

Lucretius IV. 1255 "Crassaque conveniunt
liquidis et liquida crassis". And the quantity
ier in the various wds. liqueo, liquidus,
etc notoriously varies. liquidus is same as
limpidus. Now linquo, dwh. the perfect
is liqui, is certainly same as λειπω. We
may conclude that the lengthening of iqu
in the above verse arose fr. a(perhaps then
no longer existing) form or pronunciation
linquidus wh. was transmuted into limpidus. Perhaps λειπω may have passed thro'
& form λειμπω. Compare in Eng. dank
and damp, hump and hunk,

N.B. Airs of 16th century. Polly Oliver
Admiral Benbow. Charlie is my dar-
ling. Dance tune of Charles II. Watkins
Ale. Die drei Rösslein. Several beautiful
Airs without wds. in a thin smallish
Music bk. & Aunt Fanny's.

(OET No 31g / Floris in Italy cont.)

Scene. A cave in a quarry. Evening. Gabriel
comes to ask & advice & & hermit, who has
however died. He is halfmad. He runs out
and finds some nightshade berries wh. he
eats. these make him delirious. A shepherd
and his wife take refuge in the cave fr. &

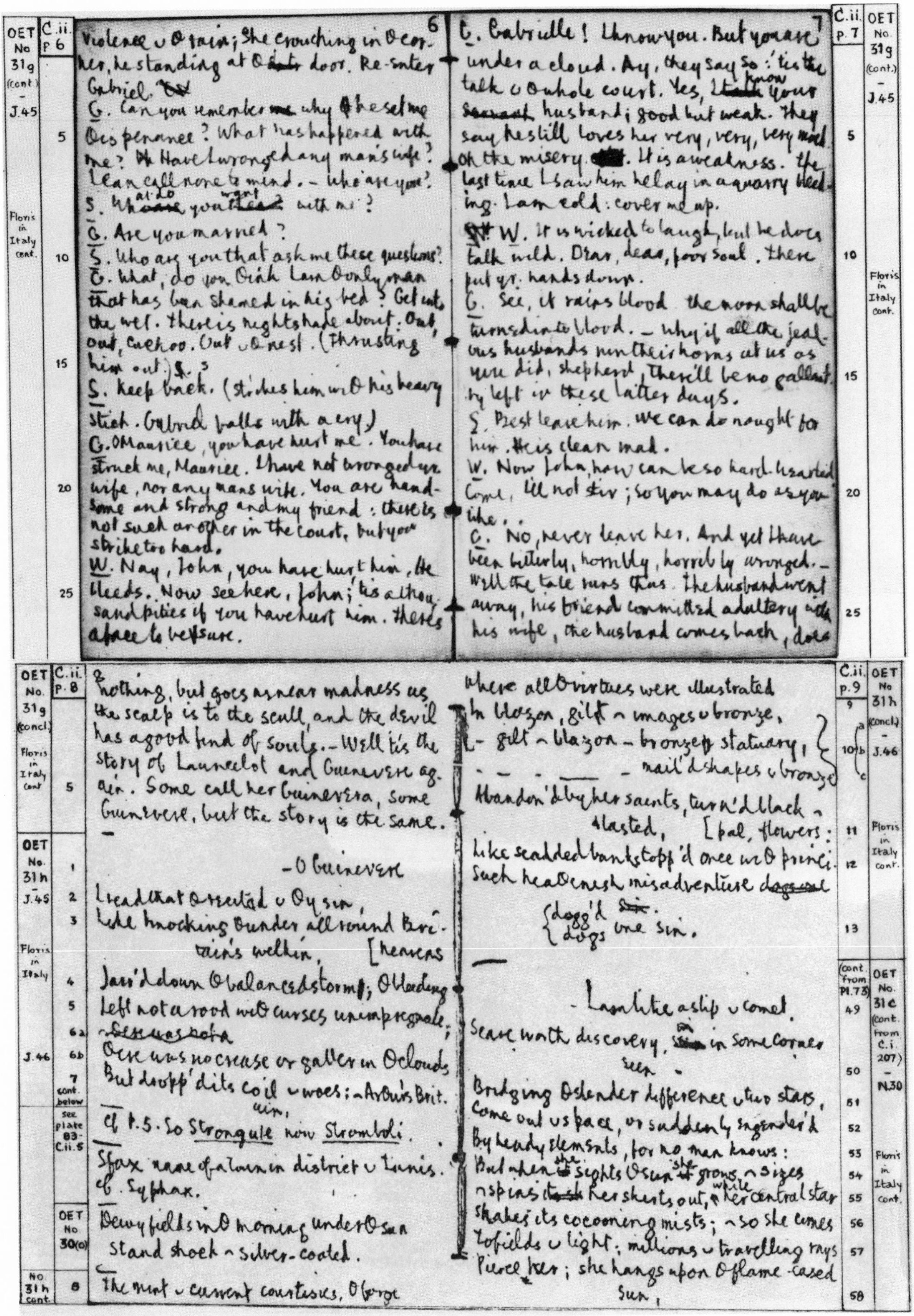

Page 6

Margin: OET No 31g (cont) - J.45 | C.ii p6 | Floris in Italy cont.

violence ⌐ ᴏ rain; she crouching in ᴏ cor-
ner, he standing at ᴏ door. Re-enter
Gabriel. ᴏ
G. Can you remember me why ᴏ he set me
ᴏis penance? What has happened with
me? Oh Have I wronged any man's wife?
I can call none to mind. — Who are you?
S. Who are you that want with me?
G. Are you married?
S. Who are you that ask me these questions?
G. What, do you think I am ᴏ only man
that has been shamed in his bed? Get out ᴏ
the wet. There is nightshade about. Out,
out, cuckoo. Out ᴏ nest. (Thrusting
him out.) S.
S. Keep back. (Strikes him w ᴏ his heavy
stick. Gabriel falls with a cry)
G. O Maurice, you have hurt me. You have
struck me, Maurice. I have not wronged your
wife, nor any man's wife. You are handsome and strong and my friend: there is
not such another in the court, but you
strike too hard.
W. Nay, John, you have hurt him, he
bleeds. Now see here, John; 'tis a thousand pities if you have hurt him. There's
a place to be sure.

Page 7

Margin: OET No 31g (cont.) - J.45 | C.ii p7 | Floris in Italy cont.

G. Gabrielle! I know you. But you are
under a cloud. Ay, they say so: 'tis the
talk ᴏ ᴏ whole court. Yes, I know your
servant husband; good but weak. They
say he still loves her very, very, very much.
Oh the misery. It is a weakness. The
last time I saw him he lay in a quarry bleeding. I am cold: cover me up.
W. It is wicked to laugh, but he does
talk wild. Dear, dear, poor soul. There
put yr. hands down.
G. See, it rains blood. The noon shall be
turned into blood. — Why if all the jeal-
ous husbands run their horns at us as
you did, shepherd, there'll be no gallantry left in these latter days.
S. Best leave him. We can do nought for
him. He is clean mad.
W. Now John, how can be so hard-hearted.
Come, I'll not stir; so you may do as you
like.
G. No, never leave her. And yet I have
been bitterly, horribly, horribly wronged. —
Well the tale runs thus. The husband went
away, his friend committed adultery with
his wife, the husband comes back, does

Page 8

Margin: OET No 31g (concl.) Floris in Italy cont. | C.ii p8

nothing, but goes as near madness as
the scalp is to the scull, and the devil
has a good kind of souls. — Well 'tis the
story of Launcelot and Guinevere again. Some call her Guinevera, some
Guinevere, but the story is the same.

— O Guinevere

Margin: OET No. 31h J.45

1
2 I read that arrested ᴏ ᴏy sin,
3 Like knocking ᴏ under all round Bri-
        tain's welkin,   [heavens

Margin: Floris in Italy

4 Jarr'd down ᴏ balanced storm; ᴏ bleeding
5 Left not a rood w ᴏ curses unimpregnable,
6a —
6b There was no crease or gather in ᴏ clouds
7 (cont below) But dropp'd its coil ᴏ woes: — Arthur's Brit-
                 ain,

see plate 83 C.ii.5

cf. P.5. So Stromgule now Stromboli.

Sfax name of a town in district ᴏ Tunis.
cf. Syphax.

Margin: OET No. 30(o)

Dewy fields in ᴏ morning under ᴏ sun
stand shock ᴏ silver-coated.

Margin: No. 31h cont.

8 The mint ᴏ current courtesies, ᴏ George

Page 9

Margin: C.ii p9 | OET No 31h (concl.) - J.46 | Floris in Italy cont.

where all ᴏ virtues were illustrated
In blazon, gilt ᴏ images ᴏ bronze,
— gilt ᴏ blazon — bronze ᴏ statuary,
— — — — mail'd shapes ᴏ bronze
Abandon'd by her saints, turn'd black ᴏ
    blasted,   [pal, flowers:
Like scalded banks topp'd once w ᴏ prince
Such heaven-ish misadventure
    dogg'd   one sin.
    dogs

Margin: (cont from Pl.73) 49 ... N.30

— Lost like a slip ᴏ comet.
Scarce worth discovery, in some corner
        seen
Bridging ᴏ slender difference ᴏ two stars,
Come out ᴏ space, or suddenly engender'd
By heady elements, for no man knows:
But when the sights ᴏ sun it grows, ᴏ sizes
ᴏ spins her skirts out, her central star
Shakes its cocooning mists; ᴏ so she comes
To fields ᴏ light. millions ᴏ travelling rays
Pierce her; she hangs upon ᴏ flame-cased
        sun,

Margin numbers: 49 50 51 52 53 54 55 56 57 58

PLATE 85. C.ii. pp 10,11 • 137

Plate 84: OET No.31(g): Floris in Italy (cont.)

Plate 84: OET No.31(g): Floris in Italy (cont.)
    C.ii.6—Deletions include 3 "Ca[n]"   8 orig. "Who are you then?"
    C.ii.7—3,4 "talk...servant"   6 "of it"   9 "S" mended to "W" then "W" rewritten
    C.ii.8--No.31(h). 2 "recited" mended to "recital"   4 orig. "storms"
    C.ii.9--10a "gild" mended to "gilt"   10b orig. "bronzen"

No.31c: "I am like a slip of comet"

The comet image suits Guilia's predicament so perfectly that I believe it belongs to the lacuna in Floris in Italy, No.31c, after ℓ.48: "let me speak this little/..." (see above, C.i.207, plate 73). Deletions ℓ.50 "seen/in" 54ff. "it", "its" rev. to "she," "her". The soliloquy breaks off top of C.ii.10, and is cont. on p.13. Further revisions or fragments of Floris in Italy occur on C.ii.24, 87, 95-97.

Plate 85. OET No.35: "No, they are come"

C.ii.10,11--This piece was also possibly intended for "Floris". Deletions are legible. Note that 9b orig. read "colums" (further confusion in spelling it in 10a)
C.ii.11   OET No.36: "Now I am minded to take pipe in hand"

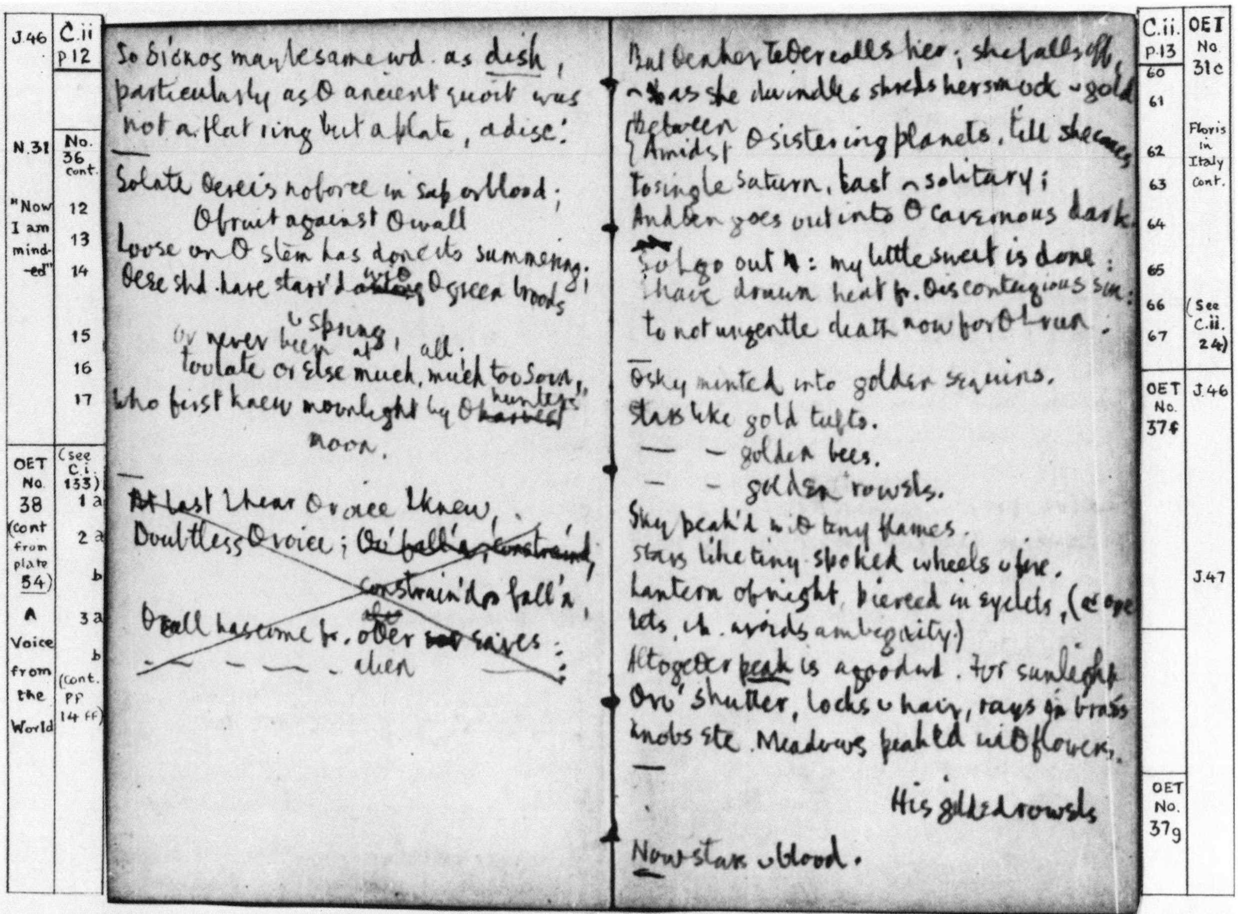

Top left panel (C.ii p12)

Margin: J.46 | C.ii p12
N.31 | No. 36 cont.
"Now I am mind-ed" | 12 13 14 15 16 17
OET No. 38 (cont from plate 54) A Voice from the World | (see C.i. 133) 1a 2a b 3a b (cont. PP 14 ff)

So διϲκος may be same wd. as dish,
particularly as ϑ ancient quoit was
not a flat ring but a plate, a disc.

Solate ϑere is noforce in sap or blood;
  Of fruit against ϑ wall
Loose on ϑ stem has done its summering.
ϑere shd. have starr'd θ green broods

Or never been at spring, all.
  too late or else much, much too soon,
Who first knew moonlight by ϑ hunter's
  moon.

At last I hear ϑ voice I knew,
Doubtless ϑ voice; ϑ' fall's constraint,
            constrain'd to fall'n
ϑ fall has come fr. over seas aïves:
    — — — alien

Top right panel (C.ii p13)

Margin: C.ii p.13 | OET No. 31c
60 61 62 63 64 65 66 67 | Floris in Italy cont. (See C.ii. 24)
OET No. 37f | J.46
 | J.47
OET No. 37g

But ϑenther ϑe ϑer calls her, she falls off,
As she dwindles sheds her smock o gold
Between ϑ sistering planets, till she came,
{Amidst ϑ sistering planets, till she came
To single Saturn, last o solitary;
And then goes out into ϑ cavernous dark.

So I go out M: my little sweet is done:
I have drawn heat fr. ϑis contagious sun:
To not ungentle death now for ϑ run.

ϑ sky minted into golden sequins.
Stars like gold tufts.
  — — golden bees.
  — — golden rowels.
Sky peak'd w iϑ tiny flames.
stars like tiny spoked wheels o fire.
Lantern of night, pierced in eyelets, (or eye
lets, th. avoids ambiguity.)
Altogether peak is a goodnt. for sunlight
Orr' shutter, locks o hair, rays o brass
knobs etc. Meadows peak'd wiϑ flowers.

          His gilded rowels

Now stars o blood.

Bottom left panel (C.ii p14)

Margin: J.47 | C.ii p.14
5 10 15
OET No. 38 (cont from p.12) A Voice Cont | 1b 2c 3c 4a 6a 9a 7a

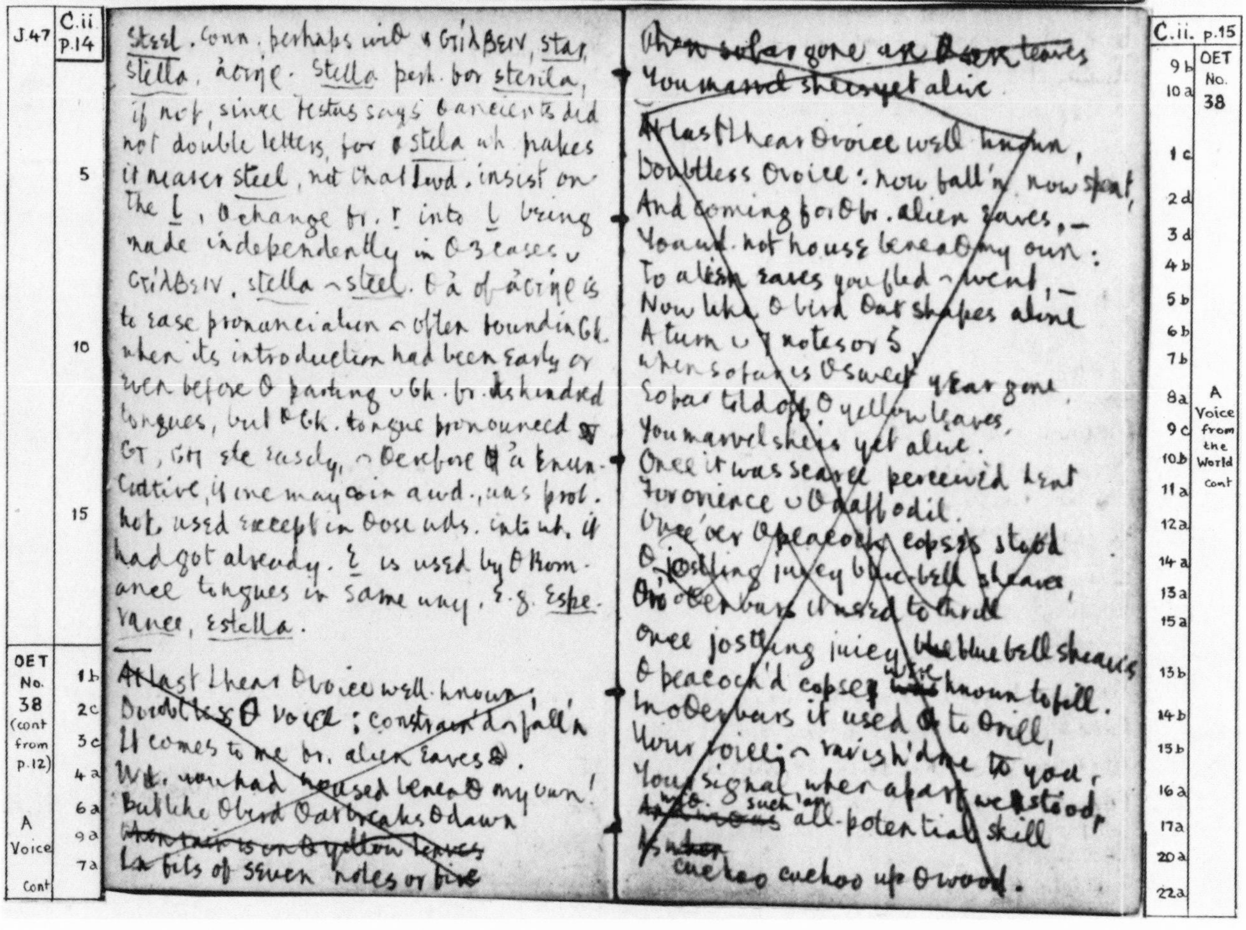

steel. conn. perhaps wiϑ ϑ GrilBeiv, star,
stella, acing. Stella perh. for sterila,
if not, since Festus says ϑ ancients did
not double letters, for ϑ stela wh. makes
it nearer steel, not that I wd. insist on
the L, ϑ change fr. r into L being
made independently in ϑ 3 cases o
GrilBeiv, stella o steel. ϑ ä of acing is
to ease pronunciation o often founding Gh
when its introduction had been early or
even before ϑ parting o Gh. fr. its kindred
tongues, but ϑ Gh. tongue pronounced st
Gt, but the easily, o ϑerefore ϑ ä enun-
ciative, if one may coin a wd., was prob.
not used except in ϑose wds. into wh. it
had got already. E is used by ϑ Romance tongues in same way, e.g. Espe-
rance, Estella.

At last I hear ϑ voice well known,
Doubtless ϑ voice; constrain'd to fall'n
It comes to me fr. alien eaves ϑ.
Wh. you had housed beneaϑ my own!
But like ϑ bird ϑat breaks ϑ dawn
                  o yellow leaves
La bils of seven notes or five

Bottom right panel (C.ii p15)

Margin: C.ii p.15
9b 10a | OET No. 38
1c 2d 3d 4b 5b 6b 7b 8a 9c 10b 11a 12a 14a 13a 15a 13b 14b 15b 16a 17a 20a 22a | A Voice from the World cont

When solar gone are Born leaves
You marvel she is yet alive

At last I hear ϑ voice well known,
Doubtless ϑ voice: now fall'n, now spent,
And coming for ϑ br. alien eaves,—
You wd. not house beneaϑ my own:
To alien eaves you fled o went,—
Now like ϑ bird ϑat shapes alone
A turn o 9 notes or 5
when so far is ϑ sweet year gone.
So far till off, ϑ yellow leaves,
You marvel she is yet alive.
Once it was scarce perceiv'd heat
for once o ϑ daffodil.
Once o'er ϑ peacock copses stood
ϑ jostling juicy bluebell sheaves
ϑ ϑe ϑ bars it used to thrill
once jostling juicy blue bluebell sheaves
ϑ peacock'd copses was known to fell.
In ϑe bars it used ϑ to thrill,
Your voice o ravish'd me to you,
Your signal when apart we stood,
      such o
     all-potential skill
cuckoo cuckoo up ϑ wood.

PLATE 87. C.ii. pp 16,17 • *139*

Plate 86. C.ii.12: No.36 (cont.). 14 "among" del.

OET No.38: A Voice from the World (cont.)

[For the earliest surviving draft (lines 135-49) see C.i.133 (plate 54).]

C.ii.12--This is the first attempt at the opening lines. The poem occupies much of C.ii.14-19, 21-24, 47-50, 75.

"Floris in Italy" cont.

C.ii.13--After line 64 GMH drew a short dividing line, then del. it and wrote a passage linking the comet image with 68 (C.i.205).

C.ii.13 cont. (Notes for Poems) Four lines from bot., "rays [in mended to] on brass knobs"

C.ii.14--A Voice from the World (cont.)   3c seems to end with "etc."   9a "When rain is on the yellow leaves" del.

C.ii.15--9b "...the sere leaves" del.   20a orig. "And with as"

Plate 87. C.ii.17--Unnumbered line following 21a "Under the wild blue"   unnumbered line following 11c "When showers on roods of flowers are sprent."   23c "Five notes or seven [; del.], [tho' del.] fall'n to few [, del.]:"
By comparing line 15c (Plate 87) with the first drafts (15a and b on Plate 86), we can see that "used the thrill" is simply a slip for "used to thrill": the poet made the same mistake in 15b, but corrected it there.

Plate 88   OET No.38: A Voice from the World cont.

C.ii.18,19 are badly smudged. Even the special plates prepared for Fr. Bischoff by a forensic department and reproduced here leave some words indecipherable. For the final versions (lines 85-88, 89b to 116), see OET text. The deleted drafts seem to read: 89a ...[?] you, had hasten'd down./90a [Some thought del.] 'Twas known the Judgment had [begun mended to] began [to rhyme with ran]/92a I thought/92b Nocturns [had del.] I thought were hurried thro'./93a Some knelt, some stood/95a They are the goats who stand, [I del.] said I./96a I stood, but does she stand or kneel?/97a I strove to look [? at del.] but lost the trick/98a Of nerve; the clammy ball was dry"

    Later deletions 89b hurried then hastened   91 cd. feel   94 st[ood?] knelt 96b orig. stood. But 102 Him [above del. word?]...[then perhaps] away in flight were gone/C.ii.19. C.103 Save me: and you were standing near.

    Lines 104-116. The draft (del. with a large X) varies from the final version below it in: 106a orig. as revised, then "heaven" and "hell" reversed to rhyme with "well", then orig. restored.   109a "but" del. before "my prize" 110,111 orig. one line: "Give him the gift: I am forgiven."   112a "And in the dream it seem'd to me". 116b (bot. line) "My fast-lodged tongue". A space and square bracket above it were left for the unfinished line. The sense ["To her the gift"] is provided by the del. drafts at top of C.ii.21: "Give her the gift/I wd. have cried"

Plate 89   No.38: A Voice from the World, cont.

C.ii.p.21--48a "love in" rev. to "love of"   From the middle of this page onward traces of erased earlier drafts are faintly visible.   33a "I cry against the pain thereof."   35 "gr[ief(?)]" del.   39a "You [hear del.] see"   42a (also 39b, next page) "sphered" mended.

C.ii.p.22--39b "But you, so sphered,"   41 note commas, ",alter'd,"   46b sign for "and" (?) del., rev. to "yea"   61 "Always"   62 "His very looks in other years;"

C.ii.p.23--70a "I rave where" del. The dot over "v" is a slip.   74 "a self-outwitted blast"

PLATE 89.   C.ii. pp 20,21,22,23   •   141

C. ii. p.20

J.47
(not
shown)
–
23
Sept
1864

Blue (delicate) and dark grey. No intermediate hues. Horizon lower. Hampstead. Sept 23.

"I yield" I wd. have cried. At last,
Something I said; I swoon'd ~ fell.
O Angel lifted us above.
O bitterness ~ dead O was past,
My love ~; ~ all was sweet ~ well.

The love in woman is not so strong ~
Falsely they sing ~ as love in men.
A thing that weeps enduring long;
But mine is dreadful leaping pain
Ruinous heart beat, wandering, death
Phrenzy but edged ~ clear ~ brain.

I know I mar my cause with wds.:
So be it, I must mar ~ mar.
Your comfort is as sharp as swords;
~ I cry ~ against ~ wounded love
And you are gone so heavenly far
You hear nor care ~ gr love ~ pain.
My tears are but a cloud ~ rain
My passion like the foolish wind
Lifts them a little way above.
But when ~ what ~ You hear no more,
Or see but ~ O a holier mind,
Being as starred apparel'd star.

C. ii. p.21

116 c
117 a
117 b
118
119
120
121

48 a
49 a
50 a
51 a
53 a
52 a

30
31
32
33 b
34
35
36
37
38
39 a
40 a
42 a

OET
No.
38
–
N.19

(rev.
C.ii
p.23)

N.17
–
A
Voice
from
the
World
cont.

C. ii. p.22

OET
No.
38

N.17

A
Voice
cont

39 b
40 b
41
42 b
44 a
45 a
46 a
47 a

54 ?

43 a
44 b
45 b
46 b
47 b

46 c

54 a
55
56
57
58
59
60
61
62

I yield, to ~ , see no more ~
You see but ~ a holier mind
You hear ~ alter'd, do not hear
Being a stored apparel'd star.
As halves ~ sweet pea-blossom are
Now as far, ~ hard to find
As O eighth Pleiad ~ behind
Sealed most remote El Khor.

You shd. have been with me as near
As halves ~ sweet-pea blossom are;
But now are fled, ~ hard to find
As O seven O Pleiad, ~ behind
Exiled most remote El Khor.

Or As O last Pleiad.

I walk towards ~ our walks again;
When lily yellow is O west.
Say O ~ o'er it hangs a water cloud
And invisible strings ~ rain.
At once I struggle with my breath
O light was so O ~ so loud
No louder, when I was with you.
Always O time remembered
~ so ~ looks in ~ eyes.

C.ii. p.23

63
64
65 a
68 a
67 a
68 b

48 b
49 b
50 b
51 b
52 b
53 b
54 b

65 b
66
67 b
68 c
69
70 a
70 b
71
72

73
74

OET
No.
38

(rev.
from
C.ii
p.21)

A
Voice
cont.

Only without is old ~ new:
I fall, I tear ~ shower O weed
I bite my lips, my locks I shroud:
Then is my misery full: I bleed
Intolerable tears, but few:
And is my misery full indeed.

The love of women is not so strong, ~
'tis falsely given ~ as love in men;
A thing that weeps, enduring long:
But mine is dreadful leaping pain
Phrenzy but edged ~ clear ~ brain
Ruinous heart beat, wandering, death.
I walk etc.

I bite my hands, my locks I shroud;
My cry is like a bleat; a few
Intolerable tears I bleed.
Then is my misery full indeed:
I die, I die, I do not live. ~
I live when
Alas! I rave where calm is due;
I would remember, love, forgive.
I cannot calm, I cannot heed.

I storm ~ cry shock you. So frail
And like a self-outwitted blast

PLATE 91. C.ii. pp 28,29 • *143*

Plate 90.   No. 38: A Voice from the World, cont.
C.ii.24--75 "portal[1]" del.   83 "And" mended   23d "etc" del.   The next draft is on C.ii.47.
    No.31(c) Floris in Italy, cont. (a bridge passage added to C.i.204). 9b orig. "All" mended to "all", then
"But" inserted with caret. # 10 "clear" then "Fine" del., rev. to "sharp"   11 "And" mended to "With"   14b
    "Unset my slender balance with a feather." del.   After 15 the stage direction "(Comes to the bed.)" replaces
the same note after 8 on C.i.204.
C.ii.25--17 to 19a orig. "[Lay del.] Fasten his eyes/That they not open"   21-22 If we take the stop after "field"
as a comma, the sentence runs "but yet/Hold him as easy and light/As..." # two lines from bot. "but" mended to
"and the outlines"
C.ii.26--OET No.39(a)--2a "hard beside" del.
C.ii.27--prose line 11 orig. "whith"   bot. line "fick" [See EDD "fike, fick"]

Plate 91   No.10: Pilate (cont. from C.i.108)
C.ii.28--Final three sts. rev. from C.i.105-6.   88b orig. "and there s[tand]" s mended to "to"
Two leaves (pp.29-32), cut from the Note-book, were restored to Campion Hall in 1949 (J.319). The inner edge of
p.29 has lost some initial letters (here restored in the margin).
C.ii.29--Below "Pilate" comes an item on Butterfield's new church, reported in "The Times" 12 Dec.1864.

C.ii. p.30	OET No.	
J.50	39 c	Her looks more moving than the peacock's eyes
		Cover is a good wd, and row, boo with ~ hora,
		though I mean no connection curiously.
	No. 39d	Spring from the branch ~ heads ordering the
		bright rows ~ the leaves, chiefly o the sun.
	No. 37h	A star most spiritual, principal, preeminent
		of all the golden press.
OET No. 37i	1 a	Or ever the early stirrings o sky-lark ~ buzzing,
	2 a	Might cover the neighbouring downs with a span o
	1 b	Or ever the early stirrings of the skylark
	2 b	Might cover the neighbour downs with a span o singing,
	3	While Phosphor, risen upon the hallowing dad,
	4	In the ruddied county of the day's up-bringing
	5	Stood capital, eminent, ... gonfalon bearer
	6	To all the starry press,—
OET No. 42a	1	I bear a basket lined with grass,
	2	I am so light, I am so fair,
	3	That men must wonder as I pass,
	4	And at the basket that I bear,
For a	5	Where in a newly-drawn green litter
Picture	6	Sweet flowers I carry — sweet for bitter.
of St	7	Lilies I shew you: Lilies none,
Doro-	8	None in Caesar's gardens blow:
thea	9	And a quince in hand: not one
	10	Is set upon your boughs below:
	11	Not set, because their buds not spring;

		C.ii. p.31	OET No. 42a
Spring not, 'cause world is wintering.		12 13	
But these were found in the East ~ South,		14	
Where winter is betime forgot.—		15	
The dew-drop on the larkspurs mouth		16 a	
O were it then be parchèd not?		17	
In starry water-meads I drew		18	For a
These drops, which be they? Stars or dew?			Picture
Had she a quince in hand? Yet gaze:		19	of St
Rather it is the sizing moon.		20	Doro-
Lo, workèd heavens with milky ways!		21	thea
That was her last year row.— So soon —		22	
Sphered so fast, sweet soul? — We see		23	see below
Nor flowers, nor fruit, nor Dorothy.		24	Plates 156-7
perhaps quenchèd. (Certainly)		16 b	J.50
I often talk to Uncle Edward Hopkins, Aunt			
Fanny, Towse, Henbrook, Mrs Cunliffe.			
Proved these prudish, selfish, hypocrite, heartless,			OET No. 43
Jo the scholar, wd be critic, a dilettante,		1	
Cream-laid, a surface, who cd quote, to startle us		2	J.50
The Anatomy, Politian, a little Dante —		3	
And so for the. Then for his looks ~ like pinkish		4	
bacon.		5	(cont. p.33)

C.ii. p.32
Not in J.50

		C.ii. p33	OET No. 43 (concl.)
Features? A watermark; other claims as scanty. [vapours		6 7	
In such mass did the gentle			
Wells, woodblock maker, Bouverie Street, Fleet Street		1	J.50
Beaumont, Arundel House, Blessington Rd., Les, S.E.		4	
As void as clouds that house ~ harbour none,			OET No. 44b (see Plate 55)
Whose gaps ~ hollows are not browzed upon,			
As void as those the gentle downs appear			
On such a season o the day ~ yr.		5	
There was no bleat o ewes, no chime o wether,			
Only the belled foxgloves lisp'd together.			Not in J.51
Yet there came one who sent his flock before him			
Alone upon the hill-top, heaven o'er her		8 a	
And where the brow in first descending bow'd		8 b	
He sat ~ wrought his outline on a cloud.			
His sheep seem'd to come to it as they stept,		10	
One ~ then one, along their walks, ~ kept			
Their changing feet in flickers all the time			Rich ard
And by their feet the narrow bells they gave their chime.			
Attired with the sweet solitudes,		15	
He was a shepherd o the Arcadian mood			
That not Arcadia knew nor harmony,			
We break no oracled melody		18 a	
He answered the day that us ~ his tendless sheep		18 b	
His tale ~ telling has been given to me.		18 c	

PLATE 93.   C.ii. pp 34,35   •   145

Plate 92--C.ii.p.30. His Moderations safely behind him, GMH is full of poetry. In No.37(i) the first two lines were rewritten (with one revision) to change the indenting.   2a "downs" mended   1b "the" del. before "skylark"
   OET No.42(a): [For a picture of St Dorothea] This is the earliest autograph : the indenting does not indicate metrical length. See below, plates 156-7, for later autographs. C.ii.p.31--20 "that" rev. to "it"   21,22 slips in writing "linkĕd" and "larkspur" have been mended.
   OET No.43: "Proved Etherege prudish"--when this leaf was cut from the Note-book, "No" at the beginning of 2 (foll. by earlier "No" del. to correct the indenting), and 5 "paper" [foll. by ? colon or semicolon, lower half lost] were both affected.   C.ii.32--drawings of window tracery, etc. not shown J.50.
   C.ii.33--OET No.44b:[Richard]. Cf. the earlier draft in C.i.137-139, plate 55 (OET No.44a).   8a (del.) "Along the hill-top, only heaven was o'er him"   9 after "first" MS. has tiny flaw, not a hyphen.   14 "kept" begun but del. because already used in 12; 18a "With break of unexpected melody"   18b "He answer'd the dry tinkles of his [tinkles del.] sheep"--these lines revise first draft in C.i.138.

Plate 93   C.ii.34--OET No.44c: [Richard, cont.].
   1a "downs" is apparently mended to "towns" though the poem develops in the opposite direction.   2a "And [gave del.] bred acquaintance of unusèd towns?"   1b "brought" rev. to "drew"   3 query del. after "lip"   6 sign for "of" after "humanities" is prob. meant for "and" (a fairly frequent slip)   After "Oxenham" three unimportant lines were omitted in error from J.51.   OET No.45: "All as the moth".   1a "called" mended to "call'd"   C.ii.35 3a orig. "How she [?]...of underplighting"   5a (del.) "With watchet staid"   5b "with" del.   2b "Pac[ing?]" mended to "Travelling".
   OET No.46: The Queen's Crowning. This poem occupies C.ii.35-42 without interruption.   C.ii.35: 1 "wedded a" del.   5 "may" del.

C.ii. p36 OET No 46 — N.34	C.ii. P37 OET No 46 — N.35

[Left column — C.ii. p36]

3 "Heaven make O time be short," she said,
  "Altho' it were yrs. three.
Heaven make ~~it were~~ it sweet to you," she said,
  "And make it short to me.

4 ~ what is your true name? she said,
  "Your name ~ your degree?
"How shall I call my love, she said,
  "When he is over O sea?"

5 O I am ~~the~~ O king's son," he said,
  "Lord William they call me.
"I give you my love ~ I give you my land,
  And ~~you shall be queen~~
  When I come home fr. sea".

6 He yearn'd, he yearn'd to have his love,
  For two yrs. ~ for three.
Then he set sail on a golden ship
  With a golden company.

7 Or ever he set his foot to O land,
  He saw his brothers three.
O have you here a foreign lady
  Come wth you fr. over O sea?"

8 "O I have here no foreign lady
  Come wth ~~her~~ fr. over O sea".

(margin: 12, 16, 20a, 20b, 24, 30 — "The Queen's Crowning Cont.")

[Right column — C.ii. P37]

"Oen will you wed wth an English lady,
  As wedded you must be?"
9 Says "Get you, get you a lady to wed
  Oat has both gold ~ fee.
Ere you set sail O king was dead.
  O crown has come to Oee."
10 "And if I chose a love to wed
  Oat was o low degree?
O crown shd. be unto her head
  And what were Oat to Oee?"
11 One ~~went~~ to O king's stewart,
  Shewn him both gold ~ fee;
Said "Who o Oen is Ois lowly woman,
  And truly tell to me".
12 O king's friend told O king Oat was hid
  because o gold ~ fee.
Said it was not meet O king sh. wed
  wth one o low degree.
13 Oey have held his eyes wth O blindfold bands
  Because he shd. not see.   [hands:
Oey have bound his feet, Oey have bound his
  It was but one O Oree.

(margin: 32, 36, 40, 44, 48, 52 — "The Queen's Crowning Cont.")

OET No 46 — N.35	C.ii. p38

[Left column — C.ii. p38]

14 Oey have taken out Oeir long brands
  Oey bow'd him on his hass.
  {~ made ~ hass ton ~.
"It is for O shame of O lowly woman
  Oat Ois has come to Oee".
15 Oey have happ'd them wth O sand ~ stone
  Oat was beside O sea.
In his heart said everyone
  O crown shall be for me.
16 Lowly Alice sat in her bower
  wth a two yrs. child at her knee.
"I think it is seven days", she said,
  "Oy fader Oou shalt see".
17 Lowly Alice look'd abroad
  Over field ~ tree,
And she was ware of a servingman
  Came running over O lea.
18 "O what will you now good servingman
  O what will you now wth O me?""
Says "Are you not ~~King~~ Lord Williams love
  Oat is o low degree?"
19 "I am Lord William's love," she said,
  "And Alice Oey call me".

(margin: 54a, 54b, 56, 60, 64, 68, 72 — "The Queen's Crowning cont." N.36)

[Right column — C.ii. p39]

~~Say~~ "Lord William comes hunting to morrow morning,
  And hen he'll come to Oee.
20 But how will you Lord William know
  Beside his brothers three?"
  "Because he is my love", she said,
  "And is so fair to see."
21 Yet how will you Lord William know
  Beside his brothers Oree?
His Oree brothers are each as tall
  ~ each as fair as he.
22 ~~Oyf love~~
  If it be a white rose in his hand,
  O lily if it ~~be~~, shd. be,   your lord
  In Ois wise you may know ~~Oeray~~
  Beside his brothers Oree:
23 If he wear O crown upon his head
  Among his brothers Oree,
If he wear O crown upon his head
  And bring a crown for Oss."
24 She heard O hunt the morrow morning
  And she came out to see.
And Oere she never saw O king,
  But saw his brothers Oree.
25 She stood before Oen in O glen,
  She kneel'd upon her knee.

(margin: C.ii. P39, OET No 46 — N.36; 76, 80, 84, 85a, 85b, 88, 92, 96 — "The Queen's Crowning cont." N.37)

PLATE 95.   C.ii. pp 40,41   •   *147*

OET No. 46 — N.37 | C.ii. P40

"O where is Lord William, my lords" she said,
    "I pray you tell to me."
26. Two made answer in one breath
    reach said "I am he".
"Fie, you are not Lord William", she said;
    "O fie, that this shd. be."
27. Then up ~ spake O bird brother,
    said, "Listen now to me.
Lord William is king v all this land
    ~ thou v low degree."
28. "Fie", she said unto them all,
    "No truth between you three.
If he [were] is king v all this land
    He wd. have come for me."
29. As she lay weeping at O night
    She heard but knockings three
"It is as cold as death without:
    Open O door to me."
30. Said "Who is this that stands without?"
    Said "Open, open to me"
When she had made O door wide
    Her true love she might see

The Queen's Crowning cont.

C.ii. P.41 | OET No. 46 — N.38

31. "O why art thou so hard she said, she said,
    ~ why so short with me?
~ art [thou] come fr. English land,
    Or come fr. over Sea?"
32. I am not come fr. English land,
    Nor yet fr. over Sea
If I were come fr. Paradise,
    It were more like to be."
33. "Is it a lily in your hand,
    Is it a rose & less?
Did you pull it in O king's garden
    when you came forth for me?"
34. "I did not pull it in king's garden
    when I came forth for thee.
If it were a flower v Paradise,
    It were more like to be."
35. "Is that O king's crown on your head,
    ~ have you a crown for me?"
"If it were a crown v Paradise,
    It were more like to be".
36. O more she ask'd, O more he spoke,
    O fairer waxed he.
O more he told, O less she spoke,
    O wanner waned she.

The Queen's Crowning cont.

Plate 94 [opposite]   OET No.46: The Queen's Crowning (cont.)
    C.ii.36: 11 "the time" del.   17 "lord" del.   20a "And you shall be queen to me'"   32 "you" del.
    C.ii.37: 41 "went" del.   52 "the three" slip for "to three"
    C.ii.39: 75 "Say" del.   85a "O if he bore" del.   91 "the crown" rev. to "a crown"

Plate 95 [above]   OET No.46: The Queen's Crowning (cont.)
    C.ii.40: 111 "is" rev. to "were"   120 "Her" mended from "Lord[d]"
    C.ii.41: 122 orig. "so so" mended to "so short"   123 orig. "are you" rev. to "art thou"

Plate 96. OET No.46: The Queen's Crowning (concl.)

C.ii.42--Top and bot. lines smudged. 145 st.37 "Wilt thou follow me, my true love [? del.]," 151 "O I" mended to "Sweeter" and "t[o ?] mended to "my"

OET No.39e: "Tomorrow meet you?" The tiny stop at end of first line is possibly a comma, or a minute colon. # 4b was added after deletion of marginal dividing rule. Last line on page: "Henry V. iii.v"

C.ii.43--top line smudged: "Rush on his host, as doth the melted snow"

OET No.47: Stephen and Barberie. C.ii.43 Bot. of page smudged: 3-5 "To the often takings of desirous winds,/Sits without consolation, marking not/The time save when her tears wh. still descend" [last word not quite certain]

Plate 97--C.ii.44--In 6 the grave on "barrèd" is on the top edge of the page. 8 "litter" the dot over the i makes l seem crossed. 10a, 11a "O weary Martinmas! wd. it were summer./Poor, poor afflicted [grave del.] soul." In 11b grave is restored.

OET No.48: "Boughs being pruned". C.ii.44 1 "better show" del. 2a "Builders to grace their spires shave" del. 6 "valued" rev. to "rated".

C.ii.46 is completely blank, but smudged by p.47.

C.ii.47. Top line "So[uthern]" del. before "4 Southern Hill, Reading".

OET No.38: A Voice from the World (cont. from C.ii.24, plate 90). 157a "etce" del. 159a "in" del. 164a "Freelong y" (cf. No.60, ℓ.44--Plate 144). 152b to 154b are partly smudged: "For my thought/No house of Rimmon may I take,/To bow but little, and worship not?"

PLATE 97.　C.ii. pp 44,45,46,47　•　149

OET No. 47 – J.52 Stephen and Barberie	C.ii. 6 7 8 9 10 a 11 a 10 b 11 b 12 13 14 15

Her barrèd fingers clasp'd upon her eyes,
Shape on O under side ~ size ~ drop,'
Meanwhile a litter ~ O jaggèd leaves
Lies in her lap, wh. she anon sweeps off.
Ouercome Martinmas! nd at once ~
weary
"This Martinmas, wd. it were summer,"
I heard her say, poor poor afflicted soul,
Wd. it were summer-time". Anon she sang
O country song ~ Willow." The poor soul _
(like me) _ sat sighing by a sycamore-tree"
Perhaps it was for O~ she chose O place.

OET No. 48 "Boughs being pruned"	1 2 a b 3 4 5 6 7 8

"Boughs being pruned, birds prunèd,
show show note fair;
To grace O~ spires are shaped with
corner squinches;
Enrichèd posts are chamfer'd; every where
He heightens wor O who guardedly di-
minishes;
Diamonds are better cut; who pars, repairs;
Is statuary by its inches?
Thus we shall profit, while gold coinage still
Is current ~ a lessèn'd mill".

C.ii p.45	J.P. 456, fig. 28 Not in J.

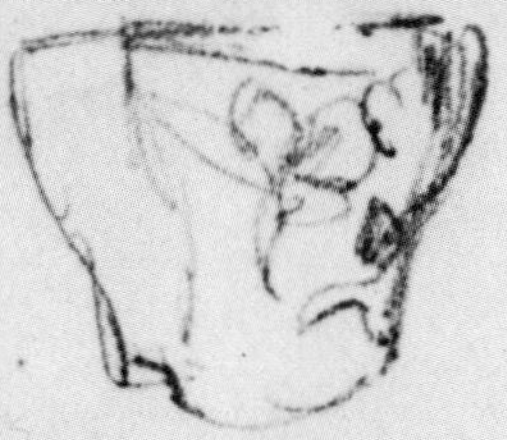

C.ii. P 46	

[page faded/illegible]

Miss Story,

The moonlight mated glowless glowworms
shine.

- to my thought
No house of Remmon may I take,
to bow but little, ~ worship not?
No little Bela? - No, not one.
O answer comes
Yea, to myself I answer make _
who waster late, on ~ slender sums,
By slender losses are undone;
Oey break not who are last to run..
O hideous vice, to haggle yet
for more wi O~ who gives Oee all
Keeping 4 forgives O monstrous debt!
Having O~ infinitely great
to hanker for O small.

But grant my penitence begun:
I need not, love, I need not break
Remember'd sweetness. for my Oou
No house ~ Remmon may I take,
to bow but little, ~ worship not?

C.ii P.47	J.52 OET NO. 39 f
	OET No. 38 (cont. from C.ii.24)
152 a	
153 a	
154 a	
155/6a	
157 a	
158 a	
159 a	
160 a	
161 a	
162 a	A Voice from the World cont.
163 a	
b	
164 a	
165 a	
166 a	
150	
151	
152 b	
153 b	
154 b	

C.ii. p48

| OET No. 38 – N.20 | | A Voice from the World cont (cont. below) |

No little Bela? — No, not one,
O heaven — enforced answer comes,
Yea, to myself I answer make

Is not some little Bela set
Before O mountain? — No, not one,
O heaven — enforced answer comes,
Yea, to myself I answer make:
Who can but barter slender sums
By slender losses are undone;
They break not who are late to run. —
O hideous vice to haggle yet
For more with Him who gives thee all,
Freely forgives O monstrous debt!
Having O infinitely great
Desired to hanker for O small

OET No. 39g

A silver scarce — call silver call gloss
Lighted O watery — plated leaves,
O watery — plated plane leaves lit.

OET No. 38 cont.

Knowledge is strong but love is sweet. —
I found O ways well sown with salt
where you — I were wont to tread;
Not further'd much my foolish feet
for — travell'd —
For all O miles that they were sped;
No flowers to find, no place to halt,

C.ii. p49

| OET No. 38 – N.21 | | A Voice from the World cont | J.52 |

No colour in O overhead,
No running in O river bed;
— passages where we used to meet, —
fruit-cloistering hyacinth-warding woods,
I call'd them — I ought them then —
When you were learner — I read,

Are waste, — had no wholesome foods
Unpalatable fruits to eat.
What have I more Vander men?,
For learning stored — garnered?

And barely to escape O curse,
I who was wise and be untaught,

How shall I search, who never sought?
How turn my passion-pastured thought

To gentle manna — simple bread?

(i) At last I hear O voice well-known.

(ii) I looking seaward, what see I?

(iii) Alas! — many times a day!

C.ii. p50

| OET No. 38 – J.52 | | (cont. p.75) |

(iv) I do not say you nothing need.
(v) You have O woman's purity.
(vi) So far, when made afflictive tears.

| J.53 | Not in J.53 | J.53 | | (9 cont line 20) | 29 Jan. 1865 | (cont. from l.9) |

Dined with Spencer on Monday.

Toothbrush, clothesbrush, slippers,
wine, Macbeth's, chalk drawing paper.

Shakes O frozen snow-drifts. Parallel
ribs Delightful curves. Saddles,
lips, leaves.

De Quincey used wake blue — trembling in O morning — languidly
ask O servant to "Wd. you pour

Breakfast with Addis on Tuesday

Drive with Woods to morrow Sunday
Name off Hall

Gk. History. Herod. Newman
Monday — Friday, at 11.

Palmer noticed in his sermon yesterday (Jan. 29.) that our language
with respect to character is that O morality, not O religion; we say virtue
not holiness, crime not sin

out some of that black mixture to O bottle Rose". O servant wd. give it him, &c.

C.ii. p51 | J.53

(xii) really not knowing what it was. After this he wd. revive. This wd. happen in Mr.
(xiii) Nicol's house, whose son told it to W. M. — &c. who told me.

De Q. borrowed two valuable bks. of him — always excused himself from sending them
back. On several times asked. He wrote that his library was in such confusion that he cd. not lay
his hand on them — so on. At last Mr. B. wrote to De Q.'s daughter who replied that she had done
her best, but O time O was her father had for two days been sitting on them — at night took them to his
room — put them under his pillow.

Latin weather proverb.
Si sol splendescat Maria purificante,
Major erit glacies post festum quam fuit ante.

Breakfast with Lake on Thursday

Boats, necktie, ink, ink-eraser, notebk.

The Epistles. Jowett.
Tuesday — Thursday at 10.
Plato's Republic. Jowett.
Thursday at 1.

Aristotle's Ethics. Wall.
Monday, Wednesday, — Friday at 10.

| 173 | 174 | 175 | 176 | 177 | 178 | 179a | 180a | 179b | 180b | 180c | 181 | 182 | 183a | 183b | 183c | 184 | 185 | 186 | 187 | 188a | 188b | (i) | (ii)a | (ii)b | (iii) |

| [Feb. 2] | Not in J.53 | J.54 |

PLATE 99. C.ii. pp 52,53 • *151*

Plate 98   OET No.38: A Voice from the World. (cont.)

C.ii.48—172 "spo[t?]" mended to "place"

C.ii.49—179a, 180a "I curse [their del.] too late the[ir del.] Sodom foods/They held" all del.   180b "I curse the unpalateable meet" [meat]   181 final query del. [183a, 183b] "How am I not perditions worse/Who sought a sin in every glen?"   184 prob. orig. "I f[ain]" from next line   "I who"   188a "To live upon the living bread?"

C.ii.49-51—These three pages have (a) a scheme for arranging six sections of the poem: only the first is extant; (ii) was transferred to (iii). This whole scheme is crossed through: (b) a thirteen-section scheme is prepared for but abandoned. The spaces are used instead for memos related to Hilary term (which began 14 Jan.1865). See Plate 115 for a further section of "A Voice from the World."

C.ii.50—for del. entries see J.53, except for lines 2,3, which dropped out of the printed Journals: "Toothbrush, clothesbrush, slippers, wine, Hachette's, chalk-drawing paper."

C.ii.51—line 19 is omitted in J.53: "Boots, necktie, ink, ink-eraser, note-bk."   24 "Thursday" mended to "Tuesday"; "Friday at 1" del.

Plate 99—C.ii.52: 11 "Artic[les]" del.

OET No.49: "I hear a noise of waters"—3 "cope" mended to "copse" #

C.ii.53: 6 "sods" mended to "clods"   7 "hilted" ("1" crossed in error as a "t")   8b orig. "ended"   9a "in" del. 11 "pledged"; "purple" mended to "purply"   1 "The dented primrose. Slight-edged." orig. "primsose, slight-edged." (Comma after "primrose" mended to period?)

C.ii p 54 | J.55

cloth backs for Dem, wiO cardboard; but
how? Shd. not I write home for Dem?
brass-headed nails. Red cord. Arranging pictures.

5 — Walking to Lydden on Tuesday at 30. But
how about Jowell's lecture?

To breakfast wiO me on thursday, Ur.
Urquhart Muirhead, Marshall, Madan,
10 — To ask Whitaker, Hood, Addis, Plummer,
Macfarlane, Wood, No not Hood and
Whittaker.

(Not in J.55)

Alea ~ Maclaverly

Baillies Cross, Coldash, Lovell,
Hardy for the Memorial.

15 — Phelps, 9 Orchard St, Fra Bartolom-
meos portrait ~ Savonarola.

Breakfast wiO Professor Wednesday.

Breakfast wiO Macfarlane on Monday.
Dolben's cards.

20 — Waistcoats.

more precision now ~ light ~ dark
O heightening dawn wiO milky orience
Rounds its still purpling centrerings ~

(OET No 39 (J)) 1a 2a 3a

C.ii p 55

... cloud.

Now more precisely touch'd in light ~ dark,
O place ~ O East wiO milky morn
earliest [cloud.

Rounds it still ~ purpling centredarks ~

(3a, 1b (J), 2b, ~ J.55, 3b) — OET No. 39 (J)

Dawn Oat O pebbly low down East
covers wiO shallow silver, Oat unsets
O lock ~ clouds betimes ~ hangs O day.

Dawn Dawn Oat O low down pebbly East
covers wiO shallow silver, O lock ~ clouds
Oat early 'spenses, ~ high hangs O day.

(1a, 2a, 3a, 1b ~ J.56, 2b, 3b) OET No. 39 (K)

When eyes Oat cast about O heights wishy-heaven
To canvass O retirement ~ O lask
(Because O music p. his bill ter O driven
so takes O sister sense) can find no mark,
But many a silver visionary spark
Springs in O floating air ~ O skies swim, —
Then often O ears in a new fashion hark,
Beside Oem, about O hedges, hearing him:
At last O bird is found a flickering shape aflight,

(1,2,3,4,5,6,7,8,9) OET No. 50 "When eyes that cast about"

At once O senses give O music back,
Nor absolute residue
So proper sweet is attributing above.
Oat sweetness is attributing above.—
whorled wave, whorled wave, — ~ drift.

(10, 11a, 11b, 11c) OET 39 (L)

C.ii. p 56 | (Not in J.56) | J.56 N.41

Bks. to be read — Bacon's essays; Browning's Paracelsus; the Apocryphal New
5 — Testament; King Henry V, VI (parti, ii,
~ iii), Richard III, ~ Henry VIII; Words-
worth; the Spiritual Combat; Villani's
Life ~ Savonarola, vol ii; Beresford
Hope's English Cathedral; S.B. Denison's
10 — book on church-restoring or some line
~ O kind; Le Morte Arthur; Tracts for
O Times; Essays ~ Reviews; "La Kouata-
la; the life ~ Lacordaire; Matthew
Arnold's Essays; Haen Creswells Life
15 — portraits ~ Shakspere; Modern Paint-
ers; The Newcomes; Dombey ~ Son; Our
Mutual Friend; the story ~ Elizabeth;
Silas Marner; the Mill on O Floss; Evelina

(cont. C.ii.63)

The Summer Malison.
Maidens shall weep at merry morn,
And hedges break, ~ lose O kine,
~ field flowers make O fields forlorn,
~ noonday have ~ shallow shine,
~ barley turn to weed ~ wild,
~ seven ears crown O hedged corn

(OET No. 51 ~ N.41) 1 2 3 4 5 6

C.ii. p57 | 7,8,9,10,11,12,13,14,15,16 OET No. 51 cont. N.41 The Summer Malison

~ mothers have no milk for child,
~ father be oversworn.

~ John shall lie, whose winds are dead,
~ hate O ill-visaged cursing tars,
~ James shall hate his faded red,
Grown wicked in O wicked wars.
No rains shall fresh O flats ~ sea,
Nor O clayfield's shasded sores,
~ every least ought to loathingly
Its dearest changed to bores.

Charteris, Phipson, kitson, Grant,
Boevey L Maclangford, Bell.
Bagnold, Butterworth,
Papillon, Reid, Hannah, Cope.
Nischter. St. George's Mission.
Mamma's present, pencil.

(Not in J.56) 5

In the Times ~ today (March 2, 1865) it is
said Oat some prisoners belonging to O
Old Papal states were brought to Rome
~ to O French extradition treaty. Some
were political, ~ one had been 15 yrs and
5 months in prison without a sentence.

(J.56 2 Mar. 1865) 10

Wootton church just restored by Butterfield.

(15) J.57

PLATE 101. C.ii. pp 58,59 • 153

Plate 100--C.ii.54: 9,11 "Whittaker"   12 (missing from J.55) "Allen and Maclaverty"   17 "Breakfast with Fyffe on Wednesday."

OET No.39(j): "In more precision". 3a only pencil smudges from p.54 occur between "centreings of" and "cloud" at the top of C.ii.55. 1b "with" and "dark" rev. to "in" and "gloom"

OET No.39(k)--"Dawn that the pebbly..." 2a "siilver"   1b "Dawn" del. and rewritten to show first foot is missing.   OET No.50--"When eyes that cast about"   11a "Re-attribute his due" del. (stress on "at"?)

OET No.39(1): "whelkèd wave,--and drift." [Note. The date printed above this line in J.56, "February-March 1865", is not in the MS.. C.ii.50-51 record events at the end of Jan. and beginning of Feb.. See OET Introd.]

C.ii.56: 1,2 [missing from J.56] "Letters to Mamma [her birthday was 3 March; see p.57, prose, line 6 and p.58, top line] (or Cyril and Gurney) The Rawlinsons."   18 The list of books to be read,begun on p.56, is cont. on C.ii.63, where the last title is completed, "Emilia in England'.

OET No.51: The Summer Malison--6 "crown the lodgèd corn,"   14 "melt" rev. to "close"   15 "be sick to"   16 "turned" ⟶ "changed" [Note: J.56 omits the list of nineteen names (middle C.ii.57), and the two-line entry which follows it.] "Charteris, Phipson, Kitson, Lovell, Grant, Boevie [slip for Boevey?], La Man Langford, Lang [prob. Andrew Lang], Bell, Bagnold, Langford, Lewis, Butterworth, Papillon, Secker, Reid, Hannah, Cope." 5,6 "Gill and Ward's bill. Necktie. St. George's Mission. Mamma's present. Grote, pencil."

Plate 101—C.ii.58: 8 the second "i" in "lilies", though dotted, is squeezed in almost invisibly   9 "Owed to Addis 6d" del.

OET No.53; Easter Communion (first draft: see C.ii.79-80 for title and rev.). 1a "come" ⟶ "draw"   3a "scored" rev. to "striped"   5a "at the least" del.   6a (del.) "You whom the pursuant [East del.] cold so wastes and nips,"   7a (del.) "Breathe Easter now. Ye serge-clad fellowships," 8a (del.) "Ye..." rest as 8b 10a "oil of gladness"--not "oil and" as in J.57   12a "Give fragrant-threaded g[old]"   12b "change of fragrant-threaded gold raiment," grave accent over "-ment" is del.   13a "for" rev. to "since"   13b "faint being" del.

OET No.39(n): 1 "cope" mended to "copse" (as in C.ii.52)

OET No.54: 0 Death, Death, He is come"   2 "grounds" (s squeezed in)   3 "Who" rewritten to correct indenting. 6 "thou" and "lord" both seem l.c.—contr. "Lay", "Lift" top of next page in next two lines

C.ii. p60		
OET No. 54 - J.58	7 8 9 10	Lay open Oine estates. / Lift up your heads, O Gates; / Be ye lift up, ye everlasting doors / The King of Glory will come in.
OET No. 42(b)	1 2 3 4 5 6 7 8	A. A basket broad of woven white rods / I have fill'd, But hard to fill is, / Wi' O multitude of O lily-buds / of O brakes of lilies. / B. And I came laden wt. such floods / of flowers Oat counting closes, / Wi' O warm'd of O water'd buds / of O press of roses.
Not in J.58 N.41 March 12 1865	5 10	5, St. Colme Street, Edinburgh. / March 12. A day of the great mercy of God. / Addis says my arguments are coloured & lose their value by personal feeling. This ought to be repressed. / Addis' debt, I mean debt to Addis, 6d. / Hexameron subscription 1s. Kidlington — 1s. Beggar 1d.

C.ii. p.61	J.58
	OET 39(P)
	N.41
	OET No. 55
1	
5	Omitted J.59 MAR.25 1865 (cont. top p.62)
10	
15	

Cyril's present and letter. Drawing. / Palms dotted into silver. / The sun just risen / Flares his wet brilliance in O dintless heaven. / His shaking eye. / The moon glassy.

Love me as I love thee. O double sweet! / But if thou hate me who love thee, albeit / Even thus I have O better of thee: [thee, / thou canst not hate so much as I do love / thans. of Gk. epigram.

g, Binswood Terrace, Leamington, Warwickshire. — A. Wood.

I confessed on Saturday, Lady Day, March 25.

Dawdling in going to bed (not very much). / March 25. Inattentions at morning chapel. 26 ... at night prayers, 26 Conceited forecasts ... evening church. Sitting late in ...

To ask about lay baptism (in the tract) & about justification &c. About betting. About mortification.

Liddon's tracts. The testimonial. Necklie. Boots. Cripps' bill. Letter to Harrison.

Plate 102—C.ii.60: line 7 of memos (del.) "Addis' debt, I mean debt to Addis, 6d." 9 "Kidlington—1s." (railway station 5 miles N. of Oxford).
   C.ii.61: top line (del.) "Cyril's present and letter. Pencil." Memos 4 to 10 <u>The earliest confession note</u> (though GMH had confessed to Liddon at least three times before); it is cont. top p.62. "I confessed on Saturday, Lady Day, March 25./S[ins]. Dawdling in going to bed (not very much), March 25.—Inattentions at morning chapel. 26 [Sun.]. Rubbing my eyes in irreverent inattention at night prayers, 26 [? mended to "25"?]—Conceited forecasts. Inattention at aft. evening church. Sitting late in [C.ii.62, top line] Geldart's room.--Since then proud thoughts" [prob. about his status in the Ireland exams, p.62, ℓ.8]

PLATE 103.   C.ii. pp 62,63   •   155

Plate 103--C.ii.62: lines 2 to 5 (omitted J.59) "Manson, Southby, Wilkinson, Leach, Bullock, Ranken, Gwyon, Maclaverty, Richardson."

S[ins. Mar. 26-29] "Dr. Pusey's story of the stable boy: repeating this. Repeating my ~~success~~ doing well in the Ireland [exam for a prestigious classical scholarship, written in March] ag[ain]st a scruple. Missing morning chapel thro' lateness to bed twice. Inattention at evening chapel. Falling into old habit. Speaking impertinently to Liddon (about Jowett). Was it deception about my Plato paper? March 29. [Cont. ℓ.18] E.s. [? Emissio seminis; see Plate 151] in morning not without sin [wet dream?]. Inat. at chapel. Incautiousness in dispute. Lateness to bed. March 30."

Line 15 "the Revd." del   20 1s., entrance to lecture [by Brother Vincent, p.63, ℓ.8]   24 was
→ were bot. line, cont. top p.63: "The altar-piece is by Tin/toret."

C.ii.63. "The [nave del] transept-roof also must be by Butterfield."   ℓ.3 "Gerald [Massie, ℓ.18].

S[ins]. March 31 [1865]. Inat. at chapel in morn. Wasting morning. Intemperance in food—biscuits. Wine twice a day. Relapsing into old impurities. Irreverence at a prayer. Altogether self-indulgence. On 30, anger agst. the man at Brother Vincent's lecture.—31. Talking unwisely on dangerous subject. Resolution. Breaking into work by scribbling [drawing? (cf. p.65, ℓℓ.32-3) writing poetry?]. April 1. [cont. 11] Wasting much of morning in quad. Wicked thoughts have occurred and not been at once driven away.—Earlier, talking about Williams of Ch[rist] Ch[urch] more than [one del.] I needed. Not acknowledging at once a P.O.O. fr. Papa.—Wasting time away fr. work. April 1. Inattention at chapel.—2 [Sun.]. Inattentions at church in morning. Intem-[cont. ℓ.24]perance in food at Addis' desert. No reading done or anything. Evil thoughts, partly abt. Urquhart. Repeating abt. the man at Brother Vincent's by speaking of him earlier.--April 3. Writing letter in morning when I shd. have read. Drawing in Taylor's letter [L.iii.229?] and going on obstinately, even when a wicked thought came wh. I scrup[led over" cont. p.64].

Line 18. Gerald [ℓ.3] Massie's books at Union [Gerald Massey, Poems (Lon. 1854), Craigcrook Castle (1856), Havelock's March and other Poems (1861), all in Union].

Plate 104--C.ii.64: S[ins. April 3 1865 cont.,   lines 1 to 14 "scrup]led over so to speak.
After drawing Carlyle I went to the Union near 7 o'clock when I should have read or at least stayed
there as above. Not sending Muirhead from my room [till] late. Falling into old habits.—4. Laziness
in bed. [Line 5] Waste of time, both by talking over work in morning, in Baillie's room by putting
off going out, and after coming from the Scotts' by idling in the quad.—3. Talking either unkindly
of Fyffe or near it.—4. Eating two biscuits at the Master's.—5th. Laziness in getting up, getting
little [Line 10] work done, and staying talking to Addis in evening (and on a dangerous subject, pursued
more than it need have been), no drawing. Despondency and ill humour in walking to and from near
Abingdon. Looking at a dreadful word in Lexicon.—6. Conceited thoughts arising. Idling [cont. ℓ.20]
somewhat in morning, and in going to bed, so as not to be there till after 12. Irritation agst.
Urquhart and unkind talking abt. him. Dangerous thing in The Saturday wh. I wd. read twice, anxiety
to hear about [Prof.] Robinson Ellis.—7. Idling in morning, inattention at [Line 25] psalms in chapel,
falling into old habits. Looking at and thinking of stallions.—8. Lateness in getting up. Idleness
in morning and no work at all in the evening. Not good humour in walking with Urquhart. Looking
at a man who tempted me. Lateness to bed. The N[ew] T[estament] lessons not [Line 30] read. Talking
abt. Urquhart less kindly than I cd. have. [Cont. ℓ.34] Saying unkind things abt. Monro.—Enquiring
(9 [April, Sun.]) abt. Voltaire's death. To ask abt. this, mem. Inattention at church. No evening
d[itt]o. Waste of time talking and before [going to bed." cont. p.65, top]

PLATE 105. C.ii. p 65 • *157*

Plate 105   C.ii.65 [Sins cont. from p.64, April 9 1865] "going to bed. Intemperance at dessert at Brooke's.—10. Wasting a good deal of time in morning, some in the evening. Lessons not read, very little work done.—[Cont. ℓ.6] 11. Scarcely any work done in morning and so on the 12th, on both wh. days I got up late, being unwell, but this not enough. Lounging on the river too much. Wasting evening in Baillie's room after coming fr. [Line 10] Union. All or half the lessons unread.—12. Half lessons unread. Indulging feeling of weariness agst. Urquhart. Evil thoughts in dictionary etc. No self-denial to speak of. E.s. on 11th, I fear not without sin. [Cont. ℓ.19] S.13. Maundy Thursday. Wasting time after coming [Line 20] fr. Merton in Addis' room and again after Psalms at 12. Little work done. Reading O[ld] T[estament] in foolish way in evening. Falling into old habits and before. Evil thoughts of wh. more or less guilty. Story abt. Fyffe in unkind spirit.—14, Good Friday. Self-indulgence in not getting up at [Line 25] once. Inattention at church in morning. Being late for St. Philip's so as to turn back when I got out. The evil thought in writing on our Lord's passion. Speaking lightly of the lie [i.e. the state] of Society, some time ago (more than once) and 14. Parker's boy at Merton: evil thoughts. [Line 30] Foolish and proud thoughts abt. fasting. Inattention at St. Giles's.--15. Easter Eve. In looking over the above poem [? Easter Communion, pp.58-9] an evil thought seemed to rise from the line before. Idling over architectural scribbling at lunch time. Unclean habits, not exactly the old ones. Looking at a cart-boy fr. Standen's shopdoor. Wasting time in evening. Lapses into idleness."

Plate 106—C.ii.66: Top lines badly smudged. Illegible except [ℓ.1] "thought at chapel [?].   16th" [of April, Easter Sunday]   [ℓ.2] "Ch. at Holy Communion"   [ℓ.3] "agst. communicating. Going to Merton[?]" [ℓ.4] "...ch. Intemperance at tea with Baillie and/ [ℓ.5] afterwards at Green's dinner. Sitting late in B's room [ℓ.6] against warning of conscience. No reading done. Impatience (17) about scruple [?] against Urquhart and all things in [ℓ.8] [...?] from Dorchester. Some intemperance at Macfarlane's. Clamour in arguing with Baillie.—16 Rubbing eyes with fingers [cf. p.61, ℓ.8] in evening and again 18, evening, and for a [ℓ.11]...[?] on the 19th, morning.—18 Idleness in getting up. Delay in going to town [London: home to Hampstead].—19 Frivolous talk to Arthur [GMH's brother] in morning. Idleness. Lessons unread. Not nice way in talking to Mamma. Lateness to bed. Intemperance at dessert. — 20 Idling all day and in going to bed. An evil [ℓ.15, cont. ℓ.21] thought rose while I was making some poetry in fields but I was only guilty of not dismissing the subj/ect as far as I understand. Not down to prayers [ℓ.24]...[?] (21) at evening prayers. No lessons. Quickness with Cyril. Waste of time. Madox Brown's pictures. [ℓ.26] Looking [?] at navvies in Swiss Cottage Fields. Waste of time in going to bed. Impurities. Not in time (22) for prayers. Morning lessons unread. Evil as well as foolish and proud thoughts. Putting off Holy Communion by waste of time chiefly [end of ℓ.29, cont. ℓ.32] 22 [?] Idling and irresolution at night so as to be late to/bed. Inattention at chapel and church [April 23 was Sunday: GMH now back at Oxford]. Proud thoughts about preaching. Dangerous talking about Dolben, no [ℓ.35] reading whatever. Censoriousness, slander, etc. in/talking about [?] Powell, etc.. Speaking about holding up/[ℓ.37] my hands in prayer in Lent to Coles. —24. Foolishly being/... Indecision about [Holy Communion?]. Idling.../[ℓ.39] and idling in Coles' room in evening..." Oxford Poets (lines 16 to 20) Line 20 "Keble [Corpus and Oriel], J.H. Newman" [Trinity and Oriel].

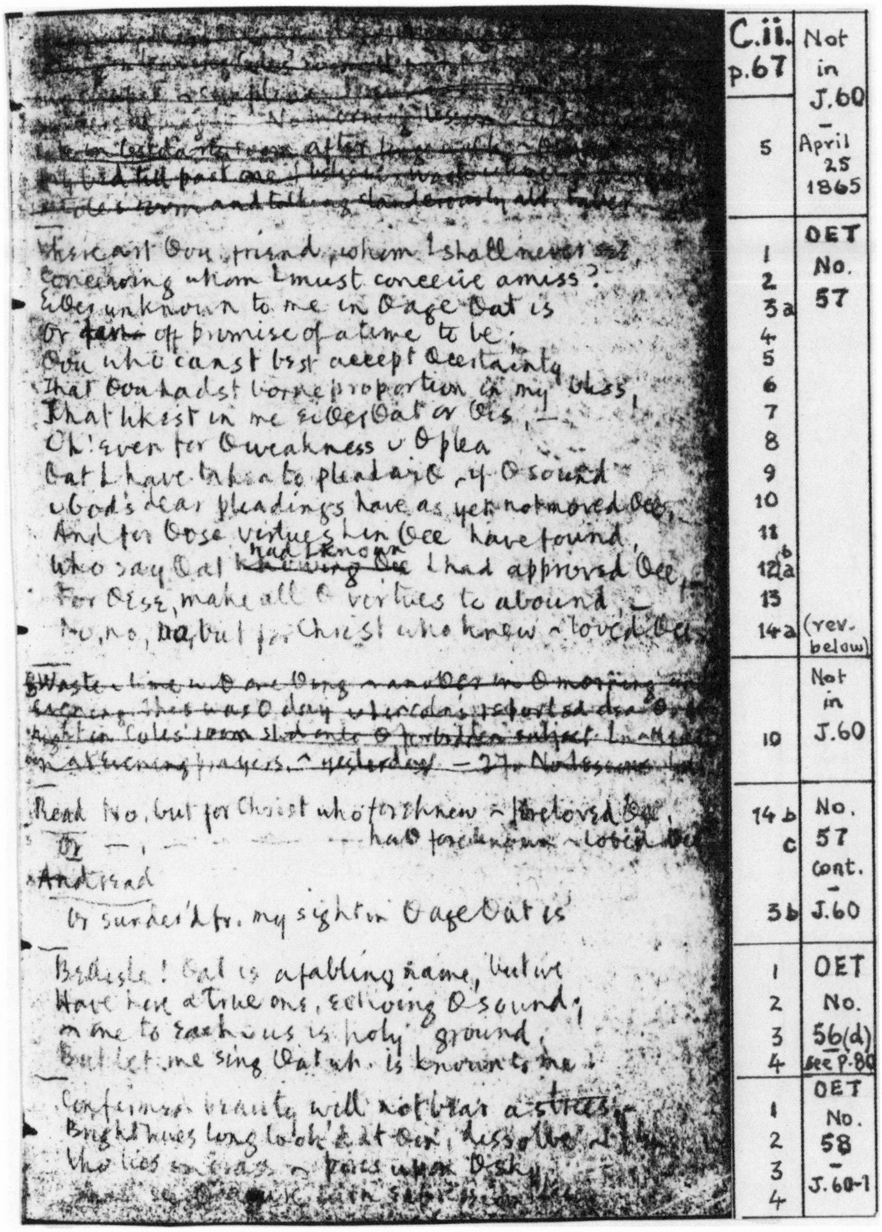
C.ii. p.67
Not in J.60 — April 25 1865
OET No. 57
(rev. below)
Not in J.60
No. 57 cont. — J.60
OET No. 56(d) see P.80
OET No. 58 — J.60-1

Plate 107--C.ii.67: [top line illegible] ℓ.2 "Idling on leaving Coles' room at night." [rest smudged] ℓ.3 [?] "no chapel and compline." [illegible to] ℓ.4 "...No morning lessons.—25 [?] Staying.../late in Geldart's room after long walk and then [not going to?]/my bed till past one I believe. Waste of time [...?]/in Coles' room and talking slanderously about Faber." [Line 7 of "Sins" cont. below OET No. 57, which has illegible words beneath "far", ℓ.4, and the third "no" in ℓ.14.] Sins, ℓ.8 ends "morning and/evening. This was the day of Lincoln's reported death. At/night in Coles' room slid into the forbidden subject. Inattention at evening prayers, and yesterday. — 27. No lessons. Intemp--[cont. p.68 after three lines of verse]. Revision of OET No. 57: 14b "foreknew and foreloved thee." OET No. 56(d) "Bellisle!" For To Oxford, sonnets (a) to (c), see plates 119, 120. # OET No. 58: "Confirmed beauty." 2 "dissolve and fly." 3 "Who lies on grass and pores upon the sky/Shall see the azure turn expressionless"

Plate 108. **C.ii.68--OET No. 58:** "<u>Confirmed beauty</u>" (cont.) 5 orig. "Tantalèan pal[est?]" The nos. 2 and 1 at their ends show that lines 7 and 6 are to be transposed. 7 "blue and be not slaked" # Confession notes break this sonnet into two 7-line units. Line 8 (bot. of page), "And" mended to "Ah! surely all who have written will profess/The sweetest sonnet five or six times read..." 11a orig. "I prove it; therefore when these lines are dead" rev. to "I prove it. What then when these lines" ["What" seems u.c.; contr. "when" and cf. "Where is it?" in Memos above, 5 and 8.] 13 "I'll lay them by, and freshly turn instead" 14 (C.ii.69) orig. "unchartèd"

<u>Sins</u>. In three paras. of confession notes, each cont. from a previous para., GMH at first forgot the "S" and had to insert it later. [Line 1]. [cont. from p.67: "Int]emperance after hall (with Emerton), talking lightly on Millais etc. Evil thoughts now and then. Idleness in morning. Nothing done all day but Papa's translation. Vanity in Union.—28. [April, Friday]. Falling into [cont. ℓ.9] old habits. Evil thoughts and various dangers. [Line 10] Wasting time in C.'s room in morning.—Note. con[cont. ℓ.12]fession for Easter Communion, it is entered: General self-indulgence. Prayers not enough reverent. Inattention at the Psalms. Imitating Christopher. Imitation. [Line 15] Malicious feelings agst. Saintsbury [the prolific author, George Edward Saintsbury, entered Merton 1863] at a celebration at Merton. Neglecting duties. Self-indulgences.—29. Got up late by il[l]ness, but might have got up earlier. Impatience with Urquhart and talking unkindly (his inattention) to Addis abt. him. [Line 20] Being late in getting to work in evening. Envy because Liddon called on Coles and not me. No lessons read.—30 [April, 1865, Sunday]. Nothing read, not very culpable per[haps"—cont. p.69].

PLATE 109.   C.ii. p 69   •   *161*

C.ii. p 69	
14	OET No.58
	Not in J.61
5	Mon. May 1st 1865
	J.61
10	
15	
20	
25	
	(Cont. p.69)

Plate 109.   # C.ii.69.   1. Confession notes cont. "[per]haps but chiefly thro' going to Bridges in the evening. Intemperance (not so much as before) at Coles' desert. Inattention at the services, even at the Holy Communion. Forgetting respect to Urquhart and saying Sh to him.—May 1. Lateness to bed, after getting up before 5. Inattention at Chapel. Wastings of time. Intemperance at lunch in Coles' room. Evening lessons unread.—2 [May]. Lateness in rising, later than excused by fatigue."

9 to bottom: Notes taken at lectures on "Shrubs of the Ancients Monday and Tuesday at 2", mentioned p.68, ℓℓ .5,6. For transcription see J.61. # 27,28 "not indigenous [o(f)? mended to] to" Notes continue on C.ii.70.

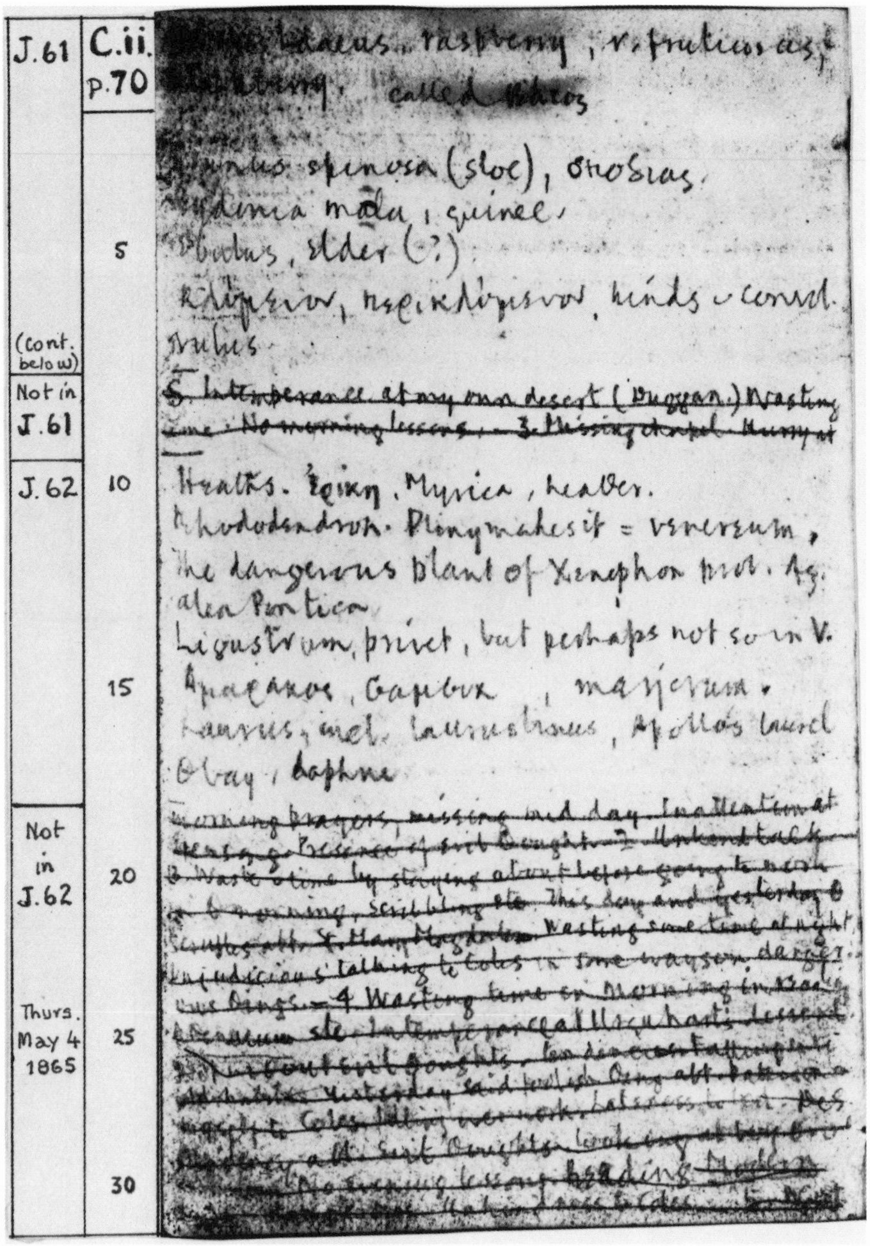

Plate 110. C.ii.70. Top lines smudged: for transcription see J.61-62. 1,2. "Rubus Idaeus, raspberry, r. fruticosus, blackberry, called Βᾶτοϛ3 Prunus spinosa (sloe), ϵπόδιαϛ

Confessions   [Line 8.] "Intemperance at my own desert (Duggan). Wasting time. No morning lessons.—3. Missing chapel. Hurry at [line 18] morning prayers, missing mid-day. Inattention at evensong. Presence of evil thought. 2 [May, Tues.] Unkind talk. 3 [May] Waste of time by staying about before going to work in the morning, scribbling etc. [drawing—cf. p.76, ℓ.2—perhaps also composing poems.]. This day and yesterday the scruples about St. Mary Magdalen. Wasting some time at night. Injudicious talking to Coles in some ways on dangerous things.—4 [May]. Wasting time in morning in reading [ℓ.25] Athenaeum, etc.. Intemperance at Urquhart's dessert. Not without evil thoughts and tendencies. Falling into old habit. Yesterday said foolish thing about Pattison and myself to Coles. Idling over work. Lateness to bed. Despondency about evil thoughts. Looking at boy thro' [ℓ.30] window. No evening lessons. Reading Modern [? Love stanzas...]"—three badly smudged words, bot. line. "Unkindness to Coles. 5 [May] Not" [cont. p.71, "getting up at once."]

PLATE 111.   C.ii. p 71   •   *163*

The beginning of O End.

My love is lessen'd and must soon be past.
I did never promised such persistency
In its condition. No, O tropic tree
Has not a chaster Out its sap shall last
Into all summers, so' no winter cast
Its happy leafing. It is so with me.
My love is less, my love is less for thee.
Cease O mourning O abject fast,
Rise Eat go about my works again,
save, by darting accidents, forget
But ah if you cd. understand how, then
How less is heavens greater every yet
Than treble-fervent more of other men,
Even your unpassion'd Euclids might be wet.

Some men may hate their rivals desire
Sensitive moats, knives, smoldering-clods, drugs, flame
But I am so consumed with my shame
I dare feel envy scarcely never use.
O worshipful O man that she sets higher

I must feed fancy. show me any one
that reads or holds O astrologic lore

	C.ii.	Not in J.62
	P.71	
5		
10		Sat. May 6
1a		OET No. 59 (a) — N.43
2		
3		
4		
5a		
6a		
7		
8		
9a		
10		
11a		
12a		
13a		
14a		
12		Not in J.62
1		OET No. 59(d)
2		
3		
4		
5		
1		No. 59(b)
2		

Plate 111. C.ii.71. Confession notes: "Inattention at morning chap/el. Idling after chapel, over work, foolishly spending [?] afternoon, etc.,—wrongly missing evening chapel. Desire to hear things connected with forbidden subject, as questions about Dolben. Disrespectful feeling towards Jowett. Languor at lecture. Generally, in preparing for Holy Comm. Impatience [ℓ.8] towards Urquhart. Unkind talking about people. Vain thoughts. One morning and two evening lessons unread. Little work in evening. Dawdling in Coles' room till later than was good.—6 [May]. No evening lessons. [Cont. below sonnet, ℓ.12 of notes] No chapel. Wasting time both in morning and evening. Scribbling. Later to bed than good. The story about D. Jerrold and Miss Sach. Inattention at compline.—8 [May]. No chapel or lessons."

   OET No. 59: The beginning of the end. Early version, autograph faircopies with a few revisions. For RB's transcript of a later revision of (a) and (c) (autographs now missing), in A. pp.21-22, see below, plate 159[B]. No. 59(a): ℓ.2 orig. "did no[t]" 9a "rise and" del. 10 "in" [?] → "by". 13 orig. reading under del. "treble-fervent" is illegible. 14 "unpassion'd"; RB misread the revised autograph as "impassioned". C.ii.71-2 are repeated on Plate 159[A].

   No. 59(d)—the start of a fourth sonnet.

   No. 59(b)—smudged lines at the bottom: "I must feed Fancy. Show me any one/That reads or holds the astrologic lore,"

Plate 112. C.ii.72—OET No. 59: The beginning of the end (cont.)

No. 59(b). 5 "that's" apostrophe s squeezed in. 12 a (del.) "No hopes were so ill-heaven'd as mine are"—adapted for ℓ.14. 7b foot-note revision: "Saturn-swayèd" (accent obscured by interlined "influential").

No. 59(c). 5 "assured" grave accent on "ed" del. 8 "And" → "But" 10 "Do" → "Is"..."plea" →"plain" 13 sign for "And", a slip for "A [boy etc.]."

Sins [May 8, cont. from p.71] "Some vain thoughts. Wasting of time. "Good heavens" [quotes del.?]./Seeking occasion agst. Macinnon [cf. L.iii.255].—9 [May, Tues.]. No chapel, but not/my fault in evening, doubtful in morning. Wasting/time by going for tea to Baillie. Anger and impatience [ℓ.5] uncurbed. Fyffe. Wicked feeling.—10 [May]. No chapel. Wasting time in morning talking to Coles about Fyffe. Lateness/to bed. I think only one of the lessons.—11 Lateness to bed.—[12 mended to] 13 [but the dates seem confused when cont. p.73].

PLATE 113. C.ii. p 73 • *165*

	C.ii p.73	Not in J.62
		5	Sun. May 14 1865
	10	

The Alchemist in City.
My window shews the travelling clouds,
Leaves spent, new seasons, alter'd sky,
The making and the melting crowds:
The whole world passes; I stand by.

They do not waste their meted hours,
But men and masters plan and build:
I see the crowning of their towers,
And happy promises fulfill'd.

And I — perhaps if my intent
Cd. count on prediluvian age,
The labours I shd. then have spent
Might so attain their heritage,

But now before the pot can glow
With not to be discover'd gold,
At length the bellows shall not blow,
The furnace shall at last be cold.

Yet it is now too late to heal
The incapable and cumbrous shame
Wh. makes me when with men I deal
More powerless than the blind or lame.

No, I should love the city less,
Even than this my thankless love;
But I desire the wilderness
And weeded landships of the shore.

Poem margin
OET No. 60
4 — N:44
8
12
16 — N.45
20
21a / 22a
21b / 22b
24

Plate 113. C.ii.73. [11? May cont.] "No evening lessons. Idling in looking out of window in Geldart's upper room. Intemperance at dinner. Lateness to/bed after yesterday.—12 (no chapel, only a little of the lessons)—13. Conceited talking to Geldart (as often) about Ilbert [Courtenay Peregrine, Fellow of Balliol, Presid. of the Union, winner of the Ireland Schol.] and Art, and to Coles. Conceited things.—14 [May, Sunday]. Despondency leading to want of devotion at H[oly] C[ommunion]. Inattention at that and matins. Provoked at Coles singing. Managed so as to have no evensong or reading of any sort. Discussion with Geldart with faults of manner. [C.10] Joking at and deceiving Emerton. Looking at a temptation in Newman's friend.—15 [May]. Staying up late, very wrongly. No lessons (unwell). Reading a dangerous thing."

OET No. 60: The Alchemist in the city. Sole MS.. 9 "But" → "And" # 21a, 22a (del.). "I cannot love the city, less/Will I pursue my thankless" 24 "And" rev. to "Or"

OET	C.ii.	
No. 60 (cont.) – N.45	p.74	*I walk my crazy belvedere*
		To watch O law or levant sun,
		I see O city pigeons veer,
	28	*I mark O tower swallows run*
		Betw. O tower-top & O ground
		Below me in O bearing air;
	32	*Oen find in O horizon-round*
		One spot & hunger to be oen.
	33a	~~Then hate~~
	b	*& Oen I hate O most Oat love*
		Oat holds no promise & success;
	36	*Oen sweetest seems O houseless shore,*
		— free & kind O wilderness,
		Or ancient mounds Oat cover bones,
		Or rocks where rockdoves do repair
		& trees & terebint & stones
	40	*& silence & a gulf v. air.*
	41a	~~There~~
	b	~~For there some~~ *long & squared height*
	c	*Here on a*
		After O sunset I wd. lie,
		& pierce O yellow waxen light
	44	*wO free long looking, ere I die.*
Not in J.62	5	*(Sins entries — heavily deleted manuscript)*
	10	
Sun. May 21	15	

Plate 114. C.ii.74--OET No. 60: <u>The Alchemist in the city</u> (cont.)

26 Sign for "And" → "To" 28 "tower" misread as "lower" till 4th. edn. (very small cross to
t) 33a (del.) "Then hate" 41a "There" (del.) 41b "For there some" (del.).

<u>Sins</u>: "16 [May, 1865, Tuesday]. Waste of time in evening. Ill temper at being quizzed. Two
lessons unread. Later to bed than good.—17 [May]. Quarrel with Coles in morning, unkind words.
Waste of time (very much) in morning. No work done in evening through going to Addis [ℓ.5] about
the Canada business. Looking at temptations.—18 [May]. Wasting time in morning--very late to bed
through not turning people out of my room. Bad way with Urquhart. Self-indulgence at a dessert.
(Walk from Bicester to Islip.) Talking about Urquhart.—19. No lessons. Foolish waste of time in
evening. Forgetting God, leading to self-indulgence. [ℓ.11]--20. No evening lessons. Unwisely wasting
time. Presence of evil thought. [Foolish <u>del.</u>] conceited looking forward. Self-indulgence at
S. Davidson's dessert. Impatience with U[rquhart]. Looking at temptations (then reading about
buckles.) [cf. No.120, ℓ.10]—21 [May, Sunday]. Inattention at chapel. Lateness to bed. Leaving
Emerton in my room, and talking about him.--Wasting time in evening and going to bed late. 22. Talking
dangerously of Benson.—23. Inattention in chapel in" (cont. p.75, ℓ.6).

PLATE 115. C.ii. p 75 • 167

Plate 115.   C.ii.75: 1,2 Mrs. Edward Hopkins [Aunt Frances, Canadian artist, on a visit to London in 1865], 7 Palace Gardens Terrace, Kensington.   5 Point-feather elms.

Sins [cont. from p.74, 23 May, 1865:"Inattention in chapel in] morning chapel. No evening lessons, nor penitential psalms either today or yesterday. Greediness from having had no dinner towards some dessert I saw and with my own biscuits. Wasting time.—24 [May, Wed.]. Scarcely attending at all to its/[Line 10] being a fast day. Wasting time. Laughing at U[rquhart]. Inattention at chapel.—25 Ascension Day. The same, even with want of faith at reception of the H[oly] C[ommunion]. Killing a spider. No evening lessons. Impurities of thought.—26. Putting off penintential psalms till late at night. Thinking little of the/[Line 15] Fast. Malice towards Jeffreys. Evil thought slightly in drawing made worse by drawing a crucified arm on same page.—27. No lessons. Wasting and foolishly using time. Sin in dream perhaps.—28 [May, Sunday]. Inattention at services. Waste of time.—29. Intemperance at Wilkinson's dinner. Wasting of time. Conceited thoughts,/[Line 20] and last night.—30. Wasting time in   evening, if I remember, and on 31.—31 Some intemperance at my own dessert. No evening lessons. (Late up on 30, not all my fault.) Looking at F. (but?). [Fyffe—see p.76, ℓ.25] Looking at the Lancet (and long ago temptation in drawing Baillie, before May 12).—June 1 [Thursday]. No evening [lessons", p.76].

OET No. 38: A Voice from the World (cont.). "But what indeed is ask'd of me?" Formerly printed as a separate fragment (4th edn. No. 118) in spite of its acknowledged affinities with No. 38. It seems to help fill the gap after ℓ.121 of the uncompleted poem.   124 "will'd" over l or t.   131a (del.) "I knew at last, and [that success del.] with excess "—the final s is smaller than a comma. The marginal X is repeated below next to the revised opening, ℓ.131b.   134 orig. "And then I thought"

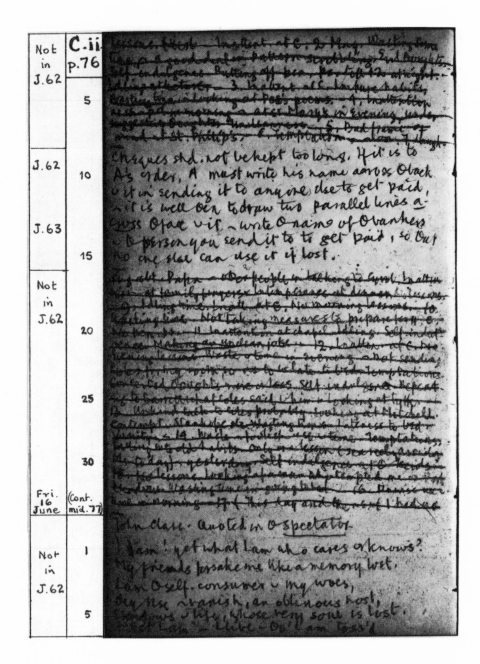

Plate 116. C.ii.76. Sins [cont. from middle of p.75: "June 1. No evening] lessons. (Yest[erday? del.] Inattentive at C[hapel]. 2 May [slip for June]. Wasting some time and a good deal in pattern scribbling. Evil thoughts. Self-indulgence. Putting off pen[itential] ps[alms] till 12 at night. Idling at lecture.—3 [June]. Inattent. at C[hapel]. Impure habits. Wasting time in looking at Poe's poems.—4 [June, Sunday]. Inattention at chapel in morning and at St. Mary's in evening, under suggestive thoughts. Uncleanness.—5. Bad frame of mind at St. Philip's.—6. Temptation and on 7. Laughing [Cont. ℓ.16] about Papa and other people in talking to Cyril. [Easter Term ended Frid. June 2, and Trinity Term began on Sat. 3; GMH went home to Hampstead briefly.] Inattention at family prayers. Intemperance at dinner. No lessons.—9. Idling time. Inatt. at C.. No morning lessons.—10. Wasting time. Not taking measures to prepare for H[oly] C[ommunion]. [ℓ.20] No pen. ps..—11 [June, Sun.]. Inattention at chapel. Idling. Self-indulgence. Making an unclean joke.—12. Inatten. at C.. No evening lessons. Waste of time in evening and not sending Coles from my room, so as to be late to bed. Temptations. Conceited thoughts more or less self-indulgent [mended from "indulgence"]. Repeating to Garrett what Coles said of him. Looking at Fyffe.[13] Unkind talk to Coles probably. Looking at Mitchell. Contempt of Stanhope, etc. Wasting time. Lateness to bed. Vanity.—14. Waste and foolish use of time. Temptations. Falling into old habits. Only one lesson (scarcely avoidable today) and yesterday. Self-indulgence at the Reids' [see p.52, ℓ.2, plate 99].—15. No lessons. Looking at a man who tempted me on Port Meadow. Wasting time in going to bed.—16. Unwise use of time in morning.—17 (This day and the next I had no [cont. p.77] pencil..."/John Clare's poem, "I am", quoted from the Spectator, [28 May 1864].

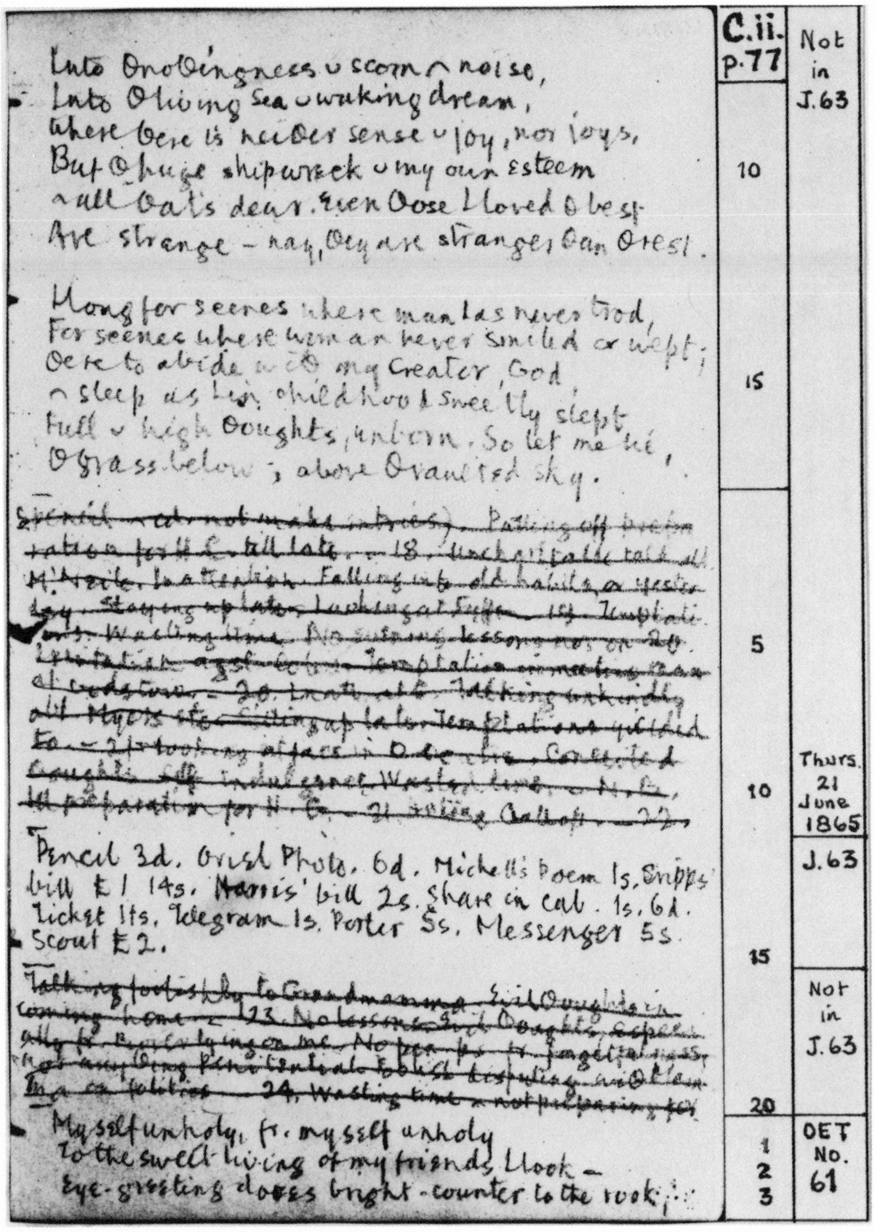

PLATE 117.   C.ii. p 77   •   *169*

	C.ii. p.77	Not in J.63
(handwritten verse)	10	
(handwritten verse)	15	
(handwritten prose, struck through)	5	
	10	Thurs. 21 June 1865
(handwritten expense list)		J.63
	15	
(handwritten prose, struck through)		Not in J.63
	20	
(handwritten verse)	1 2 3	OET NO. 61

Into moodingness & scorn & noise,
Into O living sea & waking dream,
where there is neither sense & joy, nor joys,
But O huge shipwreck & my own esteem
& all O's dear. Even Oose I loved O best
Are strange — nay, O's are stranger than O rest.

I long for scenes where man has never trod,
For scenes where woman never smiled or wept;
O're to abide with my Creator, God,
& sleep as in my childhood sweetly slept
Full & high O thoughts unborn. So let me lie,
O grass below; above O vaulted sky.

Pencil 3d. Ogist Photo. 6d. Michell's Poem 1s. Snipps
bill £1 14s. Harris' bill 2s. Share in cab. 1s.6d.
Ticket 1s. Telegram 1s. Porter 5s. Messenger 5s.
Scout £2.

Myself unholy, fr. myself unholy
To the sweet living of my friends I look —
Eye-greeting doves bright-counter to the rook;

Plate 117.   C.ii.77.   John Clare's "I am", cont.
    Sins, cont. [On 17 and 18 of June 1865 GMH had no] "pencil and could not make entries). Putting off preparation for H.C. till late.—18 [Sun.]. Uncharitable talk about M'Neile [D.A. M'Neill, Balliol 1861-66; died 1866]. Inattention. Falling into old habits, or yesterday. Staying up late. Looking at Fyffe.—19. Temptations. Wasting time. No evening lessons nor on 20./[ℓ.6] Irritation against Coles. Temptation in meeting man at Godstow.--20. Inatt. at C[hapel] Talking unkindly about Myers etc. Sitting up late. Temptations yielded to.—21. Looking at face in the theatre. Conceited thoughts. Self-indulgence. Wasted time, of [on?] N.B. ["North British"? see C.ii.64, ℓ.16]. Ill preparation for H[oly] C[ommunion].—21. Hating Gallop.—22. [cont. ℓ.16] Talking foolishly to Grandmamma. Evil thoughts in coming home.—23. No lessons. Evil thoughts, especially from Rover lying on me. No pen[itential] ps[alms] from forgetfulness, nor anything penitential. Foolish disputing with Mamma on politics.—24. Wasting time and not preparing for" [cont. p.78, "the H.C."].
    Line 12. "Cripps'" apparently mended from "Sripps'" [cf. p.61, ℓ.15]
    OET No. 61: "Myself unholy"

Plate 118. C.ii.78--OET No. 61: "Myself unholy, from myself unholy" (cont.)

4a "Brig[ht]" del. 4b "White clouds to furnace-eaten regions coaly:" 7a "And so my trust confusedly is shook" Below 7b the del. "S" marks space he had allocated for confession notes. 4d "to saltsa[nd]" 7d "confusèd" 9a "Yie[lds]", rev. to "He", then del., prob. to leave a line space after octave. "He has a [fault rev. to] sin of mine" 11a "In him this", then ital. del. 12a "one," then comma del. 13a "This time it serves not. I can seek no [brother ? mended to] other/Than Christ; to Christ I look, on Christ I call." 9a to 14a all del. 13b "save best; no [brother? del.]" "on Christ I [fall mended to] call." 10c "And partly I hate, partly condone that fall;" is replaced at the foot of the poem by 10d, "Knowing them well..."; but this change of syntax calls for 9 to end with a semi-colon (editorial), not the comma which preceded three versions of the next line (10) all beginning with "And".

Sins [cont. from 77, C.20, "not preparing for] the H[oly] C[ommunion]. No lessons.—25 [Sun.]. Inattention and bad frame of mind at Mr. West's ch[urch], self-indulgence. Idling in going to bed. Nothing done.—26. No lessons. Morning spent" [cont. p.81].

OET No. 56: To Oxford. Dated "Low Sunday and Monday, 1865" (i.e., April 23-24), two months earlier. 4 "were send" (slip for "sent")

PLATE 119. C.ii. p 79 • *171*

TO OXFORD.

New-dated fr. O terms Oat reappear,
More sweet-familiar grows my love to Oee
nstill Oou bind'st me to fresh fealty
wiO long-superfluous ties, for noOing here
Nor elsewhere can Oy sweetness unendear.
This is my park, my pleasaunce; Oi's to me
As public is my greater privacy,
All mine, yet common to my every peer.

Those charms accepted of my inmost thought,
The towers musical, quiet-walled grove,
O window-circles, Oese may all be sought
By oOer eyes, noOer suitors move,
n all like me may boast, impeach'd not,
Their special-general title to Oy love.

(Continued.)

Thus, I come underneath Oi's chapel-side,
To that O mason's levels, courses, all
Ovigorous horizontals, each way fall
In bows above my head, as falsified
By visual compulsion, till I hide
O steep-up roof at last behind O small
Eclipsing parapet; yet above O wall
Osumptuous ridge-crest leave to poise n ride.

None besides me this bye-ways beauty try.
Or, if Oey try it, I am happier Oen:
O shapen flags n drilled holes n sky,
Just seen, may be many unknown men
O one peculiar n Oeir pleasured eye,
n I have only set O same to pen.
                    Low Sunday n Monday, 1865.

EASTER COMMUNION
Pure fasted faces draw unto Oi's feast:
God comes all sweetness to yr. Lenten lips.

C.ii. P.79	OET No. 56 (a) - N.46
5	
10	No. 56 (b)
5	
10	see P.80 for 56(c)
1 b 2 b	OET No. 53 (revis. from C.ii.59)

Plate 119. C.ii.79—OET No. 56: To Oxford

No. 56(a): "New-dated from the terms that reappear" 10 "quiet-wallèd"—note grave. 13 "impeachèd"—note grave accent.

No. 56(b): "Thus, I come underneath this chapel-side" 6 "small" m mended from w 9 "bye-ways" no apostrophe in ms. 12 "may be [to omitted in error] many"

No. 53: Easter Communion (MS.2). Revised autograph. (For earlier draft see C.ii.58-59, plate 101.) # 1b,2b "Pure fasted faces draw unto this feast:/God comes all sweetness to your Lenten lips."

Plate 120. C.ii.80: Easter Communion--revised version, cont.

3b "You striped in secret with breath-taking whips,"—the stroke above "breath" in the plate is not part of the text.   6d "With [thin del.] draught"   10b "gladness"—ms. prob. intends comma, not semi-colon.   11b "ever-fretting"—a minute dot represents the hyphen.

No. 56(c): To Oxford--"As Devonshire letters, earlier [th(an) del.] in the year"   The last two lines, which he had forgotten, are not recorded elsewhere, leaving the sonnet in an unfinished state. (See plate 107 for No. 56d, "Bellisle! that is a fabling name", which was perhaps an alternative opening quatrain for No. 56c).   5 "So is it with my friends, I note, to hear"

OET No. 62: "See how Spring opens with disabling cold"   3,4 "Is it a wonder [that they ? del.] if the buds are slow?/Or where is strength to make the leaf unfold?"

PLATE 121. C.ii. p 81 • 173

Plate 121. C.ii.81--OET No. 62: "See how Spring opens" (cont.)

Sins (cont. from p.78: 26 June. "Morning spent) foolishly. Weakness about self-denial. That sonnet beginning "See how Spring opens with disabling cold"—scruple.—27. No lessons. Morning wasted almost and afternoon misspent. No self-denial.—28. Vigil of St. Peter. Self-indulgence at dinner not altogether intentional but with consequence of making me feel unwell. No lessons. Nor evening ditto on 28 [slip for 29?]. Falling into old habits. Temptation violent. Too affect. signature to Addis. Idling. Lateness./[ℓ.9] Inattent. at church.—30 [June]. Self-indulgence. No lessons. Foolish spending of time.—July 1 [1865]. Self-exam. Despair of God. Talking against Aunt Frances [see plate 115, ℓ.1]. Waste of time. Temptations and last night in bed. Self-indulgence in kitchen garden. Foolish and weak self-indulgence. Idling in going to bed. No lessons. Nor evening ch[urch] or lessons on 2 [Sun.]. Inatt. at ch. Self-indulgence./[ℓ.15] Old habits. Lateness.—3. No lessons. Impurities. Time wasted in dressing. Anger. Talking unkindly of people.—4. Lateness in undressing. Temptations.—5. No lessons [? read]. Looking at boys, several instances, and foolishness [?] also. Vanity,/[line 19] after looking in glass.—6. No morning lessons. Misspent time. Irritation agst. Frank Geldart. [GMH stayed with the Geldarts near Manchester, July 6-20, 1865; see L.i.1; J.339.] Temptation, but less. Vanity on 7. Laziness. Some idleness. Temptations yielded to. Old habits."

OET No. 63: Continuation of R. Garnet[t]'s "Nix". 5,6 "I see her riving fingers tear/A branch of walnut-leaves, and that"....

OET No.	C.ii p.82		
		More sweetly shades her stolen hair	
		Than fan or hood or strawy plait.	
63	9	He sees her, O but he must miss	
—	10	A something in her face v guile,	
J.64	11a	~ relish not her loveless kiss	
	12	~ wonder at — shallow smile.	
	11b	Or ~ half mislike her loveless kiss.	
	13	. Ah no! ~she who sits beside	
	14	, Bids him his way his gazes fix .	
	15a	Then she seems sweet who seems his bride,	
	16a	She sour who seems the slighted Nix.	
	15b	Then sweetest seems the seeming bride	
	16b	When maddest looks – slighted Nix.	
Not in J.64	1	~~8. Self-righteousness towards Ernest Geldart~~	
	2		
	3		
No. 63 (cont.)	17	I know v the bored ~ bitten rocks	
		Not so far outward in the sea :	
		One lives O witch shall win my locks	
	20	~ my blue eyes again for me .	
		Alas! but I am all at fault,	
		Nor locks nor eyes shall win again .	
		I dare not taste the thickening salt,	
		I cannot meet the swallowing main .	
	25	Or if I go, she stays meanwhile,	
		Who means to wed or means to kill,	
		~ speeds unchseck'd her murderous guile	
		Or wholly winds him to her will .	
Not in J.64	4		
	5		
	6		
	7		

Plate 122. C.ii.82--OET No. 63: Continuation of R. Garnet[t]'s "Nix" (cont.)

  7,8 "More sweetly shades her stolen hair/Than fan or hood or strawy plait." 16b orig. ditto mark (a long dash) under "seems"; rev. to "looks". Cont. after confession notes.

  Sins. 8 [July]. Self-righteousness towards Ernest Geldart [younger brother of E.M. Geldart of Balliol; J.339]. Imprudent looking at organ-boy and other boys. Inatt. at prayers (family.)—9 [Sun.]. And at them [prayers] and twice at church. Censoriousness [cont. below poem, ℓ. 4] towards Jeffreys (at least unkind saying), or yesterday. Looking at temptations, esp. at E.Geldart naked. Foolish talk yesterday and partly today about Mrs. Geldart.—10. Conduct in playing with Nash [see J.135, 348] and the Geldarts unwise. Telling [cont. p.83] story"....

PLATE 123. C.ii. p 83 • 175

Plate 123. C.ii.83. Confession notes (10 July 1865, cont. from p.82: "Telling) story about Grose. Inatt. at family prayers. Some temptation. Old habits. Waste of time. Conceited thoughts.—11. Vacillation about drawing. Carelessness about time. Self-satisfaction. Laughing at Lee. Repeating what Coles said of Urquhart.—12. [ℓ.5] Feeling contempt for Mr. Ransome's friend and for the Leighs. Irritation with Geldart about pock-bitten. Self-indulgence.—13. and today. Hating Mrs. Leigh and Leigh, and talking about that and other things unreticently to Geldart.—14. Ill feeling towards Geldart, and towards Leigh. Lateness to bed. One lesson unread.—15. Inattention at prayers (family). Waste of time at night. Hurry and excitement over my prayers and Old habits, badly in going to bed, not duly checked.—16 [Sun.]. Inatt. at ch. twice and fam. prayers. Speaking with [cont. p.84] unadvised warmth to Geldart."

OET No. 44(d): Richard--"Sylvester, come, Sylvester". For earliest drafts, see C.i.137-39, rev. C.ii.33-34 (No. 44, a,b, and c). 3 "Crisped" rev. to "Crisp'd" 12a (del.) "His steady wheel" 12b "horn" rev. to "wheel" 13 "brushe[s]" rev. to "brush" 16 "shelder" slip for "shelter"

OET No. 44(e): Richard--"There was a meadow" 3a (del.) "On the other s[ide]" 6-10 "Their highest sprays were drawn as fine as lashes,/With centres duly touch'd and nest-like spots,—/And oaks,—but these were leaved [with del.] in sharper knots./Great butter-burr-leaves floor'd the slope corpse [for copse] ground/Beyond the river, all the meadows round," cont. p.84. In 9 "corpse-ground" is not hyphenated.

Plate 124. C.11.84--OET No. 44(e): Richard--"There was a meadow"
11,12,13 "And each a dinted circle. The grass was red/And long, the trees were colour'd, but the o'er-head,/Milky [and sober—del.] and dark, with an attuning stress" The stop after "head" is a comma, but appears a semi-colon through the infra-red filter. In 13 "and sober-dark" is confusingly mended and rev., with a very large sign for "and" drawn above "sober" 17a (del.) "Made Richard" [cont. below Confession notes] 20 "on that", not "in that"—the dot is irrelevant; the apparent comma after "bay" is the apostrophe after "Keats". 23 "meadows" del., rev. to "fields" 24 "came."—faint period 28—end of poem.

Confession notes [cont. from p.83, 16 July 1865, "Speaking with] unadvised warmth to Geldart. Old habits. Feeling against Pollock of self-righteousness etc and ill-feeling against a woman. Wasting time at night. Nothing done.—17. Anger against Ernest Geldart [E.M.G.'s younger brother]. Old habits. Inatt. at fam. prayers. Lateness in morning [ℓ.5] (often) and at night.—18. Heat in argument. Not in bed till past 1. Cruelty to a moth. Old habits badly at night.—19. Old habits and acts of uncleanness. Temptations somewhat yielded to. Bad manner with Ernest Geldart. Self-indulgence. No lessons.—20 [July, 1865, Thurs.].Temptations partly yielded to. Old habits. Despising fellow passengers [on the journey back home to London].—21. Imitating and laughing at Herclots. [ℓ.11] Wasting time at night. No lessons. Putting off pen[itential] ps[alms] till the last thing. Ill temper with Cyril at dinner. Inattention at family prayers.—22. Affectation in manner. No lessons. Idling time. Speaking unkindly of Durnford and Herclots.—23 [Sun.]. Bad inattent. at morning ch[urch], not quite so bad at evening. Ditto at family prayers. Making Mamma unhappy about my poems. Wasting time. No bible read. Old habits and on 24. Waste of time. No lessons. [Cont. after "Richard".] Waste of time in going to bed. Temptations—25. No lessons. Temptations partly yielded to. Old habits at night. Temper [cont. p.87] with Cyril." Rest of page has poetic jottings.
20 "Mems. The opposite sunset [see plate 126]. The barrow clouds. The valves [grave prob. meant for 'Valvèd' in ℓ.21]. The rail. Mallowy. Peace. Valvèd eyes. Bats' wings and images. Lobes of leaf. Theory of trees. Temper in art." Next line divided off:
OET No. 64a: [Fragments IV—July, August 1865]. "[It ? mended to] He shook with racing notes the standing air."

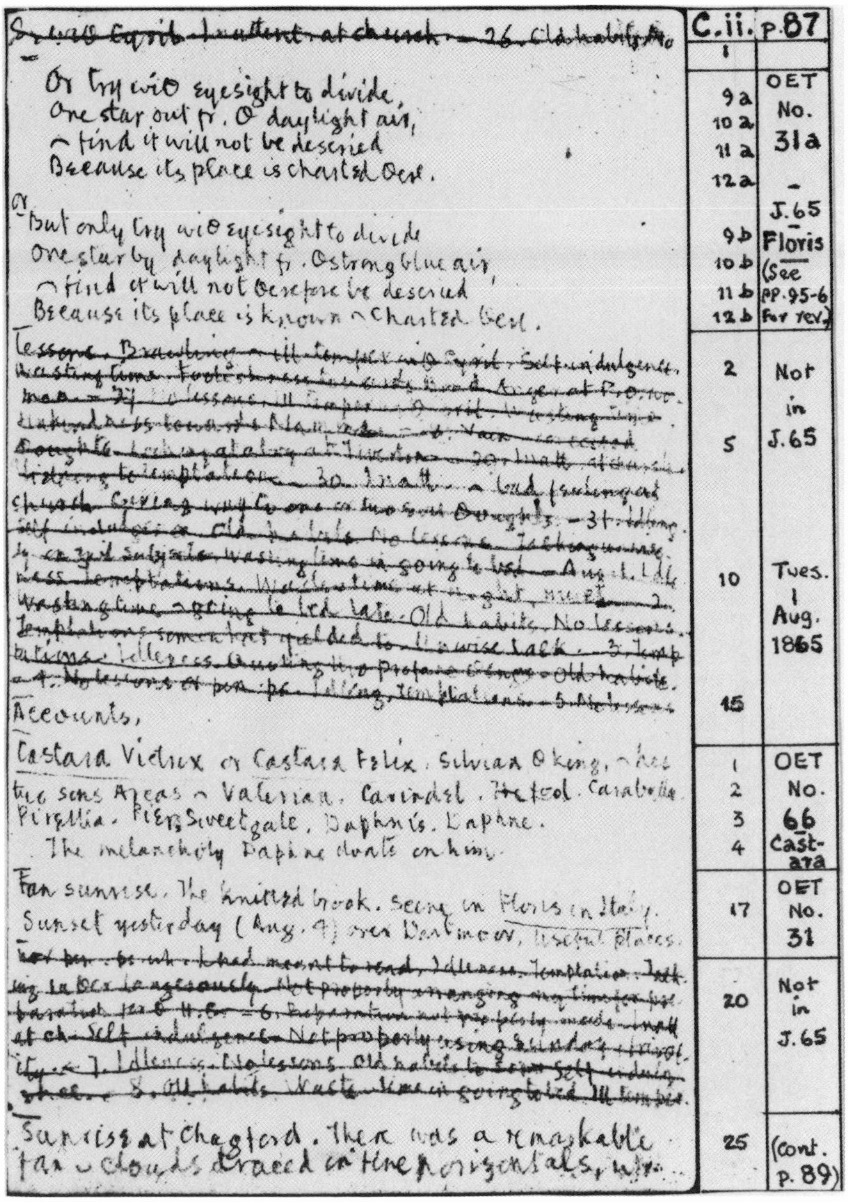

PLATE 125. C.ii p 87 • 177

The manuscript facsimile shows handwritten notes with a right-hand column table:

	C.ii p 87
9 a / 10 a / 11 a / 12 a	OET No. 31a
9 b / 10 b / 11 b / 12 b	J.65 Floris (see pp. 95-6 for rev.)
2 / 5 / 10 / 15	Not in J.65 — Tues. 1 Aug. 1865
1 / 2 / 3 / 4	OET No. 66 Castara
17	OET No. 31
20	Not in J.65
25	(cont. p. 89)

Plate 125 Cii.85,86. This leaf was cut out. The stub (see plate 124) reveals that it bore the sketch headed "Blue with rosy clouds", "a rougher drawing made at the time on the torn out page" (see note p.88). The continuity of the notes is not affected.

C.ii.87—OET No. 31(a): Floris in Italy. First draft towards a passage developed on C.ii.95-96. Another fragment towards the play occurs below this draft.

Confession notes [cont. from p.84, "Temper] with Cyril [his brother: see J.310]. Inattent. at church.—26. Old habits. [Cont. below drafts of No. 31] No lessons. Brawling and ill-temper with Cyril. Self-indulgence. Wasting time. Foolishness towards Bond [Edward Bond lived in Hampstead also: see J.302-3]. Anger at P[ost] O[ffice] woman.—27. No lessons. Ill temper with Cyril. Wasting time. [ℓ.5]. Unkindness towards Mamma.—28. Vain and conceited thoughts. Looking at a boy at Tiverton [see L.iii.89-90, and L.i.1 for GMH's visit to Devon, July-Aug. 1865].—29. Inatt. at church. Yielding to temptation.—30 [Sun.]. Inatt. and bad feeling at church. Giving way to one or two evil thoughts.—31. Idling. Self-indulgence. Old habits. No lessons. Talking unwisely on evil subjects. Wasting time in going to bed.—Aug. 1 [1865]. Idleness. Temptations. Waste of time at night, much.—2. Wasting time and going to bed late. Old habits. No lessons. Temptations somewhat yielded to. Unwise talk.—3. Temptations. Idleness. Quoting two profane things. Old habits.—4. No lessons or pen[itential] ps[alms]. Idling. Temptations.—5. No lessons [Cont. below notes for poems, ℓ.17] nor pen. ps. which I had meant to read. Idleness. Temptation. Talking rather dangerously. Not properly arranging my time for preparation for the H[oly] C[ommunion].—6 [Sun.]. Preparation not properly made. Inatt. at ch. Self-indulgence. Not properly using Sunday, frivolity.—7. Idleness. No lessons. Old habits to some Self-indulgence.—8. Old habits. Waste of time in going to bed. Ill temper."

OET No. 66: Castara Victrix. "The fool" del. "Piers Sweet⌣gale" (not "-gate" as in J.65). "The melancholy Daphne [not "Daphnis" as in J.] doats on him."

<u>Plate 126.</u> <u>C.ii.88</u> "Blue with rosy clouds"--<u>A sunset seen at Hampstead</u> on July 20 (see enigmatic note, C.ii.84, bot., ℓ.20, "The opposite sunset"). In ℓ.11 he explains that a rougher drawing [on p.85] was torn out and used to guide this one. See J.65 for transcription of the description. Neither sketch is reproduced **in J**./ **4**"Green under the red."

<u>Plate 127</u> <u>C.ii.89.</u> The Hampstead sunset, seen in company with the Dugmores, is reproduced on a smaller scale, but only lines 1 to 5 describe it (see J.65-66 for description). Lines 6 to 8 continue the account of a su<u>nrise</u>, begun at the bot. of C.ii.87, witnessed at Chagford "on the borders of Dartmoor" (L.i.1).

Lines 9 to 13 begin a description of a <u>Chagford sunset</u> (cont. top C.ii.90).

9 "Over the nearest [ridge <u>as J.66 reads</u>, <u>but</u> <u>this</u> <u>is</u> <u>mended to</u>] ledge...trail of bronze-lit   10 (<u>del</u>.) "but this   not the por[tion?]"

12 "a field with an angle"

PLATE 127. C.ii. p 89 • *179*

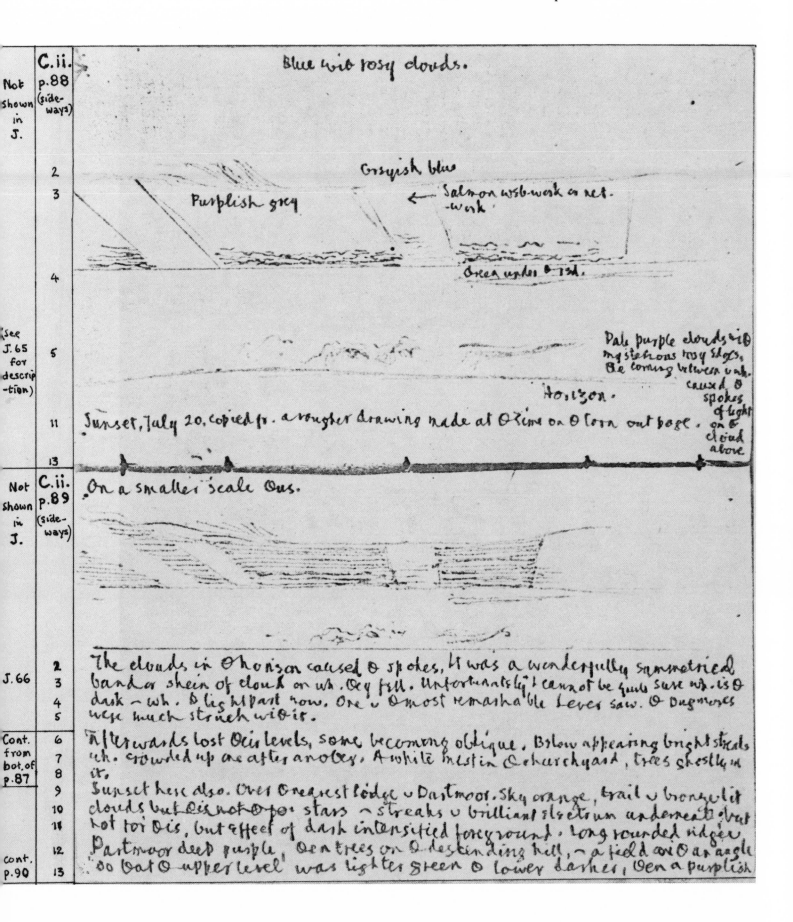

Blue wit rosy clouds.

Greyish blue

Purplish grey

← Salmon web-work or net-work

Green under ⊙ set.

Pale purple clouds wit mysterious rosy edges. These coming between & also caused ⊙ spokes of light on ⊙ cloud above

Horizon.

Sunset, July 20, copied fr. a rougher drawing made at ⊙ time on ⊙ corn out bags.

On a smaller scale Ours.

The clouds in ⊙ horizon caused ⊙ spokes. It was a wonderfully symmetried band or skein of cloud on wh. ⊙ey fell. Unfortunately I cannot be quite sure wh. is ⊙ dark — wh. ⊙ light part now. One ⊙ ⊙ most remarkable I ever saw. ⊙ Dugmores were much struck wi⊙ it.

Afterwards lost ⊙eir levels, some becoming oblique. Below appearing bright streaks wh. crowded up one after another. A white mist in ⊙ churchyard, trees ghostly in it.

Sunset here also. Over ⊙ nearest lodge ⊙ Dartmoor. Sky orange, trail ⊙ bronze lit clouds but ⊙is not ⊙ for stars — streaks ⊙ brilliant electrum underneath ⊙ but not for ⊙is, but effect of dusk intensified foreground. Long rounded ridges Dartmoor deep purple, ⊙en trees on ⊙ descending hill, — a field over ⊙ an angle 'so ⊙at ⊙ upper level' was lighter green ⊙ lower darker, ⊙en a purplish

(cont. from p.89)	C.ii. p.90	
J.66	5	
	10	
Not in J.66 [Aug 12 1865]	15 17	
OET No. 64b J.66	1 2 3 4 5	a b
OET No. 65 J.66	1 2 3 4 5a 6 7 8 9 10a 11a	
(Rev. p.91)	10b	
J.67	18 19	

Plate 128 C.ii.90. Chagford sunset (cont. from p.89) 1-3 "great brown field, then the manufactory with grey white timbers.../grey shingle (?) roofs." 4 The reference to Hampstead is retrospective: he spent a month at Chagford (L.i.1). "Clouds shewing" 5 "compared" (contr. J.66).

    <u>Confession notes</u> [Aug.] "9. [1865]. Waste of time at night. No lessons. Heat in argument. Some temptations.—10. No lessons. Unkindness to Phillimore [see J.159, 378] Ill-temper in argument. Self-indulgence. Waste of time at night. [Line 15]—11. No pen[itential] ps[alms] but not wholly my fault. No less[ons]. Ill-temper uncapt (?). Old habits. Waste of time on going to bed.—12. Bad i/dleness Vanity (or yesterday). Ill-temper. No lessons.—13 [Aug. Sunday]. Weak-/ness" [? cont. p.91, middle]

    OET No. 64(b): <u>"A noise of falls"</u> 2a "of [water <u>del</u>.]" 4 "oak" [?] → "ash-tops"

    OET No. 65: <u>"O what a silence"</u> 2 "[those <u>del</u>.] the sweet" 3 "or that" → "and his" 5a, 11a—see p.91, lower half, for 5b, 11b etc. The line-space after 5a was prob. left for alternative. 6 "sky?" del. 8 "[their <u>del</u>.] such" 10a ("X" indicates rev. below) "fol[ded?]" <u>del</u>.

    Prose 18,19: "Brush and comb (how vastly absurd it is) both apply to [? the rough sprays] of water ribs." Line is badly smudged.

PLATE 129. C.ii. p 91 • *181*

The right-hand column of the facsimile reads:

	C.ii. p.91
2	J.67
1	OET
2	No.
3	64c
4	—
5	
6	J.67
3	
5	OET
	64d
10	OET
	64e
12	Not in J.67
5b	OET
11b	No.
12	65
13	(cont.)
14	
15	
16	
15	Not in J.67
20	Thurs. Aug. 17
	(cont. line 27)
25	J.67
30	Not in J.67

Plate 129 # # C.ii.91: 1 "Sprigged white on breast of an iron-grey horse." 2 "Mealy clouds"

OET No. 64c: "Mothers are doubtless happier" Line 4 contains one of the most difficult cruxes in GMH's poems, where two words have been mended. After innumerable re-examinations I now read "come by" → "hold to".

Lines 3 to 11 mix prose and verse. 9 "Oakroots are...solid..." # 10 "Water" del.

S[ins]. "Weak-[p.90]ness or temptation about dangerous sweetness of singing in ch[urch]. Inatt[ention]. Waste of time. Old habits. Bed late.—14 [Aug. 1865] Old habits. No [cont. below] lessons"

OET No. 65 (cont). 11b "As [slip for "of"] the wood-sorrel..." I do not find the "A." prefixed to this line in other edns.

[Sins, cont.. ℓ.14] lessons. Faults of manner to Bond and Phillimore. Almost despair. [Line 15] Temptation in thinking over boy I saw. Another about drawing Phillimore. Loss of faith in God.—15. Looking at men in church at Moreton. Lateness to bed. ˄No lessons. Sharp temper. O.H.—And [?] badly on 16. Bad temper. Lateness to bed. No lessons. Idling. Talking [? with guile] [Line 20] of Burrows [? See J.54], the Church Union, Grey (of SS. Philip's) etc. —17. Idling in going to bed. O.H.. No   lessons and on 18, nor pen[itential] ps[alms]. Evil thoughts at the [?] Holmes'. Self-indulgence at dinner it being Friday, [? O.H. at night.] Idling .—19. Self-indulgence. Idleness.—20 [Aug. Sunday] Inatt. at ch[urch]. O.H. Unkindness to Phillimore. Wasting time at night. [? Idling.]—21. O.H. Lateness to bed. Bad manner. Wasting time." [cont. ℓ.27] S[ins]. No l[essons]—Nor on 22. Waste of time. Unkindness to Phillimore in [? teasing and] imitation at the pic-nic. Self-indulgence.—23. Snappishness in [Line 29] talking with Phillimore. Speaking (yesterday) [rest of page heavily smudged] [?? intemperately abt.....Idleness]—24. [? Waste of time....Phillimore]

The manuscript, with left-hand reference column reading:

Not in J.68 · C.ii. p.92 · 5 · Sun. Aug 27 1865 · 10

OET No. 66a – J.68, with line numbers 1, 2, 3, 4a,4b, 5a, 6a, 7a, 8a, 5b, 6b, 7b, 8b, 9, 10, 11, 12, 17, 18, 19, 20, 13, 14, 15, 16.

Daphne.

who loves me here and has my love,
I think he will not tire of me,
But sing contented as O dove
Oat houses ~~in the wild wood tree~~ trees again to O
woodland tree.

He shall have summer sweets ~ dress
His pleasure to O changing clime,
I ~~shall~~ teach him happiness
That shall not fail in winter-time.

He shall have summer goods, ~ trim
His pleasure to O changing clime,
And I shall know ~ sweets for him
Oat are not less in winter-time.

His cap shall be shining far,
~ stain'd, ~ knots of golden Oread,
He shall be warm wiO miniver
Lined all wiO silk of juicy red.

But if Oese cannot tempt his Ought
WiO wealO Oat mocks his high estate degree,
The shepherds, Ohom I value not,
Have told me I am fair to see.

In spring our river-banks we dept
WiO yellow flags will suit his brow,
In summer are our orchards knopt
WiO green-white apples on O bough

Plate 130   C.ii.92 [Sins], cont.] "Temptation, Contempt for Palk. Talking ag[ain]st Phillimore more or less in spite of intention to the contrary.—25 [Aug. 1865]. Late to bed. Looking at temptations. Conceit. Talking agst. people esp. Lechmere and Durnford [see pp.84, ℓ.14; 105, ℓ.42]. Inatt. at pen[itential] ps[alms]. And Aitken.—26. Having to [Line 5] give up the H[oly] C[ommunion] by not coming home to prepare self for it. Conceited forecasts. Uncleannesses. Inatt. at ch[urch]. Irritated feeling (literary) agst. Carlyle.—27 [Aug., Sunday]. Inatt. at ch[urch] twice. Forecasting. Weakness at dinner. Idleness in afternoon. Nothing read. Temptation to adultery of the heart with Mrs. Gurney listened to [see J.385, L.I.p.1; at Torquay. GMH returned home to Hampstead Aug.28].—28. O[ld] H[abits]. [Line 10] Waste of time in going to bed. Temptations.—29. Waste of time at night. Temptations. No l[essons]. Nor on 30. O.H. Wasting time. 31. O.H. No l[essons]. Waste of time at night. Killing earwig. W.O.T. [? Waste of Time].—Sept. 1. O.H. Waste. Temptations. Lateness down. Despising Bel [? Byl...   ]. [? Name cont. in line below, then del., but completed top of next page.]

OET No. 66a: Daphne. [Song for "Castara Victrix"—see plate 125.] 4 "houses in the wild wood tree" (del.)   7a "shall" del.   5b "goods" prob. not foll. by comma   12 Began with "C" → "Lined". The "X" and dots indicate that the stanza from the bot. of page must follow here.   17 "these" del. 18 "wealth that...[estate del.]"19 "tho'" → "whom"

PLATE 131. C.ii. p 93 • *183*

C.ii
p.93

Not in
J.68

(cont.
below)

4

For Castara,

Enter Castara and her Esquire

	OET No. 66b
	—
	J.68
	—
	Castara —
	—
	J.69

C. What was it we shd. strike O id. again? — 1
E. There was a wood ʌ dwarf ʌ sour'd oaks — 2
Crept all along a hill upon our left, — 3
A wander in O country, ʌ a landmark — 4
O eg. said we cd. not miss. A pushing brook, — 5
Ran O'ro' it, following wh. we shd. have sight — 6
Of mile-long reaches ʌ our road below us. — 7
My O ought was, here to rest against O trees — 8
And watch until O our horses ʌ O men — 9
Circled O safe flanks ʌ O bulky hills. — 10
C. And how long was O way? This shorter way? — 11
E. Two miles indeed. — 12
C. We have gone four, do you O ink? — 13
Somewhere we have slipt astray, you cannot doubt. — 14
E. True, madam, I am sorry now to see — 15
I belie'd all our path O sanguine eyes.

5
6

Not in J.69

Fr. Castara.

At O picnic or whatever we call it. Daphnis Castara

	OET No. 66c
	—
	Castara —

D. — Can I do any harm? — 1
E. If you are silent, that I know of, none. — 2
D. Ill meant, but true. I best shd. flatter O sin, — 3
I'm copying well what you have begun. — 4
C. In copying? how? — 5
D. Must I give tongue again? — 6
In copying yr. sweet silence. Am I so
C. Guilty ʌ silence? — 7
D. Quite, as ladies go. — 8
Yet what you are, O world wd. say, remain: — 9
It never yet so sweetly was put on — 10
By any landed statue, nor again — 11
By speech, so sweetly broken up ʌ gone. — 12
C. What if I hated flattery? Say you do:
D.

Plate 131.   C.ii.93 [Sins, cont. from top of p.92: "Despising Bel/w?]...—2. Anger at something Mamma said. Evil thought. Idleness. Lateness to bed. O.H. And on 3 [Sept. 1865, Sunday]. Inatt. at ch[urch]. Despising Wadmore [Perpetual curate, All Souls, Hampstead, 1865—] and Herklots. Looking at tempting pictures and idling over <u>Once a Week</u>.—4. O.H. Looking with [<u>cont. after No. 66b</u>] wicked curiosity at things in W.S. Landor. Idling. No l[essons]. Late to bed. And on 5, O.H. Idleness. Impurities and often. Temptations.

OET No. 66b: <u>Castara Victrix</u>. With four mended words on this page it is sometimes hard to tell which is on top. Line 1 "What [is →] was" slip for "Where was" 4 "A land[mark]" → "A wonder" [J.68 "wander"]. 6 "Ran" (mended in absent-mindedness to "Than"?) 9 "the ho[rses]" del. 12 "Three" → "Two" [J.69 "Three"] "gone" → "come". 13 "have" del. 15 "path with"

OET No. 66c: <u>Castara Victrix</u>. "Daphis" del. # 3 "yet [...?]" → "but true" 4 "best begun"→ "well begun"

C.ii. p.94	
OET 66c	14
No. 66d	
J.69	
Cast-ara	5
	10
J.70	
	15
	20
	25
Not in J.70	5
OET No. 67 – N.49	1 2 3 4

[Manuscript in Hopkins's hand:]

the latch comes with a good grace to you:
Flattery's all out of place where praise is true.

Valerian, Daphnis.
V. Come, Daphnis.
D. Good Valerian, I will come. [Exit V.
Why shd. I go because Castara goes?
I do not, but to please Valerian.
But why then shd. Castara weigh with me?
Why ... an interest and sweet soul in beauty
wh. makes us eye-attentive to the eye
that has it; ~ she is fairer than ...
Selvaggia, Orinda, and Adela, ~ the rest.
Fairer? these are the flaring shows unlovely
that make my eyes sore ~ cross-colour things
with fickle spots ... sadness; accessories
{ familiar ~ so hated by the sick;
{ hated ~ too familiar to ...
these are my very text ... discontent.
these names, these faces? They are customary
~ kindred ... to my lamentable days,
... wh. I say there is no joy in them.
To these Castara is rain or breeze or spring,
— dew, is dawn, is day,
shot lightning to the stifling lid ~ night
Bright-lifted ... a little-lasting smile
~ breath upon it. That is, her face is theirs.
And if it is why there is cause enough
To say I go because Castara goes.
Yet I'd not say it is her face alone
that this is true of: 'tis Castara's self,
But this distemper'd court will change it all. –
Wh. sees at least then while go while all is fresh
Much cause to go because Castara goes. –

My prayers must meet a brazen heaven
~ fail or scatter all away.
Unclean ~ seeming unforgiven
My prayers I scarcely call to pray.

Plate 132 # # C.ii.94. OET No. 66: Castara Victrix—(c) concl., 13, 14.
    OET 66 (d), also part of Castara Victrix. 5 "there is" rev. to "there's" 15 "of" del. 17 "Spring" prob. u.c. 18 "sheet lightning" (till 1984 printed "shot")..."lid and night" slip for "lid of night" 19 "lifted" → "lifting" 20 "upon" rev. to "on" 26 "sees" → "says"..."while" del. before "go"
    [Sins] 6 [Sept. 1865]. No l[essons]. Lateness to bed, in writing the above, in the last lines of which a wholly (not put down) a wholly illogical association or alarm came, not relinquished soon enough. O.H. Lateness to get up. Weakness if not idleness in evening. Slight tempt. in Shakspere.—7. Idling much over work. Unkindness in talking" (cont. p.95 "with Mamma").
    OET No. 67: "My prayers must meet a brazen heaven" 2 "o[r?]" rev. to "and" 3,4 "Unclean" not del., two unrelated strokes: "Unclean and seeming unforgiven/My prayers I scarcely call to pray."

PLATE 133. C.ii. p 95 • 185

I cannot buoy my heart above;
Above it cannot entrance win,
I reckon precedents ₒ love,
But test ⊙ long success ₒ sin.

My heaven is brass ₐ iron my earⱅⱈ;
Yea, iron is mingled wiⱅⱈ my clay,
So harden'd ʟⁱ⁵ it in ⊙is deaⱅⱈ
ut. praying fails to do away.
Nor tears, nor tears ⊙is clay uncouⱅⱈ
Cₐ mould, if any tears ⊙ere were.
A battle ₒₒ lips in true ,
warfarce ₒₒ God .
A warfarce of my lips in truⱅⱈ,
Battling wiⱅⱈ God, is now my prayer.

After" Because its place is known ₐ chastd ⊙ere"
My My love in lists of loves I wiⱅⱈ, not fend,
Much less all love in one conscribèd spot,
Oo' true love is by narrowest bands confined,
New love is free love, or true love tis not.

~~[deleted struck-through lines]~~
~~[deleted struck-through lines]~~
~~[deleted struck-through lines]~~
~~[deleted struck-through lines]~~

Floris in Italy -- Floris having found by deavicc that Giu
-lia loves him reasons wiⱅⱈ himself (or perh. with Henry)
in defence of his not returning her love. Her beauty is urged.
Beauty it maybe is ⊙ meet ₒ lines,
Or careful-spaced sequences ₒ sound,
These rather are ⊙ are where beauty shines,
⊙ temper'd soil where only her flower is found.
~~At least ᵃlow it has a term ₐ part~~
Allow at least it has one term ₐ past
Beyond, and one wiⱅin ⊙ ᵍ lookers eye;
And I must ᵃᶫʷᵃʸˢ center in my heart
To spread ⊙ compass on ⊙ all-starr'd sky
For only try by gazing to divide

5	OET
6	No.
7	67
8	
9	N.50
10	—
11	"My
12	prayers
13	must
14	meet"
15a	—
16a	
15b	
16b	
(cont. from p.87)	OET No 31 (a)
[13a]	—
[16a]	J.70
[15a]	(cont below)
20a	
1	Not in J.70
2	
3	
4	
5	OET No. 31a (cont.)
6	—
7	N.50
1a	
2a	—
3	
4	
5a	—
5b	Floris
6a	—
7a	
8a	
9 c	

Plate 133 # # C.ii.95--OET No. 67 cont.: "My prayers must meet a brazen heaven" 6 "it" → "I" (i del. by oblique stroke, I on top of t; corrected Poems, 4th edn. reprint 1984) 12 "away" badly blotted 13 "Nor tears," comma half hidden by d of "mould" 15a "lips" the dot over the i (cf. next word, "in") makes l look like a t. 15b Note Freudian slip "warfarce" for "warfare".

OET No. 31(a): Floris in Italy (cont. from C.ii.87) These four lines were later replaced by ℓℓ.13 to 20. [13a] "My" del. to correct indenting "will" → "wd." (would) 20a "freedom" → "free love"

S[ins. cont. from p.94: "Unkindness in talking] with Mamma. O.H.. Forecasts. Dawdling at night. Contemptuous temper at lunch etc. Talking unkindly of Mrs. Reid.—8. O.H. Imitating Papa at the office. Idling in going to and over work. Scrupulosity. Lateness in morning.—9. Waste of time in dawdling"[cont. p.96 "and worse"]

OET No. 31(a): Floris in Italy (cont.) Prose introd. 5 "by acci[dent]" → "chance" 1a "lines," comma del. and then restored 2a "sound" u.c. may not be intended 5a (del.) "At least allow it has a term, a part" 6a "ga[zer's?]" rev. to "looker's" 7a-9c "And I must [always del.] have the centre in my heart/To spread the compass on the all-starr'd sky./[Or →] For only try by gazing to divide"

C.ii.	**p.96**	One star by daylight fr. O strong blue air,
OET	11 c	~ find it will not OckJon be descried
No.	12 c	Because its place is known ~ charted there.
31a	13 b	No, love prescriptive, love ... place assign'd,
(cont.)	14 a	Love by monition, heritage, or lot,
—	15 b	Love by prenatal serfdom still confined
N.50	16 b	Even to O tillage ~ O sweetest spot,—
	17 a	It is a regimen on O imperfect wind,
Floris	18 a	Piecing O elements out by plan ~ plot. [bind,
—	19	Though self-made bands at last may true love
(alternatives below)	20 b	New love is free love or true love 'tis not .
Not in J.70 Sun. Sept. 10	5	*(heavily struck-through lines)*
OET No. 31a (cont.)	1 b	I say beauty lies but in O meet .....
	2 b	In careful-spaced sequences ~ sound'
	8 b	To turn O compass on O all-stain'd day
	17 b	Is to give regimen to O imperfect wind,
N.51	18 b	~ slender element to piece ~ plot,
	18 c	O — elements ~
	20 c	New love is free love or true love 'tis not. [Exit.
	21 a	Thus he ties spider's web across his sight
	22 a	~ gives for tropes his judgment all away,
	23 a	Gilds wi O some sparky fancies his black night
	24 a	~ stumbling swears he walks by light ~ day.
	25 a	Blindness! A learned fool ~ well-bred churl
(rev. p.97)	26 a	Oat swinishly refuses such a pearl !
Not in J.70	10	*(heavily struck-through lines)*

Plate 134   C.ii.96--OET No. 31(a): <u>Floris in Italy</u> cont. 10c to 20b.
    S[ins cont. from p.95. "...dawdling] and worse in idleness both morn. and evening. Scrupulosity. Temptations. Weakly reading a stupid story. Putting off preparing for H[oly] C[ommunion].—10 [Sept., 1865, Sunday]. (I received the H.C.) Want of faith, weakness. I had also a horrible thought but I doubt if it was a temptation. It was about personal love of Ch. Inatt[ention] at ch[urch] twice (and often at fam[ily] prayers.) Some contempt for Herklots. O.H. Waste of time. Temptations." [cont. bot. of page]
    OET No. 31(a): <u>Floris in Italy</u>, some alternatives: <u>X</u>s mark omitted lines with no alternatives. 21a "upon" del.
    S[ins, cont.] 11 [Sept. 1865]. Lateness up and to bed. Temptations, a good many. Wasting much time in morning. Talking unkindly of Aunt Frances. Want of faith in God about temptations—And some on 12 perh[aps]. Lateness to bed. Self-indulgence at Croydon in fruit. O.H. Some unkindness in disputing "[cont. p.97: "with Mamma"].

PLATE 135. C.ii. p 97 • *187*

	C.ii. P.97	Not in J.70
~~[struck through line]~~ 13. O.H. A good deal of idleness ~~[struck through]~~	2	
Or Such spiders web he ties across his sight,	21 b	OET
~ gives for tropes his judgment all away,	22 b	No.
Gilds wi° some sparky fancies blinding right,	23 b	31 a
~ stumbling swears he walks by light o' day.	24 b	(concl)
A learned fool indeed ~ well-bred churl	25 b	End
O at swinishly refuses such a pearl!	26 b	of Floris
Shakspere.		OET No. 68
In °lodges ~ O perishable souls	1	Shaks-
he has his portion. God, who stretch'd apart	2	pere
Doomsday and death — whose dateless Oought		
must chart	3	
All time at once ~ span O dic's lanced goals,	4	
Sees what his place is; but for us O rolls	5	
Are shut agst. O canvassing ~ cast.	6	
Something we guess or know: some spirits start	7	
upwards at once ~ win Oeir aureoles	8	
. . . . . .		
~~14. C.H. ... going to work. Grumbl...~~ ~~...last night ab...~~		Not in J.70
~~...bed. Sept. 15, O.H. Idling! ...knowledge~~	5	15 Sept 1865
Edward O confessor had a vision. F.G. Lee's ser-		J.70
mon in O second series ~ O A.P.U.C. sermons		
quoted in O Union R. says, Oat England		
shd. be afflicted ~ not restored to God's mercy		
till "a green tree, cut down fr. O root, ~ removed	10	
3 furlongs distant fr. its own stock, shd., weOout		
O help ~ any man's hand, return to its own rt. a-		
gain, ~ bring for O fruit ~ flourish." This is re-		
counted in O Salisbury Breviary. Taking 1325		
as O date ~ O Reformation ~ a furlong as	15	

Plate 135   C.ii.97.   [Sins, cont. from p.96 "disputing] with Mamma.—13. O.H. A good deal of idleness
o-/ver work. Reading weakly a thing in <u>Love's Labour</u> [sic] <u>Lost.</u>"
    OET No. 31(a): <u>Floris in Italy</u> (last surviving draft). Alternatives to 21 to 26.
    OET No. 68: <u>Shakspere</u>. The octave of an unfinished sonnet (note the row of dots below it and
the space left.
[<u>Sins</u> cont.] 14 [Sept. 1865]. "O.H. No 1[essons]. Idleness in going to work. Grumbling last night
ab[ou]t Arthur being put into my bed. Lateness to bed. 15. O.H. Idling, [? tho' with knowledge]"
   <u>"Edward the Confessor</u>..." 12 "its own rt." [root] 14 "Taking 1525" (looks like "1325")

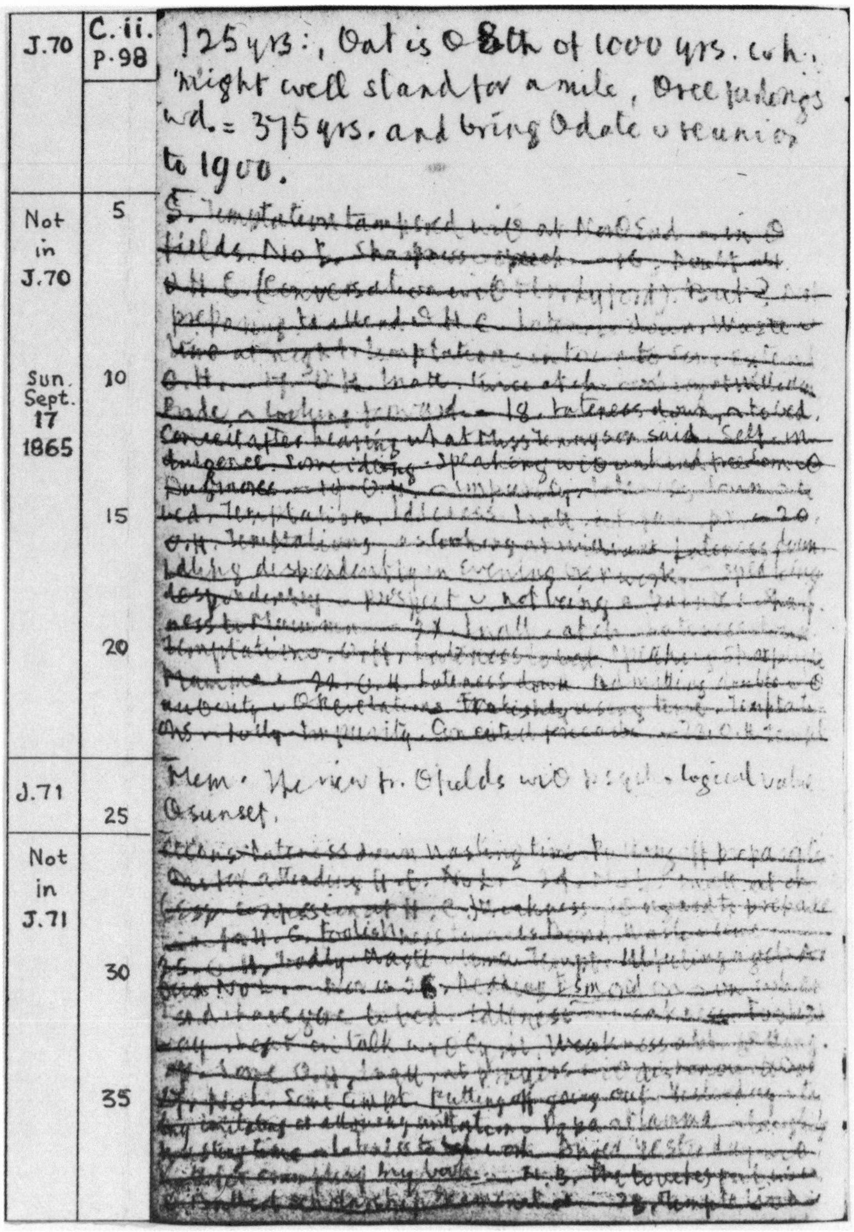

Plate 136   C.ii.98. 1 the ei[gth] → 8th.

    S[ins 15 Sept. 1865 cont.]. "Temptation tampered with at North End [in Hampstead] and in the fields. No L[essons]. Sharpness of speech.—16. Doubt about the H[oly] C[ommunion] (Conversation with Mr. Lyford). But? Not preparing to attend the H.C.. Lateness down. Waste of time at night. Temptations in town to some extent. [Line 10] O.H.—17 [Sept., Sunday]. O.H. Inatt[ention] twice at ch[urch]. Looking at William. Pride and looking forward.—18. Lateness down, and to bed. Conceit after hearing what Miss Tennyson said. Self-indulgence. Some idling. Speaking with unkind freedom of the Dugmores [J.66, (Plate 127), 150,168,338].—19. O.H. and impurity. Lateness down and to [Line 15] bed. Temptation. Idleness. Inatt. at fam[ily] pr[ayers].—20. O.H. Temptations as looking at William. Lateness down. Idling despondently in evening over work and speaking despondently of prospect of not being a painter. Sharpness to Mamma.—21 [1 del.?]. Inatt. at ch[urch]. Lateness down. [Line 20]. Temptations. O.H. Lateness to bed. Speaking sharply to Mamma.—22. O.H. Lateness down. Admitting doubts of the authority of the Revelations [sic]. Foolishly [mended?] using time. Temptations and folly. Impurity. Conceited forecasts—23. O.H. Tempt[cont. ℓ.26]ations. Lateness down. Wasting time. Putting off preparations for attending H[oly] C]ommunion]. No L[essons].—24 [Sept., Sunday]. No L[essons]. Inatt[ention] at ch[urch] (esp. confession at H.C.). Weakness with regard to preparation for H[oly] C[ommunion]. Foolishness towards Bond. Waste of time. [Line 30]—25. O.H. badly. Waste of time. Tempt[ation]. Ill-feeling ag[ain]st Arthur. No L[essons]. Nor on 26. Reading [Henry] Esmond on and on when I should have gone to bed. Idleness and weakness. Foolish way and heat in talk with Cyril. Weakness ab[ou]t getting up. Some O.H. Inatt. at prayers with dishonour to God. [Line 35]—27. No L[essons]. Some tempt. Putting off going out. Yesterday and today imitating and allowing imitation of Papa and Mamma and laughing. Wasting time and lateness to [bed del.] work. Anger yesterday with Kate for crumpling my book. N.B. The touches put [? into/the] Balliol scholarship examinations.—28. Temptations."

PLATE 137. C.ii. p 99 • *189*

	C.ii p.99	OET No. 69 – N.51 "Trees by their yield"
A verse or more has to be prefixed.		
Trees by their yield		
Are known; but I –		
My sap is sealed,		
My root is dry.		
If life within	5	
I none can shew		
(Except for sin),		
Nor fruit above, –		
It must be so –		
I do not love.	10	
Will some one show — *no*		
I argued ill?		
Because, although		
Self-sentenced, still		
I keep my trust.	15	
If He wd. prove		
And search me through		
Wd He not find		
(What yet there must		
Be hid behind	20	

	Not in J.71	Sun. Oct 1
[heavily deleted lines]		
	5	
	10	
	15	

Plate 137   C.ii.99--OET No. 69: "Trees by their yield"

    3 "seal'd" → "sealed". Prob. l.c. <u>s</u> intended; cf. ℓ.14, "Self," where a smaller u.c. <u>S</u> has been mended to a much larger one   11 "some" del. 20 neither the main clause nor the parenthesis is completed: no further drafts.

    S[ins, cont. from p.98, 28 Sept. 1865]. "Unwise use of time,—29. Doubt ab[ou]t the <u>Revelation</u> returning [Plate 136, ℓ.22]. Bad waste of time over a bk. before going to work. Inatt. at ch[urch]. Some idleness. Waste of time in going to [ditto marks repeat two words in line above] bed to prepare for H[oly] C[ommunion]. Scrupulosity. Talking against Walford. Late-[<u>Line 5</u>] ness down. Generally, pride and foolish self-will in thinking of preaching unaccepted Catholic truths. Speaking with foolish, if not bad, double meaning to Arthur. Quarrelsomeness with Cyril. Gen[erally] ill-spent Sundays.—30. Waste of time in dressing and over work. Temptations. Imitating Papa. Talking with Arthur [<u>Line 10</u>] ag[ain]st Cyril in the affair of the cold beef. Cruelty to insects gen[erally]. Vanity. Putting off answering Miss Robinson. Spiritual pride. Lateness down.—Oct. 1 [1865, Sunday]. (I communicated) Spending much time in evening in imitating and listening to imitations of kinsfolk. Wasted time and in going to bed.—2. Idling in [<u>Line 15</u>] getting up. Wasting time. Provoking and not considering Nurse, who is ill. Criticising Papa and Mamma. Impurities as often. Imitating Papa once, less respectfully [?]. 3. O.H."

Plate 138   C.ii.100--[Sins cont.—3 Oct. 1865]"Lateness down. Idling. Provoked feeling ag[ain]st Mamma, and agst. Arthur and the children. Forecasting.—4. O.H. Idleness. Unkind feeling and petulance towards Mamma and speaking harshly to Cyril. No L[essons]. Nor on 5. O.H. Idleness in going to work [Line 5] in the evening. Temptation over dictionary. Unwisely speaking long ab[ou]t leaving our Church. And on 6 some of this and more or less forecasting. Dictionary, once I think. Heat in argum. with Cyril. Impurity and O.H. No L[essons]. Idleness in going to work. Lateness down. Inatt. at fam. pr[ayer]s. Putting off preparing for [Line 10] H[oly] C[ommunion].—7. Intemp. [?] O.H. Laziness. Lateness to bed. Wasting time over work.—8 [Sunday] Inatt. at ch. services. Laughing at Mr. Ayre's sermon [cf. p.107, ℓ.17]. Repeated forecasting about Ch[urch] of Rome. Talking about Dr. Newman at dinner etc in a foolish way likely to produce unhappiness and harm. Two or three tempts. [Lines 15] given some way to. Ill feelings towards Rivington (of **J.**) [?: see J.296] and Herklots—9. Lateness down. Idling over work and in going to it and to bed. O.H. And on 10. Dangerous forecasting. [Cont. below copy of Newman's "Lead, kindly light"] Grumbling abt. food. Roughness with Cyril. Idling much. Lateness down and wasting time in going to bed."[cont. p.101].

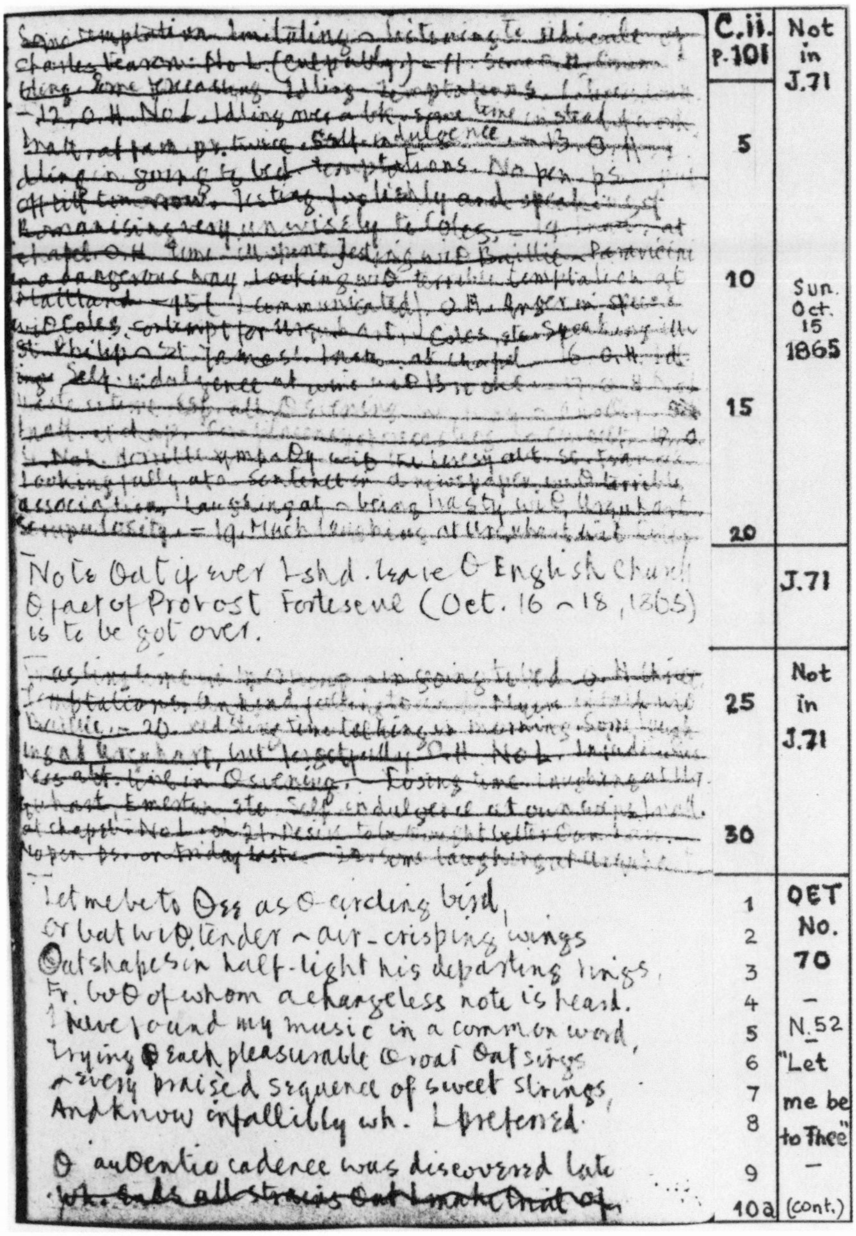

PLATE 139. C.ii. p 101 • *191*

The manuscript page (C.ii. p.101) with marginal column headings: **C.ii. P.101** — lines 5, 10, 15, 20 marked "Not in J.71 / Sun. Oct. 15 1865"; a three-line entry marked **J.71**; lines 25, 30 marked "Not in J.71"; and lines 1–10a of the poem marked **OET No. 70 / N.52 / "Let me be to Thee" — (cont.)**.

Three-line entry (J.71):

Note that if ever I shd. leave O English church
O part of Provost Fortescue (Oct. 16 ~ 18, 1865)
is to be got over.

Poem (OET No. 70):

Let me be to Thee as the circling bird,
Or bat with Ø tender ~ air-crisping wings
Outshapes in half-light his departing rings.
Fr. God of whom a changeless note is heard.
I have found my music in a common word,
Trying Ø each pleasurable throat that sings
~ every praised sequence of sweet strings,
And know infallibly wh. I preferred.

O authentic cadence was discovered late
Which ends all strains that I make trial of.

Plate 139   C.ii.101. [Sins, 10 Oct. 1865 cont.] "Some temptation. Imitating and listening to ridicule of Charles Fearon [Vearon?]. No L[essons] (culpably.)—11. Some O.H.. Grumbling. Some forecasting. Idling. Temptations. Lateness down.—12. O.H. No L[essons]. Idling over a bk. sometime instead of work. [Line 5] Inatt. at fam[ily] pr[ayers] twice. Self-indulgence.—13.   [Michaelmas Term began on 10 Oct.. GMH at Balliol on 13.] O.H. Idling in going to bed. Temptations. No pen[itential] ps[alms], put off till tomorrow. Jesting foolishly and speaking of Romanising very unwisely to Coles.—14. Inatt. at chapel. O.H. Time ill-spent. Jesting with Baillie and Paravicini [Line 10] in a dangerous way. Looking with terrible temptation at Maitland.--15 [Oct. 1865, Sunday]. (I communicated). O.H. Anger in speech with Coles, contempt for Urquhart, Coles, etc.. Speaking ill of St. Philip and St. James' [Church]. Inatt[ention] at chapel.—16. O.H. Idling. Self-indulgence at wine with Brooke [Samuel Brooke, **Corp. Christi**].—17. O.H. No l[essons]. [Line 15] Waste of time, esp. all the evening one way and another. Inatt. at chap[el]. Complacency and forecasting and conceit.—18. O.H. No l[essons]. Horrible sympathy with the heresy ab[ou]t St. Francis. Looking fully at a sentence in a newspaper with terrible associations. Laughing at, and being hasty with Urquhart. [Line 20] Scrupulosity.—19. Much laughing at Urquhart with Coles. [Cont. after three-line entry on Provost Fortescue.] Wasting time in the morning and in going to bed. O.H. thrice. [Line 25] Temptations. Unkind feeling towards Myers in talk with Baillie.—20. Wasting time talking in morning. Some laughing at Urquhart, but forgetfully. O.H. No L[essons]. Injudiciousness ab[out] line in the evening. Losing time. Laughing at Urquhart, Emerton, etc. Self-indulgence at own wine. Inatt(ention) at chapel. No l[essons] on 21. Desire to be thought better than I am. No pen[itential] ps[alms] on Friday last [20].—22 [Oct., Sunday]. Some laughing at Urquhart."[cont. p.102.]

OET No. 70: "Let me be to Thee as the circling bird" Note the extra-large thetas in 1 and 3 to emphasise upper-case.   6 Theta <u>del</u>.   10a del. "Wh[ich] ends all strains that I make trial of"

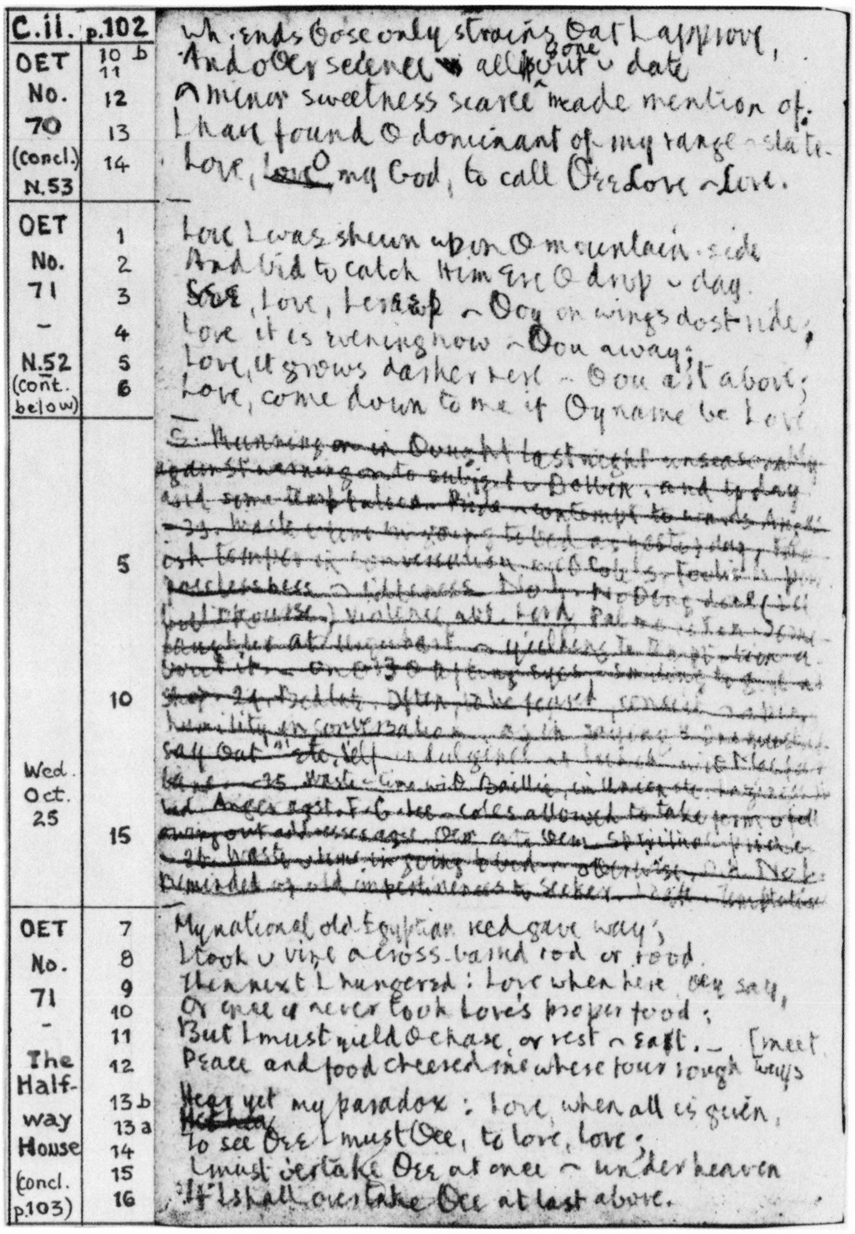

Plate 140   C.ii.102--OET No. 70: "Let me be to Thee as the circling bird" concl.   11 "science [is del.] all [is squeezed in, then del.] gone"   12 "me" → "made"; "of" period → colon   14 second "Love" del....."Thee" theta del. and rewritten larger (u.c.).   "Love and Love" l.c. 1 → L in both cases.

    OET No. 71: The Half-way House (title recorded at end of poem, top p.103).   3 "Love" → "See"..."crawl" → "creep"..."Thou" theta enlarged (as also in 4)..."ride;" → "ride:"? [cont. below confession notes]   10 "love's" l.c. makes better sense.   11 "east" → "eat"   13a "Yet hea[r]" → "He[ar]", then del. and revised above.   14 "To see Thee I must [see supplied by eds.] Thee"

    "S[ins of Oct. 22 1865, Sun., cont. from p.101]. "Running on in thought last night unseasonably against warning on to subject of Dolben, and today and some temptation. Pride and contempt towards Angus. [ℓ.4] —23. Waste of time in going to bed as yesterday. Fool/[Line 5] -ish temper in conversation with Coles. Foolish purposelessness and idleness. No l(essons). Nothing done (Ill will of course) Violence ab[ou]t Lord Palmerston. Some laughter at Urquhart and yielding to temptation about it. On the 13 lifting eyes and smiling to girl at [Line 10] shop.—24. Bed late. Often, to be feared, conceit and aping humility in conversation, as in saying 'One must'nt say that' etc. Self-indulgence at lunch with Macfarlane.—25. Waste of time with Baillie, in Union etc. Laziness in bed. Anger ag[ain]st F.G. Lee [See p.97, ℓ.6; 103, ℓ.27; J.70, 338] and Coles allowed to take form of following [Line 15] out addresses ag[ain]st them or to them. Spiritual pride.—26. Waste of time in going to bed and otherwise. O.H. No l[essons]. Reminded of old impertinences to Secker [see p.103, ℓℓ.23-5; L.iii.70:3 Class Mods., 4 Law and Hist.]. Inatt[ention]. Temptation"

PLATE 141. C.ii. p.103 • 193

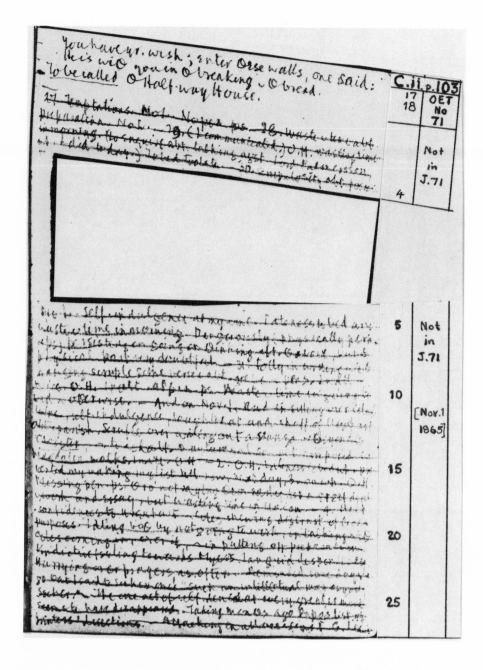

Plate 141   C.ii.103--OET No. 71: The Half-way House, concl.

[Sins] 27 [Oct. 1865]. "Temptations. No l[essons]. No pen[itential] ps[alms]—28. Waste of time ab[ou]t preparation [for Holy Communion]. No L[essons].—29 [Oct., Sunday]. (I communicated.) O.H. Wasting time in morning. (To enquire abt. talking agst. Lord Palmerston, wh. I did to-day.) To bed too late.—30. Scrupulosity abt. poems. [Cont. below excision. The missing part of the leaf may have had some humorous "verses on geese and peas" referred to as causing him a scruple in ℓ.9 below. No confession notes seem to have been lost: those for Oct. 30 (4 lines) and Nov. 4 (over 9 lines) appear complete.] [Line 5] No L[essons]. Self-indulgence at my wine. Lateness to bed and waste of time in morning. Dangerously (physically perhaps) persisting on going on thinking ab[ou]t the above [? "The Half-way House"], but the physical part very doubtful.—31. Folly in writing with hanging scruple some verses ab[out] geese and peas. Inatt[ention] [Line 10] twice. O.H. Inatt. at pen[itential] ps[alms]. Waste of time in going to bed and otherwise.—And on Nov. 1. And in sitting over Coles' wine, self-indulgence, laughter at and chaff of Urquhart ab[ou]t parish. Scruple over writing out a stanza of Beyond the Cloister, [see OET No. 38, headnote] and to ask about the autumnal sonnet composed in [Line 15] Magdalen Walks. Inatt. O.H.—2 [Nov.]. O.H. Lateness to bed wh[ich] prevented my making my list [of sins?] till now, next day, 3 [Frid.]. on wh. O.H. Missing pen. ps. thro' not saying them early, for a great deal of work and essay, but wasting time in Union.—4. Half-confidences to Urquhart and Coles, shewing distrust of God's [Line 20] purposes. Idling both by not going to work, in talking with Coles coming in, over it, and in putting off preparation [for H.C.]. Vindictive feeling towards Myers. Languid despondency. Hurrying over prayers, as often. Reminded some days ago that I said to Secker once "such an intellectual man as you, [Line 25] Secker" [see p.102, ℓ.17]. The one act of self-denial at every greater meal seems to have disappeared. Taking months ago Papa's list of printers' directions [for proof corrections?]. Attacking on all occasions F.G. Lee."

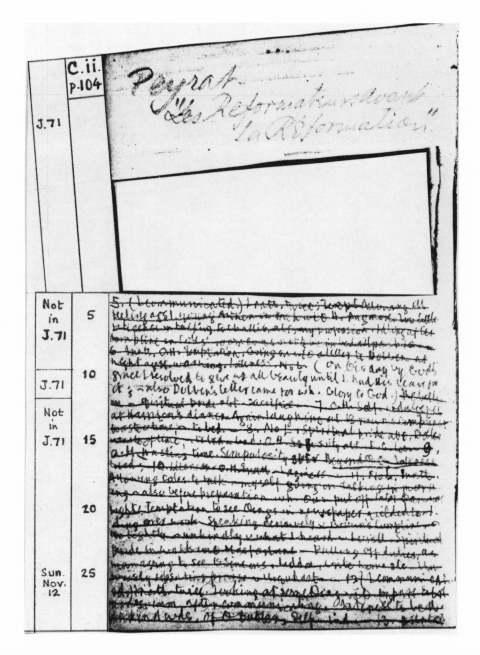

Plate 142   C.ii.104. The top entry was prob. written by the person recommending GMH to read the book. Fr. A. Bischoff suggests it was Manley Hopkins, but the hand is different from his transcript of "The Escorial" (plates 3, etc). The vol. was in the Union Library: "Peyrat 'Les Reformateurs avant La Reformation.'"/ [Sins, Sunday, Nov.]"5. (I communicated.) Inatt[ention] twice; tempt. [?] Allowing ill feeling agst. young Aitken [cf. p.92, ℓ.4] in talk with H. Dugmore [J.338]. Too little reticence in talking to Challis [J.158-9, 218,329,378] abt. my profession. Idling after compline in Coles' room so as not to be in bed till past 12. [Line 8] 6 [Nov.]. Inatt. O.H. Temptation. Going on into a letter to Dolben at night agst. warning. Lateness. No L[essons]."

[Not del.] "(On this day by God's grace I resolved to give up all beauty until I had His leave for it; and also Dolben's letter came for wh. Glory to God.)"

"Rebellion and spiritual pride abt. sacrifice.—7. O.H. Self-indulgence at [Line 13] Harrison's dinner. Again laughing at Brown's complines [cf. ℓ.18]. Waste of time, and to bed.—8. No L[essons]. Spiritual pride abt. Dolben. Waste of time, and to bed—bad. O.H. Severity abt. F.G. Lee.—9. O.H. Wasting time. Scrupulosity over Beyond the C[loister] [see p.103, ℓℓ .13,14]. Lateness to bed.—10. Idleness. O.H. Inatt. Laziness.—11. No L[essons]. Inatt. [Line 18] Allowing Coles to talk and myself going on talking in morning and also before preparation [for H.C.] wh. thus put off later than was [Line 20] right. Temptation to see things in newspaper yielded to. Id[l]ing over work. Speaking derisively of Brown's Compline, and too lightly and unkindly of what I heard of Lovell. Spiritual pride in walk with Macfarlane [cf. J.147,329, etc; L.iii. index]. Putting off duties, as managing to see the Simeons, Liddon, write home, etc. [Line 25] Unwisely repeating praise of Urquhart.—12 [Nov. 1865, Sun.]. (I communicated.) Inatt. twice. Looking at some thing with impure curiousness immed. after communicating. Lateness to bed. Unkind words of the Butler [?]. Self-ind[ulgence]. 13. Dilatori[ness" cont. p.105].

PLATE 143. C.ii. p 105 • *195*

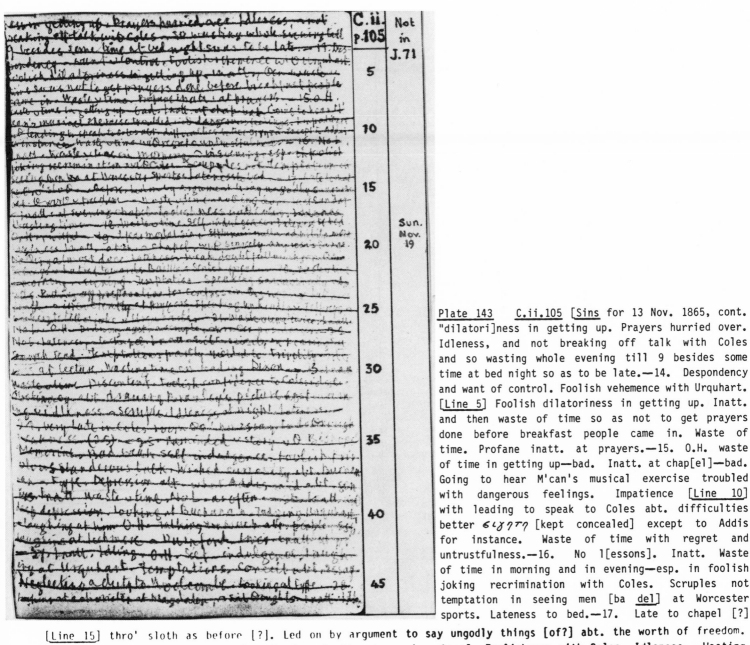

Plate 143   C.ii.105 [Sins for 13 Nov. 1865, cont.
"dilatori]ness in getting up. Prayers hurried over.
Idleness, and not breaking off talk with Coles
and so wasting whole evening till 9 besides some
time at bed night so as to be late.—14. Despondency
and want of control. Foolish vehemence with Urquhart.
[Line 5] Foolish dilatoriness in getting up. Inatt.
and then waste of time so as not to get prayers
done before breakfast people came in. Waste of
time. Profane inatt. at prayers.—15. O.H. waste
of time in getting up—bad. Inatt. at chap[el]—bad.
Going to hear M'can's musical exercise troubled
with dangerous feelings. Impatience [Line 10]
with leading to speak to Coles abt. difficulties
better εὐχητη [kept concealed] except to Addis
for instance. Waste of time with regret and
untrustfulness.—16. No l[essons]. Inatt. Waste
of time in morning and in evening—esp. in foolish
joking recrimination with Coles. Scruples not
temptation in seeing men [ba del] at Worcester
sports. Lateness to bed.—17. Late to chapel [?]

[Line 15] thro' sloth as before [?]. Led on by argument to say ungodly things [of?] abt. the worth of freedom.
Waste of time and nothing done last Sunday. Inatt. at evening chapel. Foolishness with Coles. Idleness. Wasting
time.—18. Waste of time. Self-indulgence. Lateness to bed. O.H., wilful.—19 (Nov., 1865, Sun.). I fear mortal
sin, effluximina nulla adhibita mora [night emissions to which no restraint was applied]. [Line 20] Laziness.
Inatt. at ch[urch] and chapel, with scarcely any resistance. Nothing almost done. Lateness. Weak doubt following
on the sin [?]. Feelings of hatred towards Baillie's Scotch friend.—20. Waste of time in morning and evening.
Temptation. Speaking sarcastically of Amcotts [see L.III.77, J.9,16,297]. Putting off preparation for confession
this evening. Lateness. [Line 25] Inatt. and irreverent[ly del.?] at prayers. Speaking unkindly of Jeffreys and
wishing to tell a joke of Urquhart's.—21. Waste of time twice. Inatt. No L[essons]. O.H. Drawing against a scruple
or rather pos[sible] danger.—22 No L[essons]. Lateness to chapel. Inatt. Evil curiosity in hearing Susannah read
[Apocrypha: one of the Lessons for Nov. 22] Temptations partly yielded to. Frivolity. Idle [Line 30] -ness at
lecture. Wasting time in reading Dixon.—23. Inatt. Waste of time. Discontent. Foolish confidence to Coleridge.
Obstinacy abt. drawing Bramley's picture [p.106, ℓ.25; cf. J.329, ℓ.5] agst. warning of idleness and scruple.
Idleness at night. Lateness.—24. Very late in Coles' room tho' no essay to do through weakness. (25)—25. Reminded
of story of the Bishops' [Line 35] Memorial [Ridley, Martyr's Memorial, St Giles?]. Bad weak self-indulgence,
foolish frivolous slanderous talk. Wicked curiosity abt. Buchanan [cf. line 40] and Fyffe [J.55,159,325]. Depression
abt. what Addis said abt. genius. Inatt. Waste of time. No L[essons] as often.—26 [Nov., Sun.]. Inatt. with
[Line 40] deep depression. Looking at Buchanan. Judging Urquhart and laughing at him. O.H. Talking too much
abt. people, esp. laughing at Lechmere and Durnford [cf. p.92, ℓℓ .3,4]. Irrev[erent] inatt. at ps[alms]—27.
Inatt. Idling. O.H. Self-indulgence. Laughing at Urquhart. Temptations. Conceit abt. essay. Neglecting a duty
to Woolcombe. Looking at Fyffe.—28. Looking at a chorister at Magdalen, and evil thoughts. Inatt. Idle[ness]"

Not in J.71	C. ii. p.106
	5
[1 Dec. 1865]	10
	15
	20
	25
	30
	35
[10 Dec. Sun.]	40
	44

Plate 144   C.ii.106 [Sins, cont. from p.105, 28 Nov. 1865, "Idle]ness. Evil curiosity. No l[essons]. Dwelling conceitedly on thought of my essay. Bad lateness. Wasting evening at Marshall's [J.55]. Inatt. at compl[ine].—29. Temptation of force [?] and smaller ones. Dryness [lack of interest?] little resisted. Dawdling losing morning chapel. Inatt. [Line 5] Wasting whole evening.—30. Late. Inatt. at H[oly] C[ommunion] and matins. Idling and great lateness. Tempt. Self-indulgence. Foolish censorious talk with Gent [J.159,329,378] abt. people at Palmer's dinner [J.12,16,53,298]. Evil feelings towards Monro [p.64, l.34], Cobham, Grose [p.83, l.1] O.H. Self-indulgence also at lunch.—[31 del.] 1 [Dec. 1865]. Inatt., wasting time, esp. [Line 10] in writing essay wh. kept me very late. O.H. Folly in not resisting thoughts doing no good and leading to danger. Wick/ed curiosity in reading.—Dec. 2. Waste of time and energy [and ?] scrupulosity over the poem abt. Bristow. Wasting time. Self-indulgence. Lateness by putting off prep. for H[oly] C[ommunion]. [Line 15] Laughing at Urquhart. Telling a story abt. Philip the Eunuch. Inatt. O.H. Contempt for men I met at the Reid's. State of prep[aration] very bad.— 3[Dec. Sun.]. Lateness in not taking more pains to send Northcote away from my rooms and getting unnecessarily on a dangerous subject. Waste [Line 20] of time. Inatt. (I communicated.) Brawling in Coles' rooms. O.H. And on 4. Physical danger while having my arm in Baillie's and speaking affectionately. Temptation from looking at my own feet. Despondencies. Lateness. No L[essons]. Self-indulgence. Wasting whole morning.—5, Going on [Line 25] idly and against scruples studying for Bramley's picture [J.329]. Waste of time. Self-indulgence. No L[essons]. Wrangling with Coles. Lateness. Tempt. in washing.—6. Wasting time in morning, idling [?] in Northcote's room in evening, and later. No L[essons]. Temptations. Letting myself talk on dangerous subj. with Oxenham [J.51,135,320]. [Line 30] Speaking with ridicule of Monro.—7. Wasting time. Hurrying over morning prayers as one way or another has several times happened of late. Impurity. Unkind talk abt. Urquhart. Saying most unprofitably speculation abt. Geldart. Despondency after hearing something agst. me.—8. Staying hearing [Line 35] Oxenham talk in Coles' room so as to be late. Waste of time. Inatt. No l[essons]. Tempt. Evil thoughts.—9. Inatt. No l[essons]. Impurities. Putting off confession till late. Anger with Urquhart and joking abt. him. Scrupulosity abt. Punch. Conceited thoughts.—10 [Dec. 1865, Sun.]. (I communicated.) Inatt. then and at matins where [Line 40] I had [evil del.] unkind proud thoughts abt. Urquhart. Wasting time. Nothing done. Looking with evil curiosity at a picture of Rosseti's [?]. O.H. Foolish gossipy way with Bridges.—11. Waste of time. Inatt. twice. Contempt for Wells [J.17,87?] and Urquhart and impatience. Imp. Talking too much abt. [cont. p.107]ᴹ

PLATE 145.   C.ii. p 107   •   *197*

Plate 145   **C.ii.107** [Sins, cont., 11 Dec. 1865, "Talking too much abt.] Urquhart. Affectation. Mentioning something improper in a story. Heat in defending Oxenham.—12 [cont. below Wood's address]. Inatt. No l[essons]. Indolent waste of time. Unkind way [Line 5] to and abt. Urquhart. Bad lateness.—And on 13, chiefly thro' weakness in talking to Oxenham (wh. in itself unwise partly) abt. dangerous things. Waste of time. Drawing agst. scruples. Weakness in getting up. No chapel or l[essons].—14. O.H. Waste of time in evening, conceit over letter [Line 10] to Dolben. Laziness."

"I confessed...Dec. 15" ⟶ "16," entered in middle of sins of 14: no entries for 15, 16 Dec. [Sins of 14, cont.] "Two temptations. Laughing at 'O dear Doctor.' Dawdling in going to bed. [Return to home in Hampstead].—17 [Dec., Sun.] Inatt. Unwisely mentioning Mr. Ayre's [cf. p.100, ℓℓ.11,12] praise of Luther at dinner. Despising Weir. Proud thoughts crossing me. Affectation and unwisdom at Victoria Road [Grandmamma's house, St John's Wood; J.312-3]. Evil thought abt. [Line 20] Everard and William. Indolence. Inatt. at fam[ily prayers]. Irrev. at prayers.—18. Idling over work. Languor. Dilatoriness. Despondency and untrustfulness. Temptations. Laziness.—19. Despondency leading to idleness, so that scarcely any thing done. No l[essons]. Some O.H. [Despondency del.]. Hurrying over morn. pr[ayers] [Line 25] in order to be down to family d[itt]o, having bet with Arthur.—20. No L[essons]. Impurities. Lateness down. Despondency. Unwisely arguing and speaking in other ways abt. Catholicism to Cyril, Arthur, and Mamma. Idling and weakness over work. Inatt. at fam. pr.⟶21. Lateness down. Inatt. at fam. pr. Purposelessness in [Line 30] walking abt. town to get presents. Inatt. at church, looking about, and want of devotion at H.C.—22. Inatt. (fam.) twice. Idleness and weakness in going to and over work. Dangerous scrupulosity abt. finishing a stanza of Beyond the Cloister for Dolben. Temptation in a picture and I think another. Discontent with idleness. Foolish [Line 35] -ness at Grandmamma's with talk abt. Catholicism. No l[essons]. Waste of time in afternoon. Provocation with Cyril abt. his eyes. Despising the Wadmores [p.93, ℓ.3]. Vanity. Allowing imitation of and laughter at Papa.—23. Inatt. at fam. pr. Laziness. Being wearied about Papa's illness and Cyril's eyes. Idling over work. Some temptation. Repeating [Line 40] to myself bits of Beyond the Cloister. Vehemence at Grandmamma's. Wrangling with Cyril. Vehemence and unkindness in argument with him and Mamma. Inatt. at fam. [prayers].—24 [Christmas Eve, 1865]. Allowing argum[ent] with vehemence abt. America and mira[cles"—cont. p.108].

Plate 146   C.ii.108 [Sins of Christmas Eve, 1865, cont. "argument about...mira]cles. Inatt. twice. Evil feelings towards Herklots, Lane, and laughing at them. Weakness abt. going to bed.—25 Xmas. Laziness. Lateness down. Inatten. Proud thoughts. Idling in going [to bed"—cont. after poem].

  OET No. 73: "Moonless darkness stands between." 2a del. "Be no more the [Past]"—clearly theta ("the"), not "O"   2b orig. "Past, the past, be no more seen"   6 "Make me ⌈meek →⌉ pure, Lord: thou   [l.c. → u.c.?] ⌈wert →⌉ art holy;"   9 "Day" → "day" (the vertical stroke has not been re-inforced.)

  [Sins cont. for Xmas, 1865, "Idling in going] to bed. Answering Mamma, and speaking to Cyril, angrily. [Line 5]—26. Inatt[ention] at fam[ily prayers] twice and ch[urch]. Lateness to bed. No L[essons]. Getting into argum[ent] abt. the Saints etc. with Mamma wh. brought her to tears. Idling over work. Idling in morning.—27. No L[essons]. Impurities. Lateness down. Lateness to bed. Idling abt. going out. Misusing time. Lying awake last night I was frivolous and irre [Line 10] -verent to God. Inatt. at fam. Proud thoughts somewhat yielded to. Two inst[ances] of lewd curiosity.—28. Self-indulgence at dinner. Great waste of time in going to bed. No L[?]. Inatt. at fam. and ch[urch]. (Ch. but) no (other) Bible reading. Lateness down. Idling. O.H. and impurities. Malice agst. [Line 15] Herklots. Inquiring unkindly abt. Towse's expulsion [from Clare Col., Cambridge; cf. L.iii.4].—29. Lateness down, very late. Idling and indecision. Inatt. at pen[itential] ps[alms]. Not crushing enough evil thoughts. Evil curiosity abt. twice. Vanity.—30. Idling. Laziness and lateness down. Having an evil thought in looking on a beautiful cruci/[Line 20]fix of Aunt Kate's. No l[essons]. Folly about making a scruple abt. a sugar-plum. Not preparing enough (none today) for H[oly] C[ommunion].—31 [Dec. 1865, Sun.]. Lateness down (it was at Aunt Kate's). Evil thought abt. Magdalen wh. I did not treat as I shd. Temptation fr. myself in washing. Inatt. twice with evil feeling [Line 25] abt. Mr. Hayes and the man who took the offertory. Dallying with that temptation about Magdalen, wh. indeed I think was never a tempt. in itself but a scruple and a wicked careless predisposition of
[cont. oppos.

PLATE 147. C.ii. p 109 • *199*

C.ii. p.109	Not in 71
3	
	OET No. 74
4	–
8	"The earth and heaven"
12	–
16	
20	(cont. below)
4	Not in J.71
21	
24	(cont. p.110)
5	J.71
6	

[Manuscript facsimile, Gerard Manley Hopkins notebook C.ii, p.109, with draft of OET No. 74 "The earth and heaven, so little known":]

The earth & heaven, so little known,
Are measured outwards fr. my breast.
I am ☉ midst of every zone
& justify ☉ E. & W.;

The unchanging register of change,
My all-accepting fixèd eye,
While all things else may stir & range,
All else may wheel or dive or fly.

O swallow, favourite of the gale,
Will on ☉ moulding strike & cling,
Unvalve or shut his varièd tail
& sheathe at once his tiger wing.

He drops upon ☉ wind again;
His little pennon is unfurled.
In motion is no weight or pack,
Nor permanence in ☉ solid world.

There is a vapour stands in ☉ wind;
It shapes itself in taper skeins:
You look again & cannot find,
Save in ☉ body & ☉ rains.

And ☉ sex are spent & ended quite;
☉ sky is blue & & ☉ winds pull
☉ir clouds w☉ breaking edges white
Beyond ☉ world; ☉ streams are full.

Plate 147   C.ii.109 [Sins of Jan. 2, 1866, Tues., cont.: "argum. with Mrs. Dyne [cf. L.iii.2,3].—3. [Staying with Aunt Kate again, Sussex Gardens, near Paddington, London.] Laziness. No L(essons). Idling morning and evening. Scruples abt. Magdalen and weakness, and perh. some temptations elsewhere. Abt. Magd[alen] again on 4 [cont. after ℓ.20 of poem] and over a line above. O.H. Idling. Very late to bed." [Cont. on p.110]

    OET No. 74: "The earth and heaven, so little known"   5 "change," comma del.   9 ", favourite of the gale," del., caret added for a revised version which was never added.   16 "Or" → "Nor"   22 "blue;" → "blue,"   24 "Down" → "Beyond"..."full."(the period should have been del. when the next st. was added on p.110.)

    The two last lines on the page are not del.   5 "late" del.   6 "reviewed in a letter to Archbp. Manning by [Fred. Oakley" cont. top p.110].

Plate 146, (cont. from opposite page)
mind. Irrev. at prayers.—Jan. 1, 1866. (I communicated.) Waste of time in morning. Weak scrupulosity in looking [Line 30] at Bramley's picture [pp.105, ℓ.32; 106, ℓ.25] and in thinking of our Lord on the cross. Talking abt. [Aunt? J.336] Frances, Papa etc. Speaking sharply to Mamma. Lateness to bed. No L[essons]. Nor on 2. Laziness and lateness. Scrupulous fear and two at least evil thoughts and one lewd curiosity. Idling over work. Dwelling conceitedly on argum[ent] with Mrs. [Dyne"--cont. p.109]

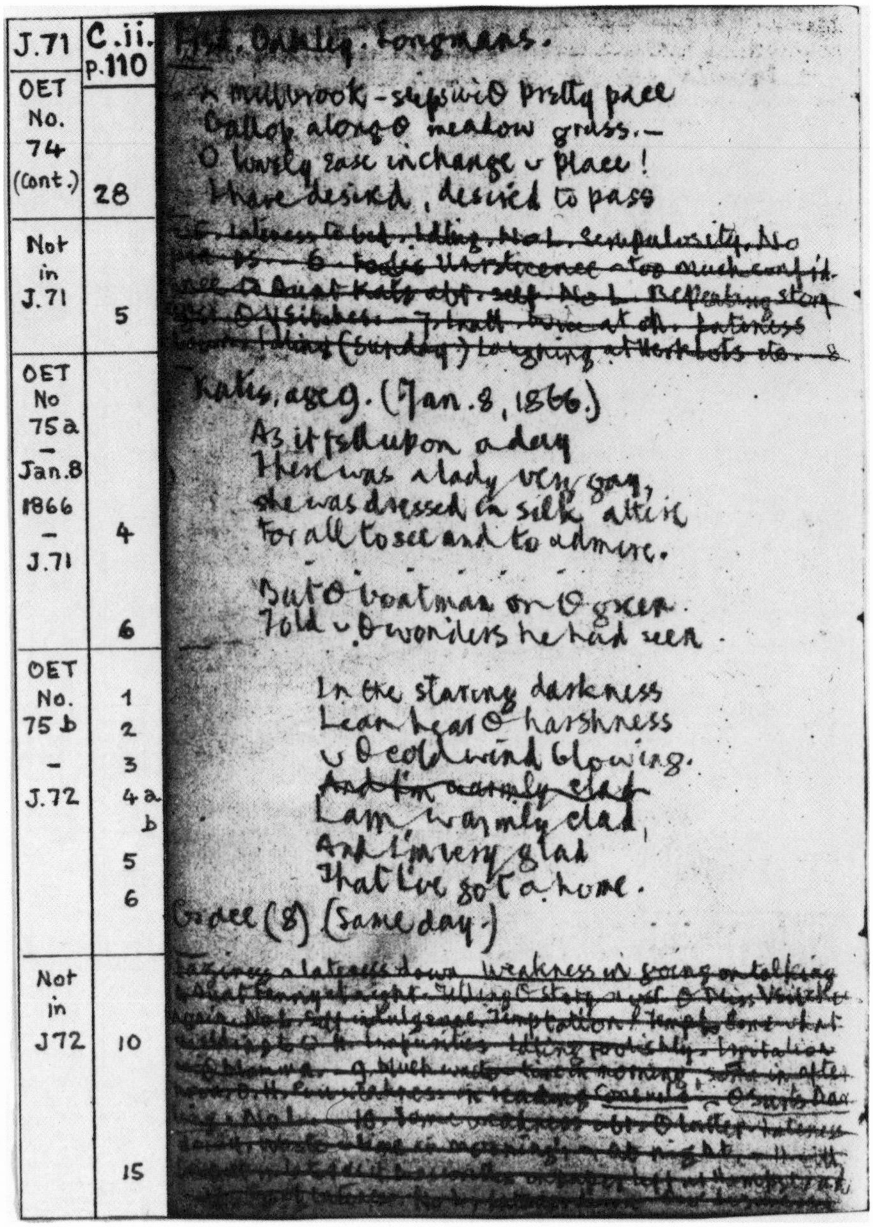

J.71 | C.ii. p.110

Fred. Oakley. Longmans.

OET No. 74 (Cont.)
The millbrook - slips with pretty pace
Gallop along the meadow grass. –
O lovely ease in change of place!
I have desired, desired to pass 28

Not in J.71 5

OET No 75a – Jan.8 1866 – J.71
Kate, aet 9. (Jan. 8, 1866.)
As it fell upon a day
There was a lady very gay,
She was dressed in silk attire
For all to see and to admire. 4

But the boatman on the green
Told of the wonders he had seen. 6

OET No. 75b – J.72
1 In the staring darkness
2 I can hear the harshness
3 Of the cold wind blowing.
4a And I'm warmly clad
b I am warmly clad,
5 And I'm very glad
6 That I've got a home.
Grace (8) (Same day.)

Not in J72 10 15

Plate 148 C.ii.110. "Fred. Oakley. Longmans"

OET No. 74: "The earth and heaven, so little known" cont.. This stanza, the last addition, begins and ends in the middle of sentences.

[Sins, cont., still staying with Aunt Kate.]—5 [Jan. 1866]. "Lateness to bed. Idling. No L[essons]. Scrupulosity. No pen[itential] ps[alms].—6. [Foolis del.] Unreticence and too much confidence to Aunt Kate abt. self. No L[essons]. Repeating story [Line 5] agst. the Veitches [Rev. H.G.J. Veitch was Vicar of St Saviour's, Paddington, 1862-73].—7 [Jan., Sun.] Inatt. twice at ch[urch]. Lateness down. Idling (Sunday.) Laughing at Herklots, etc. [Back in Hampstead.]—8." Cont. below verses.

OET No. 75(a): "As it fell upon a day". Unfinished in C.ii.

OET No. 75(b): "In the staring darkness". 4a "And I'm warmly clad"/Sins, cont., for Jan. 8. "Laziness and lateness down. Weakness in going on talking to Aunt Fanny at night. Telling the story agst. the Miss Veitches again. No L[essons]. Self-indulgence. Temptation. Tempts. somewhat [Line 10] yielding to O.H. Impurities. Idling foolishly. Irritation with Mamma.—9. Much waste of time in morning, some in afternoon. O.H. Evil weakness in reading Consuelo ["A Romance of Venice" by George Sand] and The [Surts?] Darling. No L[essons].10.Some weakness abt. the latter. Lateness down. Waste of time in morning and at night.—11. Will [Line 15] be put in later as it was written on paper left at Hampstead.—12. Great lateness. No L[essons]. Lateness down. Bad laziness.

Plate 149 [opp] C.ii.111. [Sins of 12 Jan. 1866, cont.] "Beginning argum. with Mamma abt. St. Raphael at dinner. Wasting morning. Conceited forecasting. Lewd curiosity.—13. Conceited and lewd thoughts abt. self. Wasting time. Vehemence wh. led to bad results at tea abt. the church. Laziness. [Line 5] Forecasting and pride. O.H. Idling

[cont. opp]

PLATE 149. C.ii. p 111 • *201*

	C.ii. p.111	Not in J.72
	5	Sun. Jan. 14 1866
	10	
	15	
	20	
	25	

The stars were packed so close that night
  They seemed to press and stare
  And gather in like hurdles bright
  The liberties of air.

		QET No. 75 c
	4	
	30	Not in J.72 Jan. 23 1866
	35	

For Lent. No pudding on Sundays. No tea
except if to keep me awake after without sugar.
Meat only once a day. No verses in Passion

| | | J.72 Lent- Feb.14 to Mar.30 |

Plate 149 (cont. from previous page)
before going out.—14 [Jan., Sun.] Scrupulosity abt. going to ch[urch] again. Inatt[ention]. Laziness. O.H. Waste of time.—15. Scrupulosity abt. the Pall Mall article before reading it in the Times. Evil thoughts arising therefrom and at the Giberne's [J.14, 298] party. Feeling and speaking angrily to Cyril. Wasting time. No L[essons]. [Line 10] Listening to laughing at Papa etc.—16. Waste of time in going to bed and otherwise. No L[essons]. Snappishness, and heat in argument. Talking of the stupidity of the Epsom audience [for relations at Epsom see J.298, n.14.1], of young Levick, etc. Temptations. Irrev. at prayers. Inatt.   at fam. pr.—17. No L[essons]. Laziness. Very late down. Idling at [Line 15] night. Doing no work and idling badly all day. Temptations. Discontent.—18. Idling much, twice. Weakness and indecision. Lateness to bed and down. No L[essons]. Scrupulosity (and I read the last no. of The Night in a Workhouse). Inatt.—19. No L[essons]. Lateness down. No pen[itential] ps[alms]. Idling. Several [Line 20] proud thoughts of bad kind. Irrev. at pr.—20. Idling and folly. Lateness. No L[essons] nor prep. for H.C. Resolution made to be in bed by 11 and not in bed by 12, mostly own fault. Self-indulgence. Laughing at Urquhart and saying that I had a joke tho' I did not tell it. [Hilary/Lent term began Jan.15—GMH was again up at Balliol.] Self-will in [Line 25] writing down (past 12) corrections in The Nightingale [OET No. 76] agst. warning. Effect possibly physical. Temptation. Dwelling on poems.—And in morning of 21 [Sun.]. Very little read. Inatt. at ch. Vanity, consciousness, etc.—22. No L[essons].
[Cont. after stanza, OET No, 75c, The stars were packed.] Wicked/forecasting. Idleness in morning and evening. Weak di-/[Line 30] latoriness twice. Lateness. Inatt. Tempt. fr. Fyffe and fr. pictures in Blake.—23 [Jan. 1866] No chap[el]. Short lessons. Wasting time in morn. over picture-hanging and in evening over that and wine in Coles' rooms so that almost nothing done all day. O.H. One or two proud thoughts. Weakness in not going to the Rawlinsons' [prob. Camden Prof. of Ancient Hist.] [par del] ball.

J.72	C.ii. p.112		C.ii. P.113	J.73
Good Friday Mar. 29 1866				
	5		5	
	10		8	Not in J.73
(cont. l.20) J.72	15		10	J.73
(cont. from l.16) J.73	20			
	25			
	30			

(Left-hand manuscript page, C.ii. p.112:)

Week or on Fridays. No lunch or meat on Fridays. Not to sit in armchair except can work any other way. Ash Wednesday ~ Good Friday bread ~ water.

— Drops of rain hanging on rails etc seen are only lower rim lighted like nails (v fingers). Screws of brooks ~ twines. Soft chalky look wi more shadowy middles of ⊙ slopes of cloud on a night wi a moon faint or concealed. Mealy clouds wi a not brilliant moon. Blunt buds ~ ⊙ ash. Pencil buds ~ ⊙ birch. Lobes ~ ⊙ trees. cups ~ ⊙ eyes. Gathering back ⊙ lightly ridged eyelids ~ ⊙ eyelashes. Juices of ⊙ eyeball. Eyelids like leaves, petals, caps, tufted hats, handkerchiefs, sleeves, gloves. ... of ⊙ bones sleeved in flesh. Juices of ⊙ sunrise loops and veins of ⊙ same. Vermilion look v ⊙ hand.

A. Wood, 62 N. Marine Parade, Scarborough.

E. R. Wharton, The Parsonage, Chidlock near Bridport Dorset.

Held agst. a candle wi ⊙ ⊙ dashes parts as ⊙ middles of fingers ~ esp. ⊙ knuckles veined wi ⊙ ash.

Coincidence, fr. a correspondent v ⊙ Pall Mall Gazette. Louis Philippe ascended ⊙ throne in

1830	1830	1830
His length	His eyes' width	His age
1 7 3	1 7 8 2	1 8 0 9
‾‾‾‾	‾‾‾‾	‾‾‾‾
1848	1848	1848

when he abdicated.

Louis Napolen became emperor in 1852.

(Right-hand manuscript page, C.ii. p.113:)

1852	1852	1852
His length	His eyes' width	His age
1 8 0 8	1 8 2 6	1 8 5 3
‾‾‾‾	‾‾‾‾	‾‾‾‾
1869	1869	1869

when ?

— 4 Westbourne Villas, Harrow Rd, W

Revd. R. W. Dixon, 1 Albert Street, Carlisle. He has written also Historical Odes.

Plate 150   C.ii.112. 7 "brooks." The afterthought "and twines" goes better perhaps with "Screws" than "brooks" 8 "moon" second (open) o absent-mindedly dotted like an "i"   10 "ash" (GMH's open a like u) E 16 "Joins" (o like v) cf. 21 "covered"   18 "Brid[port]" del...."Chidlock" an easy mistake in transcribing "Chideock" in another hand.   32 "Louis Napolen" (second o omitted).
    C.ii.113. This is the last page of regular entries in the Note-book. 8,9 were omitted in J.73 because the address had no name attached. Over fifty blank leaves (half the note-book) remain, unused apart from the two pages which follow, unnumbered at the end.

PLATE 151.   C.ii. pp 114,115   •   203

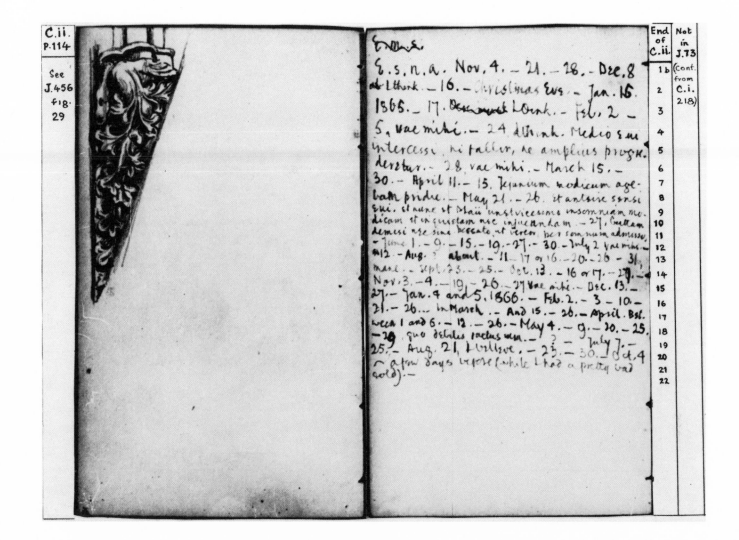

Plate 151   C.ii. unpaginated, at end.   Blank, except for this architectural detail occupying the top left corner, here reproduced on a smaller scale. This is inverted as Fig. 29 in J.

   End of Notebook C.ii.   [cf. C.i.217-8, Plate 76] Notes on physical emissions during sleep, with his subjective judgement as to whether he had been sufficiently conscious to make them sinful. See end of Introduction, Medical Commentary.   Lines 1a, 1b "E.m.s.(del.)/E.s.n.a. Nov.4." [etc.] (Cf. Plates 103, left, ℓ.18; 143, ℓ.19) perhaps "emissio seminis nocte ante Nov.4"--emission of semen on the night before Nov.4 (etc.).   He notes cases where weakness (e.g. ℓℓ.7,8, from fasting moderately on Good Friday, April 14) or insomnia and restlessness (ℓℓ.8-10), or "a pretty bad cold" (ℓ.21), had made him more conscious during a dream and so more responsible. vae mihi (ℓℓ.4,6,12,15) "alas!": this phrase in the Vulgate, e.g. Isaiah 6:5, etc., is translated "Woe is me." His uncertainties as to guilt or date are indicated by "I think" (ℓℓ.3,4), "ni fallor" (if I am not mistaken, ℓ.5), "ut vereor" (as I fear, ℓ.11), "I believe" (20).   The entry for May 27 (ℓℓ.10,11) "I released a drop not without sin, I fear, committed during sleep"), corresponds with a confession note "Sin in dream perhaps." (Plate 115, ℓ.17). Confession notes, which survive for only half the period covered here, correlate poorly with these physiological entries: e.g., Plate 143 with its recurrent "Old habits" must be a reference to something else. See Introduction.

12

of any one? was it quite necessary for me to speak it? was there anything ill chosen in the time or circumstances? Did I say it to gratify myself in any way? should I have said it of my friend, my brother, or myself?

Have I encouraged others in such conversation?

Have I been glad to hear, or think, or suspect, evil of others?

Have I acted so as to cast suspicion on others, or lessen the value in which they ought to be held?

Have I thought much of myself?

Have I concealed anything which was for another's credit?

COMMANDMENT X.—*Duties respecting our desires.*

Have I wished for anything which GOD has not given me? not been quite contented?

Have I thought of any real or supposed pleasure which I cannot now gratify without sin?

Am I truly "learning and labouring to get my own living," that I may not be a burden to others?

Do I earnestly try to serve and please GOD in my worldly work and station?

Do I seek money, worldly respect, or a high place, instead of simply trying to do my duty and leave all else to GOD?

Has the object of my life been the world, or GOD?

Have I sanctified all my acts and motives by offering them in prayer to GOD?

61

QUESTIONS

for Self-Examination.

FOR COMMON USE.

LONDON:
G. J. PALMER, 32, LITTLE QUEEN ST.
LINCOLN'S INN FIELDS.
1861.

NOTE.

IT is intended that the following questions should serve for common use:—i. Daily; ii. At stated times, as weekly, or before each Communion, at the least once a month.

i. For daily use, questions are given on p. 5. All of these, except the last three, will help to a general view of the past day.

It is good for those who wish to please GOD, besides watching over their life generally, by the use of such general questions, to fight specially against some one particular sin. They will choose for this purpose the one which at the time most hinders them from giving themselves wholly to GOD—e. g. a quick temper—love of money—rash speaking—some subtle form of impurity—censoriousness—or anything which may resist their progress. This object of special watchfulness will be changed when considerable progress has been made in that particular.

The conquest of this sin should be the object of especial prayer, particularly before Our Lord Present in His Holy Sacrament.

ii. At other times the questions on the Commandments should be used. By this means sometimes sin will be discovered which had been overlooked

---

3

before: sometimes it will be seen that sins which could be despised once are now beginning to be troublesome.

A more searching set of questions should be used before Confirmation, a First Confession, and once a year, in Lent.

Persons using questions for Self-Examination must beware of thinking that, because one question does not reveal a sin, therefore others will not. We must try ourselves by each question *separately*. When we find ourselves free from the sins mentioned in one question, we may thank GOD that HE has kept us from a sin into which our own evil nature would have cast us. When we find that we have done the wrong thing spoken of, we must humble ourselves before GOD, because we have repaid His kindness, in keeping us from former sins, with the ingratitude of this one.

It is hardly necessary to say that those who use these questions should do so with a real desire to know their sins; with prayer to God, before beginning, for help; with a real intention to give up, at any cost, whatever sins are shown to them by HIM. They should end with a confession to GOD of those sins which they have discovered, a prayer for pardon, and an act of contrition.

All who use them are specially asked occasionally to remember the Compiler in their prayers, particularly at the Blessed Sacrament.

Plates 152 to 154. This now rare pamphlet was found among Canon H.P. Liddon's papers in Keble College Library (Misc. Pamphlets F) by Lesley Higgins. It is probable that Hopkins used this or a similar list of questions when he first began to record his "Sins": they are based on a searching extension of the Ten Commandments.

PLATE 153. *Questions for Self-Examination* • 205

4

Prayer before Self-Examination.

Open, Lord, mine eyes, that I may see my sins: Examine me and prove me: Try out my reins and my heart: Look well if there be any way of wickedness in me; and lead me in the way everlasting, for Jesus Christ, His sake. Amen.

Prayer after Self-Examination.

O Lord, Thou knowest all my sins, and my faults are not hid from Thee. Give me ever true penitence and faith, that with a holy disposition of mind, I may make my confession and obtain pardon of Thee, the just and merciful God, through the atoning Blood of Thy dear Son, Jesus Christ. Amen.

Act of Contrition.

O Eternal Father, the Just and Righteous Judge, Who art of purer eyes than to behold iniquity; in deep contrition I offer unto Thee with fullest confidence the precious Blood of Thy dear Son as the perfect atonement for all my numberless offences. I beseech Thee that Thou wouldest apply It both now and ever to my heart, that It may give me deeper contrition, may purify me yet more and more from my iniquities, and cleanse me from all my sins, through the same Thy Son Jesus Christ our Lord. Amen.

5

QUESTIONS.

Did I rise in good time and make all my accustomed acts of devotion to-day? Did I say them as really speaking to God? If I have been to Church, did I join openly in the Service, and with my whole heart?

Have I tried in everything to do God's will? Have I truly loved Him? Did I think of Him first this morning?

Have I given way at all to evil thoughts? against God? against my neighbour? against myself?

Have I said anything wrong? to the injury of religion? of my neighbour?

Have I knowingly said or done what I knew God would not have me say or do?

Have I been thoroughly patient, contented, and trustful? not been self-satisfied?

Have I been temperate in all things?

Have I been thoroughly honest in all my dealings?

Have I made the Life of Jesus my Pattern in all things?

The following questions should be asked every night as to the besetting sin.

How often have I committed it to-day? Is this more or less than before?

How often have I overcome when tempted?

How often have I resisted before being overcome? with what resolution?

6

Commandment I.— *The worship of the spiritual life.*

i. Do I try to know God as He has revealed Himself, and to believe in Him as such?

Have I indulged any thoughts contrary to that belief?

Have I read books, or kept company dangerous to my faith?

ii. Do I trust in Him for all spiritual and temporal success?

Have I accepted with patience and thankfulness all difficulties, as sent by Him for my good?

iii. Do I try to love Him as my Father, reconciled in Jesus.

Do I naturally think of Him first when I awake in the morning?

Has the love of God been the motive of all, or even any, of my actions?

Have I done right things (acted honestly, spoken the truth, checked anger, gone to Church, or even received the Blessed Sacrament) for any motive short of the love of God? thought of any good work as my own?

Have I despaired of mercy, or presumed on God's goodness?

Have I feared in any way to lose His favour?

iv. Have I cared for anything, or the opinion of any person, more than for God?

7

Have I made it my one object to know and do His will?

If I have sinned, have I, out of love, hastened to repent?

Do I try to long for death that I may see Him? have I therefore been carefully preparing with fear and trembling, to meet the dreadful and searching judgment of God?

Have I valued life as a means to this end?

Commandment II.— *The worship of the bodily life.*

Do I go to Church regularly?

Have I ever wilfully and without due cause missed being present at the Holy Eucharist on Sunday or Festival? Have I omitted to communicate at stated times?

Have I, without serious cause, staid away from the Morning and Evening Services on Sunday?

Have I tried to go to some at least of the week-day services, according as my business will allow?

Have I been outwardly reverent, bowing, kneeling, standing, according to custom, and doing everything quietly, without haste or display?

Have I gone to any worship other than that of the Church of England? or in any way encouraged such schismatical worship?

Commandment III.— *Reverence for God's Holy Name and Word.*

Have I ever named God—either the Holy Trinity, or any one Person of the Godhead—irreverently, or sworn in word or thought?

8

Have I made a superstitious use of Holy Names or things?

If I have been kept from profane swearing, have I not used expressions which are a kind of substitute for it, or contain some profane corruption of, or allusion to, sacred things?

If I have had to take an oath, or make any declaration or solemn promise, have I been careful to observe strict truth in it?

Have I remembered that a Christian's word is an oath, and therefore kept from falsehood told in jest or otherwise?

Have I been careful to keep the vows of my Baptism, renewed at Confirmation, ("in the Presence of GOD," and the Church, and in GOD's Holy Name), at Holy Communion, from day to day, &c.? *Note* that every sin is aggravated by being a breach of these vows.

Have I had any doubts about the Bible? used expressions from it, or like it, as a joke? read it for amusement or impure curiosity? or omitted daily to read some portion of it reverently?

Have I taken its teaching as spoken specially to *me* by GOD?

Have I shortened my prayers for the sake of worldly business or pleasure?

Have I said my prayers either privately, or in the Public Service, without full and earnest consciousness of GOD, and an entire lifting up of my soul to HIM? How far have I resisted?

Have I acted in holy things either more or less re-

9

verently than usual out of respect for man, i. e. hypocritically?

COMMANDMENT IV.—*Observance of Holy Days.*

Have I observed the special duties of each Sunday, Festival, and day of Fasting or Abstinence?

Have I done any unnecessary work on a Sunday?

Have I tried to sanctify to GOD by a holy Christian service "all the days of my life?"

COMMANDMENT V.—*Duties of our social position.*

Have I loved my parents? been ready to help them?

Have I been obedient to those over me without disputing (e. g. as a son or daughter, servant, &c.)?

Have I been really in heart and mind humble, meek, and poor in spirit?

Have I followed the directions and advice of my Spiritual Guide?

Have I acted lovingly, as husband or wife, brother or sister, or other relation?

Have I been selfish? or neglected to be of use?

Have I been gentle, courteous, and civil to all, especially to those under me?

Have I, as a parent, teacher, or ruler, made a conscience of my life, example, discipline? have I tried never to speak harshly, because I have been angry, nor yet to be weakly indulgent to faults? have I taken care to correct each fault, according to its real greatness and danger, not in proportion to the vexation which it has caused me, nor in anger? Have I chiefly sought for those under me spiritual blessings?

10

COMMANDMENT VI—*Sins of Temper, &c.*

Have I given way to anger by thought, unadvised speaking, or violent action?

Have I been sullen; ill-tempered; proud; or done anything malicious?

Have I tried to make the lives of my companions pleasant, taking everything in the best part, not being contentious?

Have I endangered any one's soul, by bad example, bad advice, or putting temptation in his way?

COMMANDMENT VII.—*Duties of Purity.*
Purify, O LORD, and cleanse my heart by the inspiration of THY HOLY SPIRIT.

Have I been quite pure in thought, word, and deed?

Have I kept the example of our LORD and the Blessed Virgin in this respect before me?

If there is any special line of thought, or circumstance of life, or mode of speech which tempts me, have I avoided it as I would the fire of the pit?

Have I joined in talking of such sins in a worldly way? have I looked at immodest pictures or other objects of the kind?

Have I been vain of my person or anything belonging to me?

Have I been fond of dress? thought of it more than so as that it be decent, modest, and unobtrusive?

Have I sought to be noticed, especially by the opposite sex? have I taken undue notice of them? not "made a covenant with mine eyes"?

11

Have I been too fond of food? eating or drinking too much or too greedily? criticizing the quality of my food? talking or thinking about it? neglected to say grace before or after?

Have I been slothful, by taking too much sleep? by idling? by neglecting work or doing it carelessly and without heart?

Have I denied myself in any thing?

COMMANDMENT VIII.—*Duties of Honesty.*

Have I taken anything which does not belong to me? did I know to whom it did belong? have I kept any thing which I had found, without trying duly, in proportion to its value, to find the owner.

Have I bought or sold unfairly, or so as I knew or suspected might probably be unfairly?

Have I wilfully incurred debts which I cannot pay?

Have I said anything with intention to deceive? have I taken credit to myself which belonged to another?

Have I professed powers which I do not possess, to make a gain of them?

Have I refused to give alms according to my means? Have I avoided it?

COMMANDMENT IX.—*Duties respecting another's good name.*

Have I spoken evil of any one? if so, am I quite certain that what I said was strictly and literally true? not in any way liable to misconstruction to the hurt

NOTE ON PLATES 155 TO 165. The second Early Note-book (C.ii), presented in unbroken continuity above (Plates 82 to 151), contains drafts, etc., of poems ranging from Nos.31 to 75, written between Sept.9 1864 and Jan.8 1866. The next eleven plates reproduce other MSS of poems which also probably fall within that same period. "St. Dorothea" was revised repeatedly between Dec.1864 and about 1871: as its versions require two facing double-pages, "St. Thecla" is reproduced first (Plate 155).

PLATE 155. OET 52. *St. Thecla* • 207

DUBLIN MS

OET No.52

St. Thecla

L.D.S.

1	That his fast-flowing hours with sandy silt
2	Should choke ^sweet up virtue's glory is Time's great guilt.
3	Who thinks of Thecla? Yet her name was known,
4	Time was, next whitest after Mary's own.
5	To that first golden age of Gospel times
6	And bright Iconium eastwards reach my rhymes.
7	Near by is Paul's free Tarsus, fabled where
8	Spent Pegasus down the ^stark ^tous precipi~tous~ ~of stark~ air
9	Flung rider and wings away; though these were none,
10	And Paul is Tarsus' true Bellerophon,
13a	~She, high on the housetop seated, as they say,~
14a	~Young Thecla, scanned the dazzling streets one day~
11	They are neighbours; but (what nearness could not do)
12	Christ's only charity charmed and chained these two.
13b	She, high ^at on the housetop ^sitting ~seated~, as they say,
14b	Young Thecla, scanned the dazzling streets one day;
15	^Twice ~Most~ lovely, tinted eastern, turnèd Greek—
16	Crisp lips, ~str~ straight nose, and tender-slanted cheek.
17	Her weeds all mark her maiden, though to wed,
18	And bridegroom waits and ready are bower and bed.
19	Withal her mien is x ^modest; ~moles~ ways x are wise, x
20	And grave past girlhood earnest in her eyes.
21	Firm accents strike her fine and scrollèd ear,
22	A man's voice and a new voice speaking near.
23	The words came from a court across the way.
24	She looked, she listened: Paul ^taught ~spoke~ long that day.
25	He spoke of God the Father and His Son,
26	Of world made, marred, and mended, lost and won;
27	Of virtue and vice; but most (it seemed his sense)
28	He praised the lovely lot of continence:
29	All over, some such words as these, though dark,
30	The world was saved by virgins, made the mark.
31	He taught another time there and a third.
32	The earnest-hearted maiden sat and heard,
33	And called to come at mealtime she would not:
34	They rose at last and forced her from the spot.

Plate 155   No. 52: "St. Thecla"

Sole MS. (Society of Jesus, Dublin) is an autograph copy made about 1876 of a poem written 1864-65, transcribed on a double sheet facing his Latin translation of part of it (OET. No.106), for display at a festival.   8 orig. "the precipice of stark air"   13a,14a copied in error two lines too soon   15 "turnèd"   16 "str" [de]. because the ink blotted]   19 The poem orig. ended with 18, and five omission marks (x x,etc.) can be seen del. in 19, the first below the first letter in the line.   "moles" a slip for "modest" (due to Latin "mollis": see No. 106, ℓ.15).   31 final colon rev. to period.

| C.ii. P.30 | For C.ii.30 to 31 see Plate 92 | OET No.42a | H.i. 25ʳ | 25 |

1	I bear a basket linèd with grass,
2	I am so light, I am so fair,
3	That men must wonder as I pass,
4	And at the basket that I bear,
5	Where in a newly-drawn 'green litter
6	Sweet flowers I carry — sweet for bitter.
7	Lilies I shew you : lilies none,
8	None in Caesar's gardens blow:
9	And a quince in hand : not one
10	Is set upon your boughs below:
11	Not set, because their buds not spring:

P.31

12	Spring not, 'cause world is wintering. ³¹
13	But these were found in the East & South,
14	Where Winter is the clime forgot. —
15	O dewdrop on the larkspur's mouth,
16a	O shd. it then be parchèd not ?
17	In starry water-meads I drew
18	These drops. which be they ? Stars a dew ?
19	Had she a quince in hand ? Yet gaze :
20	Rather it is the sizing moon.
21	Lo, linkèd heavens wi the milky ways !
22	That was her larkspur row. — So soon ! —
23	Sphered so fast, sweet soul ? — We see
24	Nor flowers nor fruit, nor Dorothy.
16b	perhaps quenchèd. (Certainly)

| OET No. 42(b) C.ii. p.60 (see Plate 102) | 1 2 3 4 | A. A basket broad of woven white rods I have fill'd, that hard to fill is, wi the multitude of the lily-buds of the brakes & lilies. |
| | 5 6 7 8 | B. And I came laden w. such floods of flowers that counting closes, wi the warm'd & water'd buds of the press of roses. |

OET No. 42a	
1	I bear a basket linèd with grass:
2	I am so light, I am so fair,
3	That men must wonder as I pass,
4	And at the basket that I bear,
5	Where in a newly-drawn green litter
6	Sweet flowers I carry, sweet for [bitter.
7	Lilies I shew you : lilies none,
8	None in Caesar's gardens blow;
9	And a quince in hand : not one
10	Is set upon your boughs below;
11	Not set, because their buds not spring; [ing.
12	Spring not, 'cause world is winter.
13	But these were found in the East and South,
14	Where winter is the clime forgot. —
15	The dewdrop on the larkspur's mouth
16	O shd. it then be quenchèd not ?

25 ᵛ

17	In starry water-meads they drew
18	These drops: which be they — stars, or dew ?
19	Had she a quince in hand ? Yet gaze :
20	Rather it is the sizing moon.
21	Lo, linkèd heavens with milky ways!
22	That was her larkspur row. So soon !
23	Sphered so fast, sweet. soul ? — We see
24	Nor flowers nor fruit nor Dorothy.

For a picture of St. Dorothea.

Plates 156,157   No.42(a). Lines for a picture of St. Dorothea.
[Above left]. MS.1. C.ii.pp.30-31. (See plate 92 for context).
    The pattern of indenting is purely aesthetic, matching neither line lengths nor rhymes. 7 Lilies none (u.c. L]   14 w→Winter   16a were del.   parchèd rev. to quenchèd below poem   20 that del.rev.it   21,22 linkèd...larkspur both mended.   24 flowers s squeezed in?

[Above right] MS.2. H.i.25r,v. 21 ways! [exclamation partly obscured by hinge--here restored]

[Opposite left]. MS.3. A, pp.310-11. Autograph in ink; RB's pencil collation with MS.H in margin.
Title. [First letter obscured by hinge--here pencilled in] 7 dash del.

[Opposite right] MS.4. Transcript by Digby Dolben.
    Note error in title and careless punctuation in 1,2,4,12,21; but interesting readings occur in 6,13,17-18, 23. In 12 lines it has variants (mostly minor) found in no other ms.

    For OET No.42(b): "A basket broad of woven white rods"—see above left—repeated from Plate 102.

PLATE 157.   OET 42b.   *For a Picture of St. Dorothea*   •   209

A
P. 310
OET
No.
42a

The contemp autograph of this on H
is earlier. ~ does not differ.

FOR A PICTURE OF SAINT DOROTHEA.

1	I bear a basket lined with grass;	H grass :
2	I am so light, I am so fair,	
3	That men must wonder as I pass	pass,
4	And at the basket that I bear,	
5	Where in a newly-drawn green litter	
6	Sweet flowers I carry,—sweets for bitter.	Sweet
7	Lilies I shew you, lilies none,	
8	None in Caesar's gardens blow,—	
9	And a quince in hand,—not one	hand : a.
10	Is set upon your boughs below;	
11	Not set, because their buds not spring;	
12	Spring not, 'cause world is wintering.	
13	But these were found in the East and South	
14	Where Winter is the clime forgot.—	
15	The dewdrop on the larkspur's mouth	
16	O should it then be quenchèd not?	
17	In starry water-meads they drew	
18	These drops: which be they? stars or dew?	they – stars

P. 311

H

19	Had she a quince in hand? Yet gaze:	
20	Rather it is the sizing moon.	
21	Lo, linkèd heavens with milky ways!	
22	That was her larkspur row.— So soon?	ways : soon –
23	Sphered so fast, sweet soul?—We see	
24	Nor fruit, nor flowers, nor Dorothy.	nor flower nor fruit

OET
NO.
42a

For a picture of S. Dorothy.

—

1	I bear a basket lined with grass
2	I am so light I am so fair
3	That men must wonder as I pass
4	And at the basket that I bear
5	Where in a newly drawn green litter
6	Sweet flowers I carry—Sweets fr bitter.

—

7	Lilies I show you – lilies none
8	None in Caesars gardens blow.
9	And a quince in hand – not one
10	Is set upon yr. boughs below.
11	Not set because their buds not Spring.
12	Spring not. 'Cause world is wintering.

—

13	But these were brought fr the East & South.
14	Where winter is the clime forgot –
15	The dewdrop on the larkspurs mouth
16	O should it then be quenchèd not?
17	In starry watermeads I drew
18	The drops – Wh. be they stars or dew?

19	Had she a quince in hand? yet gaze –
20	Rather it is the sizing moon.
21	Lo linkèd heavens with milky ways
22	This was her larkspur row – so soon?
23	What sphered so fast sweet soul? we see
24	No fruit. nor flowers. nor Dorothy.

OET No. 42c

A. P. 58 | A. P. 59

St. Dorothea

(Lines for a picture)

The Angel

1 I bear a basket lined with grass.
2 I am so light and fair
3 Men must start to see me pass
4 And the basket I bear,
5 Which in newly-drawn green litter
6 Carries treats of sweet for litter.

7 See my lilies: lilies none,
8 None in Caesar's gardens blow —
9 Quinces, look, when not one
10 Is set in any orchard, no;
11 Not set because their buds not spring;
12 Spring not! 'cause world is wintering.

— [T.O.

The Protonotary Theophilus

But they came from the south,   13
where winter's out and all forgot.   14

The Angel

The Gill-drops in my mallow's mouth   15
How are they quenchèd not? —   16
These drops in starry shire they drew: 17
Which are they? stars or dew?   18

A Catechumen

That a quince we pore upon?   19
O no, it is the sizing moon.   20
Now her mallow-row is gone   21
In floats of evening sky. — So soon?   22
Sphered so fast, sweet soul? — We see   23
Nor fruit nor flowers nor Dorothy.   24

Theophilus

25 How to name it, blessed it,
26 suiting its grace by *him* and *her*?

27 Dorothea — or was your word
28 Served by sweet seconder? —
29 Your parley was not done and there!
30 You fell into the pathless air.

31 You waned into the world of light,
32 Yet made your market here as well:
33 My eyes hold yet the rinds and bright
34 Remainder of a miracle.
35 O this is braving! tears may swarm
36 While such a wonder's wet and warm!

37 Ah myrtle-wand never set,
38 Set no more these bookish brows!
39 I want, I want, if I were fit,
40 What the cold month allows —
41 Nothing green or growing but
42 A pale and perished palmtree-cut.

Pip in blood the palmtree-pen   43
And wordy warrants are flawed enough;   44
And moss shall wear this wand and then   45
The warpèd world it will undo. —   46

Proconsul, — call him near — ?   47
I find another Christian here.   48

— Ball. Coll. Oxford.

handwriting: 66-68

See letter of Aug 7/68
...

PLATE 159. OET 42d. *Lines for a Picture of St. Dorothea* • 211

STONYHURST MS.

OET No. 42d

Lines for a picture of
St. Dorothea

DOROTHEA AND THEOPHILUS

1 I bear a basket lined with grass.
2 I am so' light' and fair'
3 Men are amazed to watch me pass
4 With' the basket I bear,
5 Which in newly drawn green litter
6 Carries treats of sweet for bitter.

7 See my lilies : lilies none,
8 None in Caesar's garden blow.
9 Quinces, look', when' not one'
10 Is set in any orchard; no,
11 Not set because their buds not
       spring;
12 Spring not for world is wintering.

13 But' they came' from' the south',
14 Where winter-while is all forgot.—
15 The dewbell in the mallow's mouth

16 Is' it quenched or not'?
17 In starry, starry shire it grow:
18 Which' is it', star' or dew'?—

19 That a quince I pose upon?
20 O no it is the sizing moon.
21 Now her mallow-row is gone
22 In tufts of *evening* ~~purply~~ sky. — So soon?
23 Sphered so fast, sweet soul? — we
       see
24 Fruit nor flower nor Dorothy.

25 How to name it, blessed it!
26 Suiting its grace with him or her?
27 Dorothea—or was your wit
28 Served by' messenger'?
29 Your parley was not done and
       there !
30 You went into the pathless air.

31 It crossed into the world of light,
32 Yet made its market here as well:
33 My eyes hold yet the rinds and
       bright

34 Remainder of a miracle.
35 O this is bringing! Tears may
       swarm
36 Indeed awhile such a wonder's warm.

37 Ah dip in blood the palmtree pen
38 And wordy warrants are flawed
       through.
39 More will wear this wand and then
40 The warped world we shall undo.
41 Proconsul ! — Is Sapricius near ?—
42 I find another Christian here.

[opposite] Plate 158 No.42(c): St. Dorothea (Lines for a picture)

MS.A, pp.58-61 in ink on four sheets, written one side only, mounted in album A. Lines 25,26, on a strip cut from the bot. of previous sheet, were accidentally pasted too far to the right (no indenting intended). 6 s partly erased after "bitter". For the new rhythms, brought out by stresses (in contemporary ink) in 2,4,9,13,16,18,40, see L.i.24. After 47 "near—" a flaw in paper looks like a query.

RB added in pencil after poem, "handwriting of [18]66-68/See letter of Aug 7/68 [L.i.24] when he burnt his old Summa etc/This copy of that date"

[above] Plate 159 No.42(d): Lines for a picture of St. Dorothea (Dorothea and Theophilus). Stonyhurst MS. Note the stresses (to indicate metrical experiments anticipating Sprung Rhythm) here placed, as in most dictionaries, at the ends of stressed syllables. He reverted by mistake to the normal placing of stresses in 9 "Quínces" (stress del. and replaced) and 28 "méssenger'" (one stress in old position).

	See Plate 111	C.ii. P·71	OET No.
The beginning of the End.			
My love is lessen'd and must soon be past.		1a	59
I did never promised such persistency		2	(a)
In its condition. No, the tropic tree		3	—
Has not a taster but its sap shall last		4	N.43
Into all summers, ou' no winter cast		5a	
Its happy leafing. It is so with me.		6a	
My love is less, my love is less for thee		7	
I cease the mourning ~ the abject fast,		8	
~ ... eat ~ go abt. my work: again.		9a	
~ save by darting accidents, forget		10	
But ... if you cd. understand how, then		11a	
~ less is heavens greater every yet		12a	
Than ... treble-fervent more of other men,—		13a	
Even your unpassion'd eyelids might be wet.		14a	
[crossed-out lines]			Not in J.62

			OET No.
Some men may hate their rivals ~ desire		1	59
Secretive meats, knives, smouldering-clothes, drugs, flame,		2	(d)
But I am so consumed with my shame		3	
I don't feel envy scarcely ~ never ire.		4	
O worshipful ~ man that she sets higher		5	
I must feed fancy. show me any one		1	No. 59(b)
That reads or holds the astrologic lore,		2	

C.ii. p.72 OET No. 59(b) — N.43		See Plate 112
And I'll pretend the credit given of yore;	3	
~ let him ... that my love	4 a	
Prove my passion was begun	b	
In the worst hour that measured by the sun,	5	
With such malign conjunctions as before	6	
No Saturn-dominated sky e'er wore;	7a	
That no recorded devilish thing was done	8	
With such a seconding, nor Saturn took	9	
Such opposition to the Lady-star	10	
In the most murderous passage of his book;	11	
No hopes were ...	12a	
And I'll love my distinction: Near or far	b	
He says his science helps him not to look	13	
At hopes so evil-heaven'd as mine are.	14	
influential		
No Saturn ... heaven ever wore;	7 c/b	

No. 59(c)		
You see ... that I have come to passion's end.	1	
This means, you need not the storms, the cries, ..	2 a	
that were yr. vantage when you wd. despise:	3 a	
~ save you	b	
My bankrupt heart has no more tears to spend,	4	
Else, I am well assured I shd. offend	5	
with fiercer weepings ~ these desperate eyes	6	
For love's poor failure than his hopeless rise.	7a	
But now I am so tired I soon shall send	8	
Barely a sigh in thinkings of things gone.	9a	
Is this made plain? What have I come across	10	
That here will serve me for comparison?	11	
O sceptic disappointment ~ O loss	12	
~ boy feels when the poet he dotes upon	13 a	
Grows less ~ less sweet to him without cause.	14 a	

A.
21

OET
No.
59
a

Two Sonnets.
"The beginning of the end"
(a neglected lover's address to his mistress.)

I

1b My love is lessened and must soon be past,
2 I never promised such persistency
3 In its condition. No, the tropic tree
4 Has not a charter that its sap shall last
5b Into all seasons, though no Winter cast
6b The happy leafing. It is so with me :
7 My love is less, my love is less for thee.
8 I cease the mourning and the abject fast
9b And rise and go about my works again
10 And, save by darting accidents, forget.
11b But, ah! if you could understand how yet then
12b That less is heavens higher even yet
13b Than treble-fervent more of other men,
14b Even your impassioned eyelids might be wet.

A.
p.22

OET
No.
59c

II

1 You see that I have come to passion's end;
2b This means you need not fear the storms, the cries,
3 That gave you vantage when you would despise:
4 My bankrupt heart has no more tears to spend.
5 Else I am well assured I should offend
6 With fiercer weepings of these desperate eyes
7b For poor love's failure than his hopeless rise.
8 But now I am so tired I soon shall send
9b Barely a sigh to thought of hopes forgone.
10 Is this made plain? what have I come across
11 That here will serve me for comparison?
12 The sceptic disappointment and the loss
13b A boy feels when the poet he pores upon
14b Grows less and less sweet to him, and knows no cause.

Here two sonnets
must never be printed
R.B.

C M N. Ball Coll
Oxf [sent to the Corn-
hill magazine & re-
fused. MB]

22

[opposite] Plate 159^A   OET No.59: The Beginning of the End.

C.ii.71-2 (repeated from Plates 111 and 112)—Early version of three sonnets and five lines of another: autograph faircopies in pencil with a few revisions, in GMH's second early Note-book.

No.59(a): "My love is lessen'd"—MS.1.   ℓ.2 orig. "did no[t]"   9a "rise and" del.   10 "in" [?] → 'by'   13 orig. reading under del. "treble-fervent" is illegible   14 "unpassion'd"; RB misread the revised autograph as "impassioned" [Plate 159^B].

No.59(d): "Some men may hate their rivals"—(sole MS.) the first five lines of an uncompleted sonnet.

No.59(b): "I must feed Fancy" sole MS. of a second sonnet—the opening lines are badly smudged: "Show me any one/That reads or holds the astrologic lore," cont. C.ii.72. 5 "that's" apostrophe s squeezed in   7a The x refers to the revisions, 7b and 7c at the foot.   12a del. "No hopes were so ill-heaven'd as mine are"—adapted for ℓ.14.   7b footnote revision: "Saturn-swayèd" (accent obscured by the interlined replacement, 'influential")

No.59(c): "You see that I have come to passion's end"   3b—the usual dashes used as ditto marks. 5 "assured" grave accent on "ed" del.   8 "And" → "But"   10 "Do" → "Is"..."plea" → "plain"   13 sign for "And", a slip for "A" ("boy" etc.).

[above]   Plate 159^B   OET No. 59(a): The Beginning of the End—"My love is lessened"
MS.2—Transcript of a revised version (autograph now missing), copied into album A, p.21, by RB. It provides the sub-title, and verbal variants in 5, 6, 9, 11 to 14. In 11 "yet" was a slip from the line below, and in 14 "impassioned" a misreading of "unpassion'd" which reverses the sense: some editor has pencilled "un(?)" below "im".

[above right]   No. 59(c): "You see that I have come to passion's end"
MS.2—RB's transcript, A.p.22—of an autograph now missing.   2b "you need not fear" is so much more natural rhythmically than 2a "you need fear not" that I wonder if GMH inserted "fear" by oversight in the wrong place in C.ii.72. In 13b the original "And boy" error is corrected. Other changes in 7, 9, 14. RB's note is interesting: "Sent to the Cornhill magazine and refused"; but this otherwise unknown fact proves that GMH while an undergraduate wanted the two sonnets printed. L.i.24, however, on the burning of some of his verses before he entered the Novitiate, shows a change of attitude which RB tried to respect. RB's note "These two sonnets must never be printed" was added much later.

H.i.
24r

24

A COMPLAINT.

1 I thought that you wd. have written; my
   birthday came and went, [sent.
2 And with the last post over I knew no letter was
3 And if you write at last, it never can be the same:
4 what would be a birthday letter that after the
   birthday came?

5 I know what you will tell me — neglectful that
   you were not. [and you forgot?
6 But is not that my grievance — you promised
7 It's the day that makes the charm; no aft-
   er-words could succeed
8 though they took till the seventeenth of next
   October to read.

9 Think this, my birthday falls in saddening
   time of year;   [here
10 Only the dahlias blow, and all is Autumn
11 Hampstead was never bright; and whatever
   Miss Cully's charms
12 It is hardly a proper treat for a birthday to
   rest in her arms.

13 Our son shd. be born in April perhaps or the
   lily-time; [not in its prime:
14 But the lily is past, as I say, and the rose is

24v

15 What I did ask then was a circle of rose-red
   sealing-wax
16 And a few leaves not lily-white but charact-
   ered over with blacks.

17 But late is better than never : you see you
   have managed so,
18 You have made me quote almost the dismal-
   est proverb I know :
19 For a letter comes at last : (shall I say before
   Christmas is come ?)
20 And I must take yr. amends, cry Pardon,
   and then be dumb.

PLATE 161. OET 72. *A Complaint* • 215

A.
p. 67

A.
p. 68

68

A COMPLAINT.

1 I thought that you wd. have written : my birth.
- day came and went,   [sent.
2 And with the last post over, I knew no letter was
3 And now if at last you write it never can be
the same; [the birthday came?
4 What *would* be a birthday letter that after

5 I know what you will tell me, Neglectful you
were not ;   [and you forgot?
6 But is not that my grievance — you promised
7 It's the day that makes the charm ; no after.
- words can succeed [October to read.
8 Though they took till the seventeenth of next

9 Think this, my birthday falls in a saddening
time of year ;
10 Only the dahlias blow , and all is Autumn here.
11 Hampstead was never bright, and whatever
Miss Cully's charms, [in her arms.
12 It's hardly a proper treat for a birthday to rest

13 Our sex shd. be born in April perhaps or the
lily time , [not in its prime :
14 But the lily is past , as I say , and the rose is
15 What I *did* ask then was a circle of rose.
- 'sd sealing-wax [over with blacks.
16 And a few leaves not lily-white but character'd.

17 But late is better than never. You see you have
managed so, [est proved I know;
18 You have made me quote almost the dismal.
19 For a letter comes at last (shall I say before Christmas is come ?),
20 And I must take yr. amends, cry " Pardon," and
then be dumb.

must not be printed RB

[left] Plate 160   No.72: A Complaint—MS.1
H.i.24r,v.--Autograph on two sides of cream laid note-paper. Fair-copy with no corrections—formerly
owned by the family, so probably the verse-letter sent to Milicent. No punctuation ends 10. This
MS. was taken as copy text in Poems 3rd and 4th edns.

Plate 161   No.72: A Complaint—MS.2
A.pp.67-68. Autograph faircopy on two sheets embossed "Oxford Union Society" and watermarked "1865,"
mounted in album A. RB added "Must not be printed." See L.i.87 for RB's discovery of what was probably
this poem, which GMH (a trifle defensively) described as "birthday lines to me sister,
I fancy." This probably revised autograph is taken as text in the OET.

H.i.
23r

OET
No.
76

The Nightingale.

23

1. "From nine o'clock till morning light
2. The ~~wood~~ *copse* was never more than grey.
3. The darkness did not close that night
4.   But day passed into day.
5a,b ~~At last I saw the day-spring new~~   And soon I saw it shewing new
6a,b ~~Show in the East with such a hue~~   Beyond the hurst with such a hue
7. As silky garden-poppies do.

8. A crimson ~~dawn~~ *East*, that bids for rain,
9. So fr. the ~~first~~ *dawn* was ill begun
10. The day that brought my lasting pain
11.   And put away my sun.
12. But watching while the colour grew
13a,b ~~And glad at least that no gale blew~~   I only feared the wet for you
14a,b ~~I only feared the wet for you~~   Bound for the Harbour and yr. crew.

15. I did not mean to sleep, but found
16. I had slept a little and was chill.
17. And I could hear the ~~smallest~~ *unwist* sound,
18.   The morning was so still —
19. The bats' wings lisping as they flew
20. And water draining through and through
21. The ~~copse~~ *wood* : but not a dove wd. coo.

22. You know you said the nightingale
23. In all our western shires was rare,
24. That more he shuns our special dale
25.   Or never lodges there:
26. And I had thought so hitherto —
27. Up till that morning's fall of dew,
28. And now I wish that it were true.

29. For he began at once and shook
30. My head to hear. He might have strung
31. A row of ripples on the brook,
32.   So forcibly he sung,
33. The mist upon the ~~trees~~ *leaves* have strewed,
34. And danced the balls of dew that stood
35. In acres all above the wood.

36. I thought the air must cut and strain
37. The windpipe when he sucked his breath
38. And when he turned it back again
39.   The music must be death.

PLATE 163. OET 76. *The Nightingale* • 217

H.i.

23v

40 With not a thing to make me fear,
41 A singing bird in morning clear
42 To me was terrible to hear.

43 Yet as he changed his mighty stops
44 Between I heard the water still
45 All down the stair-way of the copse
46   And churning in the mill.
47 But that sweet sound wh. I preferred,
48 Yr. passing steps, I never heard
49 For warbling of the warbling bird,"

50 Thus Frances ~~spoke~~ sighed at home, while Luke
51 Made headway in the frothy deep,
52 She listened how the sea-gust shook
53   And then lay back to sleep.
54 While ~~Luke~~ he was washing fr. on deck
55 She pillowing low her lily neck
56 Timed her sad visions with his wreck,

Jan. 18, 19. 1866.

OET
No.
76

[opposite] Plate 162   No.76: The Nightingale (Sole MS.)
   H.i.23r. See Plate 149, ℓ.25, for his guilty feeling over working till past midnight on Jan.20,
1866, making corrections. Original readings (del.): 2 wood   5a At last I saw the day-spring new
[hyphen revealed by infra-red]   6a Shew in the East with such a hue   8 dawn   9 first
13a,14a And glad at least that no gale blew,/I only feared the wet for you.   17 smallest rev. to
tiniest   21 copse   23 Western mended to western   33 trees [36-39 bad blot, with smudges above
and below 37 "his breath"]. Final punct. in 7 "do." though a stray dot above the period seems to
convert it to a colon: cf. end of 11, and contr. colons in 21,25.

[above] Plate 163 The Nightingale (concl.). H.i.23v.
   40 Note the obscure f in "fear"; cf. 13b.   50 orig. "spoke"   54 orig. "Luke"

A¹
P.307

OET No. 77a

The Habit of Perfection.

(The Novice).

1 Elected Silence, sing to me
2 And beat upon my whorlèd ear,
3 Pipe me to pastures still, and be
4 The music that I care to hear.

5a Frame nothing, lips; be sweetly dumb:
6a It is the shutting message sent
7 Fr. there where all surrenders come
8 Which only makes you eloquent,

9a Be shellèd, eyes, with blinding dark
10a To look on the uncreated Light;
11a The coloured shows wh. else you mark
12a Tangle and break the field of sight.

13a Palate, the fleshly roof of lust,
14a Desire not to be rinsed with wine:
15a Fresh flour shall taste the seven days'
        crust
16a When thou art fed with fasts divine.

A.
P.308

17a Nostrils, the breath of life that spend
18a Buoying the wings of death and pride,

19a What relish shall the censers send
20 Along the sanctuary side !

21a Feeling voluptuous hands, and feet
22a That love the yield of plushy grass,
For 23a Triumph amidst the hail and beat
24a ~~with~~ joy the thorns you have to pass,

25 And, Poverty, be thou the bride,
26a With now the marriage feast begun,
27a And lily-coloured clothes provide
28a Your spouse, untoiled at and unspun.

        Jan. 18, 19. 1866.

OET No. 77a

A²
P.65

A(2)

The Habit of Perfection

1 Elected Silence, sing to me
2 And beat upon my whorlèd ear,
3 Pipe me to pastures still and be
4 The music that I care to hear.

5b Shape nothing, lips; be lovely-dumb :
6b It is the shut, the curfew sent
7 From there where all surrenders come
8 Which only makes you eloquent.

9b Be shellèd, eyes, with double dark
10b And find the uncreated light :
11b This ruck and reel which you remark
12b Coils, keeps, and teases simple sight.

A.
P.66

13b Palate, the hutch of tasty lust,
14a Desire not to be rinsed with wine:
15b The can must be so ~~fresh~~ sweet, the crust
16b So ~~sweet~~ fresh that come in fasts divine !

17b Nostrils, your careless breath that spend
18b Upon the stir and keep of pride,
19a What relish shall the censers send
20 Along the sanctuary side !

21b O feel-of-primrose hands, O feet
22b That want the yield of plushy sward
23b But you shall walk the golden street
24b And you unhouse and house the Lord

25 And, Poverty, be thou the bride
26b And now the marriage feast begun,
27b And lily-coloured clothes provide
28b Your spouse not laboured-at nor spun

OET No. 77a

PLATE 165. OET 77b. *The Kind Betrothal* • 219

The Kind Betrothal

1

1 Elected silence sing to me
2 And beat upon my whorlèd ear,
3 Pipe me to pastures still and be
4 The music that I care to hear.

2

5(b) Shape nothing lips, be lovely dumb:
6 c It is the shut, the curfew sent
7 From there where all surrenders come
8 Which only makes you eloquent.

3

9(b) Be shellèd eyes with double dark
10 c That brings the uncreated light:
11 c These pied shows they make their
       mask,   [sight.
12 c Tease, charge, and coil the simple

4

13 c Palate, the hutch of Like and Lust,
14 b Wish now no tasty rinse of wine:
15 c The flask will be so clear, the crust
16 b So fresh that come in fasts divine!

5

Nostrils, that dainty breathing spend
On all the stir and keep of pride,
What relish will the censers send
Along the sanctuary side!

6

O feel-of-primrose hands, O feet
That want the yield of plushy sward,
The handling of His hands is sweet
And dear the footing of the Lord.

7

And Poverty be thou the bride
And now the wedding weeds begun
And lily-coloured wear provide
Your spouse not toiled at nor spun.

(left margin) Stonyhurst MS f.1 OET NO. 77b

(right margin) Stonyhurst MS f.2 17 c / 18 c / 19 b / 20 / 21 b / 22 b / 23 c / 24 c / 25 / 26 c / 27 b / 28 c / OET No. 77b

[opposite] Plate 164   No.77(a): The Habit of Perfection. Lines are lettered (a,b,c) to indicate the principal revisions.
[top] MS.1. [A']—A.pp.307-8.   Subtitled "The Novice". Earliest autograph, mounted in album A; fair-copy with one revision, 24 "With" changed to "For" (see 26a, "With"). # 7 "there" → "where"

[bot.] MS.2 [A²]—A. pp.65-66. Revised autograph, probably written out while GMH was a novice, late 1867, early 1868.   15b "fresh" del.   16b "sweet" del. This is the version printed in Poems 1st to 4th edns.; and in OET as No.77(a).

[above]   Plate 165

MS.3—No.77(b): The Kind Betrothal. Stonyhurst College MS. Latest autograph, c.1870-71, on two small sheets of cream laid paper; with rev. title and revisions in some 16 lines. This, not ms.2, is the final version. A transcript, by Fr. F.E. Bacon, at Campion Hall, misreads "charge" (12) as "change".

CAMPION
HALL
MS.

f.1 r

OET
No.
78

Nondum.

Verily Thou art a God that hidest Thyself. — Is. XLV, 15.

1   God, though to Thee our psalm we raise
2   No answering voice comes fr. the skies;
3   To Thee the trembling sinner prays
4   But no forgiving voice replies;
5   Our prayer seems lost in desert ways,
6   Our hymn in the vast silence dies.

7   We see the glories of the earth
8   But not the hand that wrought them all:
9   Night to a myriad worlds gives birth,
10 Yet like a lighted empty hall
11 Where stands no host at door or hearth
12 Vacant creation's lamps appal.

13 We guess; we clothe Thee, unseen King,
14 With attributes we deem are meet;
15 Each in his own imagining
16 Sets up a shadow in Thy seat;
17 Yet know not how our gifts to bring,
18 Where seek Thee with unsandalled feet.

f.1 v

19 And still th' unbroken silence broods
20 While ages and while aeons run,
21 As erst upon chaotic floods
22 The Spirit hovered ere the sun
23 Had called the seasons' changeful moods
24 And life's first germs fr. death had won.

25 And still th' abysses infinite
26 Surround the peak fr. wh. we gaze.
27 Deep calls to deep, and blackest night
28 Giddies the soul with blinding daze
29 That dares to cast its searching sight
30 On being's dread and vacant maze.

31 And Thou art silent, whilst Thy world
32 Contends about its many creeds
33 And Hosts confront with flags unfurled
34 And zeal is flushed and pity bleeds
35 And truth is heard, with tears impearled,
36 A moaning voice among the reeds.

37 My hand upon my lips I lay;
38 The breast's desponding sob I quell;
39 I move along life's tomb-decked way
40 And listen to the passing bell
41 Summoning men fr. speechless day
42 To death's more silent, darker spell.

(Cont.
pl.167)

Plates 166,167   No.78: Nondum.
   Campion Hall MS. H 2(a). Sole autograph, on a large double sheet, probably written about the
date below the poem ("Lent, 1866"), judging from the handwriting and the abbreviations (24,26, etc.):
"fr.", "yr.", "wh".   In 33 "Hosts" appears to be given an u.c.. Note the irregularities in the
sizes of letters: 32 "contends" (which must be intended as u.c.), 42 "death's" (very large a)

PLATE 167. OET 78. *Nondum;* OET 79. *Easter* • 221

CAMPION HALL f.2ᵛ

43 Oh! till thou givest that sense beyond,
44 To shew thee that Thou art, and near,
45 Let patience with her chastening wand
46 Dispel the doubt and dry the tear;
47 And lead me child-like by the hand
48 If still in darkness not in fear.

49 Speak! whisper to my watching heart
50 One word — as when a mother speaks
51 Soft, when she sees her infant start,
52 Till dimpled joy steals o'er its cheeks.
53 Then, to behold Thee as thou art,
54 I'll wait till morn eternal breaks.

Lent, 1866.

OET No. 79

Easter.

1 Break the box and shed the nard;
2 Stop not now to count the cost;
3 Hither bring pearl, opal, sard;
4 Reck not what the poor have lost;
5 Upon Christ throw all away:
6 Know ye, this is Easter Day.

7 Build His church and deck His shrine,
8 Empty though it be on earth;

f.2ᵛ

9 Ye have kept yr. choicest wine —
10 Let it flow for heavenly mirth;
11 Pluck the harp and breathe the horn:
12 Know ye not 'tis Easter morn?

13 Gather gladness fr. the skies;
14 Take a lesson fr. the ground;
15 Flowers do ope their heavenward eyes
16 And a spring-time joy have found;
17 Earth throws Winter's robes away,
18 Decks herself for Easter Day.

19 Beauty now for ashes wear,
20 Perfumes for the garb of woe;
21 Chaplets for dishevelled hair,
22 Dances for sad footsteps slow;
23 Open wide yr. hearts that they
24 Let in joy this Easter Day.

25 Seeks God's house in happy throng;
26 Crowded let His table be;
27 Mingle praises, prayer, and song,
28 Singing to the Trinity.
29 Henceforth let yr. souls alway
30 Make each morn an Easter Day.

Plate 167   No. 79: Easter
    Campion Hall MS. H 2(b). Sole autograph, cont. after "Nondum," in writing of the same date and same abbreviations, common in 1865-66 (9,13,14, etc.). 25 "Seeks" final s del.

2 verso

1 a Jesus to cast one thought upon
2 a Makes gladness after He is gone;
3 a Not honey and honeycomb come
near [here.
4 a Its sweetness though when He is

5 a There's no such touching music
heard, [word,
6 a There's never spoke so ~~no~~ glad a
7 a So sweet a thought ~~there is~~
not one,
8 a As Jesus God the Father's Son.

CAMPION
HALL
P.iv.f

OET
NO.
81

25 Who tastes of thee with hunger most,
26 Who drink be thirsty as before:
27 What else to ask they never know
28 But Jesus' self, they love Him so.

29 Thou art the hope, Jesu my sweet,
30 ~~My~~ the soul has in its sighing-fit;
31 Their loving tears for thee are spent,
32 Their inner cry for thee is meant,

1 recto

No music so can touch the ear,
No news is heard of such sweet cheer,
So sweet a thought there is not one
A thought half so sweet there is not one
As Jesus God the Father's Son.   5 d / 6 d / 7 f / 7 g / 8 d

Jesus to cast one thought upon   1 c
Makes gladness after He is
gone, [comb   2 c
But more than honey and honey-   3 c
Is to come near and take Him
home.   4 c

Campion
Hall
P.IV.f

OET
NO.
81

folio

1 verso ↓

3 d Is more than honey and honeycomb.

1 b Jesus to cast one thought upon
2 b Makes gladness after He is gone,
3 b But more than honey and honeycomb
4 b Is to come near and take Him home.

5 {c Song never
{c Never was song so sweet in ear
6 {c Never was such news to hear,
{b
7 {c Thought did not thought by any one
{d Half so sweet was thought by
none never as
8 b As Jesus God the Father's Son

7 e Thought half so sweet there is not one
8 c As Jesus God the Father's Son.

folio
1 verso

2 recto

Jesus their hope who so astray,   9
So kind to those ~~that~~ ask the way,   10

So good to those ~~that~~ who look for thee,   11
To those ~~that~~ find what ~~wilt~~ thou be?   12

To speak of that no tongue will do   13 {a
Speak that is more than tongue can do;   14 a
Letters can never spell it true   15 a
They that have loved know something of   16 a
All that is meant by Jesus' love.

Speak that is more than tongue can do;   13 c
Letters can never spell it true: 14 b
They only that have loved know of   15 b
What Jesus is and what is love.   16 c

To speak of that no tongue will do   13 d
Nor letters out to spell it true: 14 c
They who have loved have tasted of   15 c
What Jesus is and what is love.   16 d
But they can guess who have tasted of   15 d
what Jesus is and what is love.   16 e

Be our delight, O Jesu, now   37
As ~~after~~ 38 {a
by and by our prize art thou,   {b

And grant our glorying may be   39
world without end alone in thee.   40

PLATE 169. OET 81. *Jesu Dulcis Memoria* • 223

fol.3r

17 a Jesu, like dainties to the heart
18 a Daylight & running brooks Thou art,
19 a And matched with Thee there's nothing glad
20 a That can be wished or can be had.

[21]
22 And a sweet singing in the ear
23 And in the mouth a honey zest
24 And & drinks of heaven in the breast

33 Wish us Good morning when we wake
34 And light us, Lord, with Thy day-break.
35 Beat fr. our brains the chicky night
36 And fill the world up with delight,

17 b Jesu, a springing well Thou art,
18 b Daylight to read and Great to heart;
19 b And matched with Thee there's nothing glad
20 b That men have wished for or have had.

Campion Hall MS. P.IV.f. 3r

OET No. 81

Campion Hall MS. P.IV.f. 3v

Plates 168, 169   No.81: Jesu Dulcis Memoria. The OET text arranges the scattered drafts in the sequence of the Latin originals in the Breviary.

Campion Hall MS P.IV.f. Autograph drafts on two scraps of paper; one, watermarked "STOWFORD MILLS 1866," had a corner with further drafted lines torn off. The second (blue paper) has on its verso notes on logic and seven lines of a translation from classical prose (Plate 169, on slightly smaller scale). Mostly in pencil, but in ink are 1a to 8a, 1c to 4c, and 22 to 24. The sequence of the drafts is sometimes conjectural.

Obscurities and Deletions include: 3d (folio 1 verso)—this was fourth line of a deleted version of st.1; the rest was above it on the missing quarter sheet. 5b "Never was song" rev. 5c "Song never was"   6b "Never was word" rev. 6c "Word never was"   7b "Thought was not thought [an →] by any one" del. rev. 7c "[Thought] half so sweet was thought by none" rev. 7d "[sweet was] never o[ne]"   "Sweet" was replaced: fol. 2v, 6a "sw[eet]" del.; fol. 1r, 7f orig.   "No sweet[er]" rev. "So dear"   7g "sweet" del. rev. to "dear"   Draft cont. on 2 recto: 9 "Jesus" → "Jesu"   10,11 and 12 "that" rev. to "who"   12 "wilt thou" rev. to "must Thou"   13b "To speak of that [tongue w/del.] no tongue will do" all del.   15a "who" → "that"   Between 16a and 13c is a blot caused by del. of "sw" on verso (6a).   16b "All" mended to "What" then del.   15c,16d "They who have tried have tasted of/What Jesus [mea del.] is and what is love." del.   Draft cont. on 3 recto: 17a "dainties"   18a "or ... thou → Thou"   19a "Thee" orig. written with theta.   21 missing.   24 "a" del. and blotted.   Draft cont. on 2 verso: 30 "My" del.   31 "These" → "The", "for Thee are meant" rev. to "on Thee are spent"   32 orig. "These inner cries" (partly erased). Draft ends on 2 recto: 38a "afterw[ards]" del.

Summa

A.
p.309

OET No. 80

1 The best ideal is the true
2 And other truth is none,
3 All glory be ascribed to
4 The holy Three in One,

5 Man is most low, God is most high,
6 As sure as heaven it is
7 There must be something to supply
8 All insufficiencies,
9 For souls that might have blessed the
   time
10 And breathed delightful breath

11 In sordidness of care and crime
12 The city tires to death,
13 And faces fit for leisure gaze
14 And daylight and sweet air,
15 Missing prosperity and praise,
16 Are never known for fair,

Inundatio Oxoniana

Mr. Hopkins

Campion Hall P. IV.a recto

OET No. 82

1 Verna diu ~~tristes~~ *saevas* senserunt pascua nubes
2 Imbribus assiduis, et aquosi copia caeli
3 Ingruit et spretae ~~perrupto~~ *dirapto* limine ripae
4 Fit mare per patulos ventisque ferentibus agros.
5 Interrupta locis candenti gramina surgunt
6 Laetius in pelago, pars lenibus edita dorsis
7 Quae vim f[i]at vacuus jam caetera condidit hu-
   mor,
8 Vix indiscretis *as* proprio deducitur alveo
9 Isis aquis; liquidos exercent libera tractus
10 Flabra, vadisque novis Austro juvat ire secund[o];
   o;   [aeas
11 Invia vilificant nemorum et penetralur op-
12 La salices; inter discussae culmina silvae
13 Populus insolitis dat currere mersa carinis.
14 At quinto tandem si sol equitaverit orbi
15 Per purum, toties si riserit igneus aether,
16 Deficient reduces undae. Tum saepe marinus
17 Fertur odor campo et madidas levis occupat
   auras,
18 Urbem qui subsat mediam lustretque domorum
19 Intima; tristem adeo non usquam avertens
   algam,   [us
20 Hinc quota vis morbi, quoties adusta quaerent.

Plate 170   No. 80: Summa
[above] MS. A. p.309. Sole autograph, unfinished. Commas and periods are in places indistinguishable. The slight curl in the stop ending 2, and the sense, persuade me it is a comma. The OET text also takes as commas stops following "low" (5), "air" (14) and "praise" (15), which are the longest strokes measured on a highly magnified scale. Those following "death" (12) and "insufficiencies" (8) are the next longest: the OET reads them as commas also. In 9 "For" means "Because," making that line part of the two lines before it. The sense runs from 12 into 13.

[right] No.82: Inundatio Oxoniana.
    Campion Hall MS. P. IV.a—sole autograph, faircopy, in ink, on paper watermarked "STOWFORD MILLS 1866" (cf. No.81). "Mr. Hopkins" added top left, probably by a tutor. Original Readings include: 1 tristes   3 perrupto
    7 colon beneath blot ... iam → jam   8,9 indiscretis ... aquis   10 iuvat· → juvat ... secund [blot obliterating original o ?]

[opposite left] Plate 171 23 Iam → Jam   25 different u.c. "T" superimposed on Tutior   29 Sed loca, sed
34 [ink] limum ... sequacem corrected in pencil to limos ... sequaces   Signature is pencil autograph.

VERSO

21	Freta petis nostri vicinam obnoxia febrem,
22	At vicibus vertisse solum est, aegrosque calores [umbris.
23	Jam fugere: his non perpetui versamur in
24	Pars ascripta solo sedes servabit avitas
25	Tutior, indigenae plebes assueta periclo;
26	Hinc almo certe submotae numine pestes,
27	Namque licet tepidos in nostra Favonius imbres
28	Arva ferat pernox, resupina impune fatigat
29	Sed loca sed campis obducitur aequor inerme,
30	Vix rubeant immo siccis sua lilia pratis,
31	Quot capita ad notos agitari videris amnes,
32	Debita ni paullum fecundo luserit unda
33	Diluvio interea, dubii se pandere fluctus
34	Ni poterint prius et limum posuisse sequae.
35	Dulcia sic fluvius praetendit fortior arbos
36	Vimena; sic crescant salices; eques avia quaerit [herbas,
37	Aequora sic, tumidasque libentius itur in
	G. M. Hopkins

CAMPION HALL P.IV.a — OET No. 82

OET No. 83b

How well ~~thou~~ Thou comfortest!
And art the soul's sweet guest,
Guest and refreshment sweet

OET No. 83a

Ecquis binas

1 O for a pair like turtles wear,
2 O wings my spirit cd. put on!
3 And where I see O sweet cross-tree
4a {I in an instant wd. be gone
4b {In instant time I wd. be gone

CAMPION HALL P.IV.g

[above, right] Plate 171   No.83: (b) "How well Thou comfortest!"
    Campion Hall MS. P.IV.g--autograph translation in ink of "Veni, Sancte Spiritus," lines 7 to
9. In 1 "thou" del and final comma (rev. to exclamation mark). The mark over "Guest" (3) may be
a music sign (crescendo) or simply deletion lines through a dot absent-mindedly placed over a u

    No.83(a): Ecquis binas. Autograph translation in pencil of "De Passione Domini," first 4 lines
out of 40. The paper bearing these two fragments is watermarked "[JOY]NSON [18]66" (cf. No.87), like
the crested Hopkins family notepaper on which he wrote letters to Bridges on 22 Dec.1866 and 30
Aug.1867. Line 3 "I hat" mended to "And"

Plate 172   [left] OET No.84(a): "Tristi tu, memini"--Campion Hall MS P.IV.b. folio 1 recto. Autograph drafts in pencil on dark blue sheet watermarked "E. TOWGOOD". 1a final question-mark del.   2a orig. "stetarat" 2b "N" → "Illo"   3a "Non" → "Iamque abeo" del.

The ink entry del. is from OET No.85: "An memor et req[uies]"--the beginning of ℓ.30 of "Fraterno nobis"

OET No.84(e): "Alget honos". Deletions are clear except 1c "... tandem deperditus" [For verso, see Plate 173]

[right] P.IV.b--folio 3r. OET No.84(c): "Quo rubeant". Autograph draft in ink (two versions), a palimpsest at right angles over a pencil draft of the opening to a letter to RB about Dolben's death (after beginning "Dear" in ink, he reverted to pencil): "Dear Bridges, I heard of Dolben's death [the day I came back fr. Paris inserted] by a letter fr. Coles wh. had been a week waiting for me [the day I returned fr. Paris del.]. A letter from Edgell has since given me a few more particulars." Cf. final version, L.i.16, 30 Aug.1867. Doodles run vertically down the middle of the Latin text and "rubor" is written across another scroll.   1a "Ille" del.

OET No.84(b): "Tristis eras"--another version of No.84(a).   1 final colon rev. to period.   4 two pencil revisions, "vacuas" and "stella"

PLATE 173.   OET 84. Elegiacs in Latin   •   227

Plate 173   [left] OET No.84(d): "At tu me madidis". Campion Hall MS. P.IV.b. folio 3 verso.   Autograph
fragment of an epithalamium in ink. 1 "At" del. and rewritten to emphasise the longer hexameter in the elegiac
distich.   "petiisse" rev. to "vexare"   2b pencil alternative: "Non mea per lacrimas"   2a "Pa" del.
3a "Parce crede mihi tu" del.   3b "ne[c del.] dederis" canc. ... "tu" rev. to "ne".   4 "Hic" mended to "His"
    6 "vehitur" del.

      [right, lower sections]   OET No.84(f): "Non ibi sol nobis"-- MS. P.IV.b. folio 2.r,v   Autograph pencil
draft. Deletions legible, except 1a "admoverit"   1b "versas...umbras" rev. to "versos...aestus"   3a "Et"
rev. to "Nos," ... "suetos" rev. to "notos"   4a "Non" rev. to "Nos"   5a "sublustris"   8a "exul ero"
8b "[inter del. separately] exul et umbra" ... "sequor" → "sequar"

      [right, upper section] OET No.85: "Fraterno nobis"--draft of ℓℓ.13-18.   13a "curae" added during revision
and bracketed with "fletus"   14a "Et" del. and rewritten to improve layout   17a "caeco possis" rev. to "caecum
possim"   See Plate 174.

      [left, lower MS.]--OET No.85: Fraterno nobis--del. autograph pencil draft of ℓℓ.23-24. Campion Hall MS. P.IV.b.
folio 1 verso. (See Plate 172,left,for recto.)   23a "optatas" rev. to "exstructo" then "sit exstructo"
24a "secat[?] → "subit"   23d "optatas [rev. to optatum] conscendere limite sedes" del.   24b "Mec[um]"→
"Conscendas"

Campion Hall
P.IV.C. recto

OET
No. 85

1 Fraterno nobis interluit unda cruore
2   Et novus exstincti stat patris, Aule, cruor.
3 O mihi Tu summæ et semper suavissima rerum,
4   Divisam longe jam cruor ille tenet,
5 Et via per stellas sublimis et aureus ordo
6   Excipiens noctem nocte disque diem:
7 Hanc ingressa poli seras elabar ad arces
8   Sub vitreasque domos ad vitreumque mare
9 Candida quos perhibes praecellere lilia forma
10   Purpurei infecta sunt male labe pedes.
11 Purpurea sunt labe pedes et Tristibus exsto
12   Indicio guttis criminis ipsa mei,

15b ~~At neque habent illi tantum nec sanguis id~~
                    ~~habet~~

16b ~~Scilicet admotis ille abolendus aquis:~~
17b ~~Si penitus caecum possim recludere pectus~~
18b ~~Hanc penitus caeco pectore culpa latet.~~

13b Gaudia quae fuerint et qui post gaudia fletus
14b   Et qui concident nec recidivus amor.
15c At neque habent illi tantum nec sanguis inhaer.
                    et
16c   Scilicet admotis ille abolendus aquis:
17c Si penitus caecum possim recludere pectus
18c   Hanc penitus caeco pectore culpa latet.
19 Sed mare quod mixta ~~luce~~ *rutilat* flammaque vitro-
                    que —
20   Illud molle vitrum, limpidus ignis erat —
21 Afferat ah captis oro medicamina plantis
22   Infectaeque notae suppositique doli.
23f Quemque sit exstructo monstratum limite cae-
                    lum
                Aurea
24d ~~Ignea mecum adeas~~ quas subit astra viam.
e   O adeas mecum

PLATE 175. OET 85. "Fraterno nobis" • 229

OET No. 85 cont.	
P.IV.c VERSO	
25	Hesternas referam quot vidi insomnia noctis
26	Ambiguaeque umbrae noxve diesve foret.
27	Plurima tum nobis gelido coma rore madebat.
28	Creverat ex gelida ~~ros~~ ros liquefactus humo.
29	Huc ades atque tua num tangar imagine quaeris,
30b	An memor et requies hactenus illa tui.
31	Ista quod quondam saliebat imagine pectus
32	Urgenti dictis stat tibi pulvis iners.
33	Percipio quaesita tamen, nec reddere vocem
34	Non erat, et cardo pauca sopore dabam:
35	Sunt tristes thalami, funesta toralia nobis,
36	Impositoque rigent frigida saxa toro.
37	Tu dulces thalamos, tu quaere novos hymenaeos,
38	Adde, licet, grato mollia membra toro.
39	Est tibi quae melius te foveat altera conjunx,
40	Suavior exstat amor qui sit amore meo.
41	Perculeras validis crepidas ad talia palmas
42	Visaque sunt subitis membra labare modis.
43	Extrema haec sensi; crassas simul intima terras
44	Volvor et in vacuos praecipitata locos.
45	Ah neque te festis plausu dare signa choreis
46	Nec rata sum nimio membra labare mero.

[opposite] Plates 174, OET No. 85: "Fraterno nobis" (elegiacs based on Christina Rossetti's "The Convent Threshold", which is reprinted in OET Appendix B).

Campion Hall MS. P.IV.c.recto. Autograph faircopy in ink with a few revisions. For lines 13a to 18a see Plate 173 right; for 23 a to e and 24 a to c, Plate 173 lower left; 30a is on Plate 172 left. In this faircopy, 13 and 14 were overlooked, so 15b to 18b had to be del. and rewritten. Other changes: 3 "summa...suavissima" rev. to "summe...suavissime" 19 "lucet" rev. to "rutilat" 24d "Ignea mecum adeas" rev. to "Aurea" then to 24e

[above] Plate 175 "Fraterno nobis" cont. The x x x x x mark the omission of verse paras 2 to 8 in "The Convent Threshold". 28 "ros" blotted and del.. Last word is "humo" (m like n) 35 final stop prob. blotted comma, not semi-colon as in printings before 1984.

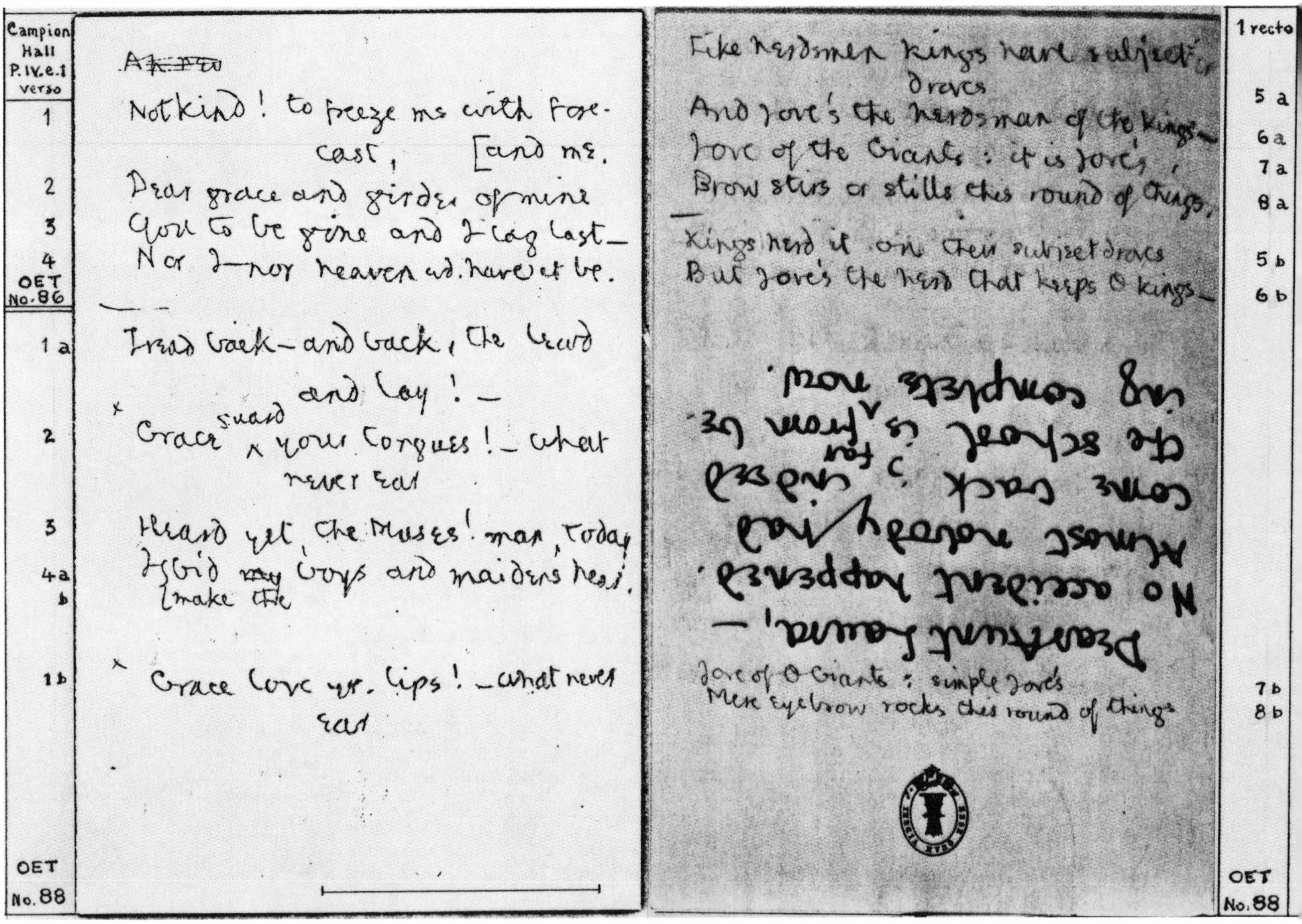

Plate 176 [left] OET No.86: "Not kind! to freeze me with forecast"
Campion Hall MS. P.IV.e,folio 1 verso—pencil autograph faircopy; discovered in 1983 by NHM and Ross Kilpatrick to be a very free translation of Horace _Odes_, II, no.17, st.1 (see _E.L.N._, 23.3, March 1986, 41-2). The del. line above it may belong to No.87, ℓ.3 (see Plate 177).

OET No.88: translation of "Odi profanum volgus", MS.1—st.1. Partly erased original readings: 1a "O back and back" 2 "Grace to your tongues!—What" The letter to Aunt Laura on the recto, in ink, shows through. Poem continues above and below the letter (see right half).

[right] OET No.88: "Odi profanum volgus", MS.2—st.2 (two versions): on folio 1 recto. Hopkins crest in red with tower and family motto: "Esse quam videre" ["To be rather than to seem"]. # 5a orig. "kings have each their droves"

Campion Hall P.IV.d recto	
1	Ah child, no Persian- perfect art!
2	Crowns composite and braided bast
3	They tease me . Never know the past
4	Where roses linger last.
5	Bring natural myrtle, and ~~have done~~
	have done :
6	Myrtle will suit your place and mine ;
7	And set the glasses from O sun
8	Beneath O tackled vine ,

OET No. 87

P.IV.d verso

most of F. Ignatius Ryder, whose name perhaps you know : he comes to see us . the other Fathers are not. He is the youngest of the ʃ priests. But I was forgetting that you must have seen him. I do not expect to be long here : if I get a vocation to the priesthood I shd. go away (I shd. to be an Orato and if not I better myself I knew for cer was not to be

1

5

10

15

J.534,
537-8

Plate 177   [left] OET No.87: "Ah child, no Persian-perfect art!"
    Campion Hall MS. P.IV.d.recto. Autograph faircopy in pencil of translation of Horace, Odes I.38; the paper is watermarked "[JOY]NSON [18]66". Erased original versions: 3 "Tease me"   5 "Bring me". The opening was understandably printed as "Ah child, no Persian—[dash] perfect art!" (a conundrum) till 1967 when I restored the hyphenated adjective.

[right] verso. Autograph letter in ink to unidentified correspondent, written from the Oratory, Birmingham, where GMH was teaching Latin, Sept.1867 to April 1868. Printed J.534, with commentary 537-8. The corner cut out leaves us biographical uncertainties, but ℓ.12 seems to have the beginning of "not"

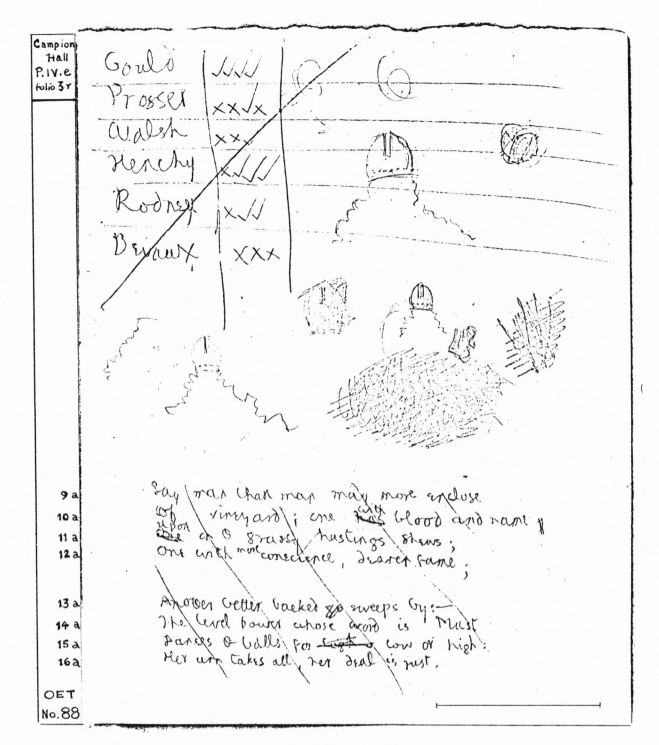

Plate 178   OET No.88: translation of "Odi profanum volgus" (Horace). MS.3.
    Campion Hall MS. P.IV.e. folio 3 recto. Pencil. Attendance at one of the classes which GMH taught at Oratory School, Egbaston, Birmingham (Gould, [Wegg-] Prosser, Walsh, Henchy, Rodney, Devaux). From plates 182-3 it would appear that these were not the five boys in the fifth form (which included C. Wild, W. Sparrow and J.B. Simeon) [L.iii.45]. Doodles of monograms and mitres. Translation cont. from Plate 176.   10a "has" rev. to "with" ...line orig. ended with semi-colon   11a orig. "One on" (only "one" del.)   12a orig. "with a conscience"   13a "go[es]" del.   15a "high and [shorthand sign]" del.

[opposite, top] Plate 179   OET No.88: "Odi profanum volgus". MS. 4
    Campion Hall MS. P.IV.e. 3 verso. Variants legible, except: 13b orig. "Another better backed" erased. 9c "than man the [theta] rankèd"   9d "the" erased below "his"   11c "b" del.   13c "filing" rev. to "crowding" 14c "etc" del. and line completed in full.   17 "that knew" rev. to "who saw"   21a orig. "sleeps that's"   22a "O[f]" → "At"   24a "Or" del.

(opposite, bottom) MS. 5—P.IV.e. folio 2 recto: Autograph pencil fragment of an essay on Comte, or draft of a letter. Deletions legible. 21d "un" → "afraid". This line, though the last revision, cannot form the text because it fails to link with 20.   22d "At" → "Of"

PLATE 179. OET 88. "Odi profanum volgus" • 233

folio 3ᵛ	
9 b	Say man can man may ~~more~~ enclose.
10 b	In ranked vineyards ; one rich claim
11 b	Of blood or our own hustings strews ;
12 b	One with more conscience, braver fame ;
13 b	There's one but better backed sweeps by :—
14 b	That level power whose word is Must
15 b	Shakes up O-balls for low or high ;
16 b	Her urn takes all, her deal is just.
9 c	~~Say may can man a ranked rows~~
9 d	Say man can man may rank his rows
10 c	Wider, more wholesale ; one no claim
11 c	Of blood into our green hustings goes ;
12 c	One with more conscience, cleaner fame ;
13 c	One better backed comes ~~along~~ ^crowding^ by :—
14 c	That ~~the~~ level power whose word is Must
15 c	Dances O-balls etc
17 a	Sinner ~~Oat~~ knew ^who saw^ O ~~sword~~ ^blade that^ was hung
18	Vertical none, cd. Sicily fare
19	Be managed tasty to Oat tongue?
20	Or bird and pipe, viol with air
21 a	Have sleep back ? — sleep Oat's not afraid
22 a	At country caller's bids or low
23 a	Entries or banks all over shade
24 a	~~Or~~ ^and^ tempe with O west to blow
P.IV.e	
OET No. 88	

Campion Hall P.IV.e. Folio 2 recto	Must last in some form as long as O world, I
	think, for it is so consistent, so courageous, and
	so realist. But I see no reason to think Comtism
	will last long. It has ~~no~~ ^little^ intellectual enchant-
5	ment and ^makes^ no moral headway. And it is not on-
	ly Oat Comte is to O English a stumbling-block
	and to O Germans foolishness but that, I suppose,
9	people say of him what they do not say of their
	greatest enemies otherwise — that he is a quack.
OET No. 88	
21 b	~~sleep not afr~~
22 b	^a low^
23 b	(Entries a banks all over shade
	.
	)
21 c	Bring sleep round then? sleep not afraid
22 c	~~that~~ ^Of^ country bids a entries low ,
23 c	Tempe with winds, ~~and~~ ^or^ banks with ^in^ shade,
24 b	But light to come and light to go.
21 d	Sleep that comes light and not afraid
22 d	Of country bidder's calls, or low
23 d	Entries a banks all over * shade
24 c	Or tempe with O west to blow.

Campion Hall P.IV.e folio 4r		P IV - e - 4
29 a	Or ~~Nor~~ hail upon O vine or break	
30 a	His heart at farming, what between	
31 a	The dog-days wiO O fields, alake	
32 a	And spiting hosts that ~~chaks~~ O green.	
32 b	[And spiteful snows to choke O green.	
		stops
25	Who ~~builds~~ his asking mood at par	
26	The burly seas may quite forget	
27	Nor ~~watch~~ fear O violent calendar	
28 a	~~Nor~~ Haedus-rise, Arcturus-set ↑ ,	
b	At	
29 b	For hail upon the vine nor break	
30 b	His heart at farming, what between	
31 b	The dog~~days~~star wiO O fields abake	
32 c	And spiting snows to choke O green .	
OET No. 88		
37-39 →		
41 a	O it ~~flens~~ that ash, Phrygian stone	
42 a	~~Nor~~ starry "shot" in crimson wear	
43 a	~~Sleeks off nor first Falernian-grown~~	
44 a	~~Nor Shushan out to gloss the hair~~	
43 b	Not comforts nor Falernian-grown	
44 b	Nor Shushan glosses ~~for~~ O hair —	

(right-margin, written at right angles)
For motions of their last account
Hangs [?] masters care on board
The brazed barge

For motions [?] [?] [?] some last account
Keep suits and follow : O watch his reins,
[?] Carr, his brazed barge and

(box, lower right) 37 a | 38 a | 39 a | 37 b | 38 b | 39 b

Plate 180 OET No.88: "Odi profanum volgus"—MS. 6

P.IV.e. folio 4 recto. Autograph pencil draft of lines 25 to 32, 37-39, 41-44. Changes include: 30a "h → farming" 31a "dog['s del.]" 32a orig. "frosts to cheeks" → "that choke" 26 "Sea[s del.]" 27 "watch" rev. to "fear" 28 "For" rev. to "At" ...final dash rev. to comma. 29b orig. "his vine" 31b "dogdays" rev. to "dogstar" (no hyphen) ...orig. "to bake"

[written at right angles] 37a "black" rev. to "last" 39a "His" → "The brazed" 37b "last" rev. to "some"

[upright] 42a orig. "Nor" ... "of" rev. to "in" 43a "Sleeks off nor first Falernian-grown" del. 43b "Nor" →"Not" 44b "for" rev. to "in"

PLATE 181. OET 88. "Odi profanum volgus" • 235

Campion Hall P.IV.e. folio 4ᵛ	
37c	For -molions, summers to account
38c	Tread quits and follow him : she boards,
39c	Gay Car, his crazed barge ~~and moo~~
37d	But ~~The~~ Trak, fire-moteons of omind one boards O master there
38d e,f	Climb quits : ~~there's one that boards him there~~
39d	On crazed barge and said behind
	seats
40	Sits to ~~his~~ the beast that ~~bears~~ him _ Care
41b	O if there's Oal ash. Phrygian stone
42b	And crimson wear of starry "shot"
43c	which Not smooth, ~~not~~ that Falernian - grown
44c	~~Nor shushan oils can comfort not~~
44d	And oils of shushan comfort not,
33 b a	{Fish feel Our waters drawing to {O fishes feel O seas draw to
34	With our abutments : there we see
35	The labes discharged and laded new,
36a b	~~For feet~~ And Italy flies from Italy
41c	O if there's Oal ash. Phrygian stone
42c	And crimson wear of ~~shot~~ starry shot
43d	Not sleeks away ; Falernian - grown
44e	And oils of shushan comfort not,
45-48 →	
OET No.88	

(right margin, vertical text) Why / Why sh'd. I change a sabine dale / For wealth that went into weariness? / so join so

(bottom boxes) 45 | [46] | 47 | 48a b [c]

Plate 181   OET No.88: "Odi profanum volgus"--MS. 7.
    P.IV.e. folio 4 verso. Autograph draft in pencil of lines 33 to 48 (45-46 uncompleted). Deletions etc. include: 39c "and mou[nts]"   38d "there's one that boards him there" # 38e "O watch her board him there" # 38f "one boards the master there"   39d "His" → "On"   40 "his" and "bears" del.   A period should follow "Care" 43c "nor" del.   44c "Nor" rev. to "Or" ... comma del. after "oils" and rest of line revised then del.   34 "while" rev. to "there"   36a "For feet"   42c "shot" del.   43d "sleek[s del.]"   [at right angles] 45 "Why [in new erased]" Space left for rest of stanza and further revision of 48.

Oratory
School
Mag.
No .13
Nov.
1895

OET
No.
89

EARGLY MAGAZINES.

—

Page
5

5

TO the readers of the O. S. Magazine an account of some of the previous attempts to start a periodical in the School may be of interest, and we have been able to obtain reliable and certain information of all the efforts in this line from the foundation of the O. S.

The first attempt was made by J. R. Weguelin, of whom it might well be said "Nihil tetigit

---

Page
6

6   THE ORATORY SCHOOL MAGAZINE.

quod non ornavit," in the winter of 1863-64. The publication was called the *Stale News*, and only *one* copy was prepared. This was read to the admiring school on Sunday evenings in the small schoolroom. Acrostics, charades and riddles formed a large part of its contents, but so far as we can learn no copy exists nor have we been able to meet with anyone who has preserved in his memory any of the articles. It had only a short life, not lasting for more than a month or so.

The next effort in this direction took place in the beginning of 1868, when two of the fifth form, C. Wild (now, alas, dead) and W. Sparrow, joined with one of the junior masters, Mr. J. Scott Stokes, in editing a weekly journal called *The Early Bird* or *The Tuesday Tomtit*. The first number appeared on February 18th, 1868. Three copies were published every Tuesday, laboriously written out by the editors, one was placed in the library, one in the studies, and one was handed to the masters.

The Tomtit was rather, we believe, a heavy production. It contained some capital contributions by Mr. Kelke and others of the masters, and had a "leading article," "Notes on News," poetry, and correspondence.

However, the fourth form, which at that time contained some clever and unruly members, determined to start a sort of popular paper in opposition, and E. C. Corry was selected as editor.

This opposition journal came out on the Sunday following the first appearance of the *Tuesday Tomtit*. It described itself as the *Weekly Wasp*, and was of a decidedly spicy not to say libellous character. It began by a slashing attack on the *Tomtit's* leading article, which had been written by Mr. Stokes, and spared nothing and nobody in its denunciations. Only one copy was circulated, and this was written in an ordinary exercise book.

Of course, this warfare gave great pleasure to the school generally, more especially as the articles were supposed to be anonymous in both papers, but everyone knew that Mr. Stokes was the author of the attacked "leader." Perhaps the unkindest cut of all was when the *Wasp* dubbed him a Neophyte in composition, and declared it had found a "pleonasm" in his first ten lines. Poor Mr. Stokes, who was absurdly touchy, threw up his position as editor of *The Tomtit*, but his place was filled by J. B. Simeon, another of the fifth form, and the war went merrily on.

The following lines in *The Tomtit* were perhaps the gem of the controversy :—

"Honoured Sir and dear Mr. Editor,

"Our Bill has an amazing notion to see hisself in print, and I hev promised that he shall make his debutt in one of our leading noos-papers. I hev been for some time wobbling so to speak between the quarto pages of that amoozing little cuss the *Wasp* and your own more classick columns. What has finally indoosed me to give the preference to the *Early Bird* is that quadruped's strictly moral and conservative character alongside of the reverlootionary tendencies of that caterwamptious insec' which I do believe is in the pay of Mr. John Bright. The voluntary principel won't work I calkerlate nohow neither in Church nor State.

"If I had a donkey what wouldn't go
Do you think I'd wallop him, oh, no no,"

as Shakespeare says. Just wouldn't I, some few. But let's have no more meandering. My old woman thinks Bill has a great gift for poetry and between you and me I believe she's right. So here goes. The subjec' cannot but please as it's your noble self. If Bill don't beat that ere bilious nightingale out of the field I'm a biled owl.

THE EARLY BIRD.

The *Early Bird* he finds the worms,
The sweetest thoughts, the choicest terms,
The cut and outest fine new rhymes,
By taking thought to rise betimes.
Could you but see his bill of fare
You'd all be clamouring for a share.

Wasp grubs in heaps like Greenwich bait
Served hot and hot upon his plate,
A plethoric spider, dainty roast
Dressed like a woodcock upon toast,
Rich patè of the harvest bug,
The simpler luxury of a slug.

A hard run beetle baked in mud,
A dish of worts to cool the blood,
Bloom scrapings from the damson blue
And copious draughts of garden dew.
With such a choice of grub, old feller,
No wonder that his throat is meller.

A *Weekly Wasp* or fretful bee
Is just the jockey to suit he.
The little insect kicks no doubt
And jerks his little sting about ;
But the idea is quite absurd
That he can hurt the *Early Bird*.

Our philosophic early fowl
With mien composed as any owl
Sits still as opium-chewing Turk,
While calm digestion does its work,
Then flying on from tree to tree
Enjoys hisself amazingly.

Bravo, Bill, that's what I call music and nature too. There's more where that comes from.

Forgive, honoured Sir and dear Mister Editor the natural emotions of a parent.

Yours to command,
JOSIAH MUGGINS."

5
10
15
20
25
30
35
40
45
50
55
60
65
70
75
80

(Cont.
page 7)

PLATE 183. OET 89. *The Elopement* • 237

No.13
Nov.
1895

OET
No.
89

THE ORATORY SCHOOL MAGAZINE.   7

Some verses in *The Tomtit* by Mr. Hopkins, one of the masters, were followed by a parody in the same paper by R. Bellasis and W. Sparrow. We append the poem and the parody.

THE ELOPEMENT.

All slumbered whom our rud red tiles
Do cover from the starry spread,
When I with never-needed wiles
    Crept trembling out of bed.
Then at the door what work there was, good lack,
To keep the loaded bolt from plunging back.

When that was done and I could look
I saw the stars like flash of fire.
My heart irregularly shook.
    I cried with my desire.
I put the door to with the bolts unpinned,
Upon my forehead hit the burly wind.

No tumbler woke and shook the cot,
The rookery never stirred a wing,
At roost and rest they shifted not.
    Blessed be everything.
And all within the house were sound as posts,
Or listening thought of linen winded ghosts.

The stars are packed so thick to night
They seem to guess and droop and stare,
And gather in like hurdles bright
    The liberties of air.
I spy the nearest daisies through the dark,
The air smells strong of sweetbriar in the park.

I knew the brook that parts in two
The cart road with a shallowy bed
Of small and sugar flints, I knew
    The footway, Stephen said,
And where cold daffodils in April are
Think you want daffodils and follow as far.

As where the little hurling sound
To the point of silence in the air
Dies off in hyacinthed ground,
    And I should find him there.
O heart, have done, you beat you beat so high,
You spoil the plot I find my true love by.

THE ROBBERY.

He stumbled, and his soft silk tile
Straight to the rushing gutter sped,
When I in pugilistic style
    Began to punch his head.
Then as he reeled, what work there was, good lack,
To keep the bloated snob from hitting back.

THE ORATORY SCHOOL MAGAZINE.

8

When that was done and I could look,
His blow had made my eyes shoot fire,
My fist irresolutely shook.
    I roared with my desire.
I put the snob down after him I'd pinned,
Upon my word I did get awful shinned.

No peeler woke and roused the lot,
The night birds never stirred a wing,
The neighbours did not mind the sot,
    Blessed be everything.
And all within were deaf as any post,
Or snoozing dreamed of tea and buttered toast.

The stars were packed so thick that night
They seemed to wink and blink and stare,
And nod as if I were quite right
    In doing what I were.
I spied the nearest peeler through the dark,
From out his bull's eye lantern came a spark.

I saw the kennel part in two
The footwalk with a muddy bed
Of slush and dirt which ran into
    The roadway, my pal said,

And where the cribs we cracked in April are
Think not on daffodils and follow as far,

As where the prowling bobby's lantern's flare
Down to the nearest twinkling glim
Dies off macadamised square,
    And there I should find him.
O heart, have done, you beat, you beat so high,
You spoil the plot I get my living by.

The *Tomtit*, however, published its last number on March 31st, the end of the Easter term. Simeon was leaving, and Wild and Sparrow were too devoted to cricket to spare the time necessary to carry on the paper during the summer. *The Wasp*, however, continued its career, but the account of its sad fate must be reserved for a future occasion, as this article has already exceeded the limits I had proposed to myself.

Plates 182,183   OET No.89: The Elopement
    No MS.--This anon. article in The Oratory School Magazine, No.13, Nov.1895, pp.5-8, copies from an original hand-written issue of "The Early Bird or The Tuesday Tomtit" (since vanished) "some verses in The Tomtit by Mr. Hopkins, one of the masters". The parody, by two of GMH's private pupils, proves that the period ending ℓ.30, in the middle of a sentence, was not in the original ("The Robbery" has a comma there). In ℓ.20 "guess" is a mistake for "press"--see C.ii.111, plate 149, for the orig. quatrain (OET No.75c) adapted to form ℓℓ.19-22. The period ending ℓ.15 should also be a comma. For Sir John Simeon's son (p.6, ℓ.53; p.8, ℓ.3) see L.iii.45. For R. Bellasis see J.158, 377: he and Sparrow were "private pupils" (L.iii.43-4, J.158): GMH comments on their "innocence and backwardness."

H.ii.80ᵀ   80

Ad Jesum viventem in Maria

Oratio

R . P . Condren ex Congregat.
Gallica Oratoni S. Philippi
Nerii

1   O Jesu vivens in Maria
2   Veni et vive in famulis tuis
3   In spiritu sanctitatis tuae,
4   In plenitudine virtutis tuae,
5   In perfectione viarum tuarum,
6   In veritate virtutum tuarum,
7   In communione mysteriorum tu-
       orum ;
8,9 Dominare omni adversae potestati
10   In Spiritu Sancto
11   Ad gloriam Patris . Amen .

To Jesus living in Mary

a prayer

of Fr. Condren of the French
Oratory of St. Philip Neri

1b   Jesu that dost in Mary dwell
2b   Live in Thy servants' hearts as well

OET No.90

3b   H.ii.81ᵀ   81
32
4b   In the spirit of Thy holiness,
     In the fulness of Thy force and
       stress,   [ulkest,
5b   In those most perfect ways Thou
6b   In that strong virtues that Thou
      ~~makest~~ shewest,
7b   In the sharing of Thy mysteries;
8b   And every power in us that is
9b   Against Thy power tread under
        feet
10b In the Holy Ghost the Paraclete
11b To the glory of the Father. Amen.

L . D . S .

5c   ✗ In those most perfect ways Thou
       wendest,   [wendest,
6c   In the virtues of that life Thou

or
5d   In those most perfect ~~ways~~ paths Thou
       treadest,   [leddest,
6d   In the virtues of that life Thou

or
5e   In the walking of Thy perfect ways,
6e   In the spending of Thy spotless days,

OET No.90

H.ii. 82ᵛ

1a   Jesu that dost in Mary
       dwell [as well
2a   Come down and be in us
3a   In the spirit of Thy holiness &
4a   In the fulness of Thy force &
       and stress
5a   In those most perfect ways
       Thou takest [makest
6a   In that strong sanctity Thou
7a   In the fellowship of Thy mys-
     ~~And~~ teries
8a   ~~And~~ every power in us that is
9a   Against Thy power tread under
       feet
10a In the Holy Ghost the Paraclete
11a To the glory of the Father.
       Amen.

      In the ~~perfect~~ faultless footsteps
       of Thy feet,
      In Thy making all the
       virtues meet

5f
6f

32

OET No.90

PLATE 185. OET 90. *Oratio Patris Condren* • 239

[B.41r panel:]

A.M.D.G.   et   B.M.V.

Ad Jesum viventem in Maria

oratio R. P. Condren ex Congregatione Gallica Oratorii S.
Philippi S̶.̶P̶. Nerii

1   O Jesu vivens in Maria
2   Veni et vive in famulis tuis
3   In spiritu sanctitatis tuae,
4   In plenitudine virtutis tuae,
5   In perfectione viarum tuarum,
6   In veritate virtutum tuarum,
7   In communione mysteriorum
         tuorum; [estati
8,9   Dominare omni adversae pot-
10   In Spiritu Sancto
11   Ad gloriam Patris. Amen.

OET No.90

[Turn over

[B.40r panel:]

To Jesus living in Mary

a prayer by Fr. Condren
of the French Congregation
of the Oratory of St. Philip.
Neri

1c   Jesu that dost in Mary dwell
2c   Live in Thy servants' hearts as well
3c   In the spirit of Thy holiness,
4c   In the fulness of Thy power and stress,
5g   In those most perfect ways thou
       wendest,   [spendest,
6g   In the virtues of that life thou
7c   In the sharing of Thy mysteries;
8c   And every power in us that is
9c   Against Thy power tread under foot
10c   In the Holy Ghost the Paraclete
11c   to the glory of the Fath
11d   To the glory of the Father. Amen

OET No.90

L.D.S.

[H.ii.76v panel:]

Oratio Patris Condren : O Jesu vivens in Maria
Jesu that dost in Mary dwell,
Be in thy servants' hearts as well,
In the spirit of thy holiness,
In the fulness of thy force and stress,
In the very ways that thy life goes,
and in the virtues which that thy pattern shows,
In the sharing of thy mysteries;
and every power in us that is
against thy power put under feet
In the Holy Ghost the Paraclete
     To the glory of the Father. Amen.

H.ii. 76v
1d
2d
3d
4d
5h
6h
7d
8d
9d
10d
11e

OET No. 90

Plate 185   OET No.90: To Jesus Living in Mary (Oratio Patris Condren)

[left] MS.4--B.41r: autograph faircopy in ink; written out for public display with Jesuit headings ("A.M.D.G. et B.M.V.": "Ad Majorem Dei Gloriam et Beatae Mariae Virginis"--To the greater glory of God and of the Blessed Virgin Mary) and ending ("L.D.S.": "Laus Deo Semper"--Praise ever to God) Latin heading omits second "g" in "Congregatione"; "S.P." deleted and written out in full around it. 10 "A" begun, then mended to "In", and "s" → "Spiritu"

MS.5--B.40r. English translation. 2c "thy" → "Thy" 11c line del. to correct indentation.

[right] MS.6--H.ii.76v [H³] final autograph, on the back of del. draft for OET No.100 ("Godhead I adore thee") 1d "that" not del. 2d "Be" blotted, del. and rewritten. 3d "fulne" confused with 4 and del. 5h "those", "which" and final comma all del.. 6h "In the", "which" all del. 7d "on" → "of" 9d blot above "power" "tread" rev. to "put"

Plate 184   OET No.90: To Jesus Living in Mary (Oratio Patris Condren).

[opposite] MS. 1--H.ii.82v [H¹]. Autograph in pencil. First col. is faircopy of his earliest translation, with no stops before the end (comma after "Jesu" in 1 is del.). "Thy", "Thou" are capitalised throughout. In 8 "And", and "Tread" del. Second column is later, about same time as MS.2: in 5f "perfect" rev. to "faultless" and "thy" → "Thy". In 6f stroke below "virtues" marks the end of the variants, not italics. The no. "32b" added by RB.

MS.2--H.ii.80r,81r [H²], orig. one sheet watermarked VALLEY/FIELD. Later autograph in ink (1871-74), with the Latin original (lines here numbered to correspond with the English). 5b "takest" mended to "goest" 6b "that" → "those" 5d "ways" del. [5b-X refers to alternatives for 5,6 at foot.]

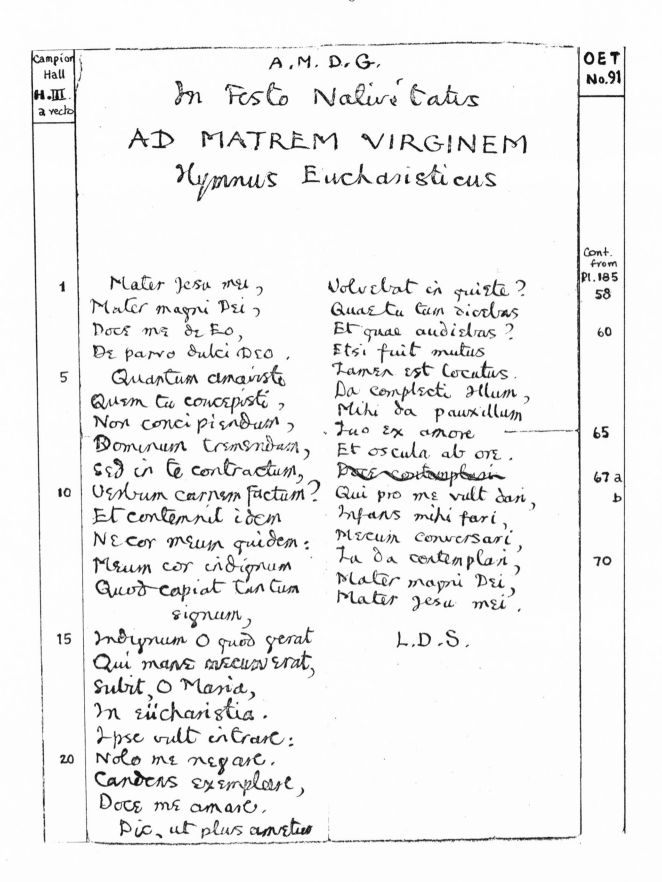

[above and opposite] <u>Plates 186,187</u>   <u>OET No.91</u>: <u>Ad Matrem Virginem</u>

<u>Campion Hall MS.H.III(a)</u>--autograph faircopy in ink, on one long sheet, written out for display at a Christmas festival to the Virgin Mother. The left hand column of Plate 186 is cont. on Plate 187; the right col. above is the end of the poem. Undated (1870?).

   8 "R" mended to "Dominum"   48 slip in copying ("carne" before "mea") corrected   67a "Doce contemplari" del.

PLATE 187.   OET 91.   *Ad Matrem Virginem*   •   241

Campion Hall
H. III. a. γ (cont)

OET No. 91

25 Qualis videretur
   Vulva dum lateret,
   Necdum appareret,
   Cum tua fecit laetam
   Vox Elisabetham,

30 Laetam matre matrem,
   Laetum fratre fratrem.
   Doce me gaudere,
   Rosa, tuo vere,
   Virga, tuo flore,
   Vellus, tuo rore,

35 Arca, tua lege,
   Thronus, tuo rege,
   Acies, tuo duce,
   Luna, tua luce,
   Stella, tuo sole,

40 Parens, tua prole.
   Nam timeo et abundo
   Immundo adhuc mundo,
   Dum contristatus Sanctum
   Spiritum et planctum

45 Custodi feci meo
   Cum exhiberem Deo
   Laesum atque caesum
   In mea carne Jesum.
      Denuum quid sensisti

50 Ipsum cum vidisti
   Tandem visu pleno
   Parvulum in foeno,
   Ecce tremebundum
   Qui fixum firmat mundum

55 Et involutum pannos
   Qui aeternos annos
   Nondum natus de te

OET No. 91

H.ii
86r   86

1a   Salvere Haec te quod possint,
c
b   Haec te salutant ~~~~   quod possint, loc

2a   Dilata multis imbribus,

3a   jubet, valebatur, jubet valere   desserens

4a   Infecta prata foenisex.

1d   Haec te jubent salvere, quod possunt, loca
2b   Diluta nimius imbribus,
3b   Multum, Pater, salvere deserens jubet
4b   Infecta prata foenisex.

5a   Sed candidatus ille quem cernis chorus
6a   Ipso colore prospera
7a   Et auguratur et per ora optat mea
8a   Et gratias et gaudia

87r   87
7b   Et auguratur et tibi ore optat meo
8b   Et gratias et gaudia.
9a   Intonsus ergo hic cum suis pastoribus
10a   Bene et vestat oro grex tuus
7c

88r   88
5b   Sed candidatus quem vides nostrum chorus
6b   Ipso colore prospera
7d   videtur augurari et ore optat meo
8c   Et gratias et gaudia.
10b Bene optat
9b   Intonsus ergo hic cum suis pastoribus
10c   Bene vestat oro grex tuus
11d Et quae tuae novella cura dextera
12b   Remittitur provincia.

         R. Reposi

OET
NO.
92

PLATE 189.   OET 92. "Haec te jubent salvere"   •   *243*

[facsimile, upper portion, H.ii.88v — labelled in right margin: 11 a / H.ii. 88v / 11b / 11c / 12a / OET No.92]

[facsimile, lower portion, H.ii.86v — draft essay on the philosophy of language]

[opposite] <u>Plate 188</u>   <u>OET No.92</u>: <u>"Haec te jubent salvere"</u>
    H.ii.86r,87r,88r--Autograph draft in ink on three scraps of cheap paper (with blots from deletions and from the other side, making transcription hazardous), now mounted one above the other. The last two lines are drafted on the verso of 88. 1a to 4a, all deleted: 1a "Salutat haec te, quod potest, ···ager"   1b "Haec te salutant mad[   ], quod possunt, loc[a" <u>cut off when page was trimmed to fit album H</u>]   1c "jubent salv[? del.]ere"   2a "Diluta mult[u →]is imbribus,"   3a "Jubet [rev. to "Multum"], valere Pater, jubet valere···deserens"   4a "<u>Infecta</u> ~~prata foenisex~~"
1d blot above "loca"   7a,8a "Et auguratur et per ora optat mea/Et gratias et gaudia" del.   9a prob. "pastoribus"
10a "ve[?] del.   5b "noster" del.   10b "Bene vertat" del. (he had missed 9)   Draft of 11,12 on 88 verso, Plate 189.   Some ornate pencilled writing at the foot ("Romano" "Reposi")
    [above] H.ii.88v (at top): No.92 cont.: 11b "Bene vertat et novella cura"   87v is blank (not reproduced). 86 verso has been turned at right angles: it has a draft of an essay or paper on the philosophy of language, perhaps written for GMH's Stonyhurst professors. It is reproduced on a smaller scale: it begins: "Words and signs mean an[d thi]s is their work and office and [of meaning they <u>del.</u>] discharge [themselves <u>del.</u>]

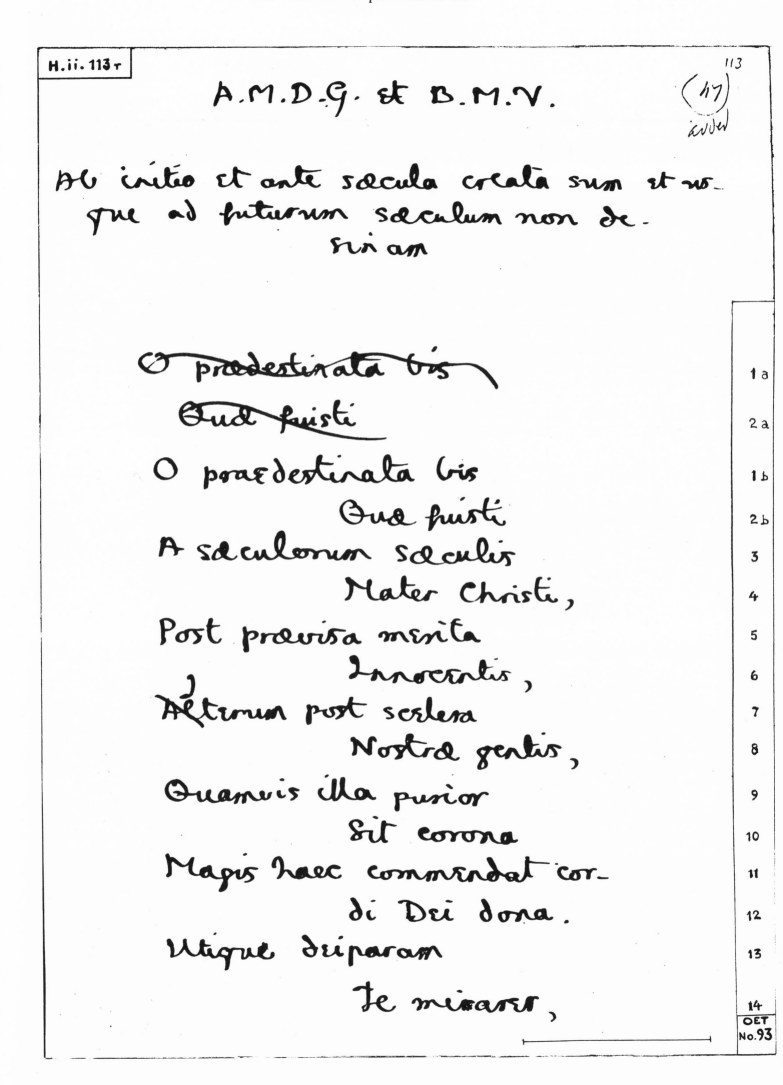

H.ii. 113r

113
(17)
illeg.

A.M.D.G. et B.M.V.

Ab initio et ante saecula creata sum et us-
que ad futurum saeculum non de-
sinam

O praedestinata bis   1 a

Qua fuisti   2 a

O praedestinata bis   1 b

      Qua fuisti   2 b

A saeculorum saeculis   3

      Mater Christi,   4

Post praevisa merita   5

      Innocentis,   6

Alterum post scelera   7

      Nostrae gentis,   8

Quamvis illa purior   9

      Sit corona   10

Magis haec commendat cor-   11

      di Dei dona.   12

Utique deiparam   13

      Te miramur,   14

OET No. 93

PLATE 191. OET 93. "O praedestinata bis" • 245

H.ii
114r

114

15 At non partu tuo Casu

16   Delectarer,

17 Confiteor virginem

18   Matrem factam

19 At non cater omnes sem-

20   per te intactam.

21 Sed bifronti gloriae

22   Tibi erunt

23 Haec quae stant et illa quae

24   Conciderunt —

25 Et redempta scelera

26   Nostrae gentis

27 Et praevisa merita

28   Innocentis.

L.D.S.

Plates 190,191   OET No.93: "O praedestinata bis"
    H.ii.113r,114r--sole autograph, in ink, copied out large for display beside an image of B.V. Mary, with "A.M.D.G." etc. A note by RB (top right corner of f.113) indicates that he added it to Album H later--see his index H.ii.126, where he inserts the date "1819" (for "1918"? as with the poem above it, or perhaps "1919"). Note the stylistic attempt to use a ligature for some of the ae diphthongs, not all.   1a,2a del. and rewritten to produce a more artistic layout, but ligature forgotten in 1b   7 "Alterum" mended to "Iterum"   15 "partu"--printed as "pastu" till reprint of 1978.   24 comma del.

Stony-hurst Mag. No.72 (Feb. 1894) p.233

OET No. 94

To the Editor of the Stonyhurst Magazine.

DEAR MR. EDITOR.—For the benefit of old Stonyhurst boys who knew, and admired the late Fr. Gerard Hopkins, S.J., I wish to call attention to the recognition his undoubted poetical talents have received in a recent Authology of English verse. In the eight volume of "The Poets and the Poetry of the Century" (Hutchinson and Co.,) a selection of his poems is printed, prefaced by a very sympathetic, biographical, and critical notice, by Mr. Robert Bridges. I venture to add to the poems printed there, the enclosed verses on our Lady, which excel in simplicity and melody any of those chosen to illustrate his powers. They were written, I believe, in 1884, and may have appeared at the school statue in their time, but have not to my knowledge been published anywhere.

I remain,
Yours, etc.,
O. S. J.

AD MARIAM.

When a sister, born for each strong month-brother,
　Spring's one daughter, the sweet child May.
Lies in the breast of the young year-mother
　With light on her face like the waves at play,
Man from the lips of him speaketh and saith,
At the touch of her wandering wondering breath
Warm on his brow: lo ! where is another
　Fairer than this one to brighten our day ?
We have suffered the sons of Winter in sorrow
　And been in their ruinous reigns oppressed,
And fain in the springtime surcease would borrow
　From all the pain of the past's unrest ;
And May has come, hair-bound in flowers,
With eyes that smile thro' the tears of the hours,
With joy for to-day and hope for to-morrow
　And the promise of Summer within her breast !

4

8

12

16

234　THE STONYHURST MAGAZINE

And we that joy in this month joy-laden,
　The gladdest thing that our eyes have seen.
Oh thou, proud mother and much proud maiden—
　Maid yet mother as May hath been—
To thee we tender the beauties all
Of the month by men called virginal.
And, where thou dwellest in deep-groved Aidenn,
　Salute thee, mother, the maid-month's Queen !
For thou, as she, wert the one fair daughter
　That came when a line of kings did cease,
Princes strong for the sword and slaughter,
　That, warring, wasted the land's increase,
And like the storm-months smote the earth
Till a maid in David's house had birth,
That was unto Judah as May, and brought her
　A son for King, whose name was peace.
Wherefore we love thee, wherefore we sing to thee,
　We, all we thro' the length of our days,
The praise of the lips and the hearts of us bring to thee,
　Thee, oh maiden, most worthy of praise ;
For lips and hearts they belong to thee
Who to us art as dew unto grass and tree.
For the fallen rise and the stricken spring to thee,
　Thee, May-hope of our darkened ways !

20

24

28

32

36

40

Blandyke Papers xxvi, May 1890, ff.130-2

OET No. 94

A May Poem.

Written by F. Gerard Hopkins S.J. in 1884.

When a sister, born for each strong month brother,
　Spring's one daughter, the sweet child May,
Lies in the breast of the young year mother
　With light on her face like the waves at play,
Man from the lips of him speaketh & saith,
At the touch of her wandering, wondering breath
Warm on his brow: lo! where is another
　Fairer than this one to brighten our day?

4

8

We have suffered the sons of Winter in sorrow
　And been in their ruinous reigns oppressed,
And fain in the springtime surcease would borrow
　From all the pain of the past's unrest.
And May has come, hair bound in flowers,
With eyes that smile through the tears of the hours,
With joy for today & hope for tomorrow
　And the promise of Summer within her breast!

12

16

And we that joy in this month joy-laden,
　The gladdest thing that our eyes have seen,
Oh thou, proud mother and meek faced maiden
　Maid yet mother, as May hath been
To thee we tender the beauties all
Of the month by men called virginal.
And, where thou dwellest in the deep groved Aidenn,
　Salute thee, maiden, the maid month's queen!

20

24

PLATE 193. OET 94. "Ad Mariam" • 247

132

OET
No.
94

For thou, as she, wert the one fair daughter
  That came when a line of kings did cease,
Princess strong for the sword & slaughter
  That, warring, wasted the lands increase,
28 And like the storm-months smote the earth,
Till a maid in David's house had birth,
Who was unto Judah as May & brought her
32   A son for king whose name was peace.

Wherefore we love thee, wherefore we sing to thee,
  We, all we through the length of our days,
The praise of the lips and the hearts of us bring to thee,
36   Thee, oh maiden, most worthy of praise:
For lips & hearts they belong to thee
Who to us art as dew unto grass & tree,
For the fallen rise and the stricken spring to thee,
40   Thee, May, hope of our darkened ways!

[opposite and above] Plates 192,193   OET No.94: "Ad Mariam"

No autograph has survived, but the poem is ascribed to Hopkins by the Hopkins family as well as by long and well-attested Jesuit tradition. Within a year of GMH's death it was included in a handwritten private magazine, The Blandyke Papers, No.xxvi, May 1890, ff.130-132, reproduced here. Joseph Keating, SJ, using an independent text, contributed the poem to the Stonyhurst Magazine (vol.72, Feb.1894, 233-4) under the pseudonym "O.S.J." Neither text can be accepted in its entirety: see headnote to OET.

The Blandyke Papers (BL.P) avoids GMH's characteristic hyphernations (lines 1,3,13,23,24,40--a later editor has lightly pencilled some of them in, but they occur in orig. ink in 17,29) and unconventional usages (19 "much proud," 24). The Stonyhurst Mag. is prob. wrong in omitting the stanza divisions embodied in the rhymes. The punct. varies considerably: a later editor has added pencil dashes to end 19,20 in BL.P. Mrs. Kate Hopkins made a copy of the poem, apparently from the Stonyhurst number.

MS.1 (H¹) [H.ii. 60ᵀ · OET No. 95]

A.M.D.G.   (21)   60

St. Francis Xavier's Hymn

1a My God I love Thee, I love Thee,
2a Not out of hope of heaven for me
3a Nor fearing not to love and be
4a In the everlasting burning.
5a Thou, Jesu, didst for me, ~~this me~~,
6a ~~Reach out Thy a~~
6b Reach out Thy arms in dying,
7a For me didst bear the nails, the
        lance,
8a And the shaming out of countenance,
9a And sorrows out of number,
10a Sad sweats, hard days, short
        slumber,
11a O and death! ~~and~~ this for me
12a ~~And Thou couldst see me sinning~~
12b And Thou couldst see me
        sinning —
13a Then I, why should not I love Thee,
14a Jesu so much in love with me?
15a Not to win heaven nor not to be
16a In hell for want of loving Thee

MS.2 = H² [H.ii. 61ᵀ · OET No. 95]   61

5b My Jesu, thou for me, mere me,
6c Didst reach Thy arms out dying,
7b/d Didst hast suffered
7c Thou ~~didst suffer~~ nails and lance,
8b Shaming out of countenance,
9b Sorrows out of number, [ver,
10b Sad sweat, hard days, short slea-
11b O and death! and this for me
12c And Thou couldst see me sinning:
13b Then I, why should not I love Thee,
14b Jesu so much in love with me?
15b Not to win heaven nor not to be
16b In hell for want of loving Thee
17a Nor any earnings I foresee, [Then?
17b Not for Thy gain or ~~and~~ gift. Why
21a For being my King and God. Amen.

17c Nor any earnings I foresee
[See f. 60V]
18,20a ~~But just~~ Are what I love Thee for. Why then?
21b For being my King and God. Amen.

5c Thou, Jesu, didst after me, mere me,
6d Didst reach Thy arms out dying,
7e Sufferedst the nails, the lance,
8c The mocked and marred countenance,
9c Sorrows out of measure,
10c Weary sweat and pressure,

MS.4 = H³ [H.ii. 58ᵀ · OET No. 95]

A.M.D.G.   58

St. Francis Xavier's Hymn

1b My God, I love Thee, I love Thee,
2b Not out of hope of heaven for me
3b Nor fearing not to love and be
4b In the everlasting burning.
5c Thou, Jesu, after me, mere me,
6d ~~Didst reach~~
6e Didst reach Thy arms out dy-
        ing, [and lance,
7f Thou didst bear ~~the nails~~ with nails
8d Mocked and marred countenance,
9d Sorrows out of measure,
10d Weary sweat and pressure,
11c O and death! and this for me
12d And Thou couldst see me sin-
        ning: [thee,
13c Well I then, should not I love
14c Jesu so much in love with me?
15c Not to win heaven nor not to be
16c In hell for want of loving Thee
17e Nor any earnings I foresee,
(cont. 58V)

MS 3 — cont. from 61 r v [H.ii. 60V bot. · OET No. 95]

~~But just~~

18a But just the say that Thou didst me
19a I mean to love and do love Thee:
17d Not for Thy gifts or gains. Why then?

MS.6 [H.ii. 60V top]

15d Not for heaven's sake nor to be
16d From thy fire eternal free
17g Nor for ~~profits~~ for any prize I see

20b And why do I love thee then?
21d For being my King and God. Amen.

20c What do I love thee, Lord, for then?
[OET No. 95]

PLATE 195. OET 95. "O Deus, ego amo te" • 249

[Left panel — H.ii 58v, M5 (H³ cont); Latin 1–21; OET No.95]

> 7 Not for Thy gifts or gains.
> Why then?
> For being my king and God. A
> > But just the way that Thou didst me
> I mean to love and do love Thee;

```
 1   Miy Deus ego amo Te:
 2   Non amo Te ut salves Me
 3   Nec quia non amantes Te
 4      Aeterno punis igne.
 5   Tu tu, mi Jesu, totum me
 6   Amplexus es in cruce,
 7   Tulisti clavos, lanceam,
 8   Multamque ignominiam,
 9      Innumeros dolores,
10      Sudores et angores,
11   Et mortem, et haec pro me
12      Ac pro me peccatore:
13   Cur igitur non amem Te
14   O Jesu amantissime,
15   Non ut in coele salves me
16   But ut inferis damnes me
17   Aut praemii ullius spe,
18   Sed sicut Tu amasti me
19   Sic amo et amabo Te
20      Solum quia rex meus es
21      Et solum quia Deus es
```

[Right panel — H.ii 74v, MS.7, OET No.95]

O Deus, ego amo te

```
 1c  O God, I love thee, I love thee —
 2c  Not out of hope of heaven for me
 3c  Nor fearing not to love and be
 4c     In the everlasting burning.
 5c  Thou, thou, my Jesus, after me
 6d     Didst reach thine arms out dying,
 7g  For my sake sufferedst [lance] and lance,
 8e  mocked and marred countenance,
 9e     Sorrows passing number,
10e     Sweat and care and cumber,
11d  Yea and death, and this all for me,
12e     And thou couldst see me sinning:
13d  Then I, why should not I love thee,
14d  Jesu, so much in love with me?
15e  Not for heaven's sake; not to be
16e  Out of hell by loving thee;
17h  Not for any gains I see;
18c  But just the way that Thou didst me
19c  I do love and will love thee:
Cont.→
```

[right margin, diagonal: Written by mistake for nails? — What must I love thee, Lord, for then? / For being my king and God. Amen.]

[opposite] Plate 194   OET No.95: "O Deus, ego amo te" ("St. Francis Xavier's Hymn").   MS.1--H.ii.60r [H']--autograph faircopy translation in ink of 1-16.   1a "I", "Thee" in italics.   Two revisions: 5a "this" rev. to "mere", 11 "and" rev. to "all this"   6,12 del. and rewritten to correct indenting.   6a "thy" → "Thy"

MS.2--H.ii.61r (with 3 lines on 60v--MS.3 [H²]--autograph ink draft of rev. 5-21, with alternatives; 17-19 are drafted on bot. 60v (here cut off and reproduced below 61r--three lines in brownish black ink: the margin of 18,20a on 61r is visible on the right).   6c "thy" → "Thy"   7 "Didst" rev. to "Thou didst suffer" rev. to "Thou hast suffered"   17b "and" rev. to "or"   17b and 17d are designed to lead to 21 without 18,19,20 intervening, but 17a and 17c fit the full version.   5c "did" del.   61 verso is blank.

MS.4--H.ii.58r cont. [above] MS.5--58v [H³]--autograph revised faircopy of whole translation in ink (except 20, omitted), followed by pencil transcript of the original Latin.   1b "I love Thee" in italics.   6 del. and rewritten with indentation to indicate the shorter line.   7f "bear the nails" rev. to "bear with nails"

[above] Plate 195:   58 verso--18,19 at first omitted.   21c "A[men]" end of word covered by the hinge pasted over it.   This page bears RB's circled number "20"--not shown. [opposite]--H.ii.60v [H⁴] (top portion of verso here shown separately)--pencil autograph draft, corrected in pencil, for the later translation in MS.7 (74v). 16d "the" mended to "thy fire" 17g "profits I fore[see]" del.   [above] MS.7: H.ii.74v [H⁴ cont] later autograph faircopy of a new translation, added to drafts of No.100: the ms. has here been cut to exclude three del. drafts of No.100, ℓ.1, written at right angles beside the title "O Deus" (see Plate 207).   RB in a pencilled balloon draws attention to GMH's dittography in 7g, the first "lance" "Written by mistake for nails?"   12e a blob of glue with paper stuck to it obscures the end of "couldst"   14d comma del. after "Jesu"   When GMH quoted the first 4 lines in a sermon in St Francis Xavier's, Liverpool, he stressed the second "I" and "thee" in 1, and "not" in 3 (see S.50).

A.M.D.G. **Rosa Mystica**

The rose is a mystery, where is it found?
Is it anything true? Is it more than a word? Does it grow upon ground?
It was made out of earth's mould but it went from men's eyes
And its place is a secret and shut in the skies.

Refrain –

In the gardens of God, in the daylight divine
Find me a place by thee, mother of mine.

Was it here once then? and where is the spot
But there was it formerly? which
blest in spot
That was it once, though now it is not?
Mary makes answer: it grew at God's will
And I broke into bloom upon Nazareth hill.

In the gardens of God, in the daylight divine
I shall look on thy loveliness, mother of mine

What was its season then? how long ago? and
What was the summer that saw the flower blow?
are near upon
Two thousand years, blow?
since its springing, its blooming, its breathing
its last.

In the gardens of God, in the daylight divine
Keep me in thy company, mother of mine
I shall keep time with thee, mother of mine.

Tell me the name now, tell me its name –
The heart guesses easily: is it the same?
Mary the Virgin, well call the heart knows,
She is that mystery, she is that rose.

In the gardens of God, in the daylight divine
Teach me thy mysteries, mother of mine –
I shall come home to thee, mother of mine.

Is Mary the rose then? Mary the tree?
The bloom that is on it who can that be?
Who can it be? O it can be but one:
The rose is Christ Jesus, her God and her son.
her God and her son.

In the gardens of God, in the daylight divine
Shew me thy son, mother, mother of mine.

5.

Is Mary the rose then? Mary the tree?
But the blossom, the blossom there, who can it be?
Who can it be? O it could be but one:
The rose is Christ Jesus, her God and her son.
In the gardens of God, in the daylight divine
Shew me thy son, mother, mother of mine.

What was the colour of that blossom bright? –
White to begin with, immaculate white.
But the flush on its flakes is to me richer hued,
When the rose ran with crimson against the cross-tree wood.
In the gardens of God, in the daylight divine
I shall worship his wounds with thee, mother of mine.

Campion
Hall
H.II.c
f.1v

Plate 196   OET No.96: Rosa Mystica—(MS.1) Campion Hall H.II.c   autograph draft in ink on a single sheet folded to make four pages (here rearranged into sequence).   Earlier Readings include: 2a Is it more than a word? 3 It was made out of earth   7 [sequence uncertain]7a Was it here once then? and where is the spot   7b Did it live among men   7c Was it found amon[g]   7d Was it growing on earth then? and where is the spot   8b That was graced by it   9a Mary makes answer, I rose   10 And I broke into flower   13 When was   14 What was the summer   that saw the flower blow   15a Nearly two thousands of years [have del.] are gone past   15b Two thousand years' time will soon have gone past   16a From its springing, its blooming, its breathing its last [? del.].   rev. its bloom, from its   16b From its birth, from its bloom, from its breathing   18a Keep mé in thy company, [note stress]   19 name: 20 easily,   24a Teach me thy mysteries,   33a,b But the flush on its flakes [looks richer to me rev. to] is to me richer hued

PLATE 197.   OET 96.   *Rosa Mystica*   •   251

Campion
Hall
H.II.c

7.

37a^b How many leaves had it? — Five they were then,
38 a^b ~~they were~~ Five, like the senses and members of men;

39 Five ~~was~~ is their number by nature, but now
40a-d they multiply, multiply ~~who can say~~ now?
41 In the gardens of God, in the daylight divine
42 Make me a leaf ~~of~~ thee, mother of mine.

31 b What ~~is~~ was the colour of that blossom bright?
32 b White to begin with, immaculate white.
33 c O rose but thy crimson, the gashes in thee
34 c they came at thy nailing against the cross-
35 b In the garden of God, in the daylight divine

8.

43 Does it smell sweet too in that holy place? —
44a^bc ~~So sweet unto~~ God, and the sweetness is grace:
45a^b ~~The breath~~ of it bathes ~~blood~~ heaven above
46 In grace that is charity, grace that is love.
47a^b To thy ~~rest~~, to thy ~~breast~~, to thy ~~glory~~ divine
48 Draw me by charity, mother of mine.

33 d But a royaller flush on the flakes of it stood
34 d when ~~with~~ the rose running crimson
34 e clasped the cross-wood.
   When the life of it crimsoned the bitter cross-wood.

6.

31 c What was the colour of that blossom bright? —
32 c White to begin with, immaculate white.
33 e But what a wild flush on the flakes of it stood
34 f ~~when the rose, running crimson, hung on the~~
   when the rose ran in crimsonings down the cross-
34 g wood!
35 c In the gardens of God, in the daylight divine
36 b I shall worship his wounds with thee, mother of mine.

33 f But how gorgeous a flush on the flakes of it stood
34 h when the rose ran in crimsonings down the cross-wood!

33 g But a royaller flush on the flakes of it stood
34 i when the rose ran in crimsonings down the cross-wood.

But the blossom, the blossom — Ah! who can it be

But what a deep flush — Sh. prefer

A very sweet & thoughtful little
poem indeed — yet not so good to sing
as to read: Too many close sounds.

OET No. 96
[26]
[33]

fol. 2 r   fol. 2 v

Plate 197   37a How many leaves [has mended to] had it?—When they began   40a who can say how?   40b who shall say how? 40c no man knows how.   42 leaf of thee   44a Sweet even to God   44b O sweet unto God   45a The breath of it   45b Breath of it.

The poem was probably meant to be hung beside an image of the Virgin: note the "A.M.D.G." heading it. The comments at the end are in an unidentified hand, probably by the person responsible for assembling the poems.

A. M. D. G.

22 13

H. ii.
63ʳ

On St. Winefred

besides her miraculous cures
filling a bath and turning a mill

———

1 As wishing all about us sweet,
2 She brims her bath in cold or heat;
3 She lends, in aid of cook and coill,
4 Her hand from heaven to turn a mill —
5 Sweet soul ! not scorning honest sweat
6 And favouring virgin freshness yet.

L. D. S.

OET
No
98a

Plate 198   OET No.98(a): On St. Winefred   Note: this Plate may be compared with the Latin version, Plate 201, by holding up the intervening leaf, while the drafts on Plate 200 are conveniently opposite the finished poem which borrowed some of their lines. RB numbered the poem "22" in album H; the Latin version, later presented to the Fourier Library, came next, No.23. Both are marked "A.M.D.G." and "L.D.S.", written out large on very poor quality paper. The semicolon ending 2 is smudged.

PLATE 199. OET 97. "Quique haec membra" • 253

H.ii. 85r — OET No. 97 — (33) b — 85

1a — *Atque* haec membra malis videas

1a cont. — obnoxia multis

2a — *Nil nimium* esse velis

1b — Quique haec membra malis vis esse ob-
nexia multis

2b — Ne nimium esse velis,

3 — Non ego namque meas haec haerentia haerentia *sorti* repugno

4 — Aut minor *em* *esse* esse piget,

5 — *Verum et* Interest mediae tantum indulgentia poenae

6 — Quamque subire *jubes* crucem

7 — Sit tua crux : tecum, qui sum torquendus,
et oro

8 — Torquear ante tua.

9a — Sed miserere tuis, *hoc multum* te deprecor, Indis

9b — Sed miserere tuis tam multis millibus Indis,

10 — Jam miserere tuis, [interea

11a — Quamque rogare alios peccat gens credula

11b (12a) — Quam *pro Deus* rogare alium properant peccantque salutem

12b — pro Deus interea.

H.ii. 85v

it *re* remains that *as* slip in silence, as
religious, we bestow the secret service of
the heart and the eloquence of our deeds
not now in month's-end praises but through
our whole life's course in her honour. So let
it be.

<u>Plate 199</u>   <u>OET No.97</u>: <u>"Quique haec membra"</u>
  <u>H.ii.85r</u>—autograph draft in pencil (numbered "33b" by RB). <u>Earlier alternatives include</u>: 1a [Atque <u>rev.</u>
<u>to</u>] Cumque haec membra malis videas obnoxia multis   2a [Ne <u>mended to</u>] Nil nimium esse velis   1b Cumque <u>mended</u>
<u>to</u> Quique   2b welis ⟶ velis   3 Na ⟶ Non ... haerentia sorti   4 esse   [After 4 a space suggests omitted
material]   5 Verum or[o?]...medii ⟶ mediae   6 jubes crucem   7 qui ⟶ quod   9a [multum te <u>rev.</u> <u>to</u>] hoc multum
deprecor, Indis   11a alios <u>rev.</u> to alium   11b (<u>written around</u> 12a)...alium properant
  <u>H.ii.85v</u>—No.97 was written on the other side of a sheet used for this autograph translation of an exhortation
to religious to honour the BV Mary in deeds rather than words.

H.ii 68 r

(26) 5ᵛ

Carissime in Christo frater,
P. C. — Facile intelliges scho-
lastica me negotia tenuisse
hactenus tenuisse ne ad bon-
as tuas litteras promptius re-
scriberem. Hodie magis vacat,
feriae menstruae aguntur.

1   Iam si rite sequor ~~veteris~~ Prisci vestigia facti
2   Haec sunt egregie numine plena. sacro

3   Quis etiam nostros non ~~deneg~~ aspernata labores
4   utilis assiduaefst, nec pudet esse, molae,
5   scilicet et sordes ut quae patiatur
       honestas
6   Et quae virgineum suadeat ipsa decus.

OET No. 98 C

H.ii 68 v

7a   Primum quod ternis erumpit fontibus unda
8a   Haec est ~~tergemini~~ tergemini credita forma Dei
9a   ~~Qui quod sincerum~~
9b   Mox quod sincerum juncti simul   aequore crescunt
10a,c   ~~simplicitas~~ tibi simplicitas quam colit alma fides
7c,b   Atque tribus primum quod fontibus exiit fontibus unda
8b   Haec est tergemini credita forma Dei,
9c   ~~Mox~~ quod sincero juncti simul aequore crescunt
10d   En tibi simplicitas quam colit, alma fides.

7d   Atque tribus primum quod flumen fontibus exiit ste

11   Quid quod ab occulta submissus origine sese
12   inque hominum adspectus fons agit inque diem?

69 r

13   Quod pulcral cernis distinctum cardine quino
14   Qua   inclusas   fronte coronet aquas
15   Hoc est quod species, ~~nobis data~~ quae fuit nuntia rerum,
16   Quinque aulit mentem, qua patet ire, viis.

OET No. 98 C

PLATE 201. OET 98b. "In S. Winefridam" • 255

A.M.D.G.

In S. Winefridam
praeter miraculorum gratiam
operam dantem
et balneis et molae,.

—

Temperat
~~Apparat~~ aestiva fessis sua balnea membris,
Hiberna *rigidis* *temperat* *alma*
~~Apparat hiberna balnea~~ rite manu;
os *dextra*
Quin etiam nostri ~~partem~~ dignata laboris
scilicet *alta* *polo*
utilis assiduae, nec pudet esse, molae;
~~Ut quae expers maculae~~ sordes non temnat
honestas
Virgineum *quamvis*
Et ~~quae virgineum~~ suadeat ipsa decus.

L.D.S.

Fourier Library, Notre Dame, Maryland.

OET No. 98b

[opposite] Plate 200 OET No.98(c): Iam si rite.

MS.1--H.ii.68r: autograph draft of a letter to a fellow scholastic, apologising for leaving the answer to his letter until the arrival of a holiday. Undated: c.1875. The discarded note, front and back, was used for elegiacs in honour of St. Winefred: 3 to 6 were modified for inclusion in No.98(b)--Plate 201.

Deletions and Revisions include: 1 sacri[us?] rev. to veteris then prisci 2 Dei 3 dedig 4 orig. assiduaeest 5 blot after Scilicet / MS.2: H.ii.68v--8a termin del. rev. to tergemini 9a Qui quod sincerum 9b sincerum →sincero 10a Simplicitas rev. to En tibi then En est ... ecce colenda fide illa 7c [x in margin refers down to revision 7d below]... fo ... fontibus del. 7b Principio 9c Mox 10d colit →colis 14 single letter del. after inclusas 15 nobis data rev. to quae fiunt [damaged surface obscures last letter]

[above] Plate 201 OET No.98(b): In S. Winefridam (Latin translation of No.98(a)—Plate 198: see note there). This ms., formerly in album H.ii., is now in the Fourier Library of the College of Notre Dame in Maryland. If it was hung in honour of St Winefred on her feast day, GMH probably revised his version (with a steel nib) afterwards. The revisions are: 1 Apparat rev. to Temperat 2 Apparat hiberna balnea rite rev. to Hiberna rigidis temperat alma 3 nostri partem ... laboris rev. to nostros dextra ... labores 5 Ut quae expers maculae ... temnat rev. to Scilicet alta polo ... temnit 6 Et quae virgineum rev. to Virgineum quamvis

OET No. 99	H.ii.89 v	
1	*Miror surgentem per puram Oriona noctem,*	
2	*Candida Luna* ~~tuens~~ *incubat* [*laetis*	
3a,b	*Adstet et exiguis* ...	
4	*Nec simul esse sinat.* [*altum et*	
5	*Verum hic Orión miror quam crescat in*	
6a	*Oxan micet igne suo*	
9a	*Quosque agitare putes septena cacumina vent[*	
10a	*septem agitantur enim,*	
11a	*Miror item suaves adeo spirantis auras*	
12	*Exclidunque Notum*	
13a,b	~~At~~ ... *hiemes primasque tepere Kalend[* *Atque hiemem median*	
14a	*Quas novus annus agitat,*	
13c	*Atque hiemem tantum primasque tepere Kalen[*	
14b	*Quas novus annus agit,* ...	
15a,b	*Nostramque ab ea quae jam* ~~non est numera-~~	
16	*Dicimus ire dies.*	
17	*O Jesu qui nos homines caelestis et alta ha[*	
18	*Contrahis astra manu,* [*annus*	
19d	*Omnia sunt de te : precor a te currat et*	
20b	*Is bonus annus erit.* [*in te,*	
21	*Omnia sunt in te : nostram vivat gen[*	
22	~~Nam~~ *tua membra sumus,* [*laud[*	
23a	*Omnes concessas exiguam quot carpimus*	

Plate 202   OET No.99: "Miror surgentem"--MS.1
    H.ii.89 verso. Undated: paper watermarked "1874"; prob. written 1 Jan.1876. Autograph faircopy in pencil (with some revisions) of lines 1 to 6, 9 to 23. Other lines are drafted or redrafted on the recto (Plate 203), so that we sometimes cannot be sure which version came first (e.g. 19,20).
    Original Readings (deleted or mended) include: 1 noctem: [or noctem.], rev. to noctem, 2 tamen   3 Adstat →Adstet ... exiguus   nimis imminet [claerior rev to] clarior   4 sinet → sinat   12 notum → Notum   13a, 13c, 15a [First letters of lines del. and rewritten to correct indenting] 13a Et → At[que?] orig. Et [tristes rev. to] rigidas hiemes ... Kalendas   rev. to Atque [hiemum →] hiemem   14a agit → agat   13c or del. and rewritten   15a ea quae jam non est numeramus et [ipsas rev. to] anni   19d in   22 Nam
    Words rubbed faint at line ends: 9a ventos   13a, 13c Kalendas   15b anni   17 haec   21 genus   23a carpimus auras

PLATE 203. OET 99. "Miror surgentem" • *257*

	H.ii. 89 r
~~omnes contestas~~ inquam ~~quot carpimus au-~~	
~~ras~~	23 b
Suspicimusque polum. [deȳt	24
Gratia ~~deest~~ ~~sed~~ ~~multis~~ cum ~~et~~ multis: ut gratia	25a b
Omnia ~~sunt~~ a te; ~~perrecor~~ pergat precor ~~annus~~ ~~currat~~	19a b / c
Non tamen omne ~~deest~~	?26 a
~~scilicet~~ alma ~~a te~~: subest etiam	27 a
~~Is bonus annus sit~~	20 a
natura	27 cont.
Quam micet igne suo, [itque	6 b
Non suas aetherium quem purpurat impetus,	7
Molle redit que decus: [tos	8
Quin versare aliquos septena cacumina ven-	9 b
turire posse putes.	10 b
Miror item etc	11 b
Gratia deest sed enim multis: ut gratia deset,	25 c
~~Attamen~~ omnibus alma ~~simul~~ tamen,	26 b
Alma ~~simul~~ etiam natura subest, cui tenditur ista	27 b
Provida cunque manus	28
	OET No. 99

Plate 203   OET No.99: "Miror surgentem"—MS.2

H.ii.89 recto—autograph in pencil: faircopy cont., 23 prob. repeated from verso in error; next five lines rough draft, some lines scarcely recognisable; lower half faircopy with a few revisions. Deletions include: 25a multis: ut multis at   19a Omnia sunt a te: [perecor rev. to] precor rev. to perga then to currat   ?26a Na→ Non ... deest   27a Alm[a] ... a te   20a Is bonus annus erit   10b putes [cf. Plate 202, 9a]   [bot. of page] 26b Attamen ... simul,   27 simul [Comma del. and rewritten after subest]

[H¹]

H.ii.

78r

OET

No.100a

1 a	
2 aᵇ	
3 a	
4 a	
St.2	
5 a	
6 a	
7 aᵇ	
8 a	
St.3	
9 aᵇ	
10 aᵇᶜ	
11 a	
12 aᵇᶜ	
St.4	
13 a	
14 a	
15 aᵇ	
16 aᵇ	
St.5	
17 a	
18 a	
19 aᵇ	
20 aᵇ	
St.6	
21a/22d	
22aᵇᶜ	
23 aᵇ	
24 a	
St.7	
25 a	
26aᵇ	
27 aᵇ	
28 a	

78

30

Godhead, I adore Thee, down on bended knee,
Who art here ~~though or~~ hiding under ~~in the shapes~~ things we see.
Wholly to Thy service I submit a heart
Wholly lost in wonder, Lord, at what Thou art.

Seeing, touching, tasting, might mislead me here
But in faith I follow what is taught the ear.
What God's son has ~~spoken~~ told me take for truth I do:
Word of Truth speaks truly or there's nothing true.

On the cross the godhead lost indeed its light ~~was concealed from sight~~
~~Here But the very~~ the manhood ~~too is hidden from the light~~ ever also here is
Both are^ my confession, both are my belief, out of sight:
And I ~~take~~ pray the ~~blessing~~ prayer of the dying thief.

I am not like Thomas, wounds I do not see,
But ~~I can~~ confess Thee Lord and God as he.
~~Grant me~~ Make this faith the deeper every day I live,
~~Stronger~~ More the hope ~~to~~ hold by, ~~greater~~ more the love to give.

Being our reminder of our Master's death,
Living bread, and giving man his life and breath,
Grant my ~~thoughts~~ mind may ~~always~~ ever find in Thee ~~their~~ its food
Tasting ~~in these~~ in Thee that sweetness Thou hast meant I should.

Make the tender tale true of the Pelican;
Nurse me weak and naked at Thy breast that ran
~~Wash my soul to life that from Thee Thy bosom ran~~
Blood ~~which one single~~ drop of has the worth to win
All the worlds redemption from its world of sin.

Jesu, whom I look at darkly here below,
Give me what my ~~soul is~~ thoughts are thirsting after so;
Take The veil away that ~~hides~~ thy face and then
I shall see Thy glory and be blest. Amen.

Plate 204   OET No.100(a): S. Thomae Aquinatis Rhythmus.
[Note: The MSS. are reproduced as full plates first, Nos.204 to 209, in chronological order; then, to make possible the tracing of each line's evolution, double-page spreads assemble all the MSS. for sts.1-3, then 4 and 5, and finally 6 and 7, on Plates 210 to 215.]
MS.1--H.ii.78r [H¹]--earliest autograph translation, in ink, of a hymn attributed to St Thomas Aquinas. Begun as a faircopy, subsequently revised. Undated; prob. c.1876. Verso blank. For transcription of deletions see Plates 210ff.. Unlike other versions, H¹ capitalises "Thee" (in 1, orig. "thee"), "Thou", "Thy". This earliest version is published separately as No.100(a).

PLATE 205. OET 100b. *S. Thomae Aquinatis Rhythmus* • 259

| [H²a] | OET No.100(b) | 74 |

H.ii
74r

1 b Godhead here in hiding, whom I do adore
2 c masked by these bare shadows, shape and nothing more,
3 b See, Lord, at thy service low lies here a heart
4 b Lost, all lost in wonder at the God thou art.

St.2
5 b Seeing, touching, tasting are in thee deceived:
6 b How says trusty hearing? that shall be believed:
7 c what God's Son has told me, take for truth I do;
8 b Truth himself speaks truly or there's nothing true.

St.3
9 c On the cross thy godhead made no sign to men;
10 d Here thy very manhood steals from or human ken:
11 b Both are my confession, both are my belief,
12 d and I pray the prayer of the dying thief.

St.4
13 b I am not like Thomas, wounds I cannot see,
14 b c
  d   But can call thee plainly Lord and God as he:
15 c make this faith the deeper every day I live,
16 c more to hope for from thee, thee more love to give.
  d   Let me hope more from thee, more love let me give.
  e   Harder to hope in thee, dearer love to give.

15 d,e This faith daily deeper make my holding of,
16 f-g Daily hope the harder, dearer let me love
  h   Daily to hope harder, and to dearer love.
  i   make me harder hope and make me dearer love.
  j   make me hope the harder, make me dearer love,

St.4
13 c I am not like Thomas, wounds I cannot see,
14 e But can plainly call thee Lord and God as he:
15 f This faith each day deeper make my holding of,
16 k Daily make me harder hope and dearer love.

St.5
(see H²b)
17 d O thou our reminder of Christ crucified,
18 c Living Bread the life for whom he died,
19 e lend this life to me then: feed and feast my mind,
20 e there be thou the sweetness man was meant to find.

Plate 205 OET No.100(b): S. Thomae Aquinatis Rhythmus (cont.)

MS.2--H.ii.74r [H²a]. Begun as a faircopy, this autograph generates twelve lines of draft before finalising st.4. The last st. on this page, and the rest of the poem (on the verso), were drafted on 76 recto, and revised sometimes even further before being copied out fair. The final form is the text of OET No.100(b). Undated, but 1879-81 seems probable. For transcriptions see Plates 210 and 212.

(29)

76

St.5
17b c

{ thou art that
{ O that {long reminder of our dear Lord's death,
18b living bread and giving ~~those~~ that too of thee breath,...
19c Grant this grace to me then, be my life of mind,
d { life blood to my mind

20c { with the love and relish I was meant to find.
d { with the relish in thee I was meant to find.

St.6
21b make the tender tale true of the Pelican,
22e Jesu Lord, and wash me with at thy breast that ran
23c Blood ~~which~~ but one drop of has the worth to win
24b all the world redemption from a world of sin.

21c Like that tender tales tell of the Pelican,
22f Wash me, Jesu Lord, with what thy bosom ran —
23d Blood that but one et

St.7
25b Jesu, whom I look at veilèd here below,
26c Bring to pass the blessing that I thirst for so,
d , I pray thee, what I thirst for so,
send me what I thirst for so
26e { Beseech thee, send } what I thirst after so,
f { bring }

27c That thy ~~one~~ face ~~beholding~~ ~~uncovered light,~~
some day to
27d' { That I may gaze on thee face to face in light
28b and be blest for ever ~~in the~~ with thy glory's sight.
amen.

[H²b]
H.ii.
76r
OET
No.100 b

Plate 206   OET No.100(b): S. Thomae Aquinatis Rhythmus (cont.)
MS.3--H.ii.76r [H²b]. Ink autographs rev. in ink--drafts for the completion of version H². On the verso is a draft of No.90 ("Jesu that dost in Mary dwell"). For transcriptions see Plates 213 and 214.

PLATE 207.   OET 100b. *S. Thomae Aquinatis Rhythmus*   •   261

St.6
21 d
22 g
23 c
24 c
21 e
Vertical 1 c,d,e
25 =d
26 g
27 f
28 c
H²c
H.ii. 74 v
OET NO. 100b
OET NO. 95 (see Plate 195)

× Drip
~~make~~ th tender tale true of the Pelican;
Bathe me, Jesu Lord, in what thy bosom ran —
Blood that but one drop of has the worth to win
all the world forgiveness of its world of sin.

× or δ
Like what tender tales tell of the Pelican;

Jesu whom I look at { shrouded / veilèd } here below,
I beseech thee send me what I thirst for so,
Some day to gaze on thee face to face in light
And be blest for ever with thy glory's sight.

———

O Deus, ego amo te

O God, I love thee, I love thee —
not out of hope of heaven for me
nor fearing not to love and be
  In the everlasting burning.
Thou, thou, my Jesus, after me
  Didst reach thine arms out dying,
For my sake sufferedst [lance] and lance,
mocked and marred countenance,
  Sorrows passing number,
  Sweat and care and cumber,
Yea and death, and this all for me,
  And thou couldst see me sinning:
Then I, why should not I love thee,
Jesu so much in love with me?
Not for heaven's sake; not to be
Out of hell by loving thee;
Not for any gains I see;
But just the way that thou didst me
I do love and I will love thee:

written 5 min. ? R.B. for Nash

What must I love thee, Lord, for then?!
For being my king and God. Amen.

Plate 207   OET No.100(b): S. Thomae Aquinatis Rhythmus (cont.)

MS.4--H.ii.74v [H²c]. Ink autograph with the final sts. of the second version, followed by three alternatives for ℓ.1, written vertically and heavily deleted: see Plates 210 and 215. These again are followed by a faircopy of No.95: "O Deus, ego amo te": see Plate 195, right, where the lower portion only of the page is reproduced.

H³a
H.ii.73v

1f
2d

OET
NO.
100(c)

This is that lent to Mr. Orby Shipley —
Godhead, I adore thee fast in hiding; thou
God in these bare shapes, poor shadows, darkling now:
Etc

MS.5 (rest blank)

OET
No.
100
(C)

THE IRISH MONTHLY   163
Vol. 31 - March 1903

SEVENTH VERSION OF " ADORO TE DEVOTE "

SEVERAL of the thirty preceding annual volumes of this magazine have contained translations by divers hands, especially of
famous hymns of the Church, and more especially still of two in
particular, the *Dies Iræ* and the *Adoro Te Devote*. The latter will
be found translated by Judge O'Hagan in our 5th volume at page
295; by Father Eyre, S.J., XV., 78; Father Coleridge, S.J.,
XXIII., 11; Father George Tyrrell, S.J., XXVI., 229; Mr.
Kegan Paul, XXX., 468; and at page 656 of our 29th volume an
excellent anonymous Anglican version is by mistake attributed to
Miss Emily Hickey. Six versions already; and now Mr. Orby
Shipley, the great hymnologist, the compiler of *Carmina Mariana*
and many other anthologies, has kindly placed at our disposal a
seventh—an unpublished version of the *Adoro Te Devote* made
about the year 1882 by the late Father Gerard Hopkins, S.J.
Father Hopkins was a very gifted man, highly appreciated by
Mr. Robert Bridges and other distinguished friends, but with some
very peculiar views on literary and other matters. There are
some traces of this originality (to call it by no worse name) in the
following version, which, however, seems worth preserving.

1 g	Godhead, I adore Thee, fast in hiding; Thou
2 e	God in these rare shapes, poor shadows, darkling now.
3 c	See, Lord, at Thy service low lies here a heart
4 c	Lost, all lost in wonder at the God Thou art.
5 c	Seeing, touching, tasting, are in Thee deceived.
6 c	How says trusty hearing? *That* shall be believed.
7 c	What God's Son has told me take for truth I do—
8 c	Truth himself speaks truly, or there's nothing true.

164   *THE IRISH MONTHLY*

9 d	On the cross Thy Godhead made no sign to men;
10 e	Here Thy very manhood steals from human ken.
11 c	Both are my confession, both are my belief,
12 e	And I pray the prayer of the dying thief.
13 d	I am not like Thomas, wounds I cannot see,
14 f	But can plainly call Thee Lord and God as he.
15 g	This faith each day deeper be my holding of,
16 l	Make me daily firmer hope and dearer love.
17 e	O, Thou our reminder of Christ crucified,
18 d	Living Bread. the life of those for whom He died.
19 f	Lend that life to me then, feed and feast my mind,
20 f	There be Thou the sweetness man was meant to find.
21 f	Bring the tender tale true of the Pelican,
22 h	Bathe me, Jesus Lord, in what Thy bosom ran—
23 f	Blood that but one drop of has the worth to win
24 d	All the world forgiveness of its world of sin.
25 e	Jesus, whom I look at veiled here below,
26 h	I beseech Thee send me what I thirst for so—
27 g	Some day to gaze on Thee face to face in light,
28 d	And be blessed for ever with Thy glory's sight.

Ad - o - ro te sup -
Do ti do re la

plex, la - tens de - i...
so fa mi

tas

③

H. ii.
16r

See
OET
NO.
146

OET
NO.
100
‾
MS. 6

PLATE 209. OET 100d. *S. Thomae Aquinatis Rhythmus* • 263

[H⁴]
H.ii.
73r

OET
No.
100
(d)

S. Thomae Aquinatis (28). ⁷⁵

Rhythmus ad SS. Sacramentum

" Adoro te supplex, latens deitas"

1 h I bow down before thee, Godhead hiding here
2 f Under only shadows, shapes that but appear:
3 d Lord, all at thy service low there lies a heart
4 d Lost, all lost in wonder at the God thou art.

5 d Seeing, touching, tasting are in thee deceived;
6 d But the trusty hearing, that may be believed:
7 d What God's Son has told me take for truth I do;
8 d Truth himself speaks truly or there's nothing true.

9 e On the cross thy godhead made no sign to men;
10 f Here thy very manhood keeps from mortal ken:
11 d Both are my confession, both are my belief,
12 f And I make the prayer of the dying thief.

13 e I am not like Thomas, wounds I cannot see,
14 g But can call thee plainly Lord and God as he:

Rest of
H⁴ lost

[opposite] Plate 208   OET No.100(c): S. Thomae Aquinatis Rhythmus (cont.)

MS.5--H.ii.73v [H³a]. The only entry (ink autograph) on the verso of *ll*.1 to 14 of H⁴. Orby Shipley did not publish GMH's translation. In the absence of a full text it was natural to assume that GMH meant by "Etc" that he had sent Shipley the version on the other side, H⁴. But in 1985 Norman White discovered that the MS. sent to Shipley was about 21 years later passed on to The Irish Monthly and publ. by Fr. Matthew Russell, SJ, who had known GMH in his Dublin days. Russell rev. the punctuation, changed "thee, thou" etc. to "Thee, Thou," and altered "bare shapes" (line 2), as too stark a reference to the bread and wine of the Eucharist to "rare shapes"; but we cannot be sure what other changes (if any) he introduced (vol.31, March 1903, 163-4). See Plates 211, 213, and 215 for larger scale reproductions.

MS.6--H.ii.16r--autograph in purple pencil of the first line in one of its Latin versions ("Adoro te supplex, latens deitas"), with tune in tonic solfa. This is written in the tiny notebook with the sole autograph of "Inversnaid," dated Sept.1881 (OET No.146). The OET headnote to No.100 reproduces the normal Latin version from the Missal.

[above] Plate 209   OET No.100(d): S. Thomae Aquinatis Rhythmus (cont.)

MS.7--H.ii.73r [H⁴]--autograph faircopy in ink of the final revised form, but only the first half of the translation, publ. as the text of OET No.100(d). The rest is missing.

OET No.100a | [H¹ H.ii. 78ʳ] | (30)

1a Godhead, I adore Thee, down on bended knee,
2aᵇ Who art here ~~through~~ hiding under things ~~in the shapes~~ we I see.
3a Wholly to thy service I submit a heart
4a Wholly lost in wonder, Lord, at what Thou art.

St.2
5a Seeing, touching, tasting, might mislead me here
6a But in faith I follow what is taught the ear.
7aᵇ What God's son has ~~spoken~~ told take for truth I do:
8a Word of Truth speaks truly or there's nothing true.

St.3
9aᵇ On the cross the godhead lost indeed its light ~~was concealed from sight~~
10aᵇᶜ ~~Here~~ But the ~~very~~ manhood ~~even cannot come to~~ ~~too is hidden from the light~~ even also here is out of sight:
11a Both are my confession, both are my belief,
12aᵇᶜ And I ~~ask~~ make the ~~blessing~~ prayer of the dying thief.
pray

OET No.100b | [H²a H.ii. 74ʳ]

1b Godhead here in hiding, whom I do adore
2c masked by these bare shadows, shape and nothing more,
3b See, lord, at thy service low lies here a heart
4b Lost, all lost in wonder at the God thou art.

St.2
5b Seeing, touching, tasting are in thee deceived:
6b How says trusty hearing? that shall be believed:
7c What God's son has told me, take for truth I do;
8b Truth himself speaks truly or there's nothing true.

St.3
9c On the cross ~~de~~ thy godhead made no sign to men;
10d Here thy very manhood steals from ~~a~~ human ken:
11b Both are my confession, both are my belief,
12d and I pray the prayer of the dying thief.

OET No.100b | [H²b H.ii. 74ᵛ]

1c ~~O I do adore thee~~
1d ~~God, I do adore thee~~
1e ~~Godhead I adore thee~~

Plate 210   OET No.100: St. Thomae Aquinatis Rhythmus, lines 1 to 12.
                     Deletions, Revisions in each MS

    MS.1--H' (see Plate 204): 1a thee → Thee   2a in rev. to though ... in the shapes I rev. to under things
we [g of things runs through h of shapes]   7a spoken rev. to told me   9a was concealed from sight del. [final
comma not del., but "even" written over it]   10a Here the manhood too is hidden from the light.   10b But the
[very with caret del.] manhood even cannot come to light.   10c But the manhood even here is out of sight: 12a
And I ask the blessing   12b I [pray del.] make the prayer   12c pray the prayer.
    MS.2--H²a(see Plate 205): 9c etc del. 10d m[ortal?] del.
    MS.4--H²b(see Plate 207): 1c O I do adore thee del.   1d God, I do adore thee del.   1e Godhead I adore thee
del.

PLATE 211. OET 100, lines 1 - 12, cont. *S. Thomae Aquinatis Rhythmus* • 265

[H³a]
H.ii.73v

1 f
2 d

This is what lent to mr. orly shipley —
Godhead, I adore thee fast in hiding; thou
God in these bare shapes, poor shadows, darkling now:
&c

OET
NO.
100(C)

1 g   Godhead, I adore Thee, fast in hiding; Thou
2 e   God in these rare shapes, poor shadows, darkling now.
3 c   See, Lord, at Thy service low lies here a heart
4 c   Lost, all lost in wonder at the God Thou art.

5 c   Seeing, touching, tasting, are in Thee deceived.
6 c   How says trusty hearing?   *That* shall be believed.
7 c   What God's Son has told me take for truth I do—
8 c   Truth himself speaks truly, or there's nothing true.

164   *THE IRISH MONTHLY*

9 d   On the cross Thy Godhead made no sign to men;
10 e Here Thy very manhood steals from human ken.
11 c Both are my confession, both are my belief,
12 e And I pray the prayer of the dying thief.

[H⁴]
H.ii.
73r
OET
NO.
100
(d)

1 h   I bow down before thee, Godhead hiding here
2 f   Under only shadows, shapes that but appear:
3 d   Lord, all at thy service low there lies a heart
4 d   Lost, all lost in wonder at the God thou art.

5 d   Seeing, touching, tasting are in thee deceived;
6 d   But what the trusty hearing, that may be believed:
7 d   What God's Son has told me take for truth I do;
8 d   Truth himself speaks truly or there's nothing true.

9 e   On the cross thy godhead made no sign to men;
10 f Here thy very manhood keeps from mortal ken:
11 d Both are my confession, both are my belief,
12 f And I make the prayer of the dying thief.

Plate 211   OET No.100: <u>S. Thomae Aquinatis Rhythmus</u>, lines 1-12 cont.
<u>MS.5</u> and <u>Irish Monthly</u>--H³ (see Plate 208, top): No deletions.
<u>MS.7</u>--H⁴ (see Plate 209): 1h Godhead [not del.; brown blot only]   6d what <u>rev.</u> <u>to</u> the   8d S <u>del.</u>

[H¹]
H. ii.
78ᵛ

OET
No.
100a

St.4
13a I am not like Thomas, wounds I do not see,
14a But I can confess Thee Lord and God as he.
15a,b ~~Grant me~~ (Make this) faith the deeper every day I live,
16a,b ~~Stronger~~ (More the) hope to hold by, ~~greater~~ (more the) love to give.

St.5
17a Being our reminder of our Master's death,
18a living bread, and giving man his life and breath,
19a,b Grant my ~~thoughts~~ (mind) may ~~always~~ (ever) find in Thee ~~their~~ (its) food
20a,b Tasting ~~there~~ (in Thee) that sweetness Thou hast meant I should.

[H²a]
H. ii.
74ʳ

OET
No.
100b

St.4
13b I am not like Thomas, wounds I cannot see,
14b,c { But as loudly own thee ~~acknowledge~~ Lord and God as he:
   d   { But can call thee plainly Lord and God as he:
15c make this faith the deeper every day I live,
16c more to hope for from thee, ~~the~~ more love to give.
   d { Let me hope more from thee, more love let me give.
   e { Harder to hope in thee, ~~higher~~ (dearer) love to give.

15d,e this faith ~~da~~ daily deeper make my holding of,
16f-g ~~Let me hope the harder, dearer let me love~~
   h   { Daily to hope harder, and to dearer love.
   i   { ~~make~~ me harder hope and make me dearer love.
   j   { make me hope the harder, make me dearer love,

St.4
13c I am not like Thomas, wounds I cannot see,
14e But can plainly call thee Lord and God as he:
15f This faith each day deeper ~~make~~ my holding of,
16k Daily make me harder hope and dearer love.

St.5
(see H²b)
17d O thou our reminder of Christ crucified,
18c living Bread the life ~~of~~ for whom he died,
19e ~~Lend~~ this life to me then: feed and feast my mind,
20e there be thou the sweetness man can meant to find.

Plate 212   OET No.100: S. Thomae Aquinatis Rhythmus, lines 13 to 20.
Deletions, Revisions in each MS.

MS.1—H' (see Plate 204) 15a Grant me   16a Stronger hope to hold by, greater love to give rev. 16b More the hope I hold by, more the love I give.   19a thoughts ... always ... their del. rev. 19b mind ... ever ... its   20a Tasting there that rev 20b Taste in Thee the

MS.2—H²a (see Plate 205)   14b with him acknowledge ... in thee del. rev. 14c as loudly own thee ... as he   16c more [for the?] rev. the more   16e higher del. rev. dearer   15d [da del.] daily deeper rev. 15e deeper daily   16f Let me hope the harder, dearer let me love. rev. 16g Daily hope the harder, daily dearer love. 16i And rev. Make   15f make rev. me   [St.5 was drafted on MS.3 before being added to MS.2]   18c bread → Bread ... those rev. to man then us   19e Gra[nt] del. rev. Lend ... feed [followed by stray dots, not a colon]

PLATE 213.   OET 100, lines 13 - 20, cont.   *S. Thomae Aquinatis Rhythmus*   •   267

St.5

17 b c
18 b

{ thou art the
{ O Thou {great long reminder of our dear Lord's death,
living bread and giving those man/our that taste of thee breath,

29

76

OET No.100 b

19 c
d

grant this grace to me then, be my life of mind,
{ life blood to my mind

20 c
d

{ with
{ and the love and relish 'twas meant to find.
{ with the relish in thee man 'twas meant to find.

[H²b]
H.ii.
76r

13 d
14 f
15 g
16 l

I am not like Thomas, wounds I cannot see,
But can plainly call Thee Lord and God as he.
This faith each day deeper be my holding of,
Make me daily firmer hope and dearer love.

17 e
18 d
19 f
20 f

O, Thou our reminder of Christ crucified,
Living Bread, the life of those for whom He died.
Lend that life to me then, feed and feast my mind,
There be Thou the sweetness man was meant to find.

THE IRISH MONTHLY
Vol. 31—March 1903

OET No. 100 c

13 e

14 g
Rest of
H⁴ lost

I am not like Thomas, wounds I cannot see,
But can call thee plainly Lord and God as he :

[H⁴]
H.ii.
73r

OET NO. 100 d

Plate 213   OET No.100: S. Thomae Aquinatis Rhythmus, lines 13 to 20 (cont.)
Deletions and Revisions in each MS include:
                                                                        ⌐great
    MS.3—H²b (see Plate 206)   17b 0 thou⌐long reminder   bracketed with Thou art the reminder   18b those
that taste   rev. to man that tastes   rev. again to them that taste [smudges after "breath,"]   20c And rev.
With ... I revision to m[an], as in 20d, begun but del.
    Irish Monthly: No deletions [16 has no MS. authority but is probably authentic]
    MS.7—H⁴ (see Plate 209) Lines 15ff., which must have been on a second sheet, have never been found.

St.6
21a/22d Make the tender tale true of the Pelican;
22aᵇc   Wash ~~my soul~~ ~~in life, that from Thee thy bosom ran~~
23aᵇ **Blood** ~~Which~~ one ~~single~~ drop of has the worth to win
24a   All the world's redemption from ~~its~~ world of ~~one~~ sin.

Nurse me weak and naked at thy
breast, that ran

St.7
25a   Jesu, whom I look at darkly here below,
26aᵇ   Give me what my thoughts are thirsting after so;
27aᵇ   Take the veil away that ~~hides~~ guards thy face and then
28a   I shall see Thy glory and be blest. Amen.

OET No.100 a

[H¹]

H.ii. 78r

St.6
21 b   make the tender tale true of the Pelican,
22 e   Jesu Lord, and wash me with at thy breast that ran
23 c   Blood which but one drop of has the worth to win
24 b   all the world redemption from a world of sin.

21 c   Like that tender tales told of the Pelican,
22 f   Wash me, Jesu Lord, with what thy bosom ran—
23 d   Blood that but one d

St.7
25 b   Jesu, whom I look at veilèd here below,
26 c
   d   Bring to pass the blessing that I thirst for so,
            I pray thee, that I thirst for so,
                         send me what I thirst for so
26 e   I beseech thee, send   what I thirst after so,
                         bring

27 c   ~~that thy once face beholding in uncovered light,~~
            some day to
27 d   That I may gaze on thee face to face in light
   e
28 b   and be blest for ever ~~in the~~ with thy glory's sight.
                         amen.

[H²b]
H.ii. 76r
OET No.100 b

St.6
21 d
22 g
23 e
24 c

✗ Bring
~~make~~ th tender tale true of the Pelican;
Bathe me, Jesu Lord, in what thy bosom ran —
Blood that but one drop of has the worth to win
All the world forgiveness of its world of sin.

✗ or θ

21 e

Like that tender tales tell of the Pelican;

St.7
25 <d/c
26 g
27 f
28 c

Jesu whom I look at {shrouded / veiled} here below,
I beseech thee send me what I thirst for so,
Some day to gaze on thee face to face in light
And be blest for ever with thy glory's sight.

[H²c]
H.ii.
74 V

OET
No.
100 b

---

21 f   Bring the tender tale true of the Pelican,
22 h   Bathe me, Jesus Lord, in what Thy bosom ran—
23 f   Blood that but one drop of has the worth to win
24 d   All the world forgiveness of its world of sin.

25 e   Jesus, whom I look at veiled here below,
26 h   I beseech Thee send me what I thirst for so—
27 g   Some day to gaze on Thee face to face in light,
28 d   And be blessed for ever with Thy glory's sight.

THE IRISH MONTHLY
Vol. 31-March 1903

OET No. 100 c

[opposite] Plate 214   OET No.100: S. Thomae Aquinatis Rhythmus, Lines 21-28.
                    Deletions and Revisions in each MS include:
    MS.1--H' (see Plate 204)--22a Wash my soul in life that from [Thee del.] Thy bosom ran,   22b Wash me white
in blood that from Thy breast there ran, 22c Turn to strength [the del.] my weakness in Thy blood that ran,   22d
Nurse me weak and naked at [thy →] Thy breast that ran [comma del.]   23a Which one single drop of rev. Bleeding
what one drop of rev.   23b Blood one single drop of   24a orig. world's ... its ... wi[n? dittography? del.
before sin]   26a soul is 27a Take the veil away that hides   27b Take away the veil that guards
    MS.3--H²b (see Plate 206)   22e with del. rev. at   23c that del. 26e send del. and rewritten   27c
That thy (unc[overed?] del.) face beholding in uncovered light,   28b in the [or thy?] del.

[above] Plate 215   OET No.100: S. Thomae Aquinatis Rhythmus, lines 21-28 (cont.)
                    Deletions, Revisions in each MS. include:
    MS.4--H²c (see Plate 207)   21d Make rev. to Bring
    Irish Monthly--no deletions. (Note that this first printing of 23 gave the correct reading "has the worth
to win/All the world forgiveness", misprinted as "has the world to win" by Charles Williams in 2nd edn. of Poems,
p.153.)

Appendix A
The Problem of How to Display
Hopkins's Variant Readings

This present work was first conceived as a fairly modest facsimile collection of the most interesting of Hopkins's drafts, to form Volume II in my Oxford English Texts edition of *The Poetical Works of Gerard Manley Hopkins*. The first volume was to contain a new text of the poems incorporating Hopkins's extensive metrical marks, along with headnotes discussing the manuscripts for each poem, and a detailed commentary. I made the suggestion of a second volume rather tentatively knowing that there was absolutely no precedent for such a companion volume in the OET series. I might have met with more support if I had proposed it after Valerie Eliot's facsimile edition of *The Waste Land* had proved an outstanding success in 1971.

The problem of how to display Hopkins's early readings generated years of perplexed discussion. The critical apparatus in most OET editions presents variant published readings, whereas very few indeed of Hopkins's poems saw print during his life-time. On the other hand, a single sonnet such as "The Starlight Night" has seven different manuscripts, some lines seething with alternative images and rhythms. No English poet seemed to the Oxford Press so mired in technical intricacies.

Delays were engendered on both sides of the Atlantic. My research time was drastically curtailed by administrative responsibilities, first as Dean and head of a department, then at Queen's University in Ontario for seven years as Director of Graduate Studies in English, followed by a stint as Chairman of the Queen's Council for Graduate Studies and Research covering all faculties. Summers and even the rare sabbatical were busy with the simultaneous supervision of ten or twelve doctoral and other dissertations, ranging from Milton's Prosody to Swedenborg's influence on W.B. Yeats—occupations that have decreased but not disappeared since my retirement.

On the Oxford University Press side, my editor was trying to cope with between one hundred and two hundred diverse editions in English literature, yet obliged by new rules—established in the seventies by the Delegates of the Clarendon Press for the safeguarding of their centuries-old reputation—to consult assessors for each of them before taking any major decision in its case. As one editor after another resigned to assume a post elsewhere, a successor would have to ask me for a new sample, which had then to be circulated with cumulative delays to the members of a new committee whose identities were protected by the editor. Opinions inevitably diverged. The editor had to coax some sort of a consensus from his committee, a process that accounted for delays of six to nine months (on one occasion a year-and-a-half) between the submission of a sample and the

verdict on it. This waiting period I could not safely devote to the edition, since the new editor was duty bound to negate any agreement reached with a predecessor if an inferior edition might in his own opinion be likely to result from it. A completely new start might then be called for.

As five successive editors and their advisers wrestled with what seemed the intractable problems of a Hopkins edition, I filled in such spare time as I had by contributing chapters to four books, producing a selected edition of Hopkins poems for the Folio Society with a new introduction and commentary, and publishing numbers of research articles. With the help of George Whalley, the Coleridge scholar, I also devised a highly economical set of sigla for the Hopkins critical apparatus, capable of compressing successive variants into remarkably few lines. Robin Skelton published in his *Malahat Review* a sample of its application to "Spelt with Sibyl's Leaves," along with one manuscript draft in facsimile. This I sent to some forty scholars for their frank reactions. Nearly everyone replied, but their praise of my compactness (made still more compact by the inadvertent closing up of all my spaces between entries) was too often accompanied by admissions that they found the apparatus hard to interpret accurately. Like Hopkins after "Tom's Garland," I realized that I "must go no farther on this road."

The committee of advisers to one Oxford editor even queried the utility of any critical apparatus whatsoever. One member felt that brackets should be avoided because Hopkins, when he overran the width of his paper, often encased the turn-over within a square bracket in the line above. Another queried the oblique sign "/" with which I separated one metrical line in a quotation from the next: might this not be confused with the medieval virgule that Hopkins pressed into service as a sort of comma near the end of "Andromeda?" A new editor also expressed himself on aesthetic grounds strongly against the disfiguring of a page of English poetry with catalogues of variants at its foot.

Since any apparatus separated from the text by relegation to the back of the book is a tax on the reader's memory, we therefore experimented instead with a full-scale typographical transcription of the manuscripts. The test poem selected this time was "The Bugler's First Communion," which has autographs spreading over ten pages, besides a transcript edited by Hopkins and occupying another three. We discovered that attempts to reproduce some drafts in print might require several times as much room as photographic facsimiles, and be extremely costly to set up. Furthermore, in spite of the immediate impact of a line of type cancelled with a rule though all the words, in the process hyphens and dashes get lost (as they also often do in Hopkins's original deleted manuscripts), and when the type is small the horizontal line bisecting a deleted entry makes *e*, *c*, and *o* confusingly similar, especially in names and incomplete words. This led us back after a long but unavoidable journey to reconsideration of a facsimile volume.

Oxford University Press generously agreed to allow me a companion volume of *Facsimiles*, to be limited if possible to about 200 plates. The discussion then focussed on some principles of selecting the variants to be cited in the headnotes to the commentaries in volume one. When the committee was apparently irreconcilably divided on this matter, my editor appealed to one of the most senior of Oxford's professors of English. After, much contemplation this professor ruled that the function of the apparatus (which had now returned as it were by a back door) was to "establish the text," not to illuminate its stages of evolution. Asking what corresponded in Hopkins to an edition published by most other poets, the adjudicator ruled that only autographs sent by Hopkins to his

friends or transcripts he checked for transmission to Coventry Patmore could be so regarded. This well-intentioned slicing of the Gordian Knot eliminated all variants for about two-thirds of the poems, including such absorbing ones as the Sonnets of Desolation. Practically every draft was also excluded. The prospects of satisfaction were so slight that I asked my daughter Catherine to rewrite the entire apparatus according to the new rule. She spent much of one summer doing this. The results were summarily rejected by my next editor, as we had indeed anticipated they might be, but meanwhile I set the OET edition aside in order to complete *A Reader's Guide to Gerard Manley Hopkins* for Thames and Hudson of London and Cornell University Press—an arduous task that occupied several years.

Good progress was made under the editorship of my old friend John Bell, but his early retirement after a long career in the Press severed a connection going back to the editing of the Hopkins fourth edition.

I have left out of this account the new technique for examining literary documents such as MS. B where an editor needs to discover which of two different people contributed particular details or changes. I was responsible for introducing the Infra-red Image Converter into Oxford, an innovation followed and greatly improved upon by the British [Museum] Library in London. The poems for which I used it were "The Wreck of the Deutschland" and the mature poetry that followed.

A dramatic turn came when Dr. Thomas Collins (now Vice-President of the University of Western Ontario) enquired on behalf of Garland Publishing whether I could edit facsimiles of Hopkins to be produced in New York. When joint publication in Oxford and New York proved impractical, Oxford withdrew in favor of Garland. The change of publisher induced me to rearrange all the plates on which I had already worked, in order to enlarge the scale of reproduction, the result of strong advice from Ralph Carlson, then Vice-President of Garland Publishing. This has produced far more legible plates. With the inclusion of the two Early Note-books at the request of the Society of Jesus the single volume of Facsimiles had to be expanded into two substantial volumes.

It is unfortunate that the critical stages of both books have coincided with some eighteen months of eye trouble, now fortunately corrected by surgery, during which my binocular vision was constantly interrupted. This was a worrying handicap to the accurate proofing not only of the copy-edited OET edition but of camera-ready material for the Garland plates. Slips seem inevitable in all human enterprises, but I trust that this physical impediment may not have impaired the usefulness of these complicated volumes.

Appendix B
Text of the OET Hopkins:
Chief Changes since 1970
Poems Nos. 1 to 100

The Oxford fourth edition of the *Poems of Gerard Manley Hopkins* (London: 1967), ed. by W.H. Gardner and N.H. MacKenzie, introduced over 400 changes to the text of Gardner's third edition of 1948, as a result of special facilities for comparing the manuscripts generously offered me by their owners: Edward, first Lord Bridges, the Society of Jesus, and the Bodleian Library. Dr. Gardner died in 1969. I was by then already working on the text of my own more specialized edition for the quite distinct Oxford English Texts series. Some corrections that resulted from the renewed study of the manuscripts could be easily incorporated in the more popular fourth edition, and this I did for its paperback reprint of 1970. Others, however, would have involved extensive resetting, especially where I had selected as the *OET* copy-text a manuscript different from the one described as the basis for the fourth edition in notes by RB, WHG, and NHM printed in the paperback. I saved other interesting changes for my own edition, and did not incorporate more than a few until the seventh impression of 1984, when many were released.

In the Oxford English Texts, instead of printing the apparently later of two readings braced together as alternatives by the undecided poet, I have usually given them both. Further, where an earlier version is of special interest or is the only autograph, I have printed it entire, along with the revised version(s)—e.g., "Heaven-Haven," "The Habit of Perfection," "New Readings," and "S. Thomas Aquinatis Rhythmus"—to mention only some of those covered in Volume One of the facsimiles. I have also re-arranged the lines in "A Soliloquy of One of the Spies," "A Voice from the World," and "Floris in Italy" (where the prose scenes have been restored to the play, but in a new order).

The Introduction to the Oxford English Texts edition sets out Hopkins's vacillation in the use of capitals, hyphens, compounds, metrical signs, and punctuation marks, facts that have emerged from my detailed scrutiny of all surviving autographs. Owing to other causes explained in this present volume, the text of poems found in the Early Note-books C.i. and C.ii. may never be finalized. Hopkins, however emphatic in theory about what was "correct," was in practice much more flexible—indeed at times almost indifferent to consistency: we may, for example, find "grey" in one line and "gray" in the next (No. 36, Plate 85). Beyond a certain point, a definitive text is defeated by the poet's ambiguities. Nor have I thought it a crime to leave the Oxford University Press single quotes (standard British practice since the first edition of his poems) in place of the double quotes favored by Victorians.

I append the chief changes after the 1970 revision which have been incorporated in the Oxford English Texts edition, occasionally mentioning the selection of a different manuscript authority as responsible for a multiplicity of small revisions (e.g., in "A Complaint," No. 72.) The revisions are in numerous cases refinements that, following the manuscripts, ease the flow and improve the logic. A comparison with the facsimiles will often reveal how obscure the manuscripts are (e.g., Plates 131–32). Most of the textual study was carried out during frequent visits to Oxford between 1964 and 1972. I am most grateful to Dr. Catherine Phillips for checking readings for me between my research visits in more recent years. Her *Oxford Authors* edition of the complete poems and selected prose was edited independently from my studies and was done directly from the manuscripts. Her edition appeared three months after my OET typescript had been submitted, but during the copy-editing stage I was able to adopt some of her corrections that I had overlooked in my revision.

OET
No.

1   <u>The Escorial</u>   The notes supplied by GMH were prob. neatly printed by the poet himself, so their spelling "Laurence" is preferred to the "Lawrence" of the copyist in the text of 11 and 15. In 9 "palace" add comma (CLP); 29 "Beyond" now l.c. 106 orig. reading restored, "continuously" instead of correction (by judges or Manley Hopkins?).   112 "sight," now "sight—"   121 "store" comma added.

2   <u>Aeschylus: Prometheus Desmotês</u>   add circumflexes in title and sub-title (CLP)   Text of 1-19 from B II, but rest from the later L.iii.6 (hence these revisions: 23 no comma   27 "destiny" now u.c.   28 "foe" for "hate"   30 "loved" for earlier "lov'd"

3   <u>Il Mystico</u>   75 "heights" for "height" (GMH's slip, corrected from orig. version)

6   <u>A Vision of the Mermaids</u>   136 "ocean" (l.c.—CLP)   7   <u>Winter with the Gulf Stream</u>   1863 version added

10   <u>Pilate</u>   7 after "keep" add "[me]" for sense and metre.   12 alternative added   23 "air" dash (removed 1970 in error) restored 73 "whom" made u.c.   76-79 (in 4th edn. notes p.298) incorporated in text.

11   <u>"She schools the flighty pupils"</u>   3 "She" now "And"

12   <u>A soliloquy of one of the spies</u>   Stanzas rearranged from MS., opening with former st.3. 7 "sand" add comma and 11 "hand" add exclam. (CLP).   15 "air," now "air."   17 "unveinèd" now "unreinèd" 20,27,34,37,42,52,54, alternatives added from MSS. 23 "Are you sandblind?" rev. "Ye sandblind!"   25 "stand," now "stand."   39 "gore," now "gore."   45 "To day" no hyphen.

13   <u>The Lover's Stars</u>   Alternatives added in 13,20. Line spaces closed except after 16 and 20. Incompatible rev. st.2 (C.i.161) printed as No.13b.

15   <u>"The peacock's eye"</u>   Two versions (a and b) in text.

17   <u>Barnfloor and Winepress</u>   Text from <u>Union Review</u> except where no MS. supports it.   11 "Those" now "Thou"   24 "Heaven" now l.c. (autograph and printed text--two transcripts have u.c.)

18   <u>New Readings</u>   Additional version, from early autograph, is printed as No.18(a). The familiar rev. version—here No.18(b)—is from a transcript by Coles of a missing revision by Hopkins. Coles's rhyme-word "shed" in 5, where early autograph has "sped," is prob. a misreading of GMH's <u>p</u> with a deficient descender—"shed" is the rhyme in 12. In 18(b) 5 "shed" now "sped"   6 "sowed," comma del. (CLP)

19   <u>"He hath abolish'd"</u>   8 "shocks" now "shooks"   10 "together," comma del.

20   a) <u>REST</u>; b) <u>Heaven-Haven</u>   Early version printed as No.20(a)

22   <u>"Why should their foolish bands"</u>   Alternatives printed in 6 and 8

25   <u>"Glimmer'd along"</u>   2 "deep." now "deep;"

27   <u>"Miss Story's character"</u>   19c, 20c (C.i.202) replace 19b, 20b. Two lines ("And, well supplied...soul"), which GMH placed in parenthesis, prob. because they had to be moved to a position marked with an X, are inserted before "Her character," with parentheses deleted: see marginal nos., Plates 70-71.

OET
No.

28   "Her prime of life"   Not in 4th. edn.

29   "Did Helen steal"   3 the version in ink, "But she's too plain," replaces alternative version in pencil below it "She is too plain."

30   [Fragments II] (e) 2 "the ready" now "thready"   (f) opening "the" now u.c.   (h) 7 "spring" also u.c.

31   Floris in Italy Poetry and prose reintegrated, but radically re-arranged: my No. 31 (a) was 4th edn. 'Floris (iii)';   (b) prose ("Giulia writing") J.42-3;   (c) was 4th edn. "Floris" (i), ℓℓ.1-60, but after ℓ.50 there I insert 4th edn. No. 103, "I am like a slip of comet" as Giulia's missing soliloquy over the sleeping Floris;   (d) was separate poem, 4th edn. No. 101;   (e) prose ("What is your name, boy?") J.44;   (f) was 4th edn. "Floris" (i), ℓℓ.61-71;   (g) prose ("A cave in a quarry") J.44-5; # (h) was 4th edn. "Floris" (ii).
        Corrections to the text of "Floris" Include: No. 30(a) Line 1 "lines," no comma   (b) C.i.221.46, "You must even" for "ever"   (c) ℓ.21 "thick in field." period now comma   (h) ℓ.7 "and" inserted before "Arthur's Britain".

32   [Epigrams]   (e) "lark" u.c., no stop.

33   Io   1,3 "leans," and "hill," commas del.   Alternatives printed in 6, 12, 14   9 "dew-lap" now one word   11 "a various brown with" rev. as "a honied brown and"   12 "damask'd with dark breaks" rev. to "damaskèd with breaks" and alternative (as in C.ii.25).

35   "No, they are come"   2 "foregone" now "forgone"   9 three alternatives printed   10 "halt" comma added

36   "Now I am minded"   Indenting corrected.   5 "boughs" semi-colon added   8 "grey" now "gray" (yet MS. has "grey" in 7)   9 "late" comma added

37(i)   "Or ever the early stirrings"   4,5 read "up-bringing" and "gonfalon-bearer" (hyphenated)   6 "press.—" now "press,—"

38   A Voice from the World   2 "fall'n" add comma   20 "sweet potential" hyphenated   22 "wood," now period   23 "seven," dash for comma   "few:" now period   24 "unlook'd for" hyphenated   "spent," no comma   36 "rain;" [;] editorial.   62 "years," now "years;"   64 "weed," no comma   85-88 (badly smudged: text uncertain) 85 "dreamed" now "dream'd"   88 "into" now "unto"   92 "through." period editorial [.]   101-2 (smudged passage) read "could not hear/Him...[? away in flight] were gone"   107 "thee" u.c. 117 "last" add comma 118 "swooned" now "swoon'd"   119 "angel" u.c.   After ℓ.121 I print "But what indeed is ask'd of me?" (4th edn. No.118), as ℓℓ.122-134, with these changes 132 (old ℓ.11) "head." comma for period, and next line "dumb," period for comma. Old line 122 then becomes 135.   179 (old 166) "foods," del. comma.

39(b) "Bringing heads of daffodillies"   1 "bringing" now u.c.

  (j)   "Now more precisely"   2 "place in the east" now "place of the East"/

  (q)   "When cuckoo calls"   2 "again." no stop. [Various other fragments have been added from C.i and C.ii.]

40(a) "A pure gold lily"   "We live to see/How Shakspere's England weds with Dante's Italy" added as ℓℓ.8,9, with GMH's spelling of "Shakespeare" restored.

41   "Although she be more white"   6 "bat's wings" hyphenated.

OET
No.

42   <u>St Dorothea</u>   Four versions assembled as <u>a</u>, <u>b</u>, <u>c</u> and <u>d</u> (4th. edn. Nos.10; 98.xix; Appendix A; and 25). Minor corrections in titles, and in the placing of stresses in (d).

43   "<u>Proved Etherege prudish</u>"   Lines 1,3,4,6,7 indented   2 "would be" hyphenated

44   <u>Richard</u>   Early version printed as No.44a (4th edn. notes p.305). Lines 4,5 closed up   8 "one drunk" rev. "drinking" 9 "In" rev. "True"   <u>Richard</u> (d) 2 "much-dreaded" no hyphen   <u>Richard</u> (e) 9 "butter-burr leaves" add second hyphen   "corpse" (GMH's slip, reflecting a northern pronunciation?) read "copse"   15 "grace" add comma

45   "<u>All as that moth</u>"   1,2 "All as the moth call'd Underwing alighted,/Turning and pacing," now replaced by later revision: "All as that moth call'd Underwing, alighted,/Travelling and turning, [braced with] Pacing and turning,"

46   <u>The Queen's Crowning</u>   54 alternative added "They bow'd him on his knee"   104 "fie" add comma 120 "true love" hyphenated (CLP)   137 "King's" changed to l.c.

47   <u>Stephen and Barberie</u>   6 "barred" rev. "barrèd"   13 "The poor soul—" ital.   14 "<u>sat</u>" u.c.

50   "<u>When eyes that cast about</u>"   1 "about in heights" now "about the heights"   lay-out now shows Spenserian st.

51   <u>The Summer Malison</u>   6 "lodged" rev. "lodgèd"

52   <u>St. Thecla</u>   31 "third:" now period

53   <u>Easter Communion</u>   Line space after octave   10 "gladness;" now comma

54   "<u>O Death, Death</u>"   6 "wide;—Thou, O Lord of Sin," rev. to "wide; and thou, O lord of Sin,"   9,10 moved to left to suit their metrical length (MS.).

56   <u>To Oxford</u>: the two completed and two incomplete sonnets (4th edn. Nos.119,116) are grouped here as <u>a</u>, <u>b</u>, <u>c</u>, and <u>d</u>. Line space after each octave.   No.56(a) "New-dated..." *ℓ*.10 "quiet-walled" and 13 "impeached" grave on <u>ed</u> in each

57   "<u>Where art thou friend</u>"   14 alternatives printed

58   "<u>Confirmed beauty</u>"   No line space after 7.   "Pharoh's" misprint, now "Pharaoh's"

59   <u>The Beginning of the End</u>   Subtitle added: "(a neglected lover's address to his mistress)". Layout for all three sonnets now follows autograph of (b) and (c). "Some men may hate their rivals" added as (d) (formerly in 4th edn. notes).

60   <u>The Alchemist in the City</u>   1 "shows" rev. "shews"

61   "<u>Myself unholy</u>"   alternatives printed in 4,7 Line space after octave.   7 "trust," no comma   9 "brother;" semicolon editorial, to suit footnote revision of 10. MS. has "brother," but this was followed by "And" in three earlier versions.

62   "<u>See how Spring opens</u>"   Line space after octave.

63   <u>Continuation of R. Garnett's "Nix"</u>   6 "walnut leaves" hyphenated

OET
No.

64(c) <u>"Mothers are doubtless happier"</u> 4 (mended phrase, uncertain) prob. "come of" mended to "hold by" 6 "thy" u.c.

65 <u>"O what a silence"</u> alternatives integrated. 15 "the" now "this"

66(a) Daphne: <u>"Who loves me here"</u> 10 "stained" now "stain'd" 66(b) <u>Castara Victrix</u>: "What was it" (GMH's slip) now "Where was it" 12 "Three" rev. "Two" 66(c) <u>At the picnic</u>. 3 "yet" mended by GMH to "but" (?). 4 "best" mended to "well" No.66(d) <u>"Come, Daphnis"</u> 16 "there" u.c. 17 "spring" u.c. 18 "Shot" now "Sheet" 20 "upon" now "on"

67 <u>"My prayers must meet"</u> 2 "or" now "and" 6 "it" rev. "I" 10 "yea" comma added

68 <u>Shakspere</u> 4 "distant" now "distanced"

69 <u>"Trees by their yield"</u> 18 "he" u.c.

70 <u>"Let me be to Thee as the circling bird"</u> line space after octave.

71 <u>The Half-way House</u> 4 editorial comma omitted 10 "Love's" rev. to l.c. for better sense (MS. uncertain).

72 <u>A Complaint</u> Copy text changed from H to A, with revisions to nearly every line.

73 <u>"Moonless darkness"</u> 3 "Bethlehem star" hyphenated

74 <u>"The earth and heaven"</u> 7 "range" add comma

76 <u>The Nightingale</u> 7 "silken" now "silky"

77(a) <u>The Habit of Pefection</u> printed as early version of No.77(b) <u>The Kind Betrothal</u>, a new final text.

78 <u>Nondum</u> 33 "hosts" mended to u.c.

79 <u>Easter</u> 21 "dishevelled" MS. "disshevelled" (obsolete)

80 <u>Summa</u> Punctuation of MS. very uncertain. See note on plate 170.

81 <u>Jesu Dulcis Memoria</u> eleven lines from other sts of the Latin hymn, assumed by WHG to be Variant Translations, have been added and arranged in Breviary order. 5,6 "Song never was so sweet in ear,/Word never was such news to hear," rev. to "No music so can touch the ear,/No news is heard of such sweet cheer," and 7 "sweet" rev. "dear". 33 "good" now u.c.

82 <u>Inundatio Oxoniana</u> 4 "Bit" typo for "Fit" 20 new para.

83(a) <u>Ecquis Binas</u> 4 alternative added: "In instant time I would be gone"

84 <u>[Latin Elegiacs]</u> sixteen lines not in 4th. edn. text or notes added.

85 <u>Elegiacs after "The Convent Threshold"</u> 35 "nobis;" now comma 45 "At" now "Ah"

87 <u>Horace: "Persicos odi"</u> No line space after 4 (CLP)

OET
No.

88   Horace: "Odi profanum volgus"   alternatives printed in 4,33,48   21 no dash (CLP) # 31 "dog-star" one word

89   The Elopement 18,19 "linen-winded" and "to-night" no hyphens.

90   To Jesus Living in Mary (Oratio Patris Condren)   4 "fullness" now "fulness"

93   "O praedestinata bis"   15 "pastu" now "partu"

94   Ad Mariam   15 "to-day", "to-morrow" each one word, no hyphen   22 "virginal." no stop   34 "all we," no comma

95   "O Deus, ego amo te"   stresses added in 1 to second "Í love thée—" and in 3 "nót"

96   Rosa Mystica   Refrain not indented (CLP)   1 dash now comma   2 ends with "?—"   12 no final period   16 no commas

97   "Quique haec membra"   2 "velis" add comma   lacuna after 4   9 "Indis" add comma   11 "prosperant" now "properant"

99   "Miror surgentem" # 1 "noctem." now comma   13 alternatives printed   28 no final stop.

100   S. Thomae Aquinatis Rhythmus   three different complete versions with one half-complete (1-14) printed for comparison. In (b)—the only text in 4th edn.—alternatives provided in 25 "shrouded/veiled"

Index of Short Titles
and First Lines

(TITLES ARE SET IN ITALIC, FIRST LINES IN ROMAN. OET POEM NUMBERS, IN PARENTHESES, ARE FOLLOWED BY REFERENCES TO THE PLATES ON WHICH THE POEMS, IN PART OR WHOLE, OCCUR.)